CUMANS AND TATARS

The Cumans and the Tatars were nomadic warriors of the Eurasian steppe who exerted an enduring impact on the medieval Balkans. With this work, István Vásáry presents the first extensive examination of their history from 1185 to the 1365. The basic instrument of Cuman and Tatar political success was their military force, over which none of the Balkan warring factions could claim victory. As a consequence, groups of the Cumans and the Tatars settled and mingled with the local population in various regions of the Balkans. The Cumans were the founders of three successive Bulgarian dynasties (Asenids, Terterids and Shishmanids), and the Wallachian dynasty (Basarabids). They also played an active role in Byzantium, Hungary and Serbia, with Cuman immigrants being integrated into each country's elite. This book also demonstrates how the prevailing political anarchy in the Balkans in the thirteenth and fourteenth centuries made it ripe for the Ottoman conquest.

ISTVÁN VÁSÁRY is Professor of Turkish and Central Asian Studies at Loránd Eötvös University, Budapest. His previous publications (in Hungarian) include *The Golden Horde* (Kossuth, 1986), and *History of Pre-Mongol Inner Asia* (1993; 2nd edition, Balassi, 2003). He served as Hungarian Ambassador to Turkey (1991–5), and to Iran (1999–2003).

CUMANS AND TATARS

Oriental Military in the Pre-Ottoman Balkans, 1185–1365

ISTVÁN VÁSÁRY

Loránd Eötvös University, Budapest

CAMBRIDGE
UNIVERSITY PRESS

PUBLISHED BY THE PRESS SYNDICATE OF THE UNIVERSITY OF CAMBRIDGE
The Pitt Building, Trumpington Street, Cambridge, United Kingdom

CAMBRIDGE UNIVERSITY PRESS
The Edinburgh Building, Cambridge, CB2 2RU, UK
40 West 20th Street, New York, NY 10011–4211, USA
477 Williamstown Road, Port Melbourne, VIC 3207, Australia
Ruiz de Alarcón 13, 28014 Madrid, Spain
Dock House, The Waterfront, Cape Town 8001, South Africa

http://www.cambridge.org

First published 2005

Printed in the United Kingdom at the University Press, Cambridge

Typeface Adobe Garamond 11/12.5 pt.   *System* LaTeX 2$_\varepsilon$ [TB]

A catalogue record for this book is available from the British Library

ISBN 0 521 83756 1

In memoriam Pál Engel

Contents

Contents   ix

Preface

From the first moment of its existence until its final fall in 1453, Byzantium had to face the imminent danger of barbaric attacks and incursions. The most frequent and dangerous of these attacks reached the empire from north of the Danube, notwithstanding that the deadly blow to Constantinople was dealt by the Ottomans arriving from the the East through Anatolia. Beginning with the Huns in the second half of the fourth century AD and ending with the Tatars in the thirteenth century, the barbaric hordes had frequently crossed the Danube and ravaged and pillaged the towns of the Balkan Peninsula, leaving them in ruins. More than once they made their incursions close to the Golden Horn, thereby endangering the imperial capital itself. Byzantium had learnt clever ways of handling the nomadic question, the most effective being the hire of nomadic warriors as auxiliaries to fight against Byzantium's enemies. But even the most cunning diplomacy could not prevent the temporary influxes of nomads, which, more often than not, proved devastating to the sedentary population of the Balkans. The nomads were generally compelled to cross the Danube by other nomads from the East, so it was a whole chain of warlike events that led to the appearance of barbaric nomads in Byzantine territory.

One major wave of nomadic tribes proved instrumental in the formation of a new state: Esperükh's nomadic warriors founded the Bulgarian Empire between the Danube and the Haimos (Balkan) Mountains in 679–80. The conquering Bulgar-Turks became slavicised in the course of the two subsequent centuries, and the adoption of Christianity by Boris in 864 meant their final assimilation into the Byzantine oecumene. But Byzantium had never acquiesced in the loss of Moesia, a former territory of the empire, and after several attempts it was Emperor Basileios II Boulgaroktonos ('Killer of the Bulgars') who finally crushed the Bulgars' resistance in 1018 and incorporated what was then Bulgaria into the Romaic Empire. Though the process of rehellenisation of the southern Slavic population began and Bulgaria lost both its political and administrative-ecclesiastical independence, Byzantium could not eliminate the nomadic question from its northern frontiers. Moreover, the annihilation of Byzantium's northern rival brought about a power gap in this region and Byzantium was again in direct confrontation with the renewed and vigorous attacks of the nomads.

In the eleventh century the Pechenegs and the Uz were the protagonists of the historical scene on the right bank of the Danube. From the second half of the same century a new nomadic confederacy entered Byzantium's sphere of interest – that of the Cumans. Following age-old techniques, Byzantium used Cuman warriors to crush Pecheneg hegemony in the Balkans. From 1091 the Cumans gained the upper hand in the Balkans, and their role in the re-establishment of the Bulgarian Empire in 1185–6 and in its eventual fate was fundamental. Furthermore, they played a pre-eminent historical role in the history of the Fourth Crusade, the Latin Kingdom of Constantinople and the Nikaian Empire. After the Tatar invasion of Eastern Europe in 1241, they were forced to flee to the West, and several groups settled in the Balkan Peninsula. Utilising their former intimate links with the Bulgarian elite, they twice appeared as founders of new dynasties (the Terterids and Šišmanids of Bulgaria). The Tatars subjugated the Second Bulgarian Empire, which was obliged to pay tribute to the new Tatar state of the Golden Horde. Towards the end of the thirteenth century and in the first decades of the fourteenth, Bulgaria was in direct dependence on the Golden Horde.

It is the Cumans and Tatars, nomadic warriors of the steppe, who are the focus of this book. I shall trace their historical fate in the Balkans, the westernmost stage of their wanderings, from 1185 until the middle of the fourteenth century. Both the chronological and the geographical frameworks of my book need some explanation. As far as the starting point is concerned, other events could equally well have been considered, such as the Cumans' first appearance in the Balkans in the second half of the eleventh century (as in the works of Michael Attaleiates, Anna Komnene and other Byzantine authors), or the first Tatar invasion, in 1241. But for the most part the early Cuman incursions did not exceed, at least in character and size, other nomadic influxes to which the Byzantines had become accustomed in the foregoing centuries. The Cuman participation in the foundation of the Second Bulgarian Empire in 1185 and the subsequent years, however, brought about basic changes in the political and ethnic map of the Balkans. Since 1185 seems to be a real turning point in the history of the Balkans, therefore, I deemed it reasonable to commence my narrative at that point. The terminus of my discussion is the middle of the fourteenth century. Although a sharp dividing line cannot be drawn, a few dates may indicate that a new era began in the history of the Balkanic lands at that time. The Tatar period of the Balkans came to a complete end with Berdibek Khan's death in 1359 and the subsequent anarchy in the Golden Horde. By contrast, the Ottoman powers' advance in Europe can be marked by the following major events: the seizure of Gallipoli in 1354, the occupation of Edirne in 1361, and finally, the loss of Serbian independence at Kosovo Polje in 1389. These events of the second half of the fourteenth century, since they herald the new Ottoman period, fall outside the scope of my work.

As far as the geographical framework of this book is concerned, it is broader than the term 'Balkans' would normally permit. The 'Balkans' as a geographical and cultural term designates the territories lying south of a line between the Sava and the Lower Danube. The western frontiers of the Balkans were rather loose: medieval Bosnia, with its mixed Catholic and Orthodox population in the pre-Ottoman period, can be regarded as a transitory territory, while Croatia and Dalmatia surely belonged to Western European civilisation. To the north, I have included medieval Wallachia and Moldavia and their historical antecedents. In the strict geographical sense, the territories between the Lower Danube, the Eastern Carpathian Mountains and the Dniester do not belong to what we call the Balkans. These territories represented the final stages of nomadic migration, and their fate was directly connected to that of the Balkans. The history and cultural traditions of these two Romanian principalities belong to that of the Balkans; they constantly stood and grew under the cultural influence of Byzantium. That is why I have included the history of these territories (within the indicated time-frame) in my book.

Finally, I must explain why I have restricted my investigations to the Cumans (a generally ethnic term) and the Tatars (generally a political one). These two peoples undoubtedly played a major role in the history of the Balkans. Their history belongs to that of the Turco-Mongolian world. A separate chapter could have been devoted to the Iranian people of the Alans or Yas, who also had a special role in the military and ethnic history of the Balkans, their role, together with that of the Catalan Company, being especially significant in the first decade of the fourteenth century. Similarly, the first Turkish mercenaries in Byzantium, often Christianised and called *Tourkopouloi*, played a significant role in the events between 1259 and 1319. Later, the first Turkish incursions into the Balkans up to the time when Orhan's son Süleyman had irrevocably set foot in Tzympe, near Gallipoli, in 1352, are also very important. The Yas, the *Tourkopouloi* and the early Balkanic activities of the Turks could equally have been included in this book. Despite having researched their history in the Balkans extensively, however, I finally decided to exclude them here. I am convinced that the *Tourkopouloi* and the Turks need separate treatment: their history belongs rather to the historical antecedents of Ottoman presence in the Balkans. Sufficient grounds could be given for the inclusion of the Alans or Yas in this book, though, since they really played an active role in the battles of the age as oriental military in the Balkans. But, after the publication of A. Alemany's excellent compilation of the sources on the history of the Alans (Alemany, *Alans*), I felt relieved of any need to include them in my treatment.

Much has been written on the history of the Balkans in this period (Ostrogorsky, *Gesch.*, pp. 285–366 (331–440); Vasiliev, *Hist. Byz.*, II, pp. 440–621; Jireček, *Serb.*, pp. 269–412; Jireček, *Bulg.*, pp. 209–90; Zlatarski, *Ist.*, II, pp. 410–83, III, pp. 1–575; Mutafčiev, *Ist.*, II, pp. 30–198; Spinei, *Moldavia*), and similarly much has been done to elucidate the history of the Cumans and the Tatars (Golubovskij, *PTP*; Marquart, *Komanen*; Rasovskij, 'Polovcy' 1–4; Rásonyi, 'Turcs non-isl.'; Hammer-Purgstall, *GH*; Howorth, *History*, II/1; Spuler, *GH*; Grekov-Jakubovskij, *ZO*; Safargaliev, *Raspad*; Kafalı, *AO*; Vásáry, *AH*), but their history in the Balkans has been rather neglected. Apart from scattered notices and hints, there are no monographs devoted to the history of the Cumans and Tatars in the Balkans, and even those works that touch on the subject have dealt with the Cumans and the Tatars from the viewpoint of different 'national' (Bulgarian, Serbian and Romanian) histories. Bulgarian researchers, especially, have shown a keen interest in the Cuman and Tatar presence in Bulgarian history (Zlatarski, Mutafčiev and Nikov). During the past twenty years the Bulgarian P. Pavlov and the Romanian E. Oberländer-Târnoveanu have made particularly important and valuable contributions to the theme (for their works, see the Bibliography). My primary aim was not to produce a history of the Balkanic lands (Byzantium, Bulgaria, Serbia, Wallachia and Moldavia), but to discover how the Cumans and Tatars bear on this history. It was difficult to determine how best to organise the heterogeneous data, since the history dealt with in this book is not that of a state, but covers the process of dispersion of nomadic tribes whose original home lay outside the Balkan peninsula. The most reasonable solution seemed to be to group the material around certain minor historical periods of Balkanic history, compromising chronological and geopolitical principles to a degree that I believe will be acceptable. The material is arranged according to what seemed to work best in practice, and, although I have tried to avoid it, there will inevitably be minor overlaps of both chronology and geography. I hope, however, that these will not detract from the book's comprehensibility. Equally, because the aim is to identify Cuman and Tatar activity and influence rather than simply to chart the history of the Balkans, and because of the fragmentary character of much of our evidence, there are evident chronological gaps. That is why Chapter 6 ('Cumans and Tatars on the Serbian scene') and Chapter 7 ('Cumans in Byzantine service after the Tatar conquest, 1242–1333') may seem to present a collection of vignettes of events in which the Cumans and Tatars participated, but which are not sufficiently linked in a meaningful way. Though I am fully aware of this unevenness of treatment, which gives rise at times to discontinuity, more often than not it is the character of the extant sources that prevents a more consistent treatment and in-depth analysis of the events. A more coherent presentation was practically impossible.

Let me say a few words about some technical details. The Abbreviations and Bibliography form two sections at the end of the book. In the Abbreviations, shorter titles refer to works whose full titles can be found in the Bibliography. Each work referred to in the text of the book has an abbreviation. The Bibliography is larger than the Abbreviations, since it includes works that have no abbreviations and that consequently are not referred to in the text. The aim of the compilation of this larger, though not exhaustive, bibliography is to offer fuller information to enable further reading and research into the various topics of the book. The transcription of Greek, Cyrillic, Arabic, Persian and Turkic words follows accepted systems of transcription and/or transliteration. Their interpretation will cause no problem to the expert. However, when longer Greek passages are cited, the original script has been used.

Proper usage of geographical names presents a special problem in medieval Balkanic history since a place may well have different names in different languages. Current state borders, more often than not, differ considerably from the medieval ones, and even within the 180 years (1185–1365) covered in this book, the overlordship of territories and cities often changed. My basic principle in each case was to use the geographical name in the dominant language of the polity to which the place belonged in the age in question. Thus I have used Greek place-names in discussing Eastern Thrace, although these territories later fell under Ottoman rule and now belong to Turkey. Geographical names of the Hungarian Kingdom are given in Hungarian, irrespective of whether these places currently belong to Romania or to Serbia. Of course, this practice could not be totally consistent. For example, the southern part of Bulgaria was a territory frequently disputed by Byzantium and Bulgaria, so the Bulgarian and Greek forms are used alternately ('Plovdiv' and 'Philippoupolis' are both correct forms).

To help readers get their bearings, I have included a comparative 'List of geographical names' as Appendix 1. In Appendix 2, the 'Chronological table of dynasties' provides a quick-reference overview of the rulers of the Golden Horde, Bulgaria, Byzantium, Serbia and Hungary. In Appendix 3, four maps help to locate the places. The maps are merely technical aids, and I do not claim to call them pieces of historical cartography.

Finally, let me express my sincere gratitude and thanks to all those friends and colleagues who, by their critical remarks and bibliographical suggestions, have helped me to improve the text of this book. Among their number are Professors Gyula Káldy-Nagy, András Róna-Tas, Peter Golden, László Solymosi, and above all Professor Pál Engel. Professor Engel was a fine and erudite historian of the Central European Middle Ages, whose untimely death was an irreparable loss for his colleagues and friends. I humbly dedicate this book to his memory.

CHAPTER ONE

Introduction

REMARKS ON THE SOURCES

The greatest difficulty in investigating the Cumans and Tatars, like that encountering anyone who investigates the Eurasian nomadic peoples, lies in the almost total lack of indigenous sources. (The *Secret History of the Mongols* is a rare and happy exception.) Chinese, Islamic, Byzantine and medieval western historiographies are severely biased against the nomadic foes, and reflect only certain aspects of nomadic life. So, willy-nilly, we must be content with a Cuman and Tatar history written mainly through the prism of the 'civilised' enemy. The most we can do is to apply an equally 'severe' criticism of the sources, thereby making an attempt to find an equilibrium between the tendentiousness of the sources and the historical reality they reflect. The basic written sources of the time-span treated in this book are undoubtedly the Byzantine narrative works. Their testimony can be corroborated and supplemented by some Latin and Slavic sources, especially in the age of the Third and Fourth Crusades (Ansbert, Robert de Clari and Geoffroi Villehardouin) and the Tatar invasion of the Balkans (Albericus Trium Fontium, Thomas of Spalato, etc.). These sources will always be referred to in the appropriate place, but the basic Byzantine sources, to which reference is made on practically every page, need a separate short treatment here, so that readers may become familiar with them. There follows a short sketch of the five basic Byzantine narrative sources relating to the period 1185–1365.[1]

Niketas Choniates (c. 1150–1213)

Born in Chonai (former Kolossai), Niketas Choniates was originally called Akominatos. He arrived in Constantinople in his childhood. He later

---

[1] Only the most essential data will be given: the critical edition (if there is one) or edition, a modern translation (if there is one) and two bibliographies (Karayan.-Weiss and *Byz.-turc.*) for further references. It must be borne in mind that all these texts and their Latin translations can also be found in the Paris, Venice and Bonn corpuses of Byzantine historians.

became secretary to Emperor Isaakios Angelos, and from 1189 was governor of the *thema* of Philippoupolis. After the capture of Constantinople by the Latins in 1204, he fled to Nikaia, and occupied important posts in the court of Emperor Theodoros Laskaris I. His works are theological and rhetorical treatises, speeches and poems, and one historical work entitled *Chronike diegesis* (Χρονικὴ διήγησις). The latter treats events between 1118 and 1206, and consists of twenty-one books, referred to under the name of the ruling emperor; for instance, Isaakios Angelos in Books I–III, Alexios III in Books I–III, Isaakios Angelos in Book I, Alexios Doukas Mourtzouphlos in Book I, capture of the City in Book I, Statues of Constantinople in Book I. For the Second Bulgarian Kingdom and the Fourth Crusade he is the primary and sometimes an eyewitness source.

Critical edition: Nik. Chon. *Hist.*/van Dieten, I–II.

Translation: Grabler, *Abenteuer*; Grabler, *Kreuzfahrer*.

Literature: Karayan.-Weiss, II, pp. 460–1; *Byz.-turc.*, I, pp. 270–5.

Georgios Akropolites (1217–1282)

Born in Constantinople, Akropolites was sent to Nikaia in 1233 and became the tutor of the eventual Emperor Theodoros Laskaris II, who, after his enthronement in 1254, entrusted Akropolites with important tasks. In 1261 Akropolites returned to the reconquered capital of Constantinople with Emperor Michael Palaiologos VIII. He was sent as a diplomat to Lyon and Trapezunt. His works include poems, rhetorical and theological treatises, and one historical work entitled *Chronike syngraphe* (Χρονικὴ συγγραφή). This is a continuation of Nik. Chon. *Hist.*, and treats events between 1203 and 1261. An objective and reliable source.

Critical edition: Georg. Akr. *Chron.*/Heisenberg, I, pp. 1–189.

Edition: Georg. Akr. *Chron.*/Bekker.

No modern translation.

Literature: Karayan.-Weiss, II, pp. 461–2; *Byz.-turc.*, I, pp. 137–9.

Georgios Pachymeres (1242–1310)

Pachymeres was born in Nikaia and moved to Constantinople in 1261, where he held high ecclesiastical and state offices. His works include rhetorical and philosophical treatises, poems, letters, and one historical work entitled *Syngraphikai historiai* (Συγγραφικαὶ ἱστορίαι). It treats events between 1261 and 1308, and consists of fifteen books (six books for Michael VIII's reign, seven for Andronikos II's reign), each of which bears the name of the ruling emperor as its title. By way of an introduction, the period between 1255 and 1261 is also discussed in brief. This work is a continuation of Georg. Akr. *Chron.* Pachymeres was the greatest polyhistor of his age, with a very solid knowledge of classical antiquity. A strong tendency to archaise and a prevalence of Greek Orthodox theological views are characteristic of his works. For the second half of the thirteenth century he is the primary Byzantine source.

> Critical edition: Pachym. *Hist.*/Failler-Laurent, I–II (the first six books only).
> Edition: Pachym. *Hist.*/Bekker, I–II.
> Translation: Pachym. *Hist.*/Failler-Laurent, I–II. (French).
> Literature: Karayan.-Weiss, II, pp. 492–3; *Byz.-turc.*, I, pp. 148–50.

Nikephoros Gregoras (c. 1290/1–1360)

Gregoras was the greatest polyhistor of the fourteenth century. Because he was an active opponent of Gregorios Palamas, Emperor Ioannes Kantakouzenos banished him to the Chora monastery in Constantinople for a certain time. Among his works are rhetorical, grammatical and philosophical treatises, poems, speeches and letters, and one historical work entitled *Historia Rhomaike* (Ἱστορία Ῥωμαϊκή). It covers events between 1204 and 1359, and so partly complements and partly continues Georg. Pach. *Hist.* It consists of thirty-seven books, the sources of the first seven being Georg. Akr. *Chron.* and Pachym. *Hist.*, together with other, unknown, sources. He is the primary authority for the first half of the fourteenth century. A strong tendency to archaise, in regard to both ethnonyms and ethnographical descriptions, can be observed.

> No critical edition.
> Edition: Nik. Greg. *Hist.*/Schopen-Bekker, I–III.
> Translation: Nik. Greg. *Hist.*/van Dieten.
> Literature: Karayan.-Weiss, II, pp. 493–4; *Byz.-turc.*, I, pp. 275–7.

Ioannes Kantakouzenos (1295/6–1383)

The offspring of a distinguished family, during the reign of Andronikos II Kantakouzenos held high offices. After Andronikos III's death in 1341 he had himself crowned, but succeeded in reaching the capital only in 1347. There he reigned as emperor under the name John VI until 1354. He was an excellent soldier and commander; in 1353 he called in the Ottomans, who set foot for the first time in Europe in Gallipoli in 1354. In the same year Ioannes V Palaiologos coerced him to abdicate from the throne, and in 1355 he became a monk at Mount Athos under the name Ioasaph. He wrote several philosophical and theological treatises, and one historical work entitled *Historia* (Ἱστορία). It consists of four books, and deals with the events between 1320 and 1356, though he glances at events as late as 1362. In general it is a reliable source, and sometimes complements Nik. Greg. *Hist.* well.

No critical edition.

Edition: Kant. *Hist.*/Schopen, I–III.

Translation: Kant. *Hist.*/Fatouros-Krischer, I–II.

Literature: Karayan.-Weiss, II, pp. 494–5; *Byz.-turc.*, I, pp. 177–9.

CUMANS AND TATARS

Before proceeding to our work proper, a few words need to be said about the historical past of the nomadic tribes that are most frequently referred to in this book. In brief: who are the Cumans and the Tatars, and where did they come from before entering the history of the Balkans?

By the 1030s the nomadic confederacy of the Kipchaks dominated the vast territories of the present-day Kazak steppe, the Uz (or Oguz) tribes (called *Torki* in the Russian sources) occupied the area between the Yayik (Ural) and the Volga rivers, while the Pecheneg tribal confederacy stretched from the Volga to the Lower Danube, including the vast steppe region of what is now the Ukraine, Moldavia and Wallachia. Considering the nomadic way of life of these peoples, these frontiers can be regarded only as approximate. The original homeland of the Kipchaks, the westernmost branch of the Turkic-speaking tribes, was the middle reaches of the Tobol and Ishim rivers in south-western Siberia in the ninth and tenth centuries, but, as mentioned above, by the 1030s they had spread further south. In the middle of the eleventh century a large-scale migration of nomadic peoples took place in the Eurasian steppe zone, a result of which was that parts of the Kipchak confederacy appeared also in the Pontic steppe region, south of the Russian principalities. This historical event was described by the Persian Marvazī (c. 1120)[2] and the Armenian Matthew of Edessa

---

[2] Marvazī/Minorsky, pp. 29–30: 'To them [the Turks] (also) belong the *Qūn*; these came from the land of Qitāy, fearing the Qitā-khan. They (were) Nestorian Christians, and had migrated from their habitat, being pressed for pastures. Of their numbers [is? or was?] *Äkinji b. *Qočqar (?) the Khwārezmshāh. The Qūn were followed [or pursued] by a people called the *Qāy*, who, being more numerous and stronger than they, drove them out of these [new?] pasture lands. They then moved on to the territory of the *Shārī*, and the Shārī migrated to the land of the *Türkmāns*, who in their

(d. 1142).[3] It is noteworthy that, while Marvazī speaks of a people called *qūn*, Matthew of Edessa mentions, instead, the people *xarteško* (the aspirated *ko* being an Armenian plural suffix) in connection with the same event. At the same time (towards the middle of the eleventh century), the new conquering nomads of the Pontic steppe appear in the Byzantine sources as Κούμανοι or Κόμανοι,[4] in the Latin sources as *Comani, Cumani*[5] or *Cuni*,[6] in the German sources as *Valwen*,[7] and in the Russian sources as *Polovci* (plural of *Polovec*).[8] The Armenian, German and Russian ethnonyms are simply translations of the self-appellation *Qoman/Quman*, meaning in Turkic (and in related languages) 'pale, fallow'.[9] This identification was quite evident to their contemporaries, since the Russian chronicles (for instance) use the phrase *Kumani, rekshe Polovci* several times,[10] and in a Latin source from 1241 the phrase *Comani, quos Theutonice Valwen appellamus* occurs.[11]

Though the new nomadic confederacy that appeared in the Pontic region in the eleventh century bore the name *Quman* in different sources, the Muslim sources consistently refer to it by the ethnonym *Qipčaq*, the only exception being Idrīsī, who must have taken the name *Quman* from a non-Muslim source.[12] What is the ethnic reality underlying this double

turn shifted to the eastern parts of the *Ghuzz* country. The Ghuzz Turks then moved to the territory of the *Bajanāk*, near the shores of the Armenian (?) sea.' For a detailed analysis of this passage, see Marvazī/Minorsky, pp. 95–104.

[3] Under the year 1050/1, see in Marquart, *Komanen*, pp. 54–5.

[4] *Byz.-turc.*, II, pp. 167–8.   [5] For its occurrences, see Gombos, *Cat.*, IV, pp. 46–7.

[6] *SRH*, I, p. 518; II, p. 646, and Györffy, 'Kun és komán', pp. 11–15. Györffy, in his later work, represented a particular view of the ethnonym *Cuni*. Since the Hungarian appellation of the Cumans, the ethnonym *Kun* (*Cunus, Cuni* in the Hungarian chronicles), was also applied to earlier nomadic tribes such as the Pechenegs and Uz, Györffy came to the conclusion that the Hungarian name *Kun* must be separated from the ethnonym *Qun* (attested in Bīrūnī and Marvazī) and can most probably be derived from the ethnonym *Hun* (Györffy, 'Kun és komán', esp. pp. 18–19). This hypothesis cannot be defended, since the identity of the ethnonyms *Quman* and *Qun* is beyond doubt. Consequently, the Hungarian name of the Cumans must go back to one of their self-appellations, i.e. to *Qun*. Further evidence of the *Quman = Qun* identity can be found in the Russian annals. In the Lavrent'evskaia letopis', under the year 6604 (= 1096), a certain Cuman occurs whose name was *Kun* (*Polovčinu imenem Kunui: PSRL*, I, p. 239). The same person is called *Kuman* in the parallel account in the Ipat'evskaja letopis' (*Polovčinu imenem Kumanu: PSRL*, II, p. 229). The form *Kunui* is probably a corruption of *Kunu*, Russian dative from *Kun*. This identification was first referred to by Marquart, *Komanen*, p. 57, but later Pelliot, 'Comans', p. 136, refuted it. Nevertheless, Pelliot's arguments are not convincing, and I see no real reason to object Marquart's conjecture.

[7] Gombos, *Cat.*, I, pp. 23, 171, 194, 269, 307–8, 424, 477, 505, 546, 776; II, pp. 852, 880, 1318, 1331; III, pp. 1732–5, 1740, 1762, 1767, 1792–5, 1826, 1858, 1863, 1880, 1884, 1903, 1957.

[8] Németh, *HMK*, pp. 142–3.   [9] See Németh, '*quman* und *qūn*', pp. 99–101.

[10] In the Lavrent'evskaja letopis': *PSRL*, I, pp. 234, 376.

[11] Fejér, *CD*, IV/1, p. 213. A few further examples can be found in the *Floridi Horti Ordinis Praemonstratensis* under the year 1227: 'Chumanorum, quos Theutonici Walwein vocant' (*MGH SS*, XXIII, p. 511), and in the *Annales Cracovienses compilati* under the year 1135: 'Plaucorum sive Comanorum' (*Mon. Pol. hist.*, II, p. 832, and III, p. 347).

[12] Idrīsī/Jaubert, II, pp. 399–401.

usage of names? On the basis of Marvazī's text we may claim that the Kipchaks and Cumans were originally two separate peoples. The Cumans must have lived to the east of the large bend of the Huanghe, in the vicinity of other Nestorian peoples such as, for example, the originally Turkic Öngüts. The Kitans spread their dominions to include this territory at the end of the tenth century, and the Kitan expansion must have expelled a large number of tribes from their former habitats. The Cumans, or Cuns, must have reached the territory of the Kipchak tribal confederacy in southeastern Siberia and the Kazak steppe round the middle of the eleventh century. The historical process is obscure, and essential data are lacking, but the final result is indisputable: two Turkic confederacies, the Kipchaks and the Cumans, had merged by the twelfth century. A cultural and political intermingling took place, and from the middle or end of the twelfth century it is impossible to detect any difference between the numerous appellations applied to the same tribal confederacy. Though they were originally the names of different components of the confederacy, by that time these appellations (*Qipčaq*, *Quman* and its various translations: *Polovec, Valwe, Xarteš*, etc.) became interchangeable: they denoted the whole confederacy irrespective of the origin of the name. As Marquart, the greatest authority on the ethnogenesis of the Cumans and Kipchaks, has put it: 'Seit dem Ende des 12. Jahrhunderts sind die Namen Qypčaq, Polowci und Komanen nicht mehr auseinander zu halten.'[13] The best example to demonstrate this fusion of different names can be found in Guillelmus Rubruc, the famous Franciscan traveller of the thirteenth century, who expressly identifies the terms *Qipčaq* and *Quman*. After he left the Crimea for the East, he wrote as follows: 'In this territory the Cumans called Kipchak used to graze their flocks, but the Germans call them Valans and their province Valania, and Isidorus calls (the region stretching) from the river Don as far as the Azov Sea and the Danube, Alania. And this land stretches from the Danube as far as the Don, the borderline of Asia and Europe; one can reach there in two months with quick riding as the Tatars ride. The whole land is inhabited by the Cumans and the Kipchaks, and even further from the Don to the Volga, which rivers are at a distance of ten days' journey.'[14] At another place: 'And in the territory between these two rivers [i.e. the Don and the

---

[13] Marquart, *Komanen*, p. 140. Cf. also pp. 78–9.

[14] 'In hac [sc. terra] solebant pascere Commani qui dicuntur Capchat [var. Capthac], a Theutonicis vero dicuntur Valani et provincia Valania, ab Ysidoro vero dicitur, a flumine Tanay usque ad paludes Meotidis et Danubium, Alania. Et durat ista terra in longitudine a Danubio usque Tanaym, qui est terminus Asie et Europe, itinere duorum mensium velociter equitando, prout equitant Tartari; que tota inhabitabatur a Commanis et Capchat, et etiam ultra a Tanay usque Etiliam, inter que flumina sunt x diete magne.' (Rubruc, *Itinerarium* XII.6, in *Sin. Franc.*, I, pp. 194–5). *Valania* as a

Volga] where we continued our way, the Cuman Kipchaks lived before the Tatars conquered them.'[15] In the twelfth century and at the beginning of the thirteenth, the Kipchak-Cuman confederacy occupied an immense land stretching from the middle reaches of the Irtysh as far as the Lower Danube. This vast territory had never been politically united by a strong central power before the advent of the Mongol conquerors in 1241. There existed no Kipchak or Cuman empire, but different Cuman groups under independent rulers, or khans, who acted on their own initiative, meddling in the political life of the surrounding areas such as the Russian principalities, Byzantium in the Balkans, the Caucasus and Khwarezm.[16] The territory of this Kipchak-Cuman realm, consisting of loosely connected tribal units, was called *Dašt-i Qipčaq* (Kipchak steppes) by the Muslim historiographers and geographers,[17] *Zemlja Poloveckaja* (Polovcian Land) or *Pole Poloveckoe* (Polovcian Plain) by the Russians,[18] and *Cumania* in the Latin sources.[19] Naturally enough, *Dašt-i Qipčaq* or *Cumania* was not known to the various sources in precise terms, but as a *pars pro toto*; the Muslim sources meant the eastern parts of *Dašt-i Qipčaq*, while the Russian and Western sources had the western parts of Cumania in mind. Depending on their region and their time, different sources each used their own word to denote different sections of the vast Cuman territory. At the beginning of the thirteenth century, for instance, when the Cuman missions of the Dominicans began to work their way to the east of the Carpathian Basin, Cumania was predominantly the territory of today's Wallachia and Moldavia, while its eastern frontiers were rather loose.[20] For the Russians, the *Pole Poloveckoe* was primarily the steppe region between the Dnieper and the Volga.

name for Cumania does not occur elsewhere, and it is probably an invention of Rubruc taken from the German ethnonym *Valwe* in order to make possible a link between *Alania* and *Valania*. The two terms have nothing to do with each other in either the linguistic or the geographical respect. For a description of *Alania* by Isidorus Hispalensis, see his *Etymologiarum libri*, in *PG* 82, p. 504.

[15] 'Et inter ista duo flumina [sc. Tanaim et Etiliam] in illis terris per quas transivimus habitabant Comani Capchac, antequam Tartari occuparent eos' (Rubruc, *Itinerarium*, XIV.3, in *Sin. Franc.*, I, p. 200).

[16] For the different Cuman groups, see Rasovskij, 'Polovcy', III: Predely 'Polja Poloveckogo', pp. 58–77. For the tribes of the Cuman-Qipchaqs, see the excellent survey of Golden, *Tribes*. For the Cuman–Russian interactions see the foundational study of Pritsak, 'Polovcians'.

[17] The Kipchaks are first mentioned as neighbours of Khwarezm in c. AD 1030 (AH 421) by Bayhaqī, and the term *Dašt-i Qipčaq* occurs for the first time in Nāṣir-i Ḫusraw's *Dīvān*, replacing the former *mafāzat al-ghuzziyya* used by Iṣṭaḫrī. For these data, see Bartol'd, 'Guzz', in *Soč.* V, p. 525, and 'Kipčaki', in *Soč.* V, p. 550.

[18] E.g. *PSRL*, I, p. 522; II, p. 781, and *passim*.

[19] For occurrences in the Greek sources, see *Byz.-turc.*, II, p. 167; in the Latin sources, see Gombos, *Cat.*, IV, p. 47. Practically all the data for *Cumania* were attested in the thirteenth century.

[20] Makkai, *Milkói püspökség*, pp. 19ff.

Cumania became known in its whole width and breadth only after the tempest of the Mongol invasion in 1241, especially in the wake of the famous Dominican and Franciscan travellers. They had fixed the territory of Cumania to the boundaries that existed on the eve of the great Mongolian thunderbolt. In 1246, Plano Carpini personally traversed the whole land of the Cumans (*totam terram Comanorum*), which is totally flat (*tota est plana*) and has four major rivers, the Dnieper, Don, Volga and Yayik (i.e. the Ural).[21] Later, he described the borders of Cumania exactly, ending with the words: 'And the above-mentioned land is vast and long.'[22] It is important to note that, while Plano Carpini did not define the eastern border of Cumania, Benedictus Polonus, who was his companion during the journey, clearly states in his own travel account that the eastern border of Cumania is the river Yayik (i.e. the Ural), where the land of the Kangits begins.[23]

Who are these Kangits? It is the other Franciscan traveller, Guillelmus Rubruc, who helps us to understand the situation clearly. In his *Itinerarium* he claims that this people is related to the Cumans (*Cangle, quedam parentela Comanorum*), and in another place he asserts that north of the Caspian Sea there is a desert in which the Tatars now live, 'but formerly certain Cumans lived there who were called *Qanglï*'.[24] Consequently, the *Qanglï*, whose name was known well before the Mongol period,[25] must have been a Turkic tribe or tribal confederacy closely related to the Kipchak-Cumans. Their name often occurs in the *Secret History of the Mongols*, where it is always linked with that of the Kipchaks (*Ķanglin Kibča'ut*).[26] In the enumeration of peoples defeated by the Tatars, Plano Carpini also placed the names of these two peoples side by side: *Kangit, Comani*.[27] All in all,

---

[21] See Plano Carpini, *Ystoria Mongalorum*, IX.13, in *Sin. Franc.*, I, pp. 107–8.

[22] 'Et est terra predicta maxima et longa' (Plano Carpini, *Ystoria Mongalorum* IX.20, in *Sin. Franc.*, I, p. 112).

[23] Benedictus Polonus, 8: 'In fine Comanie transierunt fluvium cui nomen Iarach [var. *Jajach*], ubi incipit terra Kangitarum' (*Sin. Franc.*, I, p. 138).

[24] 'Prius vero erant ibi quidam Comani qui dicebantur Cangle' (Rubruc, *Itinerarium*, XX.7 and XVIII.4, in *Sin. Franc.*, I, pp. 218, 211).

[25] See Pelliot-Hambis, *Campagnes*, I, pp. 43–114. There is an Old Turkic word *qañlï*, 'wagon, cart, carriage' (Clauson, *ED*, p. 638), and we must agree with Clauson, who claims that 'it is an open question whether the tribe was so called because it used carts, or whether, as is more prob., carts were so called because the Kañli:, a western tribe, were the first Turks to use them' (*ibid.*). Cf. also Clauson, *Uyğur*, p. 147. The tribal name *Qañlï* can most plausibly be derived from *Kang*, the Iranian name of the Middle and Lower Syr-Darya region, and would mean 'people from Kang' (cf. Marquart, *Komanen*, p. 78; but later, on pp. 168–9, he denies this possibility without referring to his former view).

[26] §§ 262, 270: *Ķanglin Kibča'ut* (*SHM*/Ligeti, pp. 235, 243); § 274: *Ķanglin Kibča'ud-i* (*SHM*/Ligeti, p. 247); § 198: *Ķanglin-i Kimča'ud-i* (*SHM*/Ligeti, p. 163). The form *qïmčaq* must have been a secondary form of the name; it is not attested elsewhere.

[27] See Plano Carpini, *Ystoria Mongalorum* VII.9, in *Sin. Franc.*, I, p. 90.

it may safely be assumed that the Qanglï were the eastern tribal group of the Kipchak-Cuman confederacy, their territory lying east of the Ural river.

After the blow at Kalka in 1223, when the Cumans first tasted defeat at Tatar hands, and then their mortal defeat in 1241, when the Kipchak-Cuman confederacy ceased to exist as a political entity, the Kipchak tribes were partly dispersed, and partly became subject to the new Tatar-Mongol conquerors. Who were these newcomers in the nomadic world? Before the thirteenth century the ethnonym *Tatar* was used to denote different ethnic realities. Its first occurrences can be found in the Orkhon inscriptions (*otuz tatar, toquz tatar*), where it was the name of tribes who, in all likelihood, spoke a Mongolian language.[28] But certain western groups of Tatar tribes became associated with Turkic tribes, as were the Kimeks at the river Irtysh, who are said by Gardīzī to have been a branch of the Tatars.[29] But the majority of Tatars remained in the vicinity of the Kerülen river, near the Buyir-nur Lake, which, according to Rašīd ad-Dīn, was their basic habitat.[30] The Tatar tribes were Chingis Khan's ancestral enemies, and the reason why the victorious Mongol conquerors of Chingis Khan were later called Tatars by most of the sources is a historical puzzle unsatisfactorily explained to this day.[31] The initial words of Plano Carpini's famous work clearly state that by the middle of the thirteenth century the ethnonyms *Mongol* and *Tatar* had become totally synonymous ('Incipit Ystoria Mongalorum quos nos Tartaros appellamus'),[32] like the ethnonyms *Qipčaq* and *Quman*. Consequently, throughout this book we may take the liberty of using these terms interchangeably, though with a certain preference for the terms *Quman* and *Tatar*, since they were favoured by our sources relating to the Balkanic area.

Having surveyed the use of the ethnonyms *Qipčaq, Quman* and *Tatar*, we may fairly ask to what extent these and other ethnonyms can be utilised in ethnic history. The brief answer is: only in a very limited way. These appellations, like those of any large nomadic confederacy or state, are primarily *political* names referring to the leading, integrating tribe or clan of the confederacy or state. The Cumans and Tatars, when they appear in written sources, are members of a confederacy irrespective of their tribal origin. Former tribal names disappear before our eyes when the tribe in question

---

[28] See Orkun, *ETY*, IV, pp. 161, 167, 169. Cf. also Thomsen, *Inscr.*, p. 140.

[29] Gardīzī/Martinez, pp. 120–1.

[30] Raš./Ali-zade, I/1, p. 159: 'va yurtī ki bā-īšān maḥṣūṣtar ast mawżi'īst ki ān-rā Būyir [var. *Būyūr*] nāvūr gūyand'.

[31] For the use of the ethnonym *Tatar*, see Bartol'd, 'Tatar', in *Soč.*, V, pp. 559–61; Pritsak, 'Two migratory movements', p. 159; Kljaštornyj, 'Das Reich der Tataren'.

[32] See Plano Carpini, *Ystoria Mongalorum*, in *Sin. Franc.*, I, p. 27.

becomes part of a political unit, and hitherto unknown tribal names may crop up in sources suddenly, though obviously they existed before the point at which they are mentioned. For instance, when we hear of an incursion of Cumans in the Balkanic territories of Byzantium, it means that certain tribes of the Cuman confederacy took part in a military enterprise. But, to our great regret, the foreign sources are silent about the ethnic composition of the nomadic marauders. It is a rare and fortunate event indeed when our source reveals any greater detail about the nomadic assailant. One such happy case occurs when Rašīd ad-Dīn describes the Tatar campaign of 1236/7. Mengü-qa'an succeeded in capturing two leaders of the rebelling Kipchaks, Bačman and Qačir-üküle. Bačman was of the *Qipčaq* people, from the *Olbirlik* tribe, while Qačir-üküle was from the *As* tribe.[33] It is evident from this description that both leaders were of the Kipchak confederacy, but their first loyalty bound them to the Olbirlik and the As tribe respectively. The As was a tribal unit within the Kipchak confederacy, but formerly also a separate political unit, the confederacy of the Iranian Alans. Whether the Olbirlik and As leaders in question were Turks or Iranians cannot be decided with any certainty, though their names may indicate that the former was a Turkic, the latter an Iranian. This small detail preserved in Rašīd ad-Dīn may demonstrate the difficulty of making an ethnic history of the steppe region. Since the written sources have mostly preserved the ethnonyms of the leading tribe of a confederacy, the most we can do is investigate the political role of the Cumans and Tatars in the political history of the Balkans. The ethnonym 'Cuman' embraces mainly Turkic ethnic components, though other elements (such as Iranian, as in the case of Qačir-üküle) may be hidden under the general designation. But in the case of the term 'Tatar', the situation is much more complicated. The Tatars, having conquered Eastern Europe in 1241, mingled with the basically Turkic population of Dašt-i Qipčaq. Consequently, the label *Tatar* will be used in this book only as a political term, without any ethnic connotation.

Finally, brief mention must be made of the phenomenon whereby ethnic names often became personal names for many reasons. A direct

---

[33] Raš./Ali-zade, II/I, p. 129: 'az jamā'at-i Qibčāqān az qavm-i Ölberlīk ['wlbrlyk] va Qačir-üküle [qajr-'wkwlh] az qavm-i Ās har du-rā bā-girift.' The same Kipchak tribe can be found in Dimašqī's list as *Ölberli* ['lbrly] (Tiz., I, pp. 539, 541; in Dimashqī/Mehren, p. 264, in the corrupt form [brkw'], read as *Bärgü* by Marquart, *Komanen*, p. 157; and *Elberli* by d'Ohsson, *Histoire*, I, p. 338, n. I). It is also attested in the *Slovo o polku Igoreve* as *Ol'bery* (Menges, *Vost. èl.*, pp. 122–4; Fasmer, III, p. 133). For a detailed description of this tribal name, see Golden, 'Cumanica'. For *Alpar, Olper* as Cuman personal names in Hungary in the thirteenth century, see Rásonyi, 'Anthrop.', p. 135; Rásonyi, 'Kuman özel ad.', p. 79.

connection between the ethnonym and its bearer cannot be established in most cases. For instance, we know of a few Mongol princes of the thirteenth century who bore the name *Majar*.[34] Though these persons had nothing to do with the Magyars, (Hungarians), they owed their names to a common Mongol practice of naming newborn babies after the ethnonyms of conquered tribes and peoples. Among the Cuman names of the twelfth and thirteenth centuries we can find *Baškord*, *Imek*, *Kitan* and *Urus*.[35] As for the name *Qipčaq*, it is unattested among the Cumans,[36] but *Quman*, *Qun*[37] and *Tatar*[38] are known. By contrast, the personal names *Qipčaq*[39] and *Tatar*[40]

---

[34] For the Mongolian names *Majar, Majartai, Majaqan*, see Ligeti, 'Magyar, baskír, király', pp. 393–4.

[35] See Rásonyi, 'Kuman özel ad.', pp. 88, 106, 113, 136.

[36] At least in the thirteenth and fourteenth centuries. But in certain family names used in Hungary among the people in Kunmadaras and Karcag, former settlements of the Cumans, the ethnonym *Qipčaq* may be concealed: *Kopcsog* and *Kapcsog* (read Kopčog and Kapčog). See Mándoky, *Hantos*, p. 74, n. 4.

[37] There was a certain *Kuman* mentioned in the Russian annals under 6604 (= 1096) (see n. 6 above), who is probably identical with that mentioned under 6611 (= 1103) in the Lavrent'evskaja letopis' as *Kumana* (acc.) (*PSRL*, I, p. 279) and in the *Ipat'evskaja letopis'* as *Kunama* (acc.) (*PSRL*, II, p. 255). However, Rasovskij, 'Polovcy', I, p. 11, n. 32, doubts the authenticity of this *Kuman*, and thinks that *Kunam* is the original form, since it also occurs as a variant of the name in the Lavrent'evskaja letopis' (*PSRL*, I, 1st edition: St Petersburg, 1842, pp. 118–19). As the name *Kunam* cannot be satisfactorily explained as a Cuman name, I think that the reading *Kuman* is much more acceptable. For the name *Kun*, see n. 9 above.

[38] In a Hungarian diploma from 1333: 'Tatar filio Vgudey' (Gyárfás, III, p. 476). It is noteworthy that both Cumans, father and son, bear a Mongol name. In ch. 159 of the Hungarian chronicle composition of the fourteenth century, a certain *Tatar* is mentioned who was prince (*dux*) of the *Kuni* during the reign of King Stephen II (1116–31) (*SRH*, I, pp. 444–5). This Tatar fled to the Hungarian king from the massacre of the Greek emperor, with a few of his people ('a cede imperatoris cum paucis ad regem fugerat'). The ethnic identity of the Kuni people who fled to Stephen II is disputed. Most scholars have thought that they must be the Pechenegs who were severely beaten by the Byzantine emperor Ioannes Komnenos in the battle at Berrhoe in 1122, but there are adherents of the opinion that these Kuni were really Cumans (e.g. Kossányi, 'Úzok és kománok', p. 532, n. 3; Horváth, 'Török int.', p. 269). I am of the latter opinion, as I see no compelling reason to identify the Kuni with the Pechenegs. Nevertheless, it is not impossible that the fugitives from the battle of Berrhoe comprised both Pecheneg and Cuman contingents. For the complete account in the chronicle, with ample literature, see Makk, 'II. István', esp. pp. 253–4.

[39] 1. *Qipčaq*, third son of Qadan-oğul, sixth son of Ögödey (Raš./Tehran, I, p. 631; Raš./Ali-zade, II/1, p. 36; Raš./Blochet, pp. 169–73, 189–91).

2. *Qipčaq*, first son of Jirgiday, first son of Maquldar, son of Joči-Qasar, second son of Yesügey-bahadur (Raš./Tehran, I, p. 277).

3. *Qipčaq*, grandson of Mönglik-Ičike from the Qongqotan clan, his father was Kökčü the falconer, myriarch of the right flank; he himself was the elder emir (*amīr-i buzurg*) of Melik-Timur, son of Ariq-Böke (Raš./Tehran, II, p. 943; Raš./Blochet, p. 575).

4. *Qipčaq*, a warrior of the Jalayir tribe in Iran (Raš./Tehran, I, p. 70; Raš./Ali-zade, I/1, pp. 143–4).

5. *Qipčaqtay*, a member of the Qurčin tribe, a branch of the Kilingut-Urna'ut; he was a cousin of Qongqotan in Khorasan (Raš./Tehran, I, p. 172; Raš./Ali-zade, I/1, p. 437).

[40] The father of Nogay, the famous emir of the Golden Horde, was Tatar, first son of Buval, seventh son of Joči (Raš./Blochet, pp. 122, 139, 203). The name *Tatar* was also known to the Uygurs of the Mongol period. One of the envoys sent by Barčuq, the Uygur *idiqut*, to Chingis, was Tatar (Raš./Ali-zade, I/1, p. 339).

were in vogue among the Mongols in the thirteenth century, but the ethnonyms *Quman* and *Qun* were not used as personal names by them.
So the territorial distribution characteristic of the ethnonyms *Quman*
and *Qipčaq* (the former was used in the west, the latter in the east)
can also be observed in the distribution of the corresponding personal
names.

CHAPTER TWO

Cumans and the Second Bulgarian Empire

THE ANTECEDENTS AND OUTBREAK OF THE LIBERATION MOVEMENT

The first half of the twelfth century was the last great flourishing period of Byzantine history. During the reign of Manuel Komnenos (1143–1180), the first signs of decadence were to be seen, and from then onwards a speedy decline led to Constantinople's capture by the Latins. Byzantium's decay in the second half of the twelfth century can be ascribed to several factors, both external and internal. By the twelfth century Byzantium was not the unrivalled world power it had been before. The emergence and development of Western European cities, especially those of Italy, severely menaced Byzantium's hegemony in the world economy. Byzantine manufacture underwent serious decay, and Byzantium's economic power decreased in every respect. Although the Komnenoi tried to pursue the old imperial policy, the re-establishment of the unity of the Roman Empire was a daydream at that time. Nevertheless, this imperial policy demanded significant financial resources, and the Komnenoi emperors did not hesitate to seize every possible means of extorting more money from the population. Taxes and levies were increasing all the time, and the pauperisation of both peasants and city-dwellers proceeded rapidly. To make the contrast even sharper, the corruption of the state apparatus further aggravated the difficult situation of the population. The employment of great numbers of mercenary troops considerably contributed to the moral degeneration of the army. The development of the commercial and naval army was neglected, and Western foreigners, especially the Venetians, gradually gained the upper hand in handling the empire's commerce. Finally, the general tendency of growing centrifugal powers in the process of feudalisation also contributed to the weakening of central power and to increasing anarchy. The social tensions could hardly be kept in order, and the townspeople's wrath and hatred towards the aristocracy and the Latin foreigners were signs of an imminent tempest. Andronikos Komnenos' short reign (1180–5) could not halt the decline; moreover, his tyrannical policy infuriated even the aristocracy. Fiascos in the empire's foreign policy (the Hungarians made considerable progress in the Balkans, and captured and ravaged Sredec in 1185, while the Serbs tried to gain independence) issued a further warning to the unsuccessful regime. The Normans of south Italy and Sicily made extraordinarily rapid progress within Byzantine territory, and, to the Byzantines' great consternation, Thessalonike, the second largest city of the empire, fell to the Norman marauders on 24 August 1185. The Norman conquerors were marching unimpeded towards the capital. Alarmed by these shocking events, the townsfolk of Constantinople ousted Emperor Andronikos from the throne in September 1185, and the aristocracy raised a new *basileus* in his stead from among their own number.

The new emperor, Isaakios II, the first member of the Angelos House to ascend the throne, was an insignificant ruler, but the circumstances were hardly conducive to his success.[1] Even so, during the first few months of his reign he succeeded in eliminating two dangerous threats. First, he sent the Byzantine commander Alexios Branas against the Normans, who had become weakened by inner discord and epidemic diseases. Branas gained a decisive victory against the Norman enemy on 7 November 1185, when they were compelled to evacuate and abandon most of the conquered territories and towns. Isaakios Angelos' second success was the pacification of the Hungarian power. Isaakios, a widower, married Margaret, the young daughter of the Hungarian king Béla III. Margaret (later named Maria in Byzantium) was under ten years old at the time.[2] The marriage must have taken place in the autumn of 1185.[3] As a dowry, Isaakios was given back some of the territories and towns that had been conquered by Béla III in 1185, including Braničevo, Niš and Sredec; but the Hungarian king retained Dalmatia, Bosnia and Srem. At the same time, Béla III ceased to support Grand Župan Stefan Nemanja and the Serbs in their fight for independence against Byzantium. As a sign of reconciliation, the relics of St John of Rila, plundered from Sredec during the campaign in 1183 and brought to the royal town Esztergom in Hungary, were returned to Sredec around that time.[4]

---

[1] For a more realistic evaluation of Isaakios Angelos, see Ostrogorsky, *Gesch.*, p. 288 (331–3).
[2] Nik. Chon. *Hist.*/van Dieten, I, p. 368,38ff. (ed. Bonn, p. 481), = Grabler, *Abenteuer*, pp. 171–2 (Stritter, II/2, pp. 672–4); Georg. Akr. *Chron.*/Heisenberg, I, p. 18,6–10.
[3] For Niketas Choniates' *Epitalamios* and *Stichoi* written on that occasion, see Moravcsik, *Árpád-kor*, pp. 259–64, with ample further references.
[4] Moravcsik, *Árpád-kor*, pp. 247–8; Bödey, *Rilai Szent Iván*.

In this moment of relative peace, when the flames of riot and enmity seemed to have been extinguished, the Bulgarian upheaval erupted and caused the Byzantines repeated trouble for more than twenty years. The exact date of the beginning of the Bulgarian movement of liberation is not known, but it must have been towards the end of 1185 or early 1186. The primary Byzantine source reporting on these events is Niketas Choniates. Since 1018, the date of the final subjugation of the Bulgars by the emperor Basileios II Boulgaroktonos ('Killer of the Bulgars'), the former Bulgaria became part of the Byzantine Empire and its inhabitants paid tax to New Rome. The general dissatisfaction felt in the 1180s throughout the Byzantine Empire must have spurred on the Bulgarian effort to gain independence. The leaders of the movement were two brothers, Peter and Asen. Niketas Choniates, the contemporary historian and sometimes eyewitness of the events, attributes the outbreak of the rebellion to two main causes. First, he thinks, the measures taken by Isaakios before his marriage to the Hungarian king's daughter gave rise to feelings of discontent. The emperor was too avaricious to pay his marriage costs from the state budget, and levied special taxes on the population.[5] According to Georgios Akropolites, 'hence sheep, pigs and oxen were collected from all the provinces of the Rhomaioi'.[6] Niketas Choniates knew that the towns near Anchialos and the inhabitants of the Haimos (Balkan) Mountains were particularly offended by this extra taxation: 'Because of his pettiness he [Isaakios] did not notice that he caused trouble also to other towns lying near Anchialos, and incited to war the barbarians living in the Balkan Mountains against himself and the Rhómaioi. [These barbarians] were formerly called Mysians (Μυσοί), and now they are named Vlakhs (Βλάχοι).'[7] This is a very important piece of information from Choniates on the beginnings of the rebellion. As for the ethnic connotations of the terms *Mysoi* and *Blachoi*, and their connections with the Bulgars, these points will be discussed in the next section of this chapter. At this juncture, it must be stated that the starting point of the 'barbarian' turbulence was in the Balkan Mountains. Choniates' argumentation, inasmuch as he ascribes major significance to Isaakios' extraordinary levies in evoking the spirit of rebellion, may be regarded as naive or one-sided, as was often the case in such accounts; but we cannot deny that the extra

---

[5] Nik. Chon. *Hist.*/van Dieten, I, p. 368 (ed. Bonn, p. 481), = Grabler, *Abenteuer*, p. 171.

[6] 'ἐντεῦθεν ἐξ ἁπάσης τῆς Ῥωμαίων ἐπαρχίας πρόβατά τε καὶ χοῖροι καὶ βόες συνήγοντο.' (Georg. Akr. *Chron.*/Heisenberg, I, p. 18₁₂–₁₃).

[7] 'καὶ ἔλαθε διὰ σμικροπρέπειαν καὶ ἄλλας μὲν πόλεις καλαμησάμενος, αἳ κατ᾽ Ἀγχίαλον συνῳκίζοντο, ἑαυτῷ δὲ μάλιστα καὶ Ῥωμαίοις ἐκπολεμώσας τοὺς κατὰ τὸν Αἷμον τὸ ὄρος βαρβάρους οἳ Μυσοὶ πρότερον ὠνομάζοντο, νυνὶ δὲ Βλάχοι κικλήσκονται' (Nik. Chon. *Hist.*/van Dieten, I, p. 368 (ed. Bonn, p. 482), = Grabler, *Abenteuer*, p. 171).

taxation must have been one of the last grievances to push the 'barbarian' population of the Balkan Mountains to take up arms against their Byzantine overlords.

The other cause of the rebellion, according to Choniates, was of a rather personal character. He writes as follows:

The leaders of the rebellion who instigated the whole people [to rebellion] were the two brothers, Petros and Asan. Both of them had their special reasons to do so. Once, they went to the emperor, who had set up his tent in Kypsella. They asked him to register them in the Roman army and to that effect to grant them – by his imperial edict – a small piece of land in the Haimos which would yield them a modest income. But their request was rejected.[8]

The two brothers were rather discontent, and Asen, especially, gave expression to his indignation, whereupon he was punished by Ioannes Sebastokrator with slaps on the face.[9] This incident must have enhanced Asen's sense of humiliation, and was one of the personal motives for his aversion to the Byzantines. What Peter and Asen wanted to obtain from the emperor was a military fief (*pronoia*) spread widely through the Byzantine Empire.[10] It also becomes clear that the centre of the revolt was in the Balkan Mountains, whence the two brothers had come to the emperor's court in Kypsella (now İpsala in Turkey).

Notwithstanding the general discontent of the people and the personal offences felt by the would-be leaders, the smouldering revolt could not immediately burst into flames, since 'in the beginning the Vlakhs shrank and turned away from the revolt to which they were incited by Petros and Asan, in their fear of the greatness of the enterprise'.[11] So the two brothers had to persuade the 'timid' Vlakhs, and the method they applied merits our admiration: it was a professional work of manipulation of which even modern politicians could be proud. The brothers had a church built in honour of the martyr St Demetrios, and a crowd of men and women 'possessed by the devil' were assembled inside. They were instructed to speak in a state of ecstasy about God's intention to remove the yoke from the shoulders of the Bulgarians and the Vlakhs (Βουλγάρων καὶ Βλάχων).

[8] Nik. Chon. *Hist.*/van Dieten, I, p. 369₅₈₋₆₄ (ed. Bonn, p. 482), = Grabler, *Abenteuer*, pp. 171–2.
[9] Nik.Chon. *Hist.*/van Dieten I, p. 369 (ed. Bonn, p. 482), = Grabler, *Abenteuer*, p. 172. It is interesting that the same story was later linked with Kaloyan (Asen and Peter's brother) by Robert de Clari.
[10] For the Byzantine *pronoia* in general, see Uspenskij, 'Pronija'; Mutafčiev, 'Vojniški zemi'; Lemerle, 'Recherches'; Ostogorski, *Pronija*. For an interpretation of the passage in question in Niketas Choniates' *History*, see Zlatarski, *Ist.*, II, pp. 435ff.; Malingoudis, 'Zweit. bulg. Staat.', pp. 83–4.
[11] 'οἱ Βλάχοι ὤκνουν τὰ πρῶτα καὶ ἀπεπήσων πρὸς τὴν ἀπόστασιν, εἰς ἣν ἐνήγοντο πρὸς τοῦ Πέτρου καὶ τοῦ Ἀσάν, τὸ τοῦ πράγματος μέγεθος ὑφορώμενοι' (Nik. Chon. *Hist.*/van Dieten, I, p. 371₁₅₋₁₇ (ed. Bonn, p. 485), = Grabler, *Abenteuer*, p. 174).

St Demetrios had obviously abandoned Thessalonike and his church there; he did not want to be with the Rhomaioi, but wanted to support them in their cause. Convinced by this impressive scene, the whole people took up arms against Byzantium, and one of the brothers, Peter, was crowned with a golden crown. The rebellion began, but the rebels could not capture the strongest fortress of the Haimos, the town of Preslav.[12] The emperor Isaakios marched against the rebels, probably some time in summer of 1186, and defeated them.[13] The rebels escaped to the mountains, and finally fled to the Istros (Danube), crossed it, and went over to the neighbouring Scythians.[14]

This was a turning point in the history of the revolt. The first onslaughts of Asen and Peter's rebellion were crushed by the Byzantine forces, and the defeated army fled to the left bank of the Danube, to the 'Scythians'. The archaic ethnonym evidently refers to the Cumans, who are mentioned throughout Choniates' work as 'Scythians' (with a few exceptions, when they are expressly called *Komanoi*). The Cumans' appearance on the historical scene marks the beginning of a new phase of the Balkanic revolt against Byzantium. Without their aid the liberation movement would soon have been extinguished. But at the invitation of Peter and Asen they crossed the Danube and overran the Balkanic countries.

Before continuing our investigation into the further warfare of the Byzantine, Cuman, and Vlakh forces, we must delve into the intricate question of the ethnic components of the Second Bulgarian Empire, for the earliest Byzantine and Latin sources attribute a major role to the Vlakhs (sometimes even omitting the Bulgars) and to the Cumans in the liberation movement.

BULGARS, VLAKHS AND CUMANS BEFORE 1185

The Cumans' presence and their role in the liberation movement since 1186 was so evident that practically everyone agrees that without their constant aid the Second Bulgarian Empire could not have come about. But as far as the Bulgars and Vlakhs are concerned, their role in the new empire is evaluated in various ways. The ethnic composition of the Second Bulgarian

---

[12] Nik. Chon. *Hist.*/van Dieten, I, pp. 371₁₇–372₄₉ (ed. Bonn, pp. 485–7), = Grabler, *Abenteuer*, pp. 174–5. Malingoudis, 'Zweit. bulg. Staat.', pp. 107–12, made an interesting attempt to connect the appearance of the possessed people to a medieval Thracian folk custom (*anastenaria*) that survived in different parts of the Balkans till the twentieth century.

[13] In problems of chronology I have leant on van Dieten's precise definitions in the footnotes of his edition of Nik. Chon. *Hist.* (these notes form the essence of his special study on the theme: van Dieten, *Erläuterungen*) and Malingoudis, 'Zweit. bulg. Staat.', pp. 113–22.

[14] Nik. Chon. *Hist.*/van Dieten, I, p. 373₅₈–9 (ed. Bonn, p. 487), = Grabler, *Abenteuer*, p. 175.

Empire has been a favourite theme of nationalistic historiography, both Bulgarian and Romanian. Sometimes diametrically opposed views have been put forward, and, sadly, most theories and arguments, sometimes even those of the best Bulgarian and Romanian scholars (Zlatarski, Mutafčiev, Jorga, Bănescu, etc.) have been strongly biased by national sentiment and by evaluation that was far from objective. On the one hand, most Bulgarian scholars have tried to minimise or sometimes to eliminate the Vlakhs' role in the re-establishment of the Bulgarian state. On the other, most Romanian scholars extol that empire as being the first (sometimes the second!) Romanian state in history. Most of these theories were unable to go beyond prejudiced concepts of nationalism, and have sought a glorious past for their respective nations through a tendentious and partisan selection and evaluation of historical data. Though many valuable analyses of minor questions have been put forward by both Bulgarian and Romanian scholars, the broader concept and tone of their works have rarely been acceptable. Their main error is that they project the modern idea of *nation* back to the Middle Ages. They attribute major significance to nationality, although it was of secondary or tertiary significance in the outworking of events. Thus, in judging the uprising of 1186, we must not be tempted to see 'national' causes behind the events. That uprising was primarily a rebellion against Byzantium's power, and the fact that different ethnic units took part in it was a secondary matter. Its primary aim was to found or re-establish a state in the former Bulgarian territories that could counteract the might of the Byzantine state. Nobody wanted a 'national' state of the Vlakhs or the Bulgars. This thought was totally alien to the mentality of the age. Since the past cannot be expropriated and monopolised by any modern nation, the Second Bulgarian Empire belongs to the *common* past and *national* heritage of the modern Bulgarian and Romanian nations. Bulgarian and Romanian historiographers, even under the disguise of Marxism, went on propagating old and sometimes new nationalistic ideas; it is the task of their successors to put aside the onerous heritage of nationalism and to adopt modern forms of national self-consciousness.[15] Our task now is to investigate the contemporary usage of ethnonyms and to find an acceptable solution to this much debated problems.

The greatest contradiction in contemporary sources, and one that has caused great difficulty for modern scholars, is the fact that in the territory of the former Bulgaria the rebels against Byzantium are mostly called Vlakhs

---

[15] For a good overview and an objective evaluation of Bulgarian and Romanian historiographies on the Second Bulgarian Empire, see Malingoudis, 'Zweit. bulg. Staat.', pp. 123–9.

(Βλάχοι in Greek, *Blaci* in Latin), and their state, the new 'Bulgaria' is called simply *Blachia, Blakia*. So the interpretation of the term 'Vlakh' has a key role in solving the problem. The Vlakhs, as is well known, were Romanised shepherds of the Balkans who lived scattered throughout the Balkan Peninsula; they were to be found in Thrace, Macedonia, Thessaly and Moesia. The basic ethnic substratum of this Vlakh population of the Balkans was undoubtedly Thracian. With the appearance of the Slavs in the Balkans from the fifth century onwards, they underwent substantial changes: a massive layer of southern Slavic loan-words in the Romanian language testifies to this effect. The term 'Vlakh' itself is of Slavic origin (Bulg., Serb. *vlach*; Sloven. *lah*; Czech, Slovak *vach*; Pol. *woch*; Russ. *волох*), where it is a Germanic borrowing meaning 'Celt, foreigner, somebody speaking a Romance language'.[16] So originally the immigrating Slavs designated the Balkanic shepherds, who spoke a neo-Latin tongue, as 'Vlakhs'. After a long while, the term 'Vlakh' became synonymous with the nomadic shepherds of the Balkans, who, for the most part, spoke a Romance language, though other Slavic elements could also mingle with them.[17] The formation of the Vlakh ethnic identity in the Balkans was accomplished by the tenth century, when they first appeared in written sources.[18] Between 976 and 1105 the Vlakhs were widespread throughout the Balkans, their territories of densest population being the south-western part of the Bulgaria *thema* of the Byzantines (Mount Grammos, the Nerečka planina, and the Bistra and Šar Mountains); the northern part of the Hellas *thema* (the valley of the Salambrias river, and the Pindos and Zygos Mountains); and the valley of the Marica river and the Balkan Mountains.[19]

It seems reasonable to glance now at certain passages in Byzantine sources that have a direct bearing on the Vlakh–Bulgar–Cuman connection. In 1020 Basileios II issued three diplomas (σιγίλλια) in which he determined the jurisdiction of the archbishopric of Ohrid, legal successor of the Bulgarian patriarchate. Having enumerated the bishoprics subjected to Ohrid, the emperor authorised the Archbishop of Ohrid 'to collect the church levy (τὸ κανονικόν) from all of them and from the Vlakhs living throughout Bulgaria and the Turks near the Vardar who are within the Bulgarian borders. They must respect and hold him in high regard and obey

---

[16] Fasmer, I, p. 345.
[17] For instance, the Vlakhs are referred to as nomadic shepherds of the Balkans in Anna Komnene's *Alexias* (cf. n. 22 below).
[18] For the seven occurrences of Vlakhs between 976 and 1105 in the Byzantine Greek sources, see Gyóni, *Paristrion*, pp. 105–6.
[19] Cf. Gyóni, *Kékaumenos*, p. 33.

his words.'[20] It is impossible to determine a more precise location for these Vlakhs, but the most important information culled from this passage is that the Vlakhs were not subjected to any fixed bishopric but only to the archbishopric of Ohrid, since they must have roamed as nomads throughout the whole territory of the former Bulgaria.[21] Anna Komnene in her *Alexias* relates that in 1091 Emperor Alexios Komnenos ordered Kaisar Nikephoros Melissenos to 'enlist as many recruits as possible from the Bulgars and from those who pursue a nomadic way of life (in common language they are called Vlakhs)'.[22] This statement of Anna Komnene is crucial, since it clearly shows that at the end of the eleventh century the primary connotation of 'Vlakh' was 'nomadic shepherd of the Balkans'. The occupation and way of life of this originally Latin-speaking group had become their characteristic feature in the eyes of their contemporaries. Nevertheless, I do not think that any significant groups of the Vlakhs spoke a Slavic tongue. The most we can assume is that Vlakh shepherds were bilingual; they must have spoken their Romance mother tongue and a southern Slavic dialect. Since the gathering place of the recruits was in Ainos, at the mouth of the Marica river, it may safely be assumed that Vlakhs between the Marica and the Balkan Mountains were in question.

The second important piece of information we can derive from this passage from the Byzantine empress's work is that Bulgars and Vlakhs have lived side by side, in close proximity. This co-existence or symbiosis of Bulgars and Vlakhs can be corroborated by other data derived from Kekaumenos' *Strategikon*. In this work there is a detailed description of a rebellion of the local population in Thessaly, the Hellas *thema* of the empire in 1066. The centre of the rebellion was in Larissa, where Greeks, Vlakhs and Bulgars tried to plot against the state, but the organisers of the riot were seemingly the Greeks of Larissa, who incited the Vlakhs.[23] The Vlakhs and Bulgars are often mentioned together as participants in the rebellion.[24] The intimate connection between these groups is shown by the fact that a

---

[20] 'Λαμβάνειν τὸ κανονικὸν αὐτῶν πάντων τῶν ἀνὰ πᾶσαν Βουλγαρίαν Βλάχων καὶ τῶν περὶ τὸν Βαρδάρειον Τουρκῶν, ὅσοι ἐντὸς Βουλγαρικῶν ὅρων εἰσὶ, τιμᾶν δε αὐτὸν καὶ σέβεσθαι μεγάλως καὶ ἀκούειν τοῦ λόγου αὐτοῦ' (Gelzer, *BZ* 2, 1893, p. 46, and Dölger, *Regesten*, I, p. 104, no. 807). For the Turks of Vardar, see Laurent, 'Bardariōtōn'.

[21] Cf. Gyóni, *Kékaumenos*, p. 31.

[22] 'Νεολέκτους καταλέγων, ὁπόσοι τε ἐκ Βουλγάρων καὶ ὁπόσοι τὸν νομάδα βίον εἵλοντο (Βλάχους τούτους ἡ κοινὴ καλεῖν οἶδε διάλεκτος)' (Anna Komn. *Alex.*/Reiffersch., II, p. 8₁₁₋₁₃).

[23] Malingoudis, 'Zweit. bulg. Staat.', pp. 62–3, in the wake of Gyóni (*Kékaumenos*, *passim*) rightly refutes the supposition of certain researchers concerning the Vlakh and Bulgarian 'national' character of this movement.

[24] Ὁ τε Βλάχοι καὶ οἱ Βούλγαροι; 'τούς τε Βλάχους καὶ Βουλγάρους' (Kekaum. *Strat.*/Wassil.-Jern., pp. 69₉₋₁₀, 70₃₋₄).

meeting was held in the house of a Vlakh whose name was Beriboos.[25] He is the first Vlakh known by name in history, and his name was the Slavic *Berivoj*.

Finally, Vlakhs and Cumans are mentioned for the first time together in 1095. Alexios Komnenos pitched camp near Anchialos, in the eastern foothills of the Balkan Mountains, when a Vlakh chief called Pudilos reported to him that the Cumans had crossed the Danube (διὰ τοῦ Δανούβεως).[26] But before long, the Vlakhs helped the Cumans too, by showing them the mountain paths where no Byzantine guard was set up.[27] This episode, preserved in Anna Komnene's work, reveals two essential features of the Byzantine–Vlakh–Cuman connection at the end of the eleventh century. First, the Vlakhs were Byzantine subjects, but they seized every opportunity to turn against their overlords. So, less than a hundred years before the outbreak of Asen and Peter's movement, the Vlakhs behaved like enemies of the empire. Secondly, they gave assistance to the Cumans, Byzantium's nomadic enemy, in attacking the empire from the north.

The historical passages analysed above yield a perfect explanation why Bulgars, Vlakhs and Cumans became the common enemies of Byzantium on the eve of the liberation movement in 1185. It is interesting to notice that all three actors in the events of 1185–6 were present a century earlier; the Bulgars and Vlakhs were subjects of the Byzantine Empire, awaiting the right moment for an uprising. The Vlakhs, as nomads, were seemingly more active in organising riots than the Bulgars. Finally, the Bulgars and Vlakhs were not powerful enough to take on the mighty empire of Byzantium until the death of the emperor Manuel Komnenos (1180). We may venture to say that the Bulgars, Vlakhs and Cumans were ready to act jointly against Byzantium at the end of the eleventh century, and it was only the empire's strength that could prevent the Bulgar–Vlakh–Cuman coalition from attaining any major success before the events of 1185–6. But as soon as the cohesion of the empire began to loosen, the Bulgar–Vlakh–Cuman coalition became a reality that could see its fight against Byzantium through to completion. Each party in this league made a special contribution to the common cause. The Bulgarians furnished the movement with ideology: the goal of the fight against Byzantium was the re-establishment of the once powerful Bulgarian Empire, with its own administration and ecclesiastical organisation. For exploited people living in desperate need, the memory of their former political power, the active and passive protagonists in which

---

[25] 'εἰς τὴν οὸκίαν Βεριβόου τοῦ Βλάχου' (Kekaum. *Strat.*/Wassil.-Jern., p. 68₁₆).
[26] Anna Komn. *Alex.*/Reiffersch., II, p. 61₂₉₋₃₁.   [27] Anna Komn. *Alex.*/Reiffersch., II, p. 62₂₈₋₉.

have long gone, may appear very attractive. The Vlakhs, as people who pursued a special nomadic way of life, transhumant pastoralism, were particularly suited to take the initiative and lead the movement. So the Vlakhs gave the initial *energy* and *impetus*. Finally, without the Cumans' war potential, no resistance against the Byzantine Empire could have been successful for any length of time. So the Cumans gave *arms* and *warriors*. The contribution of each of these components of the anti-Byzantine alliance cannot be denied,[28] but must be studied in an appropriate manner. In what follows I shall continue to develop this line of investigation.

ETHNIC NAMES AND ETHNIC REALITIES IN THE SOURCES OF
THE SECOND BULGARIAN EMPIRE

Now we may return to our starting point, namely that the Greek and Latin sources reporting on the events of the liberation movement speak only of the Vlakhs, and the Bulgarians, if they are mentioned at all, are relegated to a very insignificant subsidiary role. One Byzantine source in particular (Nik. Chon. *Hist.*) and three Latin sources (Ansbert, Robert de Clari and Villehardouin) will now be subjected to thorough scrutiny.

Niketas Choniates used the term Βούλγαροι only a few times in his work,[29] while the ethnonym Βλάχοι occurs in his work dozens of time. It is well known that no consistent and unified system of ethnonyms was used in Byzantine historical works: one ethnonym could designate several peoples, and one people could be designated by several ethnonyms within the same work. Niketas Choniates, for example, used the archaic

---

[28] It was the eminent Russian Byzantinologist, A. Vasiliev, who presented a similar evaluation of these events in his monograph on Byzantine history: 'Although the Wallachians initiated the movement of liberation, the Bulgarians without doubt took an active part in it with them, and probably contributed largely to the internal organisation of the new kingdom. The Cumans also shared in the movement. The new Bulgarian kingdom was ethnologically a Wallachian-Bulgarian-Cuman state, its dynasty, if the assertion of Nicetas Choniates is accepted, being Wallachian' (Vasiliev, *Hist. Byz.*, II, p. 442). Bănescu was also along the right lines when he stated: 'Le second empire bulgare a été créé par l'énergie active des Roumains des Balkans, dans la ligne des vieilles traditions impérialistes bulgares' and 'L'État a été créé par les Asénides pour les deux peuples également; il a été "empire bulgare", parce qu'il faisait revivre une longue tradition historique et représentait de nouveau l'État de concurrence a l'égard de Byzance' (Bănescu, *Sec. emp. bulg.*, pp. 93, 25). But he totally forgot about the Cumans who played a key role in the events after 1186. The fact that Bănescu sometimes seems more clear-sighted than his Bulgarian opponents cannot give rise to speculation about the 'milder' character of Romanian nationalism. On this particular question Romanian scholarship is nearer the truth, since the Vlakhs were really there and cannot simply be eliminated from history as Bulgarian scholars have often tried to do. On other occasions Bănescu, too, was taken in by the empty and bombastic vocabulary of Romanian nationalism.

[29] Nik. Chon. *Hist.*/van Dieten, I, pp. 371₂₃, 374₈₆, 465₂₄, 643₃₀ (ed. Bonn, pp. 485₁₅, 489₃, 612₂₂, 849₁₁).

ethnonym Σκύθαι primarily to designate the contemporary nomads, the Cumans, but sometimes he used the word to refer to the Pechenegs.[30] At the same time, the Cumans are sometimes designated by their well known self-appellation as Κούμανοι.[31] As far as the Bulgarians are concerned, their most common designation, in addition to their self-appellation the Βούλγαροι, was Μυσοί, since they were identified with the old inhabitants of Bulgaria, the former Mysia.[32] Niketas Choniates uses all these ethnonyms in his work (Σκύθαι, Κούμανοι; Βλάχοι, Βούλγαροι, Μυσοί). His usage of the first two, as we have seen, is unambiguous. His usage of the latter three is to be eludicated now. The term *Mysoi* in Choniates' work does not mean anything other than the inhabitants of Mysia, that is, Bulgaria. When he uses this archaic term,[33] he simply means the population of the former Bulgaria without any reference to the ethnic content of the term. I would call this type of archaic ethnonyms pseudo-ethnonyms. But in particular cases, when the author wants to specify the modern, contemporary meaning of such a pseudo-ethnonym, the archaic ethnonym acquires a concrete ethnic meaning. Examples are in Zonaras: Μυσῶν ἤγουν Βουλγάρων, or in a list of peoples: οἱ Μυσοὶ ἤτοι οἱ Βούλγαροι.[34] When it came to spelling out the contemporary meaning of *Mysoi*, most Byzantine sources used the term instead of *Bulgars*, but there are a few cases when *Pechenegs* and even *Hungarians* (!) are meant by that term.[35] If we look more closely at Choniates' text, what he meant by *Mysoi* when he spoke of them in the concrete ethnic sense becomes clear. He states that the barbarians of the Haimos 'were formerly called *Mysoi*, and now they are named *Blachoi*'.[36] So Choniates certainly identified the Vlakhs with the *Mysoi*, since the Vlakhs were inhabitants of what was formerly Bulgaria, and, before that, Mysia. Choniates was consistent in his usage when later he spoke of 'the power of the *Mysoi* and the *Bulgaroi*'.[37] If the Mysoi were the Vlakhs, this statement then refers to the Vlakhs and the Bulgars, the two main ethnical entities of Bulgaria. A further corroboration of this can be found in the historical works of Theodoros Skutariotes and Ephraim, which are mainly compilations of former works, including that of Niketas Choniates: the barbarians

---

[30] See the index of Nik. Chon. *Hist.*/van Dieten, II, p. 79.

[31] Nik. Chon. *Hist.*/van Dieten, I, pp. 428₆₄, 522₂₅, 523₃₅, ₃₉, ₄₀ (ed. Bonn, pp. 561₈, 691₁₄, 692₃, ₇, ₁₇).

[32] For the occurrences of Βούλγαροι and Μυσοί in the Byzantine sources, see *Byz.-turc.*, II, pp. 100–6, 207–9.

[33] E.g. Nik. Chon. *Hist.*/van Dieten, I, pp. 371₁₃, 394₁₈, 399₄₃.

[34] *Byz.-turc.*, II, pp. 207–8, with further examples.

[35] For all the examples see n. 32 above.   [36] See n. 7 above.

[37] 'Καὶ τὴν τῶν Μυσῶν καὶ τῶν Βουλγάρων δυναστείαν' (Nik. Chon. *Hist.*/van Dieten, I, p. 374₈₆₋₇; ed. Bonn, p. 489₉).

of the Haimos 'were formerly called *Mysoi*, and now they are named *Blachoi* and *Bulgaroi*'.[38] These later editors of Choniates thus complement his interpretation: both the Vlakhs and the Bulgars are called *Mysoi*. There is a passage in Choniates which shows that he himself was aware that the archaic ethnonym *Mysoi* had a rather loose connotation, and that it could embrace both Vlakhs and Bulgars. On relating the episode of building a church to St Demetrios (see above, pp. 16–17), he first states that the *Mysoi* were under the leadership of Peter and Asen. The Vlakhs (*Blachoi*) – continues Choniates, changing the name *Mysoi* to *Blachoi* – were reluctant to take part in the brothers' rebellion. Then the brothers had a church built and filled it with demoniacs who were to announce to the people that God was pleased to return freedom to the people of the *Bulgars* and *Vlakhs*.[39] This passage makes it absolutely clear that both Bulgars and Vlakhs participated in the liberation movement. There is only one question left to answer: why did Choniates use the term 'Vlakh' almost exclusively when speaking of the events in Bulgaria at the end of the twelfth century, despite the fact that he was aware of the Bulgars' presence too? The answer is very simple: the Vlakhs initiated the uprising, and the leaders of the movement were of their number; consequently, the movement was primarily identified with the Vlakh people.[40] Later, especially after the deaths of the three

---

[38] ʿΟἵ Μυσοὶ μὲν ὠνομάζοντο πρότερον, Βλάχοι δὲ νῦν καὶ Βούλγαροι' (Theod. Skut. *Syn.*/Sathas, p. 370₁₈–₁₉ and Ephraim/Bekker-Mai, p. 237₆₃).

[39] ʿΤῶν δὲ Μυσῶν . . . οἱ Βλάχοι . . . τοῦ τῶν Βουλγάρων καὶ Βλάχων γένους' (Nik. Chon. *Hist.*/van Dieten, I, p. 371₁₃, ₁₅, ₂₃). It is important that the Bulgars and the Vlakhs are mentioned as two peoples (γένος). Nik. Chon. used the terms γένος and ἔθνος indiscriminately; for this see Malingoudis, 'Zweit. bulg. Staat.', pp. 74–5, n. 67.

[40] It is impossible to prove, as Mutafčiev and Zlatarski tried to do, that Bulgars must sometimes be meant by the term 'Vlakhs'. A great many scholars have been misled by this position maintained by Bulgarian scholars, among others Ostrogorsky, who, in his Byzantine history, asserts: 'Es ist der modernen bulgarischen Forschung (vgl. insbesondere P. Mutafčiev, Proizchodûtû na Asenevci, Maked. Pregled 4, 1928, 1ff., and Zlatarski, Istorija II, 416ff.) darin beizustimmen, daß die Rolle der Wallachen nicht überschätzt werden darf, da man damals als Walachen mitunter offensichtlich auch die Bulgarern bezeichnete' (Ostrogorsky, *Gesch.*, p. 287, n. 3). Essentially he maintained this view in the third edition of his work: 'Man damals als Walachen – die Bezeichnung hatte bekanntlich nicht nur ethnische Bedeutung, sondern diente auch als Sammelbegriff für Hirtenstämme – die Bevölkerung des alten Mösien bzw. des damaligen Thema Paristrion bezeichnete, da man unter Bulgaren vor allem die Einwohner des Thema Bulgarien, d.h. Makedoniens verstand' (p. 334, n. 5). I think it is unnecessary to repeat here my arguments that the Bulgars and the Vlakhs are never confused with each other. I cannot find a single case of the Bulgars being designated as Vlakhs. If Zlatarski and the supporters of this theory think that the Bulgars are sometimes omitted from Nik. Chon. *Hist.*, and that only the Vlakhs are mentioned, they are right. But this fact does not allow us to suppose that the Vlakhs are identical with the Bulgars; rather, it clearly shows that the Vlakhs' role was so significant that sometimes only *they* are mentioned. Besides, the usage of ethnonyms in Byzantium, though it may seem chaotic at first sight, followed strict rules. A contemporary people

brothers (Kaloyan died in 1207), the original character of the movement gradually faded, since the new state regarded itself as the direct heir of the First Bulgarian Empire. This Bulgarian character triumphed over the Vlakh beginnings. That is why Georgios Akropolites (b. 1217), who, unlike Choniates, was not a contemporary of the events, described the liberation movement as a Bulgarian phenomenon, and made no mention of the Vlakhs in his work.[41] But we must not think that Akropolites deliberately eliminated the name 'Vlakh'. After the first two to three decades of the Second Bulgarian Empire, the Vlakh beginnings had lost their significance; the Vlakh hierarchy voluntarily merged with the Bulgars, since the Vlakh people had no 'national' consciousness of their own. The basic ideology of the age, Eastern Christianity, linked all the ethnic groups of the Balkans, including the Bulgars and Vlakhs.

Choniates, the Byzantine contemporary of the events, was not alone in distinguishing between the Vlakhs and the Bulgars; Western eyewitnesses do so too, though, like Choniates they give preference to the Vlakhs. Ansbert, who took part in the Third Crusade in Emperor Frederick I's army in 1189–90, mentions 'a certain Vlakh Kalopetrus and his brother Asen with their Vlakh subjects'.[42] In another place he calls Peter 'Kalopetrus, Lord of the Vlakhs'.[43] We must add that sometimes he makes a distinction between Bulgars and Vlakhs (e.g. 'Greculos *Bulgares* Seruigios et *Flachos*').[44] Finally, there is a passage in another eyewitness report of the same crusade, the anonymous *Historia peregrinorum*, which enables us to pin down the exact connotation of the term *Vlakh*: 'Kalopetrus who, together with his brother Assanius, ruled over the Vlakh peoples . . .'[45] The phrase *populi Blacorum*, 'peoples of the Vlakhs', can be interpreted in two ways. First, it may indicate that *Blaci* was a vague term, referring not only to the Romance-speaking Vlakhs but also to other ethnic elements, such as the Slavic Bulgars. Secondly, it could mean that the Vlakhs were the dominant political power in the ethnic amalgam of the Second Bulgarian Empire; other peoples, such as the Bulgars and Cumans, were subject to them. Be that as it may, all these

could be labelled by several archaic ethnonyms, and *one* archaic ethnonym could be applied to several modern people. For example, the Hungarians were termed *Getai, Dakes, Mysoi, Skythai, Sauromatai, Turkoi*, etc., and the ethnonym *Persai* was used to denote the Seljuks, Ottomans and Tatars. But no contemporary peoples were mixed up in the sources.

[41] See Georg. Akr. *Chrón.*/Heisenberg, 1, index.

[42] 'quidam Kalopetrus Flachus ac frater eius Assanius cum subditis Flachis' (Ansbert/Chroust, p. 334-5).

[43] 'Kalopetrus Blachorum domnus' (Ansbert/Chroust, p. 6924).   [44] Ansbert/Chroust, p. 285.

[45] 'Kalopetrus qui cum Assanio fratre suo dominabatur populis Blacorum' (*Hist. peregr.*/Chroust, p. 14913–14).

data seem to confirm our impression that the Vlakhs had a special role at the end of the twelfth century in Bulgaria, and the frequent occurrence of the term *Vlakh* cannot be explained away simply as a habit of using this term instead of *Bulgar*.

Geoffroi Villehardouin, who personally participated in the Fourth Crusade and the capture of Byzantium in 1204, also clearly distinguished Bulgars from Vlakhs. He asserts that in 1207, Kaloyan (whom he calls Johannis) organised a powerful army consisting of Cumans (*Comains*), Vlakhs, and Bulgars ('*Blacs et Bougres*').[46] Otherwise he calls Kaloyan '*rois de Blaquie et de Bougrie*', and adds that he was a Vlakh ('Johanis si ere uns Blas').[47] It is also noteworthy that Pope Innocent III addressed the Bulgar sovereign Kaloyan in his letter as 'rex Bulgarorum et Blacorum'.[48]

There is an interesting echo of the events that had taken place in the last two decades of the twelfth century in the Balkans. The Hungarian Anonymus, who must have written his *Gesta Ungarorum* around 1200, is hardly a first-rate historical source; he tried to write a history of the Hungarian 'Landnahme' (the conquest of the Carpathian Basin at the end of the ninth century) by projecting persons, events and ideas of his age on to a period 300 years earlier.[49] His work is full of anachronistic details, but as they shed light on events of the author's age they are sometimes very instructive. For instance, Anonymus projects a fictitious person called Glad on to the age of the Hungarian conquest of the land. This Glad was the ruler of Vidin ('quidam dux nomine Glad de Bundyn (correctly Budyn)'),[50] his country (*terra*) extending south of the Maros river towards the Danube.[51] This Glad fought against the Hungarians with Cuman auxiliaries, and when the Hungarians wanted to cross the river Temes, he marched against them 'with a vast army of cavalry and infantry, with the aid of Cumans, Bulgars and Vlakhs'.[52] These episodes are faint reminiscences of contemporary events in Bulgaria, the chief actors in which were the Cumans, Bulgars and Vlakhs.

---

[46] 'Johannis s'ere porchaciez de grant ost de Comains qui venoient à lui; et porchaça ses os de Blacs et de Bougres, si granz com il onques pot' (Villehardouin/Pauphilet, p. 193).

[47] Villehardouin/Pauphilet, p. 136.   [48] Migne, *PL* CCXV, cols. 277, 287, 290, 293.

[49] For the history of the research into Anonymus and his work, and for further bibliographical references, see Csapodi, *Anonymus*.

[50] Anonymus, *Gesta*, § 11, in *SRH*, I, p. 49₁.

[51] Anonymus, *Gesta*, § 44: 'a fluvio Morus usque ad castrum Horom' (*SRH*, I, p. 89$_{13-14}$). *Horom* is medieval Hungarian *Haram*, later called *Palánka*, now *Bačka Palanka* in Serbia, at the confluence of the rivers Krassó (Serbian *Karaš*, Romanian *Caraş*) and Danube (cf. Melich, *Honf. Magy.*, pp. 19–22, 191–4).

[52] 'Cum magno exercitu equitum peditum adiutorio Cumanorum et Bulgarorum atque Blacorum' (Anonymus, *Gesta*, §§ 11, 44, in *SRH*, I, pp. 50₁, 90$_{10-11}$).

BULGARIA, VLAKHIA AND CUMANIA IN THE TWELFTH AND THIRTEENTH CENTURIES

In accordance with the important role the Vlakhs played in the liberation movement that had led to the foundation of the Second Bulgarian Empire, the new country separating from Byzantium was called *Blacia* in the Latin sources. According to Robert de Clari, *Blakie* belonged to the Byzantine emperor, and was a well-fortified land surrounded by mountains. Later he adds: 'Cumania is a country that borders on Vlakhia.'[53] Consequently, Vlakhia must have lain between the Danube and the Balkan Mountains, and Cumania was north of it, the frontier between the two lands being the Danube. One must be careful not to confuse this Vlakhia with the historical Wallachia, which came into being only in the fourteenth century under the rule of Voivode Alexander Basarab.[54] Wallachia was on the left bank of the Danube, where former Cumania lay, while Vlakhia was on the right bank of the Danube, its territory being identical with the former and later northern Bulgaria.

It is an extremely interesting phenomenon of ethnic history that the Vlakhs, who initiated the uprising in 1185–6 and lent their name to the new Vlakho-Bulgarian state, gradually disappeared from Bulgaria, and, about 150 years after that uprising, founded the Romanian principalities of Wallachia and Moldavia, both on the territory of the former Cumania. The largest stream of the northern migration of Vlakh ethnic elements from Bulgaria must have taken place in the thirteenth century. It must have been a decisive period in the formation of the modern Romanian *ethnos* when the Romanophone Vlakh shepherds of the Balkans merged with the Cuman warriors. It is almost certain that vigorous waves of Vlakh immigration to the north of the Danube began only after the formation of the Second Bulgarian Empire, when the coalition of the Cumans, Vlakhs and Bulgars made possible an easy connection between the two banks of the Danube. From 1185 onwards, the Danube ceased to function as a border between two inimical powers (Byzantium and the nomads), and helped connect the territories lying between the southern Carpathian and the Balkan Mountains.

---

[53] 'Or est Blakie une terre qui est du domaine l'empereeur' and 'Si est Blakie une molt fort terre, qui toute est enclose de montaignes; si que on n'y puet entrer ne issir fors par un destroit', and 'Or est Commanie une terre qui marchist à Blakie' (Clari/Pauphilet, p. 60). Cf. also Bănescu, *L'ancien état*, p. 62.

[54] For the formation of the Romanian state of Wallachia, see Chapter 9 of this book. The name Wallachia first crops up in German chronicles written in Hungary in the 1330s (*Wallachei, Walachey, Wolochey*, in *SRH*, ii, pp. 220, 221, 222, 284).

It is not our task here to trace the process of the immigration and settlement of the Vlakhs north of the Danube. Suffice it to mention a few
facts that facilitate the understanding of this process. Though the Vlakhs
may have settled sporadically on the left bank of the Danube before the thirteenth century (this possibility cannot be excluded in the case of nomads
such as the Vlakhs), the fact remains that the first occurence of the term
Vlakh north of the Danube can be dated to 1222. Andrew II, king of Hungary, invited the Teutonic Order to his land in 1211 to defend the southern
borders of Transylvania against Cuman incursions. In his grant letter of
1222, the king confirms the privileges of the knights. He donates 'quondam terram Burza nomine ultra silvas versus Cumanos licet desertam et
inhabitatam'.[55] The territory granted to the knights was called *Barca* or
Barcaság in Hungarian, *Burzenland* in German and *Bîrsa* or *Jara Bîrsei*
in Romanian;[56] it was the fertile valley of the rivulet Barca, a tributary of
the river Olt. The king guarantees the knights' exemption from taxes and
tribute in the following words, 'Item concessimus, quod nullum tributum
debeant persolvere nec populi eorum, cum transierint per terram Siculo-
rum aut per terram Blacorum.'[57] The *Siculi* (in Hungarian the *Székelys*,
in German *die Szekler*) were a particular group of Hungarians who, from
the twelfth century onwards, finally settled in Transylvania. They were a
privileged group and were organised in a military system, their primary task
being the defence of the eastern and southern borders of the Hungarian
Kingdom. The disputed origins of the Székelys (whether they were purely
Hungarian or whether sizeable Turkic groups played a part in their ethnogenesis) lie outside the scope of our interests here. But where was this *terra
Blacorum*? Most scholars think that it must have been south of Fogaras
(now Făgăraş in Romania), later called *Jara Făgăraşului*.[58] There are a few
further documents from later years in which the Vlakhs are mentioned
as being in this part of Transylvania. In the most important of these, the
so-called *Andreanum* from 1224, in which King Andrew II confirmed the
privileges of the Saxons of Transylvania, mention is made of a *silva Blacorum et Bissenorum*, 'forest of the Vlakhs and Pechenegs', which was granted
to the Teutonic guests (*hospites nostri Theutonici*), who were allowed to use
it jointly with the Vlakhs and the Pechenegs.[59] This forest of the Vlakhs

---

[55] Zimm.-Werner-Müller, I, p. 18. For further literature and details, see *Doc. hist. Valach.*, pp. 1–8.
[56] For the history of Barcaság until the end of the thirteenth century, see Györffy, *Geogr. hist.*, I, pp. 821–2. For the etymology of the name, see Melich, *Barcza*; Melich, *Honf. Magy.*, pp. 269–71; Rásonyi, 'Bulaqs', p. 174; *FNESz*, p. 91.
[57] Zimm.-Werner-Müller, I, p. 18.   [58] *Doc. hist. Valach.*, pp. 3–5, n. 6.
[59] 'Preter vero supradictam silvam Blacorum et Bissenorum cum aquis usus communes exercendo cum predictis scilicet Blacis et Bissenis eisdem contulimus' (Zimm.-Werner-Müller, I, p. 32). For further details, see *Doc. hist. Valach.*, pp. 10–15.

and Pechenegs was in the Fogaras Alps, again in the south-eastern part of Transylvania. All these data prove that from the beginning of the thirteenth century we must reckon with a Vlakh presence in south-eastern Transylvania, in the territory of the Hungarian Kingdom. Consequently, by that time they must have been present in later Wallachia too, since they could reach the Carpathian ranges only through Wallachia. The 'forest of the Vlakhs and Pechenegs' yields valuable data about the symbiosis of the Vlakhs and the Pechenegs. The nomadic Turkic people of the Pechenegs, who settled in Hungary at different times and places,[60] must have used mountain pastures in common with the Vlakh shepherds. The pastoral life of both the Pechenegs and the Vlakhs may have facilitated their interrelation in Wallachia.

It is in connection with the *Blaci* of Transylvania that L. Rásonyi put forward a strange theory. He tried to prove that the *Blaci* of Transylvania had nothing to do with the Vlakhs, but were a Turkic people named *Bulaq*, and that the Vlakhs and Bulaqs were later confused in the sources.[61] Unfortunately, this theory cannot be corroborated by any sound evidence, and every historical argument speaks against it. While I do not regard it as my task to prove here that this idea cannot be sustained, I would simply remark that it was again nationalism that lay behind this theory: Hungarian nationalism has tried to minimise the Romanian presence in history, while Romanian nationalism has tried to expropriate the Hungarian and Bulgarian past. In the case of the term *Blaci*, we cannot but conclude that it was used to designate the Vlakhs.

After this short digression following the historical fates of the Vlakhs on the left bank of the Danube in later Wallachia, we may now return to Vlakhia and Bulgaria at the end of the twelfth century and the beginning of the thirteenth. In the development of the terms *Vlakhia* and *Bulgaria*, four stages can be observed in the sources between 1185 and the 1250s. First, the new Bulgarian Empire was called simply *Vlakhia*. In the *Annales Forolivienses*, for example, Emperor Frederick I, on his way to the Holy Land in 1189, 'went through Hungary, Russia, Cumania, *Vlakhia*, Durazzo, Byzantium, and Turkey'.[62] Andrea Dandolo, Doge of Venice, reports in his *Chronicon Venetum*, written in the fourteenth century, that Robert 'went

---

[60] For the history and settlements of Pechenegs in Hungary, see Györffy, 'Besenyők'.

[61] Rásonyi, 'Bulaqs'; Rásonyi, *Tuna köprüleri*. These works contain many useful ideas and details about the presence of Turkic peoples in Transylvania, but the fundamental thesis about the Bulaqs is an abortive attempt that cannot be proved.

[62] 'Eundo per Ungariam, Rosiam, Cumaram Balachiam, Dirrachiam, Romaniam et Turciam' (*Ann. Frol.*/Muratori, p. 25). The same account was repeated, almost verbatim, in Iacobus Moratinus' *Chronicon de rebus Foroliviensibus*, written in the fourteenth century (Iac. Morat. *Chron.*, p. 786).

to Constantinople through Hungary and *Vlakhia*' to have himself crowned after his parents' death.[63]

In the second stage of development, the terms *Vlakhia* and *Bulgaria* appeared. This double designation referred to the whole territory of the Second Bulgarian Empire. It occurs several times in the correspondence between Pope Innocent III and the Bulgarian Tsar Kaloyan,[64] and in Ville-hardouin's work.[65] An exact separation of the territories of Vlakhia and Bulgaria is impossible: the two names probably refer to the same territory, and indicate the two basic ethnic components of the empire.

At a later date, the overlapping terms *Vlakhia* and *Bulgaria* separated, and each was used to designate distinct parts of historical Bulgaria. It is instructive to take note of Rubruc's *Itinerarium*, which contains valuable pieces of information about the usage of these terms in the middle of the thirteenth century. In enumerating the territories that pay tribute to the Tatars he says: 'From the mouth of the Tanais [i.e. Don] as far as the Danube towards the West everything is theirs [i.e. the Tatars'], moreover beyond the Danube in the direction of Constantinople, *Vlakhia*, which is the land of Asan and *Lesser Bulgaria* as far as Slavonia, all these pay trib-ute to them [i.e. the Tatars].'[66] At another place: 'These provinces beyond Constantinople which are now called *Bulgaria*, *Vlakhia* and Slavonia, were provinces of the Greeks.'[67] Finally, in a list of peoples, Vlakhs, and Bulgars of Lesser Bulgaria, can be found side by side.[68] These appellations indicate that the term *Vlakhia* was used by Rubruc for northern Bulgaria, while the western and south-western territories of historical Bulgaria (now west-ern Bulgaria + Macedonia) were designated as *Bulgaria Minor*. Rubruc used the term *Bulgaria Maior* to denote Volga Bulgaria, and construed a sophisticated theory that the Hungarians, Bulgars and Vlakhs had arrived in their contemporary countries from earlier eastern homelands called *Ungaria Maior* and *Bulgaria Maior* respectively.[69] He did not use the term *Blacia Maior* or *Blacia Magna*, since he may have heard that Greater Vlakhia

---

[63] 'Per Hungariam et Blachiam Constantinopolim perrexit' (And. Dand. *Chron.*/Muratori, p. 342).

[64] Theiner, *Mon. Slav. merid.*, I, p. 23.

[65] 'Rois de Blaquie et de Bougrie' (Villehardouin/Pauphilet, p. 136).

[66] Rubruc, *Itinerarium*, I.5: 'Ab orificio Tanais versus occidentem usque ad Danubium totum est eorum, etiam ultra Danubium versus Constantinopolim, Blakia que est terra Assani et Minor Bulgaria usque in Sclavoniam omnes solvunt eis tributum' (*Sin. Franc.*, I, pp. 167–8).

[67] Rubruc, *Itinerarium*, XXI.5: 'Ille provincie post Constantinopolim, que modo dicuntur Bulgaria, Blakia, Sclavonia, fuerunt provincie Grecorum' (*Sin. Franc.*, I, p. 220).

[68] Rubruc, *Itinerarium*, XVIII.1: 'Ipse [sc. Sartach] enim est in itinere christianorum, scilicet Ruteno-rum, Blacorum, Bulgarorum minoris Bulgarie, Soldainorum, Kerkisorum, Alanorum, qui omnes transeunt per eum quando vadunt ad curiam patris sui [sc. Batu]' (*Sin. Franc.*, I, p. 209).

[69] Cf. Vásáry, 'Med. theories', pp. 237–8.

(Βλαχία μεγάλη) was the name of the Vlakh country in Thessaly, Lesser Vlakhia (Βλαχία μικρά) was in Aitolia and Akarnania, and Upper Vlakhia (Ἀνωβλαχία) was located in the south-eastern part of Epeiros.[70] But even if he did not know these geographical terms of the Byzantine literature of the twelfth to thirteenth centuries, his *Vlakhia* refers to Bulgaria of the Asenids. In accordance with his conception concerning the origins of the Hungarians from the Bashkirs and the Danube Bulgars from the Volga Bulgars, he derived the Vlakhs of the Second Bulgarian Empire from a certain people *Illac* living near the Bashkirs: 'Those Bulgars who live beyond the Danube near Constantinople came from this Greater Bulgaria. And near the Bashkirs live the *Illacs* which is the same as *Blac*, but the Tatars cannot pronounce B. Those who are in the land of Asan came from them [i.e. the Illac = Blac]. So both of them are called *Illac*, the former and the latter as well.'[71] There is an extensive literature on the ethnonym *Illac* and its possible connections with the Vlakhs,[72] but here we are concerned only with the fact that, according to Rubruc's knowledge, Vlakhs were living in the contemporary Bulgaria of the Asenids. But the existence of various Vlakhias (Greater, Lesser and Upper) in Byzantine literature of the twelfth to thirteenth centuries may explain why Niketas Choniates, who otherwise used the term *Vlakh* all the time, avoided speaking of *Vlakhia* in connection with the Second Bulgarian Empire. To the Byzantines several territories were known as Vlakhias (see above), so the restored Bulgarian Empire could not be called Vlakhia, although the Vlakhs had played a major part in its restoration. The western Latin sources were not handicapped in this respect, so they applied the term 'Vlakhia' to the new Bulgarian state. In a few instances, in works from the mid-fourteenth century, it is difficult to determine the exact meaning of 'Vlakhia'. In Giovanni Villani's Chronicle, for instance, Vlakhia may mean northern Bulgaria and Wallachia as well.[73]

The fourth and final phase in the history of these terms was characterised by the dominance of the term *Bulgaria* and the disappearance of *Vlakhia*. From the middle of the thirteenth century, *Vlakhia* as a designation for northern Bulgaria disappears from the sources; only *Bulgaria* is used in both

---

[70] Murnu, *Ist. Rom. Pind.*, *passim*; Žuglev, 'Blaquie'.

[71] Rubruc, *Itinerarium*, XXI.3: 'De illa enim maiori Bulgaria venerunt illi Bulgari qui sunt ultra Danubium prope Constantinopolim. Et iuxta Pascatur sunt Illac, quod iidem est quod Blac, sed B nesciunt Tartari sonare, a quibus venerunt illi qui sunt in terra Assani. Utrosque enim vocant Illac, et hos et illos' (*Sin. Franc.*, I, p. 219).

[72] See Pelliot, *Horde d'Or*, pp. 144–54.

[73] Giovanni Villani, 1.5: 'In sul qual mare [i.e. the Black Sea] è parte d'Europa si è parte di Cumania, Rossia, e Bracchia, e Bulgaria, e Alania, stendendosi sopra quel mare infino in Constantinopoli' (Villani/Racheli, I, p. 9).

the Byzantine and Western sources. This phenomenon can be explained by
two facts. First, with the death ot Michael Asen in 1257 the Vlakh dynasty
of the Asenids died out, and by that time, as we have seen, the Bulgarian
character of the state had totally suppressed the Vlakh beginnings of the
Second Bulgarian Empire. Secondly, the immigration of Vlakh masses to
the left bank of the Danube must have progressed at a rapid pace, and
consequently the Vlakh population gradually evacuated northern Bulgaria.
Between the 1250s and 1330s both *Vlakhia* and *Wallachia* were present
virtually only in history: *Vlakhia* was fading away from the historical sources
and *Wallachia* was in the process of coming into being. Between these dates
the sources keep silent about these designations.

Though the history of the terms Bulgaria and Vlakhia was rather complicated, the idea of *Cumania* was fairly unambiguous. The southern frontier of Cumania was the Danube, and it comprised what was later to
become Wallachia and Moldavia. To the north, the Russian principalities formed the frontier, and to the east it stretched as far as the Volga.
But the land of Cumania beyond the Dniester was less well known to the
Byzantines and Westerners. Transylvania was an organic part of the Hungarian Kingdom, and it is a mystery why Uspenskij and later Zlatarski had
thought that a part of Transylvania belonged to Cumania. Uspenskij wrote
that 'by that time [the beginning of the fifteenth century] the occupation of
Moldavia, Wallachia and a part of Transylvania by the Cumans must have
been completed'.[74] Zlatarski, too, asserted that at the end of the twelfth
century the Cumans settled in Moldavia, Wallachia and Transylvania, and
these territories were called Cumania.[75] The Cumans had, of course, made
several incursions in the course of the twelfth century, but we know of
no Cuman settlements in Transylvania.[76] The southern part of Transylvania in particular, the territory between Brassó (Romanian *Braşov*, German
Kronstadt) and Fogaras (Romanian *Făgăraş*), was devastated and depopulated by the plundering Cuman groups. It was precisely in this part of
Transylvania that the Teutonic knights were settled by King Andrew II
in 1211 to defend Hungary against the Cumans (see above, p. 28). Consequently, the statement of Uspenskij and Zlatarski that a part of Cumania stretched to Transylvania is unreliable and lacks any historical proof.

[74] 'Zanjatie kumanami Moldavii i Valahii i časti Transil'vanii možet k ètomu vremeni sčitat'sja uže okončennym' (Uspenskij, *Vtor. bolg. carstvo*, p. 84).
[75] 'Běha zdravo zasednali otvud Dunav v Moldova, Vlaško i Semigradsko, koito pod těhna vlast' veče nosili edno obšto ime Kumanija i predstavili edna vnušitelna sila' (Zlatarski, *Ist.*, II, p. 427).
[76] Moreover, we know that the southern part of Transylvania, later the territories Fogaras and Barcaság, became totally deserted because of the constant Cuman incursions from the south. See p. 28 above.

The appearance of a Cumania within the borders of the Hungarian King-dom can be dated to the second half of the thirteenth century, when, after the Tatar disaster in 1241, King Béla IV settled masses of Cumans in Hungary. But this Cumania was in the middle of the country, and had nothing to do with the old Cumania, which lay to the east of the Hungarian Kingdom. The old (and, let us say, historical) Cumania existed as an independent state only until 1241. After that date the Tatar hordes dispersed the Cuman groups of Cumania to Hungary and the Balkans. But Cumania as a geographical term lived on into the second half of the four-teenth century. From that time onwards the names of the newly founded Romanian (Vlakh) principalities, Wallachia and Moldavia, ousted the term *Cumania*.

Finally, there are two peculiar passages in Western chronicles where 'two Cumanias' (*utraque Cumania*) are mentioned. Iohannes, an English chron-icler of the fourteenth century, in his description of the Tatar conquest of 1241, claims that the Tatars had conquered thirty countries, among oth-ers 'Rusciam, Gazariam, Gothiam, Ziquiam, Alaniam et utramque Coma-niam'.[77] Cornelius Zantfliet, who lived a century later, also made mention of 'utramque Comaniam'.[78] The two passages must derive from an unknown common source. A closer definition of these two Cumanias is not possible, but it is certain that the division of Cumania into two parts must have been a medieval invention, like many other double designations (such as names followed by *magna/maior, minor, inferior, ulterior*, etc.).[79]

ORIGINS AND POSSIBLE CUMAN AFFILIATIONS OF THE ASEN DYNASTY

For more than a century Bulgarian and Romanian historians have debated the origins of the brothers Peter, Asen and Kaloyan. Most Bulgarian his-torians have insisted on their Bulgarian origins, in accordance with the view that the term *Vlakh* refers to Bulgars, and that the whole Bulgaro-Vlakh problem is a mere question of terminology. The second view, held mainly by Romanian historians among others, firmly maintains that the brothers were Vlakhs. Finally, there is a third view, according to which the three brothers were of Cuman descent. Let us compare the three possibilities.

---

[77] Ludewig, *Reliquiae*, xii, p. 155; Gombos, *Cat.* i, p. 1330.
[78] Martene-Durand, *Vet. SS*, v, p. 75; Gombos, *Cat.*, i, p. 796.
[79] Cf. Vásáry, 'Med. theories', pp. 230–3.

The brothers were Bulgars

The first, namely that the brothers were Bulgars, can easily be excluded. F. Uspenskij, the noted Byzantinologist, in his book on the Second Bulgarian Empire, was the first to put forward the theory that the Byzantine writers failed to mention the name *Bulgar* after the fall of the First Bulgarian Empire, substituting other ethnonyms such as that of the Vlakhs.[80] Uspenskij's view cannot be maintained. Bănescu refuted it in detail,[81] and I too have attempted to prove in the foregoing that the ethnonym *Vlakh* had a real and concrete ethnic connotation in the twelfth to thirteenth centuries.

But there is one more argument left in the arsenal of those who have tried to verify the brothers' Bulgarian descent. Pope Innocent III had an intensive correspondence with Kaloyan, the third ruler of the new Bulgarian state, about the acceptance of the Pope's jurisdiction by the Bulgarian Church. Both parties were motivated by their own interests: the Pope wanted to extend his jurisdiction in the Balkans, and Kaloyan wanted to wear the imperial crown and have a patriarch as head of the Bulgarian Church. There are two groups of statements in the Pope's correspondence, each seemingly contradicting and excluding the other. One group seems to support the Bulgarian descent of Asen's family, the other the Vlakh descent. The 'Bulgarian party' and the 'Vlakh party' could find equal arguments in favour of their respective theories, and each party has tried to conceal or minimise the significance of the other group of data. Let us first see the data, and then attempt to interpret them.

Innocent III wrote to the Hungarian King Imre, in his letter of 1204, saying that 'Peter and Joannica, who descended from the family of the former kings, began rather to regain than to occupy the land of their fathers.'[82] By contrast, the Pope wrote to Kaloyan in 1199 saying that he had heard of Kaloyan's Roman descent. In his reply, Kaloyan expressed his satisfaction that God 'made us remember our blood and fatherland from which we descended'. In another place we have, 'the people of your land who assert that they descended from Roman blood'.[83] It is obvious that these statements cannot be taken at face value, since they exclude each other. Yet this error was often committed in the past. K. Jireček, for instance, accepted the first statement, namely that the Asenids were descendants of the former Bulgarian tsars; moreover, he discovered that they were born

---

[80] Uspenskij, *Vtor. bolg. carstvo*, p. 153.   [81] Bănescu, *Sec. emp. bulg.*, pp. 13–21.

[82] 'Petrus videlicet et Johannicius, de priorum regum prosapia descendentes, terram patrum suorum non tam occupare, quam recuperare coeperunt' (Theiner, *Mon. Slav. merid.*, 1, p. 36).

[83] 'Et reduxit nos ad memoriam sanguinis et patrie nostre, a qua descendimus' and 'populus terre tue, qui de sanguine Romanorum se asserit descendisse' (Theiner, *Mon. Slav. merid.*, 1, pp. 15, 16).

in Tărnovo, capital of the old Šišmanid dynasty (though there is no reference in support of this assumption).[84] Consequently, he had to refute the second statement, namely that the brothers were of Roman descent. Jireček's explanation is clumsy and his argumentation tortuous: the fact of Roman descent was first mentioned by the Pope, and Kaloyan tacitly and cunningly accepted it since it suited his purposes.[85] Most Romanian historians, however, are gratified by the second statement, that the Bulgarian dynasty was of Roman progeny (that is, Vlakh, on their view) and often forget to mention that another statement in another letter of the same Pope annuls the validity of this statement. The solution lies in the interpretation of the texts. Medieval texts cannot be interpreted acccording to the rules of formal logic, but must be placed in their contemporary context. As far as the first statement is concerned, it is a typical medieval requirement: the ruling house is always seen as the legitimate successor of the previous one. If the Pope said that Peter and Asen were descendants of the earlier Bulgarian kings, he simply wanted to express that they were the legitimate rulers of Bulgaria. That is why they do not occupy the land, but reoccupy it as their heritage, which was usurped by the Byzantine power till then. It was the same medieval ideological demand that made Attila, king of the Huns, the first Hungarian king. Hence, Árpád and his family did not *conquer* the Carpathian Basin in 896 AD, but *reconquered* it as their paternal heritage from Attila. The Kézai Chronicle consequently represents this view.[86] To take another, similarly instructive example, Pope John XXII addressed a letter on 3 October 1329 to a certain Jeretamir (or Jeretanny, in another variant), who was the chief of the Christian Hungarians in the East. This curious letter mentions the Hungarians, Malkaites and Alans together.[87] Since the latter two peoples were inhabitants of the Northern Caucasus, the Christian Hungarians mentioned in this letter may be only a splinter group of Hungarians living north of the Caucasus. This Hungarian group was either dragged away from Hungary by the Tatars after the East European campaign of 1241, or must have been descended from Hungarian groups that did not take part in the conquest of Hungary at the end of the ninth century. The first possibility seems the most probable. Be that as it may, the Pope expressed his satisfaction that 'you, my son Jeretamir, are descended

---

[84] Jireček, *Bulg.*, p. 211.   [85] *Ibid.*, p. 219.   [86] *SRH*, I, p. 142.

[87] 'Dilectis filiis Jeretamir et universis christianis Ungaris, Malchaytis ac Alanis salutem' (Bendefy, *Gyeretyán*, p. 445). Bendefy's work is disorganised and fanciful, but the edition of the text is based on the Vatican original and is reliable. For the *editio princeps* of this bull see Raynaldus, *Ann. eccl.*, xv, no. 96.

from the tribe of the Catholic princes and kings of Hungary'.[88] It is evident
that Jeretamir could not be a descendant of the Hungarian kings, except in a
'spiritual' sense. Even the wording of the two papal letters is very similar: 'de
priorum regum prosapia descendentes' (Peter and Asan) and 'Jeretamir, de
stirpe Catholicorum Principum Regum Ungariae descendisti'. Finally, if we
take an example from another territory, the Kazan Tatar khans considered
themselves legitimate successors of the former Volga Bulgarian sovereigns,
though there was no direct connection between the Bulgars and the
Tatars.[89]

As for the Pope's second statement, according to which the Asenid family
was of Roman descent, there are several layers of interpretations. First, it was
the Pope who first called Kaloyan's attention to his family's Roman descent.
Although Kaloyan and his Vlakh subjects must have spoken a neo-Latin
language, the precursor of modern Romanian, it can almost be taken for
granted that the Vlakhs of the Balkans had no historical awareness of their
'Roman' descent. If they were Romans, this was true only in the sense
that they were subjects of Byzantium and thus called Ῥωμαῖοι (Romans)
because Byzantium regarded itself as the true heir of Rome. The Vlakhs
of the Balkans were permeated by south Slavic folk culture and Byzantine
ecclesiastical high culture, and it was only their language that linked them
to Latin, the official language of the Roman Empire. The Pope must have
known about the Latin origin of the Vlakhs' language, and consequently
identified them as descendants of the City of Rome. Since this supposition
was really favourable and flattering to Kaloyan, as Jireček thought, Kaloyan
may have agreed with it. The two contradictory statements of the Pope must
therefore be understood in the following manner: first, the Asenids' descent
from the former Bulgarian kings was a contemporary means of expressing
the legitimacy of their rule, and had nothing to do with their *de facto*
'nationality'; secondly, the Pope's assertion that the Asenids were of Roman
descent was a mere expression of the fact that the Asenids were Vlakhs, and
had nothing to do with the Vlakhs' alleged 'Roman' consciousness.

The brothers were of Vlakh descent
If that is so, one cannot neglect those statements in the works of Byzan-
tine and Latin authors that explicitly refer to the brothers' Vlakh descent.
Ansbert, for instance, called Peter 'Kalopetrus Flachus'[90] and Villehardouin

---

[88] 'Tu, fili Jeretamir, de stirpe Catholicorum Principum Regum Ungariae descendisti' (Bendefy,
  Gyeretyán, p. 446; Raynaldus, *Ann. eccl.*, xv, no. 96).
[89] Pelenski, *Russia and Kazan*, pp. 139–73.   [90] Ansbert/Chroust, p. 33, lines 4–5.

asserted that 'Johanis si ere uns Blas'.[91] Furthermore, there is a detail in Niketas Choniates' *History* that makes the nationality of Asen indisputable. Once, a Greek priest was captured by the Vlakhs and dragged to the Haimos Mountains. He implored Asen to release him from captivity, addressing Asen in his captor's language since 'he knew the language of the Vlakhs'.[92] As both the Vlakhs and the Bulgars are mentioned by separate names in Choniates, there is no possibility of confusion: Asen and his brothers really were of Vlakh descent. But we must not exaggerate, as some Romanian scholars have done, and see Vlakh traces even where none is to be found. Bănescu, for instance, rejoices that even if the name *Asen* is of Cuman origin, the names of the other two brothers, Peter and Ioannica, are 'purely Romanian', which in reality they are not.[93]

The assertion of the pure Bulgarian descent of the brothers was so clearly untenable that the best Bulgarian scholars, such as Zlatarski and Mutafčiev, tried to find another solution in order to preserve the idea of the Bulgarian descent of the Asenids. Zlatarski supposed that the Asenids belonged to a people of Cuman extraction who became Bulgars.[94] He says that the brothers came of a distinguished Cumano-Bulgarian clan (*kumano-b"lgarski znaten rod*),[95] the members of which played an important political role in Byzantium. In addition to their distinguished descent and their personal qualities, their Cuman origins, too, must have been instrumental in the liberation movement, since only with the military force of the Cumans could anyone envisage a struggle against Byzantium. While the latter argument is right, the political role of the brothers in Byzantium cannot be proved. Moreover, they must have been rather insignificant persons, since their request to get a *pronoia* in the Haimos was categorically refused by the Byzantine authorities. Besides, the term 'Cumano-Bulgarian' is rather obscure. Zlatarski's underlying thought was that the brothers were Bulgars whose ancestors were Cumans. Mutafčiev chose another way to arrive at roughly the same conclusions as Zlatarski. In a long article he tried to prove that Kievan Rus' had intimate connections with the Bulgaria of the eleventh and twelfth centuries and that a massive layer of Russian frontier guards can be detected in Danube Bulgaria.[96] Though Asen had a Turkic ('Turanian' in Mutafčiev) name, he must have been of Russian origin. As far as the Cuman

---

[91] Villehardouin/Pauphilet, p. 136.

[92] 'ἴδρις τῆς τῶν Βλάχων διαλέκτου' (Nik. Chon. *Hist.*/van Dieten, I, p. 468₂₆).

[93] 'Pierre et Ioannice, noms purement roumains' (Bănescu, *Sec. emp. bulg.*, p. 43). *Peter* is 'neutral' as to its origin, and *Ioannica* is a Slavic formation, disregarding the fact that the formant -*ica* later entered into Romanian usage also.

[94] Zlatarski, 'Potekloto'; Zlatarski, *Ist.*, II, pp. 426–7.   [95] Zlatarski, *Ist.*, II, p. 427.

[96] Mutafčiev, 'Proiz. Asen.'

affiliations of the brothers are concerned, these are easy to explain: the Russian aristocracy often intermingled with 'Turanian' peoples. In a cautious manner Mutafčiev even suggested that the Asenids were descendants of Prince Vladimir Monomakh. Later, in his monograph on Bulgarian history, Mutafčiev formulated his opinion with great clarity: 'The name of the younger [brother] of them is Cuman. They were of Russo-Cuman (*ruskokumanski*) descent, progeny of some of those prominent emigrants from the south Russian steppes who in the first half of the twelfth century found their second homeland in Danube Bulgaria and soon were to melt into the local Bulgarian environment.'[97] Mutafčiev applied a sophisticated method of minimising the significance of Asen's Turkic name: first, Asen's family was basically Russian with a very distant Cuman connection, and secondly, even this Russian family soon became assimilated in the Bulgarian environment. Mutafčiev could claim considerable success for himself: he expelled the Vlakhs, minimised the role of the Cumans, and made Asen and his brothers Russian princes who were practically Bulgars. A remarkable conjuring trick; it is a pity that his assumptions lack a scholarly basis. Besides, his ideological preconception is too evident: he wants to eliminate the Vlakhs and Cumans from Bulgarian history, thereby serving the alleged interests of Bulgarian nationalism. There is one common element in the theories of Zlatarski and Mutafčiev: both of them took the Cuman descent into consideration.

The brothers were of Cuman descent

Here we reach the third main stream of opinions concerning the Asenids' descent.

It is interesting that F. Uspenskij, fervent defender of the anti-Vlakh theory, was the first to suggest that Asen and his brothers were of Cuman extraction.[98] Later, Jireček corroborated Uspenskij's supposition by calling attention to Cuman princes in the eleventh and twelfth centuries who bore the same name.[99] Since then, most researchers (including Zlatarski and Mutafčiev) have accepted that Asen had a Cuman name, but the historical conclusions that could be drawn from this have been very different. As we have seen, Zlatarski made the Asenids Bulgars or at the best

---

[97] 'Imeto na po-malkija ot těh e kumansko. Te bili ot ruski-kumanski proizhod, navěrno potomci na někoi ot onija vidni emigranti iz južno-ruskite zemi, koito prez p"rvata polovina na XII v. namerili v Dunavska B"lgarija vtoro otečestvo i skoro se pretopili v mestnata b"lgarska sreda' (Mutafčiev, *Ist.*, II, p. 33).
[98] Uspenskij, *Vtor. bolg. carstvo*, p. 108.   [99] Jireček, *Serb.*, I, p. 269, n. 4.

Cumano-Bulgars, while Mutafčiev succeeded in making them Russians or Russo-Cumans who were practically Bulgars. To the school of Turkish and Turkic nationalism, the fact that Asen had a Turkic name was sufficient to make him and his descendants Cumans.[100]

Before proceeding to judge the question in the light of history, we must ascertain whether this Turkic etymology of Asen's name holds true, and, if so, what are the further consequences of this fact. In doing so, we must not forget that Asen and his family were Vlakhs. The basic fact that gave rise to the idea of the Cuman origin of Asen's name was that there were two Cuman princes with the same name who had lived in the second half of the eleventh century. A Cuman prince Asen (*Osen'*) died in 1082.[101] He must have been the grandfather of the daughter of a certain Ayapa (*Aepa*) who became the wife of Jurij, son of Prince Vladimir, in 1107.[102] Ayapa was either the son or the son-in-law of this Osen'. There was another Cuman prince, *Asin'*, who, together with Prince Sakz', was captured by the Russian prince Vladimir Monomakh in 1096.[103] In 1112, mention is made in the Russian Annals of the 'town of Osen".[104] The names of these Cuman princes and that of Asen and other Bulgarian rulers who followed are obviously the same. As the name is not Slavic, everybody thought that it was a Turkic name, but no satisfactory etymology was given. Mutafčiev's haphazard ideas (e.g. the comparison of *Asen* with *A-shih-na*, the Chinese transcription of the ruling clan of the Turks in the sixth to eighth centuries) cannot be taken seriously.[105] It was L. Rásonyi who posited an acceptable etymology for the name.[106] He pointed out that the name *Esen* was widespread among the Turkic peoples; it is particularly significant that it was well known to the Mamelukes in Egypt, who were undoubtedly of Cuman-Kipchak origin. The Turkic name *Esen* goes back to a common Turkic word,

---

[100] Rásonyi, *Tar. Türklük*, p. 15; Rásonyi, 'Turcs non-isl.' , p. 153.
[101] Lavrent'evskaja letopis', under 6590 (= 1082): 'Osen' umre Poloveč'skyi knjaz' (*PSRL*, i, p. 205).
[102] Ipat'evskaja letopis', under 6615 (= 1107): 'ide Volodimer i David i Oleg k Aepe i [ko] drugomu Aepe i stvoriša mir, i poja Volodimer za Jurgja Aepinu dščer' Osenevu vnuku, a Oleg poja za syna Aepinu dčer' Girgenevu [var. Gigrenevu] vnuku' (*PSRL*, ii, pp. 282–3).
[103] In the *Poučenie Vladimira Monomaha*, under 6604 (= 1096): 'I zautra na Gospožin den' idohom k Bele Veži i Bog ny pomože i svjataja Bogorodica izbiša 900 Polovec' i dva knjazja jašča Bagubarsova brata Asinja i Sakzja, i dva muža tolko utekosta, i potom na Svjatoslavl' gonihom po Polovcih' (*PSRL*, ii, pp. 248–9).
[104] Lavrent'evskaja letopis', under 6621 (= 1112): the Russian princes 'doidoša do grada Oseneva' in their campaign against the Cumans (*PSRL*, i, p. 275). This 'Osenev grad' must have been somewhere in the neighbourhood of the Don (cf. Aristov, 'Zemlja polov', pp. 9–10; Mutafčiev, 'Proiz. Asen', p. 15).
[105] Mutafčiev, 'Proiz. Asen.', pp. 11–12.   [106] Rásonyi, 'Kuman özel ad.', pp. 82–3.

esen, 'sound, safe, healthy'.[107] All the Russian forms of the name (*Osen'*, *Osěn'*, *Asěn'*, *Asin'*)[108] and the Greek forms (Ἀσάν, Ἀσάνης)[109] can be satisfactorily explained by reference to Turkic *Esen*.[110] Some members of the Bulgarian Asen family entered Byzantine service in the thirteenth to fourteenth centuries,[111] and the late descendants of these Byzantine Asenids were the Romanian boyars' clan *Asan*.[112] The name also occurs as a family name in modern Greek,[113] and probably goes back to the same name. In addition to Asen's name, another name by which he is known in a Slavic source,[114] *Bělgun'*, seems also to be of Turkic origin. According to Mladenov, this comes from Turkic *bilgün*, 'one who knows, wise'.[115]

While the Turkic origin of the name *Asen* can be taken for granted, the historical consequences drawn from this fact by earlier researchers cannot be accepted. No serious argument can be put forward in support of the Asenids' Bulgarian or Russian origin. Moreover, a Cuman name by itself cannot prove that its bearer was undoubtedly Cuman. Asen's Turkic (probably Cuman) name must be reconciled with the fact that the sources unanimously testify to his being Vlakh. This must be the basis of any further deductions: *Asen was a Vlakh and bore a Cuman name.* In addition to having pure Romanian names, Romanians of the thirteenth and fourteenth centuries in Transylvania also bore Slavic, Hungarian and Turkic names.[116] This is evidence of the various cultural influences exerted on the Romanians during their history. Since the Vlakhs (predecessors of the Romanians) lived in the Balkans before 1185 and settled on the left bank of the Danube only sporadically, only Turkic peoples of the Balkans can be considered as having lent Turkic names to the Vlakhs. Given that the Cumans were the most frequent visitors (invited or not) in the Balkans, and that Cuman princes of the eleventh and twelfth centuries bore the same name as Asen, the most probable explanation for Asen's Turkic name

---

[107] For the data, see Rásonyi, 'Kuman özel ad.', p. 83, and Clauson, *ED*, p. 248.

[108] For the Russian and Slavic forms, see above, and Mutafčiev, 'Proiz. Asen.', p. 15, nn. 2–6.

[109] For the Greek forms, see *Byz.-turc.*, II, pp. 73–5.

[110] The rendering of an initial open *e* (= *ä*) by the letter *a* in Slavic and Greek transcriptions of names of foreign origin was quite common. The letter *o* is regularly used in Russian texts to represent an unstressed *a*. The palatal *n'* (нь) and the use of the *jat'* (ѣ) in the Slavic transcriptions may indicate that the second syllable was palatal in the original Turkic word.

[111] See Uspenskij, 'Asen. viz. služ.'   [112] Mutafčiev, 'Proiz. Asen.', p. 12, n. 4.

[113] Boutouras, *Kyria onom.*, p. 102.   [114] *Sinodik Borila*, p. 77, § 91.   [115] Mladenov, 'Bělgun'.

[116] For example, in a diploma of 1383 the following Vlakh persons (*Walachi*) occur in the neighbourhood of Szeben (Romanian *Sibiu*, German *Hermanstadt*) in Transylvania: *Fladmer/Fladmir* and *Dragmer* (Slavic names), *Neg* and *Radul* (Romanian names), *Oldamar* (a Turkic name) (*Doc. hist. Valach.*, pp. 301–2). Cf. also the index to the same work. For Romanian names of Turkic origin, see Rásonyi, 'Val.-Turc.'

is that it came from the Cumans. But the Pechenegs cannot be excluded, since their language must have been very similar to that of the Cumans, and Pecheneg settlements must have come about in the Balkans in the twelfth century after the confederacy's final defeat by the Byzantines in 1041. Moreover, in the twelfth century a certain intermingling of the Vlakh and Cuman population must be reckoned with. As with most nomadic peoples who came to Europe from the east, the Cumans were marauding and plundering warriors who, after their victories or defeats, generally withdrew from the territory of their incursions. But as is also the case with most nomadic peoples, certain contingents of nomads often separated from the bulk of the confederacy. Some Cuman groups must have remained in the Balkans and merged with the Vlakhs. The fact that the nomadic way of life of both peoples displayed numerous common features may have facilitated their fusion. I might refer here to the well-known *prostagma* of Emperor Andronikos Komnenos, issued in February 1184, in which mention is made of the *Cumans*, Vlakhs and Bulgars in the province of Moglena (western Macedonia).[117] These Cumans of Moglena were engaged in animal husbandry (most probably horses and sheep), and unlike their Vlakh and Bulgar counterparts they were freemen and belonged to the elite of the province.[118] Since these Cumans of Moglena are mentioned a decade later (in October 1196) in the same province,[119] one may safely assume that they were well-established settlers of the region. Malingoudis rightly proposes that Asen and his brothers may have emerged from a local Cuman group beyond the Balkan Mountains, very similar to that of the Moglena Cumans.[120]

Taking into consideration everything that has been said so far, the most plausible supposition seems to be that Asen and his family were of Cuman origin. They stood at the head of the liberation movement in Bulgaria, and their chief supporters were their people, the Vlakhs. They must have spoken the language of their Vlakh subjects but preserved the knowledge of their Cuman predecessors' nomadic skills. Moreover, they must have been in close contact with their near relatives in Cumania. That is why they turned to their kinsfolk to help them in their fight against the Byzantine Empire. Rasovskij called the Asenids half-Cumans (*polupolovcy*),[121] and he was right. But the other half was Vlakh, so they may rightly be called *Cumano-Vlakhs*.

In sum, the Asenids were a Cuman dynasty whose members became Vlakhs in the twelfth century and Bulgars in the thirteenth. Both Bulgarian

[117] *Actes de Lavra*, pp. 341–5 (no. 66).   [118] Anastasijević-Ostrogorsky, p. 28.

[119] *Actes de Lavra*, pp. 358–60 (no. 69).   [120] Malingoudis, 'Zweit. bulg. Staat.', p. 86.

[121] Rasovskij, 'Rol' Polovcev', p. 210.

and Romanian history may claim that this Cuman dynasty is part of their common past and heritage.

PETER AND ASEN VERSUS ISAAKIOS AND ALEXIOS ANGELOI: THE FIRST PHASE OF THE CUMANO-VLAKHO-BULGARIAN LEAGUE'S FIGHT AGAINST BYZANTIUM, 1186–1197

We left the history of the Vlakho-Bulgarian revolt at the moment when the rebels crossed the Danube and turned to the Cumans for help. In what follows I shall survey the Bulgaro-Byzantine warfare during the first twenty years of the Second Bulgarian Empire, laying special emphasis on the presence and role of the Cumans in this fight for independence.

Peter and Asen's troops escaped to the Cumans on the left bank of the Danube and applied for their support. They stirred up the Cumans to come with them and lay waste the standing corn of the Byzantines.[122] This detail yields us valuable information about the chronology of events. Zlatarski called attention to the fact that the negotiations between the Asenids and Cumans must have taken place in June or July 1186, since the corn would be standing before the harvest time in August.[123] But the Cumans were willing to attack only after the summer season. Rasovskij, in a brilliant article, succeeded in pointing out that the nomadic Cumans never waged war in summer in Bulgaria, as they were camped in the foothills of the southern Carpathian Mountains at that time, their summer pastures being in that region.[124] So the Cumans could not provide immediate support, being unwilling to cross the Danube before October. But Emperor Isaakios did not take advantage of the situation that arose when the rebels' initial impulse came to a temporary standstill. Niketas Choniates bitterly rebukes the emperor for having missed the opportunity to occupy the whole of Mysia and fortify the mighty strongholds of the Haimos Mountains. Instead, he was content to set fire to the stacks of wheat and leave the country, which was now in a volatile state.[125]

In the next year, Emperor Isaakios paid little attention to Bulgarian affairs, since he had to take up arms against Alexios Branas. When the Asenids and the Cumans returned to Bulgaria in the autumn of 1186, Isaakios was not willing to march against them in person, but appointed first his paternal uncle Sebastokrator Ioannes, then his son-in-law Kaisar

---

[122] Theod. Skut. *Syn.*/Sathas, p. 78.
[123] Zlatarski, *Ist.*, II, pp. 453–455.   [124] Rasovskij, 'Rol' Polovcev'.
[125] Nik. Chon. *Hist.*/van Dieten, p. 373$_{59-67}$ (ed. Bonn, p. 487), = Grabler, *Abenteuer*, p. 176.

Ioannes Kantakouzenos, to be commander-in-chief. The latter was soon replaced by Alexios Branas, the eminent soldier who had formerly stood at the head of the Byzantine army against the Normans. But Branas quickly turned against the emperor and sought to claim the imperial throne.[126] Isaakios marched against his unfaithful commander and crushed his forces. It is interesting to note that in the clash between Isaakios and Branas, which must have taken place in the spring of 1187, Cuman warriors also participated. Niketas Choniates remarks that one of the experienced commanders of Branas' army was the Scythian Elpumes (the Cuman Alpamïš).[127] As far as I know, this is the first occurrence of the typical Kipchak name *Alpamïš*, borne also by the well-known hero of the Turkic epic poem of the same title.[128]

Emperor Isaakios marched against the Vlakho-Bulgarian forces for the second time in September 1187.[129] He heard that the Vlakhs (*Mysoi*) had left the mountains and together with the Cumans (*Skythai*) made an incursion into the neighbourhood of Agathopolis. They devastated the country and harassed Termereia. The emperor then went to Taurokomos (Ταυροκώμος), which was a rural property not far from Hadrianoupolis,[130] and sought an opportunity to encounter the enemy. When spies reported to him that the enemy had gone through the territory of Lardea (Λαρδέα), he set out with a troop of 2,000 mercenaries. They killed many inhabitants, took many captives, and were eager to return home with their large booty. At night, the emperor's troops moved forward to a place called Basternai (Βαστέρναι), where they halted. After three days, on the morning of 11 October 1187, they started to head for Beroe (Βερόη). They had advanced less than 4 parasangas (about 16 km) when a herald reported that the enemy was in the vicinity. The two parties met, and the Byzantine forces were able to rescue some of the prisoners. At this point in his narrative, Niketas Choniates reveals that he was an eyewitness of this campaign, being a secretary of the emperor (βασιλεῖ ὑπογραμματεύων). His very detailed account of this campaign can evidently be ascribed to his own participation in the events. In recording the clash between the Cumans

---

[126] Nik. Chon. *Hist.*/van Dieten, pp. 374–6 (ed. Bonn, pp. 489–91), = Grabler, *Abenteuer*, p. 177.

[127] Nik. Chon. *Hist.*/van Dieten, p. 386₈₇₋₉₁ (ed. Bonn, p. 503), = Grabler, *Abenteuer*, p. 187. Cf. also Stritter, III/2, pp. 931–2.

[128] For the variants of the Greek word Ἐλπουμής, see Nik. Chon. *Hist.*/van Dieten, p. 386, and *Byz.-turc.*, II, p. 124. For the Turkic name *Alpamïš*, see Rásonyi, 'Kuman özel ad.', p. 79.

[129] For questions of chronology relating to the above and to the following, see van Dieten, *Erläuterungen*, and Malingoudis, 'Zweit. bulg. Staat.', pp. 113–22.

[130] Nik. Chon. *Hist.*/van Dieten, p. 394₃₃ (ed. Bonn, p. 516), = Grabler, *Abenteuer*, p. 197, who translates it as 'dies ist ein dorfartiges Landgut'.

and the Byzantine troops, he gave a wonderful description of nomadic war techniques. (We shall deal with this more fully later.) After the battle, the emperor returned to Hadrianoupolis, but the enemy did not stop disquieting the countryside. The emperor was therefore compelled to march to Beroe again. According to Choniates, it was very difficult to gain any success against the 'barbarians' since they slipped out of the emperor's hands. This was a typical tactic of light cavalry, which was the main strength of the equestrian nomads. Finally, the emperor decided to go to Zagora (Ζαγορά). He left Philippoupolis and reached Triaditza (Τριάδιτζα, that is, the Sofia of the later sources), but because of the approach of winter he returned to the capital with a small retinue, leaving the army to spend the winter in Triaditza.[131]

In the spring of 1188, Emperor Isaakios rejoined his army and spent three months on the battlefield, attempting to capture Lobitzos (Λοβιτζός). But he was unsuccessful, and returned to the capital. During this spring campaign of 1188, he captured Asen's wife and younger brother Ioannes (the eventual sovereign Kaloyan), and took them as hostages to Constantinople. Nevertheless, Byzantine success in war was on the wane.[132]

In the winter of 1189–90 the Third Crusade, under the leadership of the German Emperor Frederick I, marched through Bulgarian and Byzantine territories. It is interesting that both the Vlakho-Bulgarian rebels and Byzantium wanted to exploit the situation to the detriment of the opposing party. In December 1189, Peter (whom the *Hist. peregr.* and Ansbert call Kalopetrus) sent an envoy to Frederick in Adrianople and offered him his help against the Emperor of Constantinople. He wanted to support Frederick in his fight by supplying 40,000 Cuman auxiliaries. But Frederick politely refused the offer, because his aim was to reach Jerusalem, not to meddle into the affairs of Greece.[133] (The later crusaders of the Fourth Crusade were not so fastidious, and happily rushed on Byzantium, totally forgetting about the Holy Land.) Later, in February 1190, both the Byzantines and the Vlakhs tried once more to persuade Frederick to join them against the other party, but the German emperor was steadfast and

---

[131] Nik. Chon. *Hist.*/van Dieten, pp. 396₆₈–398₄₂ (ed. Bonn, pp. 517–21), = Grabler, *Abenteuer*, pp. 198–201.

[132] Nik. Chon. *Hist.*/van Dieten, p. 399₄₃₋₅₃ (ed. Bonn, p. 21), = Grabler, *Abenteuer*, p. 201.

[133] 'Interea Kalopetrus qui cum Assanio fratre suo dominabatur populis Blacorum, misit legationem Adrianopolim, diadema regni Grecie de manu imperatoris capiti suo rogans imponi et adversus imperatorem Constantinopolitanum promittens se venturum illi in auxilium cum quadraginta milibus Cumanorum. Imperator vero illius amicabile et placens pro tempore dedit responsum . . . Amplius namque desiderabat partibus transmarinis succurrere et videre bona Hierusalem quam in Grecia demorando alienum sibi imperium vendicare' (*Hist. peregr.*/Chroust, p. 149₁₃₋₂₃).

insisted on fulfilling his original plan, the conquest of the Holy Land.[134] It is interesting that Cuman auxiliaries supported not only the Vlakhs, but also the Byzantines, who hired their warriors. Ansbert mentions that the town and castle of Didymotoichon were possessed by the Cumans and the Greeks.[135]

Since the war situation was worsening because of the constant plundering and pillage carried out by the Vlakhs and the Cumans (οἱ Βλάχοι ληϊζό-μενοι μετὰ Κομάνων), Emperor Isaakios marched against them again in 1190. He passed by Anchialos and advanced to the Haimos Mountains. But after two months he had to return, having found the towns and fortresses stronger than before. Besides, it was possible that the Cumans (Scythians) might cross the Danube, since it was a favourable season for crossing the river. So the emperor stopped waging war against the Vlakhs and decided to retreat to Beroe by a shorter route. But on the narrow mountain path he was attacked by the enemy and could hardly escape with his life. Finally, passing through Krenon (Κρήνον), he reached Beroe.[136]

The Vlakhs, encouraged by their success, conquered and pillaged not only villages but fortified towns too. They took Anchialos and Varna, subjugated Triaditza (Sofia), and pillaged Stumpion and Nisos (Niš). The emperor then rebuilt Varna and fortified Anchialos and placed garrisons in both towns, but he could not prevent further raiding by the enemy.[137] It was after the destruction of Triaditza that the Vlakho-Bulgars took the relics of St John of Rila to their capital, Tărnovo. The acquisition of the relics of the Bulgarian 'national' saint must have had a major symbolic significance for the fighting Vlakho-Bulgars.[138] At the time of the autumnal equinox Isaakios went to the eparchy of Philippoupolis, where he wanted to hamper the Vlakho-Cuman incursions. But soon he had to turn against the Serbian Grand Župan Stefan Nemanja who destroyed Skopia (Skoplje). The Byzantine emperor defeated the Serbian army at the river Moravos (Morava), then passed by Nisos and arrived at the river Savos (Sava). Here he personally met his father-in-law, the Hungarian king Béla III, who

---

[134] First the messenger of the Byzantines arrived, then 'Ipsa nichilominus die Kalopetrus Blachorum domnus' sent a messenger too, 'sed utrique nuntii a domno imperatore inefficaciter ad sua reversi' (Ansbert/Chroust, p. 69).

[135] 'Timoticon urbem munitissimam a fortioribus et animosioribus Cumanis et Grecis possessam' (Ansbert/Chroust, p. 53).

[136] Nik. Chon. *Hist.*/van Dieten, p. 428$_{63-430}$ (ed. Bonn, pp. 561–4), = Grabler, *Abenteuer*, pp. 233–6.

[137] Nik. Chon. *Hist.*/van Dieten, p. 434$_{10-24}$ (ed. Bonn, pp. 568–9), = Grabler, *Abenteuer*, p. 239.

[138] As Höfler, 'Walachen', p. 240, remarked: 'Der heil. Johannes von Ryl verdrängte bei den Bulgaren den romäisierenden heil. Demetrios.'

was his ally. After a few days' stay he returned to Philippoupolis, then to Constantinople.[139] This autumn campaign of Isaakios has generally been dated to 1190, but van Dieten preferred 1191 or 1192.[140] I see no compelling reason to change the customary dating of 1190.

Between 1190 and 1195 no precise chronicle of the Cumano-Vlakho-Bulgarian warfare can be given. Niketas Choniates gave no detailed account of the wars. Seemingly, an ongoing war was in the making in which the Byzantines were usually the losers. Not only did they fail to put down the rebellion in Bulgaria, but they had to endure constant molesting and harassing by Peter and Asen's coalition. The allies often plundered the villages and larger towns such as Philippoupolis, Sardike and Hadrianoupolis. Finally, Isaakios turned for help to his father-in-law, Béla III, who promised to send him auxiliary troops from Vidin.[141] In March 1195 Isaakios marched against the enemy, but before long his brother Alexios headed up the malcontents, ousted Isaakios from the throne and left him blind.

Alexios III's rule (1195–1203) was certainly no better than that of his brother.[142] At first, seeking to reach agreement with the Vlakh rebels, he sent envoys to Peter and Asen. But the Byzantine mission was unsuccessful, since the rebels laid down conditions unacceptable to Byzantium. So warfare continued. While the emperor was in the east, the Vlakhs overran the Bulgarian *themata* round Serrai (τοῖς περὶ τὰς Σέρρας Βουλγαρικοῖς θέμασι), defeated the Byzantine army, and captured Aspietes Alexios, the Byzantine leader of those territories. The emperor sent his son-in-law the Sebastokrator Isaakios against them, but Isaakios' war tactics were ill-chosen, and the enemy surrounded him. He himself was captured by the Cumans (Scythians). The Cuman warrior who captured the Sebastokrator tried to keep him hidden from Asen, hoping to take his distinguished captive back to his homeland and obtain a large ransom for him from the Byzantine emperor. But his plan was detected, and he was forced to hand the Byzantine captive over to Asen.[143] It is noteworthy that it was a Cuman warrior who captured this Byzantine commander. The Cumans must have been present as auxiliaries in practically all the clashes during the Vlakho-Bulgarian and Byzantine war. Even when they are not mentioned explicitly,

---

[139] Nik. Chon. *Hist.*/van Dieten, p. 434₂₅₋₃₅ (ed. Bonn, p. 569), = Grabler, *Abenteuer*, pp. 239–40.

[140] Nik. Chon. *Hist.*/van Dieten, p. 434; van Dieten, *Erläuterungen*, pp. 83ff.

[141] Nik. Chon. *Hist.*/van Dieten, p. 446₇₀₋₅ (ed. Bonn, p. 588), = Grabler, *Abenteuer*, p. 284.

[142] For Alexios III Angelos' reign, see Ostrogorsky, *Gesch.*, pp. 291–6.

[143] Nik. Chon. *Hist.*/van Dieten, pp. 465₁₈–468₂₃ (ed. Bonn, pp. 612–17), = Grabler, *Kreuzfahrer*, pp. 30–3.

their involvement is very probable. In the case just described, for example, if the Byzantine commander had not been captured by the Cumans, we would not have known of their participation in the campaign. Although an argument from silence is no argument, these considerations may render probable the Cuman presence in every Vlakho-Byzantine encounter. The Cumano-Vlakho-Bulgarian league had firm hold of the territory between the Danube and the Balkan Mountains with Tărnovo in its centre, and regularly harassed Macedonia and Thrace, which were then under Byzantine rule.

Since no breakthrough was possible in the Vlakho-Bulgarian–Byzantine war, the Byzantines turned to their proven old method of inciting one party within the enemy ranks against the other. They encouraged a certain Ivanko, who was active in the neighbourhood of Philippoupolis, to rise up against Peter and Asen.[144] Ivanko finally assassinated Asen in 1196, but Asen's brother Peter hurried to Tărnovo and took over the leadership. His reign however, was short-lived; the next year, in 1197, he too fell victim to a riot in obscure circumstances. Thus the unexpected murders of the two brothers, Peter and Asen, put an end to the first period of the Vlakho-Bulgarian liberation movement. But the Byzantines were to be bitterly disappointed if they had thought that the re-established power of the Bulgarian Empire could now be crushed. Instead of anarchy, for which Byzantium hoped, the third and youngest brother, Kaloyan, ascended the Bulgarian throne. He became an authoritative ruler and was a fervent adversary of Byzantium. With his reign a new epoch began in the history of the Cumano-Vlakho-Bulgarian league's struggle against Byzantium.

KALOYAN AND HIS CUMANS AGAINST BYZANTIUM AND THE LATINS

As I have mentioned, one of the territories most favoured by the Cumano-Vlakh raiders was Thrace. The Byzantine emperor, in response to the threat, generally moved his troops to Kypsella (now İpsala in Turkey, on the left bank of the Marica), which was one of the basic points of Byzantine defence against the barbarians. This is what happened in April 1199, when the Cumans, together with Vlakh divisions (Σκύθαι μετὰ μοίρας Βλάχων) crossed the Danube (Istros) and plundered the towns around Mesene and Tzurulon. The barbarians wanted to go to Kuperion, near Tzurulon, where

---

[144] For Ivanko, see Nik. Chon. *Hist.*/van Dieten, p. 473₆₀–₈ (ed. Bonn, p. 24), = Grabler, *Kreuzfahrer*, p. 39.

a large mass of people had gathered to celebrate St George's day (23 April). In the morning of the holiday a dense mist engulfed the land, and a great number of the barbarians lost their way and reached Rhaidestos on the sea coast. A smaller contingent of the assailants managed to reach Kuperion, but did not succeed in penetrating to the church square, around which the inhabitants had built a strong wall of carts. The Cumans (Scythians) could not break through this obstacle, since 'the Scythians have no experience in besieging walls; they rather avoid fortresses in villages and towns. Like a whirlwind they stir up everything that falls before their feet at the time of the first attack; then they return to their homes.'[145] Those Greeks who tried to escape from the church to the fortress of Tzurulon were captured by the barbarians. The Cumans withdrew in possession of a rich booty, but then encountered the Byzantine army that was defending Bizye. The Greeks defeated the Cumans, who left their booty on the battlefield and fled. The avaricious Byzantine warriors, interested solely in the booty, failed to notice that the enemy had returned; this time the Cumans were victorious.[146] This episode, described by Choniates at great length, gives a sharp insight into the character of the Cuman raids in Byzantium.

The autumn of the same year, 1199, saw the Cumans make that strongest incursion so far. Choniates does not give details, but he asserts that this was the most terrible of the barbarian raids in Macedonia. The barbarians plundered the monasteries and killed the friars.[147]

In the autumn of 1200 or spring of 1201,[148] the Vlakhs, together with the Cumans (μετὰ Κομάνων), overran the Byzantine territories, devastating the best regions and returning unhindered to their own land. This time, had the Russians not helped the Byzantines against the intruders, they might even have reached Constantinople. According to Choniates, the Russians did so partly to the request of their prelate (ἀρχιποιμήν). Roman, Prince of Galicia (ὁ τῆς Γαλίτζης ἡγεμὼν Ῥωμανός), marched against the Cumans

---

[145] Nik. Chon. *Hist./*van Dieten, p. 500₇₁₋₅ (ed. Bonn, p. 663), = Grabler, *Kreuzfahrer*, p. 72.

[146] For the account of the whole episode, see Nik. Chon. *Hist./*van Dieten, pp. 499₅₄–501₇ (ed. Bonn, pp. 662–5), = Grabler, *Kreuzfahrer*, pp. 71–3.

[147] Nik. Chon. *Hist./*van Dieten, p. 508₆₇₋₇₄ (ed. Bonn, p. 673), = Grabler, *Kreuzfahrer*, p. 80. Cf. also Stritter, III/2, pp. 982–3.

[148] Choniates says that the events took place 'next year' ('τῷ δ'ἐφεξῆς ἔτει'), which lasted from 1 September 1200 to 31 August 1201 (cf. Nik. Chon. *Hist./*van Dieten, p. 522, n.). The Cuman raids were carried out, as we have seen, always in autumn, winter or spring, but never in summer. Rasovskij, 'Rol' polovcev', p. 208, states that the Bulgars and the Cumans devastated Thrace in April 1201. I do not know where he found this precise date, since there is no more specific indication of the time in any other source.

and 'plundered and destroyed their land with ease' (τὴν γῆν αὐτῶν κατὰ πολλὴν εὐπέτειαν ἐπιὼν ἔφθειρε καὶ ἠφάνισε). He did this repeatedly, thereby putting an end to the Cuman incursions. At the same time (ὁ τότε χρόνος),[149] internal trouble broke out among the Russians, and Roman defeated Rurik, ruler of Kiev. Roman killed many Cumans, who not only were members of Rurik's retinue but formed his strongest and boldest troop.[150] The Russian sources confirm that Roman Mstislavič, Prince of Galič (1199–1205), marched against the Cumans twice, in 1201–2 and 1203–4.[151] On both occasions he led his army to the northern shores of the Black Sea during the winter period, when Russian attacks were regularly directed against the Cumans.[152] In the autumn and winter, several Cuman groups would head for the Danube and make incursions into Byzantine and Bulgarian territories. In the winter of 1187, for example, Svjatoslav and Rurik sent the Černye Klobuki against the Cumans beyond the Dnieper. They destroyed their tents, 'since the Cumans had gone to the Danube and were not at home in their tents'.[153] It is evident that Roman Mstislavič, too, chose the winter to attack the Cuman habitations in the Black Sea region, when the Cuman warriors were far away by the Danube and and in the Balkans. Rasovskij has called attention to the fact that even Choniates did not speak of a Cuman defeat, but stated that Roman 'destroyed their land with ease'.[154]

Between 1202 and 1204 the battles between the young Bulgarian state and Byzantium came to a temporary standstill. Byzantium was increasingly sliding into anarchy. Finally, the capture of Constantinople by the crusaders on 12 April 1204 put an end to the Byzantine state for more than fifty years. In the years preceding the catastrophe of 1204, Byzantium was in no position to pay attention to and deal with Bulgarian affairs. The empire fell apart, and a Latin Empire was founded in its place, ruled by the emperor Baldouin, head of the crusader knights. The Byzantine political emigrants withdrew to Asia Minor, but the Greek cause seemed to decay everywhere; the crusaders

---

[149] According to Grabler, *Kreuzfahrer*, p. 95, it was in 1202.
[150] For the whole story of the Russian campaign against the Cumans, see Nik. Chon. *Hist.*/van Dieten, pp. 522₂₅–523₄₉ (ed. Bonn, pp. 691–2), = Grabler, *Kreuzfahrer*, pp. 94–5. Cf. also Stritter, III/2, p. 983, and II/2, pp. 703–4, 1023–4.
[151] For these campaigns, see Hruševskyj, *Ist.*, III, pp. 9–10.
[152] Lavrent'evskaja letopis', under 6710 (= 1202): 'Toe že zimy hodi Roman knjaz' na Polovcy i vzja vežě Poloveč'skye i privede polona mnogo i duš' hrist'jan'skyh množestvo otpoloni ot nih i byst' radost' velika v zemli Rus'těi' (*PSRL*, I, p. 418).
[153] Ipat'evskaja letopis', under 6695 (= 1187): 'Polovci bo bjahut' šli v Dunai i ne bě ih doma v vežah svoih' (*PSRL*, II, p. 659).
[154] Rasovskij, 'Rol' Polovcev', p. 211. For the Greek text, see above in this paragraph.

were preparing to subjugate the territory of Asia Minor too. In this moment of total loss, an uprising of the Greek population of Thrace compelled the Latins to march back to the unsettled country. The Greek rebels held the towns of Adrianople and Didymotoichon, and turned to Kaloyan for help against the Latins. Kaloyan swiftly came to their aid and marched with his troops near Adrianople. According to Villehardouin, his army consisted of Vlakhs, Bulgars and some 14,000 pagan Cuman warriors.[155] Choniates also stressed that the Cuman (Scythian) auxiliaries were innumerable.[156] At this decisive moment, the customary Byzantine–Bulgarian enmity came to an end; both Kaloyan and the defeated Greeks realised that the new danger they shared was the Latin Empire.

As soon as Baldouin learnt of the Thracian uprising, he sent his army there. The Latins recaptured Bizye and Tzurulon from the Byzantine forces, and Arkadioupolis also fell to the crusaders. In March 1205, Baldouin, Louis, Earl of Blois, and Enrico Dandolo, Doge of Venice, surrounded Adrianople, which was defended by the Greeks. They tried to take the town by besieging and undermining the walls, but failed. On 12 April, a Wednesday following Easter, Kaloyan sent a troop of Cumans against the Latins to test the strength of the enemy. The crusaders pursued them vehemently, but were hit by a storm of Cuman arrows when they attempted to return.[157] The decisive battle at Adrianople took place on 14 April 1205. Kaloyan sent his Cuman warriors into battle under the commandership of a certain Qoǰa (Κοτζᾶς),[158] ordering them to follow the same nomadic tactics of feigned retreat. The Cumans ensnared the Latins by fleeing and then turning back against them. The Latins were killed in great numbers as the Cumans stabbed them with daggers or lassooed and strangled them. Louis, Earl of Blois, met his death on the battlefield, and the commander-in-chief of the knights' army, Baldouin, ruler of the Latin Empire, was captured and carried to the Bulgarian capital, Tărnovo. The third leader of the crusaders, Enrico Dandolo, Doge of Venice, succeeded in escaping.[159] Within a year of the crusaders' capture of Constantinople, they were severely defeated

[155] Villehardouin, ch. LXXIX: 'Johannis li rois de Blaquie venoit secoure ceus d'Andrinople à mult grant ost; que il amenoit Blas et Bogres, et bien quatorze mil Comains, qui n'estoient mie baptizié' (Villehardouin/Pauphilet, p. 169).

[156] Nik. Chon. *Hist.*/van Dieten, p. 613$_{80-81}$.

[157] Nik. Chon. *Hist.*/van Dieten, pp. 614$_{83}$–615$_{35}$ (ed. Bonn, pp. 810–12), = Grabler, *Kreuzfahrer*, pp. 192–4.

[158] Nik. Chon. *Hist.*/van Dieten, p. 616$_{39}$. For the name Κοτζᾶς, see Rásonyi, 'Kuman özel ad.', p. 113.

[159] Nik. Chon. *Hist.*/van Dieten, pp. 616$_{38}$–617$_{76}$ (ed. Bonn, pp. 812–14), = Grabler, *Kreuzfahrer*, pp. 194–6. Cf. also Nik. Greg. *Hist.*/Schopen-Bekker, I, pp. 142$_{4}$–163$_{5}$.

by Kaloyan's Cumans. The historical significance of this battle cannot be overestimated; it made possible the foundation of the Nikaian Empire in Asia Minor, which preserved the Byzantine heritage until the recapture of Constantinople in 1261.

After the battle of Adrianople, Kaloyan rewarded the Cumans with a gift of those towns (κωμοπόλεις) near Byzantium that had paid tribute to the Latins. Days and weeks of terror ensued for the Byzantine population. Choniates bitterly laments the calamities that afflicted the Greeks from two sides: 'two peoples devastated the same land and the same people; once they fell on us separately, once with joint forces'.[160] In less than two months Kaloyan and his Cumans pillaged and plundered the Thracian countryside, but in June he could not hold the Cuman warriors back from returning home to their summer pastures, north of the Danube.[161]

After the destruction of Thrace, Kaloyan and his army went over to Thessalonike, seeking to wrench the Thessalian towns from the Latins. First he took the town of Serrai. Then Henry, brother of Baldouin, took over the leadership of the crusaders and marched to besiege Adrianople. On the way, he punished the inhabitants of Apros who had gone over to Kaloyan's side. After a long and unsuccessful siege of Adrianople, Henry left the city and marched to Didymotoichon, but the heavy rains caused the river Hebros (Marica) to flood. The camp of the Latins was inundated. Both the knights and their Greek opponents considered this a divine sign to halt the campaign. Henry returned to Constantinople, leaving only a small garrison in castles and towns held by the Latins.[162] At the beginning of the summer of 1205, Kaloyan captured Philippoupolis and laid it waste.[163] We have no account of the events of the war in the second half of 1205, but in January 1206 Kaloyan sent large troops of Vlakh and Cuman warriors to help the defenders of Adrianople and Didymotoichon. The succeeding events were related in detail by Villehardouin. Four days before Candlemas (*la feste sainte Marie Chandelor*), Thierry de Dendermonde (*Tierris Tendremonde*) set out on a nocturnal incursion accompanied by 120 knights, leaving a small garrison in Rousion (*Rousse*). At daybreak the troops reached a village where Cumans and Vlakhs were accommodated. The knights made a surprise attack on them and made off with forty horses. During the same

---

[160] Nik. Chon. *Hist.*/van Dieten, p. 618₃₋₅.
[161] Villehardouin, ch. LXXXVIII: 'Si ne pot plus ses Comainz tenir en la terre, que il ne porent plus souffrir l'ostoier por l'esté, ainz repairièrent en lor païs' (Villehardouin/Pauphilet, p. 177).
[162] Nik. Chon. *Hist.*/van Dieten, pp. 621₆–624₁₈ (ed. Bonn, pp. 820–6), = Grabler, *Kreuzfahrer*, pp. 201–6.
[163] Nik. Chon. *Hist.*/van Dieten, p. 627₇₆₋₈₆ (ed. Bonn, pp. 829–30), = Grabler, *Kreuzfahrer*, pp. 208–9.

night, some 7,000 Cumans and Vlakhs also went out to make an incursion. On their way back, not far from Rousion, the knights met the enemy. The Cumans and Vlakhs, together with the neighbouring Greeks, attacked the small troop of knights. No more than ten of the 120 knights managed to avoid death or prison. This battle of Rousion took place one day before Candlemas, that is, on 1 February 1206.[164]

After the battle of Rousion, Kaloyan systematically ravaged and plundered eastern Thrace, especially the towns of the southern seashore. Neapolis, Rhaidestos, Panedos, Perinthos (or Herakleia), Daonion, Arkadioupolis, Mesene and Tzurulon were the main points of Kaloyan's campaign.[165] His troops consisted of Cuman, Vlakh and Greek soldiers. If a fortress surrendered, he would promise its defenders shelter and immunity, but he never kept his promise, and put the defenders to the sword. Kaloyan and his Cumans were almost at the gates of Constantinople. They captured the town of Athyras, 12 miles from Constantinople, and, according to the testimony of both Choniates and Villehardouin, they inflicted a terrible massacre on the population.[166] Only two towns of eastern Thrace, Bizye and Selymbria, were able to escape the Cumans' looting and plundering.[167] Kaloyan and his Cumans ravaged the countryside throughout the whole season of Lent and even after Easter. The Greeks came to realise that Kaloyan and his Cuman auxiliaries were even more formidable enemies than the Latin crusaders, since Kaloyan had razed all the captured towns to the ground. The harassed population of Thrace therefore turned to the Latins for help again. In June 1206 Kaloyan recommenced the siege of Didymotoichon, but the Latin knights soon appeared and compelled him to draw back.[168] Having returned to Constantinople, the knights enthroned Henry as Emperor of Constantinople on 20 August 1206. Till that time Henry had been only regent of the Latin Empire, since the news of his brother Baldouin's death had not been confirmed before then.[169] When Kaloyan learnt that the area of the two strongholds of

[164] Villehardouin/Pauphilet, pp. 180–2. The same event in brief is in Nik. Chon. *Hist.*/van Dieten, p. 628$_{21-29}$ (ed. Bonn, pp. 830–1), = Grabler, *Kreuzfahrer*, p. 210.

[165] Nik. Chon. *Hist.*/van Dieten, p. 629$_{35-60}$ (ed. Bonn, pp. 831–3), = Grabler, *Kreuzfahrer*, pp. 211–12; Villehardouin/Pauphilet, pp. 182–4.

[166] Nik. Chon. *Hist.*/van Dieten, pp. 629$_{61}$–630$_{90}$ (ed. Bonn, pp. 832–4), = Grabler, *Kreuzfahrer*, pp. 212–13; Villehardouin/Pauphilet, p. 184.

[167] Nik. Chon. *Hist.*/van Dieten, pp. 630$_{91}$–631$_{4}$ (ed. Bonn, p. 834), = Grabler, *Kreuzfahrer*, p. 213; Villehardouin/Pauphilet, p. 184.

[168] Nik. Chon. *Hist.*/van Dieten, pp. 631$_{17}$–633$_{53}$ (ed. Bonn, pp. 835–6), = Grabler, *Kreuzfahrer*, pp. 214–15.

[169] Nik. Chon. *Hist.*/van Dieten, p. 642$_{73-80}$ (ed. Bonn, p. 847), = Grabler, *Kreuzfahrer*, p. 224.

Adrianople and Didymotoichon was defended only by Branas, who was in the service of the Latins, he set out to Didymotoichon and razed the town to the ground. Then Henry hurried to the aid of the defenders of Adrianople and embarked on a short campaign against Krenon, Beroe, Agathopolis and Anchialos, returning at the beginning of November to Constantinople.[170]

Though Kaloyan had ravaged the Greek towns of Thrace and Macedonia he was the natural ally of Theodoros Laskaris, who wanted to save and revive the Byzantine imperial tradition in the east of the former Byzantine Empire centred on Nikaia. The common enemy for both was the Latin army of the crusaders. Next year (1207), at the beginning of Lent, Kaloyan set up a huge army of Cuman, Vlakh and Bulgarian warriors and raided Rhomania again. He never relinquished his ambition to take Adrianople, the centre of Thrace. He spent the whole April at Adrianople, and this time was on the verge of taking the city, but the Cumans said 'that they would not remain with Johannis [Kaloyan], but they wanted to return to their land. So the Cumans abandoned Johannis. But without them he did not dare to remain at Adrianople, so he set out and left the city.'[171] Thus, as we have seen several times, the Cumans withdrew to their summer pastures, unwilling to take part in Kaloyan's campaign. Adrianople was saved from Vlakho-Bulgarian capture again.

The summer season of 1207 passed without any major warlike events, and in autumn Kaloyan marched against Thessalonike. His stay in the capital of Macedonia, was brief, however, as he was murdered, probably by a Cuman warrior, in October 1207.[172] The three years of tumult that followed the capture of Constantinople now came to an end. With Kaloyan's death a new period opened in the history of the Bulgarian, Latin and Nikaian Empires. Greeks and Latins alike became free from the pressure of the Bulgarian Empire for a while. Kaloyan's successor was his nephew Boril, the son of the sister of the three brothers. The story of his reign will be traced in the next chapter.

---

[170] Nik. Chon. *Hist.*/van Dieten, pp. 645₈₉–646₁₁ (ed. Bonn, pp. 852–3), = Grabler, *Kreuzfahrer*, pp. 229–30; Villehardouin/Pauphilet, p. 190.

[171] Villehardouin/Pauphilet, pp. 193–6, esp. p. 196.

[172] Georg. Akr. *Chron.*/Heisenberg, I, p. 23₁₉₋₂₃. Akropolites does not state that the warrior was Cuman, nor does he mention his name. Hunfalvy, *Oláhok tört.*, I, p. 296, claims that a certain Cuman commander called *Manastras* killed Kaloyan, but he omits to give any reference. He must have thought of Μαναστράς, Cuman commander of Ivan Asen I's troops in the years around 1200 (*Byz.-turc.*, II, p. 192). This person is mentioned in Greek legends of St Demetrios (Ioannes Staurakios and Konstantinos Akropolites), the editions of which were unfortunately inaccessible to me.

Kaloyan had been a visionary ruler. He had not only sought to preserve Bulgarian independence, which had been regained by his brothers Peter and Asen, but had also tried to unite the Byzantine Empire with the Bulgarian. His dream was of a Greco-Bulgarian Empire. He had been brought up in Byzantine surroundings in Constantinople as a hostage, and the splendour of Byzantium did not leave his soul untouched. The way to realize his dream had been opened up by the crusaders, who had crushed the strength of decadent Byzantium. But it was these same crusaders who had also hindered him from bringing his ambitious plans to a conclusion. The joy of the Greek population of Thrace, which at first greeted Kaloyan as saviour from the Latin tyranny, had soon turned to hatred when his cruelty became apparent to all. His cruelty had pushed the Greeks over to the hated Latin side, and Kaloyan's strong Cumano-Vlakho-Bulgarian league was not powerful enough to crush the united efforts of the Greeks and Latins. When he saw the stubborn opposition of the Greeks, Kaloyan's admiration for Byzantium had turned to hate. According to Akropolites, Kaloyan called himself *Rhomaioktonos*, 'Killer of the Romans [Byzantines]', on the analogy of *Boulgaroktonos*, 'Killer of the Bulgars', the sobriquet of Emperor Basileios II, who had demolished the First Bulgarian Empire in 1018.[173] But the hatred of the Byzantines against Kaloyan gleamed with equal fire. The same Akropolites recounted that Kaloyan's Greek sobriquet was *Skyloioannes*, 'Canine John'.[174] The wordplay of the appelation is evident: the abusive description 'canine' (σκύλαξ, 'whelp, cub', in Greek) plays on the Greek name of the barbaric people of the Scythians, who were the chief allies of Kaloyan. When Kaloyan died, his high-flown plans of a Greco-Bulgarian Empire faded away for ever.[175]

THE CUMANS' ROLE IN THE RESTORATION OF BULGARIA

The Cumans played a special role in the history of the Balkans in the twelfth to thirteenth centuries. Their ubiquitous presence in the wars and battles of the Haimos Peninsula was well known to their contemporaries, who were quite aware that without their military aid none of the warring parties could claim victory over their opponents. Giovanni Villani, for example,

---

[173] 'Ἀντάμυναν οὖν, ὡς ἔφασκεν, ἐποιεῖτο τῶν ὧν εἰργάσατο πρὸς Βουλγάρους κακῶν ὁ βασιλεὺς Βασίλειος, καὶ καλεῖσθαι μὲν ἔλεγεν ἐκεῖνον Βουλγαροκτόνον, Ῥωμαιοκτόνον δὲ ὠνόμαζεν ἑαυτόν.' (Georg. Akr. *Chron.*/Heisenberg, I, p. 23₁₆₋₁₉).

[174] Georg. Akr. *Chron.*/Heisenberg, I, pp. 23₂₄–24₄.

[175] Uspenskij, *Vtor. bolg. carstvo*, p. 255; Ostrogorsky, *Gesch.*, p. 305.

stated that the Cumans were instrumental in the fall of the Latin Empire.[176] The party that hired Cuman warriors could be almost sure that they would not lose any major battle.

Two questions arise concerning this special role of the Cumans in the Balkanic events of the twelfth and thirteenth centuries. First, why were the Cumans hired mostly by the Vlakho-Bulgarian coalition, and secondly, what was the secret of the Cuman successes? The first question was largely answered in the section 'Origins and possible Cuman affiliations of the Asen dynasty' (above, pp. 33–42). The Asen dynasty had intimate connections with the Cumans, being itself of Cuman origin. Though the nomads were not particular about their allies (for they rendered their services to whichever party would reward them with the most booty), their common nomadic and cultural roots with the Asenids facilitated their joining forces with the Vlakho-Bulgarian Empire.

The answer to the second question needs more explanation. Rasovskij has asserted that the decisive role of the Cumans in the Balkanic wars can be put down to their number and war tactics.[177] He was basically right, though the second factor, the role of their war tactics, was far more significant than the first. The nomadic light cavalry was practically invincible in the twelfth and thirteenth centuries. Let us examine two passages from contemporary Byzantine historians who described this method of waging war, which made them so superior to their enemies. First, Georgios Akropolites identified the difference between the army of the Latin knights and the Cuman cavalry as follows:

He [Kaloyan] was not in Adrianople for long, but he sent the Scythians [the Cumans] against the Italians [the Latins] to use the Scythian war techniques against them. Now it was the habit of the Italians to ride on prancing horses that were completely covered by armour, so that their charges against the enemy were slow. The Scythians, by contrast, were armed more lightly, so they attacked the enemy more freely.[178]

Akropolites' characterisation of the difference between the light cavalry of the nomads and the heavy armour of the crusading knights needs no further elucidation. Secondly, Niketas Choniates, when describing a battle near Beroe on 11 October 1187, gave a splendid summary of the nomadic war techniques of the Cumans. This description cannot be surpassed even by a modern analysis of their methods. He writes:

---

[176] Giovanni Villani, lib. 5, cap. 28: 'Ma poco durò il detto imperio [i.e. the Latin Empire], che fu sconfitto e morto da' Cumani' (Villani/Racheli, I, p. 70).

[177] Rasovskij, 'Rol' Polovcev', p. 205.   [178] Georg. Akr. *Chron.*/Heisenberg, I, p. 22₁₋₈.

They [i.e. the Cumans] fought in their habitual manner, learnt from their fathers. They would attack, shoot their arrows and begin to fight with spears. Before long they would turn their attack into flight and induce their enemy to pursue them. Then they would show their faces instead of their backs, like birds cutting through the air, and would fight face to face with their assailants and struggle even more bravely. This they would do several times, and when they gained the upper hand over the Romans [Byzantines], they would stop turning back again. Then they would draw their swords, release an appalling roar, and fall upon the Romans quicker than a thought. They would seize and massacre those who fought bravely and those who behaved cowardly alike.[179]

The Cumans were always at their hosts' disposal except during the summer season. As Rasovskij has pointed out and as we have already noted,[180] in the summer months they were unwilling to stay in the Balkans, but would return to their homeland north of the Danube. Villehardouin has described this phenomenon clearly. After Pentecost, that is, 29 May 1205, Kaloyan 'could not keep the Cumans in the country, because they did not endure the summer heat, and returned to their country'.[181] Similarly, two years later, in May 1207, the Cumans at Adrianople said 'that they would not remain with Johannis [Kaloyan] but they wanted to return to their land. So the Cumans abandoned Johannis. But without them he did not dare to remain at Adrianople, so he set out and left the city.'[182] The latter passage clearly shows the significance attributed to the Cuman warriors even by contemporaries such as Kaloyan. He did not dare to continue with any major venture without their participation.

If we try to summarise the Cumans' historical role in the restoration of the Second Bulgarian Empire and the first two decades of its existence, we may arrive at the following conclusions. First, without the active participation of the Cumans, the Vlakho-Bulgarian rebels could never have gained the upper hand over the Byzantines. Secondly, without the Cumans' military support, the process of Bulgarian restoration could never have come to fruition. Thirdly, the Cumans had no strategic aims, their primary and short-term goal being robbery and pillage. Though their employment as mercenaries in campaigns and battles was of prime importance for both the Vlakho-Bulgarians and the Byzantines and Latins, the Cumans did not present a real menace to the statehood of Byzantium and Bulgaria.

---

[179] Nik. Chon. *Hist.*/van Dieten, p. 397₉₂₋₇; ed. Bonn, p. 519.
[180] Rasovskij, 'Rol' polovcev'.   [181] Villehardouin/Pauphilet, p. 177.   [182] *Ibid.*, p. 196.

CHAPTER THREE

Cumans in the Balkans before the Tatar conquest, 1241

CUMANS DURING THE REIGN OF BORIL, 1207–1218

As we saw in the previous chapter, Kaloyan was succeeded by his nephew Boril, the son of the sister of the three brothers. In an attempt to legitimate his rule, Boril married Kaloyan's Cuman wife, but his reign was never regarded as legitimate. Asen's sons John and Alexander fled to the Cumans, then to the Russians.[1] John was the later Ivan Asen II, who returned from exile in 1218 and became the best-known ruler of the Second Bulgarian Empire. According to the common view, 'the land of the Russians' was the Principality of Galič,[2] but P. Pavlov has successfully shown that the brothers in fact fled to Kiev.[3] Ivan Asen was to remain in Kievan Rus' as a political exile for a long time, during which he was planning to secure Russian and Cuman assistance to take back the Bulgarian throne as his paternal heritage.

Boril was considered a usurper, and internal anarchy increased throughout his reign (1208–18). Centripetal powers strengthened and the decade of his rule was characterised by the feuds of different boyar groups. Several pretenders to the throne had arisen, among whom Boril's brother Strez and Kaloyan's nephew Aleksi Slav were the most powerful. Strez was supported by the Serbian Grand Župan Stefan Nemanja II, who gave him Prosek in western Bulgaria. Aleksi Slav was the feudal lord of the Rodope region

---

[1] 'Ὡς γοῦν οὑτοσὶ ἐτεθνήκει, ὁ τῆς ἀδελφῆς αὐτοῦ παῖς Βορίλλας τοὔνομα, τὴν Σκυθίδα θείαν γαμετὴν εἰληφώς, τῆς ἀρχῆς τῶν Βουλγάρων γέγονεν ἐγκρατής· τὸν δὲ τοῦ Ἀσὰν παῖδα Ἰωάννην ἀφήλικα ἔτι ὄντα κρύφα τις λαβὼν ἐπειρήκει, ὡς περὶ τοὺς Σκύθας κεκώρηκε' (Georg. Akr. *Chron.*/Heisenberg, 1, p. 244–9). Later, in § 20: 'Ὁ πρῶτος βασιλεὺς τῶν Βουλγάρων Ἀσὰν δύο ἔσχεν υἱούς, τὸν Ἰωάννην καὶ τὸν Ἀλεξάνδρον. τοῦ γοῦν εἰρημένου Βορίλλα βασιλικῶς τῶν Βουλγάρων κατάρχοντος, ὁ τοῦ Ἀσὰν υἱὸς Ἰωάννης φυγαδείᾳ χρησάμενος περὶ τὰ τῶν Ῥώσων χωρεῖ' (Georg. Akr. *Chron.*/Heisenberg, 1, pp. 32₂₆–33₄). According to Ephraim, the children's tutor took them to the Cumans: 'Ἀσὰν δὲ παῖδα παιδαγωγός τις λάθρα, νέον κομιδῇ, παραλαβὼν ὡς τάχος πρὸς Σκύθας ἀπήγαγεν εἰς σωτηρίαν' (Ephraim/Bekker-Mai, p. 316, lines 7829–31).

[2] E.g. Cankova-Petkova, *Asenevci*, p. 88.

[3] Pavlov, 'Brodnici', pp. 226–8; Pavlov, 'Kumanite', p. 56, n. 154.

south of Philippoupolis (Plovdiv). The Latin emperor Henry, brother and
successor of Baldouin, who was a relentless adversary of the Bulgarian tsar,
granted the title *despot* to Aleksi Slav and gave him his illegitimate daughter
as a wife. Boril became more and more isolated within his own country and,
in addition, he had to face the imminent danger of an attack from the Latin
Empire of Constantinople. Boril hastened to Beroe, and in May 1208 the
united Bulgarian and Cuman troops overcame Henri's army. The Latins
then moved in the direction of Plovdiv.[4] Here the Bulgarian and Cuman
troops were unable to repeat their victory, and suffered a blow from the
Latin knights' army on 1 August 1208.[5] Northern Thrace and the fortresses
in the Rodope again fell under Latin control.

Either immediately or a few years after the defeat at Plovdiv, Boril had
to face a serious revolt in Vidin. There was practically no one he could
call upon for help: the Latins and the Serbs were his enemies, and the
Bulgarian boyars were torn apart into enemy factions. The only support
he could hope for was that of the Hungarian king, so he invited Andrew II
to give him military aid. The only source of information on these events
is a diploma of King Béla IV of Hungary, issued in Győr (*Geurini*) on
23 June 1250. Here the king confirms the sons of Count Joachim of the Türje
clan in their paternal possessions in Szolvona (today, Slanje in Croatia), in
Varasd (Varaždin) County. Those possessions had been granted to Joachim,
Count of Szeben (*Iwachino comiti Scibiniensi . . . filio comitis Beche*) by King
Andrew II, Béla IV's father, for his merits in various battles.[6] The episode
is related as follows:

When Boril Asen, once emperor of the Bulgarians, referring to their reliable friendship, asked for the help of our memorable father against his rebels in Vidin, the king
sent to his assistance Count Joachim together with Saxons, Wallachians, Székelys
and Pechenegs, and made him commander of the army. When he reached the
river Ogozt, three Cuman chieftains marched against him and entered into a fight
with him. Two of them were killed in the battle, and the third one, called Karas,
was tied up and sent to the king by Count Joachim. Then he came to the castle
of Vidin, fought ardently, and laudably reinforced the martial spirit in his army
so that he set two gates of the city on fire. After heavy fights, the horse that he
rode was killed, and he himself was mortally wounded and his life could hardly

[4] Valenciennes/Longnon, pp. 28–33. Cf. Zlatarski, *Ist.*, pp. 274–5; Dančeva-Vasileva, *Lat. imp.*,
  pp. 80–7.
[5] Valenciennes/Longnon, pp. 36–46. Cf. also Pavlov, 'Kumanite', p. 38.
[6] For the editions of the diploma, see Karácsonyi, 'Székelyek', p. 293 (in a rather corrupted form);
  Szentpétery, *Reg. Árp.*, 1, no. 926; *Szék. Okl.*, p. 4. A seventeenth-century copy of the diploma
  deriving from the Kukuljević Collection can be found in the Hungarian National Archives, Budapest
  (MODL.36.224).

be saved, but the Lord saved his army. Though four relatives and other warriors of his were slaughtered by the Bulgarians, he was able to hand over the castle of Vidin to Boril Asen with full power.[7]

There is no direct clue as to the date of the event referred to in the diploma (only *quondam*), but it must have happened between 1208 and 1213. The chronology will be examined in more detail later. There was evidently a revolt in Vidin (*infideles suos de Budinio*), and the Hungarian king sent Count Joachim there at the head of Saxon, Wallachian, Székely and Pecheneg warriors. The four peoples constituting Joachim's army were inhabitants of southern Transylvania, where Joachim had his base as Count of Szeben. Starting from Szeben (Romanian *Sibiu*, German *Hermannstadt*), they must have marched along the Olt river to Nikopolis, then along the Danube to Vidin. After they had crossed the river Ogozt, a tributary of the Danube on the right, three chieftains or princes from Cumania (*tres duces de Cumania*), attacked them. Two of them were killed, while the third one, Karas (Karaz)[8] was captured and sent to the king. Joachim's troops besieged Vidin, set fire to two gates of the fortress, and fought valiantly. Joachim himself was gravely wounded, but recovered, and four relatives and other soldiers were killed by the Bulgars.[9] In the end Vidin was given back ko Boril.[10]

There are two questions left to be answered. First, who were the three Cuman princes who attacked Joachim's troops at the river Ogozt? Several answers are possible. As they are designated as princes from Cumania (*tres duces de Cumania*), we know that they did not belong to the Cuman groups

---

[7] 'Itaque Ascenus Burul imperator quondam Bulgarorum auxilium ab inclite memorie patre nostro contra infideles suos Budino quondam ex amicitae fiducia implorasset, rex ipse comitem Iwachinum, associatis sibi Saxonibus, Olacis, Siculis, et Bissenis in subsidium illi transmisit, eum ille ductorem exercitus praeferendo; qui cum super fluvium Obozt [correctly, Ogozt] pervenisset, tres duces de Cumania ipsis occurrentes cum eis praelium commiserunt, quorum duobus in illo praelio occisis tertium nomine Karaz comes Iwachinus vinctum transmisit ad regem. Perveniens siquidem ad castrum Budin viriliter pugnans exercitum sibi subditum in facto praelii laudabiliter confortando, ita quod duas portas civitatis igni combussisset, tandem post forte praelium ibi commissum, licet equo, cui insedebat, occiso sub eo ipse acceptis laethalibus plagis vix vivus remansit, domino exercitum conservante, tamen quattuor cognatis et aliis militibus suis ibidem per Bulgaros occisis castrum Budin ad manus eidem B.[urul] Asceni cum pleno dominio restituit ante diem' (Szentpétery, *Reg. Arp.*, I, no. 926).

[8] In the Bulgarian historical literature he is referred to as Karač (e.g. Cankova-Petkova, *Asenevci*, p. 88; Pavlov, 'Kumanite', p. 39; etc.), but Hungarian 'Karaz' in the thirteenth century can be read only as *Karas*. A Cuman family name *Karász(i)* still exists in Hungary in Greater Cumania.

[9] Bulgarian research always speaks of Boril's four relatives, who were the instigators of the revolt (Cankova-Petkova, *Asenevci*, p. 88; Pavlov, 'Kumanite', p. 39), but a closer look at the Latin text shows that this is obviously a misunderstanding.

[10] This historical episode was first analysed by Karácsonyi, *Székelyek*; Nikov was then the first Bulgarian historian to pay attention to it (Nikov, 'Car Boril').

settled in Bulgaria. They must have been Cuman mercenaries coming from
the region north of the Danube, although the summer season was not the
usual time for Cuman activity south of the Danube. They were probably
invited by the rebels of Vidin to help them against Boril and the Hungarians.
But this does not rule out the possibility that they were irregular Cuman
groups who came over to Bulgaria only to plunder and incidentally crossed
along with the Hungarians. The supposition that they were sent by Ivan
Asen to fight against Boril seems far-fetched, since there is no trace of
evidence for such a conjecture.[11]

As far as the chronology of this event is concerned, several dates have
been given by different researchers. Most scholars, like Nikov,[12] put the event
between 1207 and 1211. Karácsonyi, and after him the Hungarian scholars,
have claimed that Joachim's Bulgarian campaign must have taken place in
1210, since it was mentioned in the diploma before the campaign against the
Russian prince Roman Igorevič, and that campaign can be dated to 1211.[13]
Zlatarski settles on the spring of 1211 as the possible date of the revolt,[14]
while according to Cankova-Petkova it must have followed Boril's defeat
at Plovdiv in 1208.[15] Finally, Iliev and Pavlov date the event to 1213.[16] Be
all this as it may, the time-span 1208–13 seems certain, and I myself favour
the earlier dates of 1210 or 1211 because, towards the end of 1213 and the
beginning of 1214 another event took place that also argues for an earlier
date for the Vidin revolt. This event is referred to in a Hungarian diploma
edited not long ago.[17]

At that time, Thomas, Praepositus of Székesfehérvár (Alba Regia), and
Hector, son of John, arrived in Tărnovo to make a proposal of marriage
to Boril in the name of King Andrew II of Hungary. The king's son Béla
(the future king Béla IV) was soon to be crowned co-ruler, and the king
asked for Boril's daughter as his son's bride. The two Hungarian lords left
Tărnovo, probably with the bride, and it seems that Braničevo was given to
the Hungarians. Since Braničevo belonged to Bulgaria between 1203 and
1213–14, it would appear that this gift was not a consequence of and reward
for Hungarian help afforded to Boril at Vidin, but rather a betrothal gift.[18]

[11] Cf. Pavlov, 'Kumanite', p. 39.   [12] Nikov, 'Car Boril'.
[13] Karácsonyi, *Székelyek*, pp. 292–3; *Közép. hist. okl.*, p. 284, n. 46; Érszegi, 'Neue Quelle', p. 92.
[14] Zlatarski, *Ist.*, I, p. 305, n. 2.   [15] Cankova-Petkova, *Asenevci*, p. 105, n. 10.
[16] Iliev, 'Carl Boril', pp. 85–94; Pavlov, 'Kumanite', p. 39.   [17] Érszegi, 'Neue Quelle', pp. 96–7.
[18] Érszegi, 'Neue Quelle', pp. 93, 95, n. 22. Prior to Érszegi everyone thought that Braničevo was a
    remuneration given by Boril to the Hungarian king; cf. Pauler, *Árp.*, II, p. 47; Karácsonyi, *Székelyek*,
    p. 293; Nikov, 'Car Boril', pp. 131–2; Zlatarski, *Ist.*, III, p. 306, etc.

Under the pressure of the anarchical internal situation and the imminent danger of Ivan Asen's return as the lawful claimant to the Bulgarian throne, Boril could not breathe freely. Similarly, Emperor Henry of Constantinople could only look on with growing concern as the Nikaian Empire made progress and the discontent of the Greek inhabitants of the imperial city increased. The two traditional enemies rapidly realized that they had to reach an agreement. When Henry's first wife Agnes, daughter of Boniface of Montferrat, died in 1214, the Latin Empire and Bulgaria concluded a pact that was sealed by a double marriage. Henry married Boril's daughter, while Boril took Henri's niece (daughter of Jolanta and Pierre de Courtenay) as his wife. Boril's Cuman wife disappeared from the scene; perhaps she was sent to a monastery, in accordance with the general practice of the age.[19] It is interesting that a Hungarian–Bulgarian rapprochement, too, was observable; in the same year an envoy of the Hungarian king Andrew II visited Boril to ask for his daughter's hand for his son Béla.[20] By his marital and political alliance with Boril, Henry was able to hinder any closer co-operation between Bulgaria and Nikaia. But soon both rulers disappeared from the scene: Henry was assassinated during the campaign against Thessalonike on 11 June 1216, and Boril died two years later in 1218.

CUMANS DURING THE REIGN OF IVAN ASEN II UNTIL 1237

During his exile in Russia, Ivan Asen systematically prepared to return and take possession of his paternal heritage. According to Acropolites, success was achieved only with the military help of the Russians, while Ephraim adds that the Cumans also assisted.[21] The Russians mentioned here could well be those semi-nomadic Slavic elements who are called *brodnik* in contemporary sources, and who are often regarded as the ancestors of the Kozaks.[22] Without the Cumans' active help or passive consent, the Russians (or Brodniks) could not have acted in Bulgaria. As it turned out, Ivan Asen's attempts to regain power occupied many years. Akropolites

---

[19] Cankova-Petkova, *Asenevci*, p. 108, n. 64.   [20] Érszegi, 'Neue Quelle'
[21] 'καὶ τινας τῶν συγκλύδων Ῥώσων σὺν ἑαυτῷ περιαγαγών, τὴν πατρικὴν ἀνακαλεῖται κληρονομίαν' (Georg. Akr. *Hist.*/Bekker, pp. 35–6), and 'εἶτα Σκυθικὸν Ῥωσικὸν λαβὼν στῖφος, ἐπιστρατεύσας τῷκρατοῦντι Βορίλα ἀνακαλεῖται τὴν πατρὸς κληρονομίαν,' (Ephraim/Bekker-Mai, p. 324, lines 354–6).
[22] Cankova-Petkova, *Asenevci*, p. 109, p. 132, n. 2; Pavlov, 'Brodnici', p. 226–8.

claims that he besieged Tărnovo for seven years, during 1211–18.[23] Though earlier historians such as Zlatarski interpreted this period as meaning seven months,[24] Cankova-Petkova insisted that the seven years must be understood literally.[25] Even if we cannot decide this question finally, Ivan Asen's return to Tărnovo evidently took a long time.

Ivan Asen II inherited a country troubled with inner feuds and surrounded by avaricious neighbours ready to take advantage of the weakness of the enfeebled land. But he succeeded in stabilising his country both internally and externally. His marriage to Ann Mary, daughter of Andrew II of Hungary, was an obvious political success which made a considerable contribution to the stability of Bulgaria's foreign policy. Since 1204 Ivan Asen had had to face the inveterate problem of Bulgarian foreign policy: how to maintain a balance between the Latin Empire and the Nikaian Empire. This dilemma explains the vacillation in Asen's behaviour when choosing political alliances: sometimes he turned to the Latins of Constantinople, sometimes to the Greeks of Nikaia. But one thing remained constant in his battles: he could always rely on the assistance of Cuman auxiliary or mercenary troops. In 1235, Theodoros Angelos Komnenos, Emperor of Thessalonike, broke the alliance concluded with Ivan Asen II against their rival Ioannes Doukas Batatzes of Nikaia, and from Hadrianoupolis his troops marched against the Bulgarians along the Marica river. Asen acted promptly and, together with his Bulgarian and Cuman troops, encountered Theodoros at Klokotnica (near present-day Haskovo). On 9 March 1230 the Bulgarian and Cuman forces won a splendid victory over the Greeks; Theodoros himself was captured and later blinded. The number of Cuman warriors did not exceed a thousand, but their role was crucial.[26] After the battle of Klokotnica, Bulgaria annexed Hadrianoupolis, Didymotoichon, Pelagonia, Prilep and Greater Vlakhia (i.e. Thessaly) to its own territory. Bulgaria's role and weight in the international arena grew substantially, but the Nikaian Empire also profited from the decay of the western Greek power of Thessalonike.[27] The Cumans who participated in Asen's battles came from Transdanubian Cumania;

---

[23] ʽΚαὶ πολεμεῖ τῷ Βορίλα καὶ νικᾷ τοῦτον καὶ χώρας οὐκ ὀλίγης ἐγκρατὴς γίνεται. Ὁ δὲ Βορίλας ἔνδον εἰσέρχεται τοῦ Τρινόβου, καὶ ἐπὶ ἑπτὰ ἔτεσι τειχήρης πολιορκεῖται᾽ (Georg. Akr. *Hist.*/Bekker, p. 36).

[24] Zlatarski, *Ist.*, III, pp. 318–19.   [25] Cankova-Petkova, *Asenevci*, p. 107, n. 48.

[26] ʽὈλίγον τι συμμαχικὸν ἀπὸ Σκυθῶν εἰληφώς, οὐκ εἰς χιλίους μετρούμενον᾽ (Georg. Akr. *Hist.*/Bekker, p. 45). For the battle of Klokotnica, see Georg. Akr. *Hist.*/Bekker, p. 45$_{7-19}$, = Georg. Akr. *Hist.*/Heisenberg, pp. 41–3. Cf. also Greg. *Hist.*/Schopen–Bekker, I, p. 289$_{-20}$, = Greg. *Hist.*/van Dieten, I, p. 76.

[27] Ostrogorsky, *Gesch.*, p. 311 (360–1); Cankova-Petkova, *Asenevci*, pp. 114–17.

Nikephoros Gregoras expressly stated that Batatzes did not want Asen to be his adversary, since he (Asen) was 'the neighbour of the Transdanubian Scythians [Cumans] and whenever he wanted he made incursions with them'.[28]

After Klokotnica, Asen and Batatzes made a spectacular approach, one of the results of which was the formation of an autocephalous Bulgarian Church that was also acknowledged by the Greek. The Western powers, headed by the papacy, disapproved of the Bulgarian–Greek rapprochement, considering this process unfavourable to the Latin Empire; but, for the moment, they could not interfere and did not want to do so. In the autumn of 1235, Ivan Asen and Batatzes conquered and divided almost the entire eastern Thracian territories; the Bulgarians took the region north of Tzurulon and west of the Marica.[29] They even made two unsuccessful attempts to reconquer Constantinople, but Asen realised that the rapid progress of Nikaia was not in his favour, and changed sides again, turning to the papacy, the Western powers and the Latin Empire.[30]

TWO WAVES OF CUMAN IMMIGRATION TO BULGARIA AND THE LATIN EMPIRE, 1237, 1241

Though the Cumans had been frequent actors as allied or mercenary forces in the Balkanic scene since 1185, and though minor Cuman groups, or rather military leaders with their retinue, may have settled on Byzantine and Bulgarian soil, we have no positive mention of any Cuman mass migration and/or settlement in the Balkans prior to 1237.[31] The Cumans were present in Bulgaria's political life and military history, but their power centres remained north of the Danube. The disastrous defeat of the Cuman and Russian forces at the hand of the Tatars at Kalka in 1223 changed the power relations in Eastern Europe. After the battle of Kalka, the Cuman chiefs could not be sure whether and when a new Tatar attack would appear. The Catholic Church, especially the newly founded Dominicans, launched a strong missionary effort east of the Carpathian Basin, and the result is well known: in 1227 Prince Borč was baptised, and the Cuman episcopate was founded with its centre at Milcov (Hungarian Milkó) in southern

---

[28] 'Οὕτω τοῖς παριστρίοις ὁμοροῦντα Σκύθαις, καὶ ἅμα αὐτοῖς, ὁπότε βούλοιτο, ἐπελαύνοντα' (Greg.*Hist.*/Schopen-Bekker, I, p. 29₂₀₋₂₂, = Greg.*Hist.*/van Dieten, I, p. 77).
[29] Georg. Akr. *Hist.*/Heisenberg, pp. 51₉–52₅.
[30] Zlatarski, *Ist.*, III, pp. 388–9; Cankova-Petkova, *Asenevci*, pp. 124–5.
[31] Pavlov, *Zaselvanijata na kumani*, p. 630.

Moldavia.[32] All these important events, however, are beyond the scope of our treatment.

The beginning of the great Tatar campaign in Eastern Europe in 1236 radically changed this situation. Volga Bulgaria was demolished in 1236, and the Tatar war machine crushed the Cuman principalities in the southern steppe region one by one. A large-scale westward migration of the Cumans began. In the summer of 1237 the first wave of this Cuman exodus appeared in Bulgaria. The Cumans crossed the Danube, and this time Ivan Asen II could not tame them, as he had often been able to do earlier; the only possibility left for him was to let them march through Bulgaria in a southerly direction. They proceeded through Thrace as far as Hadrianoupolis and Didymotoichon, plundering and pillaging the towns and the countryside, just as before. The whole of Thrace became, as Akropolites put it, a 'Scythian desert'.[33]

When Ivan Asen II turned his back on Batatzes and the Nikaian Empire in 1237, he first compelled the Latins to conclude a peace treaty with him. Then he launched an attack against Tzurulon, the Thracian centre of Nikaian power, in which the Cumans and the Latins also were involved. The allied forces had been assaulting the town for a long time when an unexpected occurrence changed the course of events. News arrived from Tărnovo that Asen's Hungarian wife Ann Mary, his younger son, and the patriarch of Tărnovo had died. Asen became afraid and regarded the tragic events as a sign of God's anger and a punishment for his perfidy with Batatzes. He withdrew his forces from Tzurulon, restored his alliance with the Nikaian emperor, and married Irene, daughter of Theodoros Komnenos.[34]

Later in 1240, however, the Latin and Cuman troops seized the fortress of Tzurulon. In 1239 Pope Gregory IX had succeeded in organizing a crusade against Nikaia. More than 60,000 crusaders had marched through Hungary and Italy and then passed through Bulgaria with Ivan Asen's consent.[35] They arrived in Contantinople towards the end of 1239 or the beginning of 1240. Then the Latin Emperor Baldouin II had concluded an alliance with the Cumans and had reconquered the Thracian fortresses, which had been held by the Nikaians. In May 1240 he also recaptured Tzurulon, the siege of which had been abandoned three years earlier in 1237. These Cuman allies

---

[32] For the Catholic ecclesiastical missions of this period, see Pfeiffer, *Dominikaner*, pp. 198–214; Altaner, *Dominikaner*; Makkai, *Milkói püspökség*; Ferenţ, *Kunok*; Pašuto, 'Polov. epis.'; Sibiescu, 'Milcova'.

[33] Georg. Akr. *Hist.*/Heisenberg, p. 54$_{1-17}$.

[34] Georg. Akr. *Hist.*/Heisenberg, p. 56$_{14-22}$; Dölger, *Regesten*, 1758. Cf. also Ostrogorsky, *Gesch.*, p. 312 (362).

[35] Georg. Akr. *Hist.*/Bekker, pp. 62$_{19}$–63$_{13}$; Georg. Akr. *Hist.*/Heisenberg, p. 58$_{14-15}$.

of the Latin Empire must have been recruited from the Cuman immigrants who had flooded into the Balkanic lands in 1237.

Other than this, the sources give us no information about what happened to this first massive wave of Cuman migration to the Balkans in 1237. Apart from their being hired as mercenaries by the Latins of Constantinople, we have no news of them. But four years later, in March 1241, another Cuman wave reached Bulgaria. This time they arrived, not from Cumania north of the Danube, but from the direction of Hungary. It is well known that Prince Köten (*Kötöny* in Hungarian, *Kotjan* in Russian), accompanied by 40,000 Cumans, fled to Hungary from the Tatars and gained access to the Hungarian Kingdom, and was baptised by King Béla IV in 1239. This Köten is the same Prince Kotjan Sutoevič of the Russian annals, who forged the Russian–Cuman alliance against the Tatars. Rogerius, an eyewitness of the Tatar invasion of Hungary and author of the famous *Carmen miserabile*, enumerated in detail the various factors that led to the alienation of the Hungarians from the Cumans and culminated in the unjust assassination of their leader Köten in Pest.[36] The enraged Cuman masses began to plunder the countryside, and moved southwards in the country. They crossed the Danube and reached Srem (called *Marchia* by Rogerius). After causing much destruction and havoc in Hungary they left the country for Bulgaria.[37]

These familiar events are relevant to us in two respects. First, they elucidate the direction of the Tatar infiltration into Bulgaria. According to Rogerius' description, which we have no reason to question, the Cumans' last halt in Hungary was Srem, a territory between the Danube and the Sava, so the first Bulgarian territories they entered must have been Braničevo and Vidin. This supposition is in perfect agreement with our knowledge of the later history of these regions. The Bulgarian boyar families, the Šišmans in Vidin and Dormans in Braničevo, were of Cuman extraction, and must have settled in these regions after the large immigration of 1241. Secondly, Köten's relatives and the leading figures of his royal clan settled in Bulgaria. Since Köten was a member of the Terter(oba) clan,[38] it is

---

[36] Rogerius, *Carmen miserabile*, §§ 2–12, in *SRH*, II, pp. 553–9.

[37] 'Comani vero, ut Tartari, terram postmodum destruentes et convenientes inceperunt ad Marchiam properare . . . Et destructis melioribus villis, scilicet Franka villa senatoria, Sancti Martini et aliis et recepta multa pecunia, equis et pecoribus destruendo terram in Bulgariam transierunt' (Rogerius, *Carmen miserabile*, § 26, in *SRH*, II, p. 568). *Franka villa* is Hungarian *Nagyolaszi* in the former county of Szerém (now Mandjelos in Srem, Croatia) and *Sancti Martini* is Hungarian *Szentmárton* in the county of Valkó (now Martinci in Srem, Croatia) (see Csánki, II, pp. 236, 352). For *Marchia* as a part of Srem, see *KMTL*, pp. 442–3 (Gy. Kristó).

[38] Pritsak, 'Polovcians', p. 338.

evident that George Terter I, who was elected Bulgarian tsar in Tărnovo in 1280, must have been related to Köten's family. George Terter's father must have been among the Cuman immigrants who entered Bulgaria in 1241. Though the existence of family ties with Köten's family is more than probable, there are no positive data as to the precise degree of this kinship.[39]

As we have seen, the Latins succeeded in attracting a considerable number of the Cuman immigrants of 1237 to their side, and with their help they were able to recapture Tzurulon in 1240. In the following year the alliance between the Latins of Constantinople and the Cumans became even stronger by virtue of politically motivated family ties. Albericus Trium Fontium, who must have drawn on authoritative information from Constantinople, has an interesting report on these events. He places the story after his report of Ivan Asen II's death on 24 June 1241, so these events can be related to the middle of 1241. The Cuman allies of the Latins had two princes or kings (*rex* in Albericus), Saronius and Jonah, the latter being the superior of the two. These princes married their daughters to leading members of the Latin nobility in Constantinople. Saronius had two baptised daughters, one of whom became the wife of Guillaume, son of the constable Geoffroi de Meri, while the other married Baldouin d'Hainault, one of the leading knights of Emperor Baldouin II.[40] Jonah's daughter was married to Narillaut de Toucy, the bailiff of Constantinople, whose former wife was the daughter of the famous Byzantine aristocrat Theodoros Branas.[41] But Narillaut died in 1241, and his Cuman wife became a nun (*monialis*). In the same year Prince Jonah also died, and being a pagan, was buried outside the city walls of Constantinople in a tumulus. In the pagan burial ceremony, eight volunteer warriors and twenty-six horses were sacrificed to his memory.[42]

---

[39] Pavlov's notion (Pavlov, 'Zaselvanijata', p. 634) that Terter's father may have been the brother, son, or nephew of Köten, is mere conjecture.

[40] For Baldouin d'Hainault (Balduinus de Hannonia), see Rubruc, *Itinerarium*, §§ xv/3, xxix/44 (*Sin. Franc.*, i, pp. 201, 268).

[41] Joineville/Wailly, pp. 495–6.

[42] *Sub anno* 1241: 'Saronius insuper traditor quidam duas habebat filias baptizatas in Constantinopoli, quarum unam duxit Guillelmus conestabuli filius, alteram Balduinus de Haynaco. Filiam vero regis Ione, qui videbatur esse maior in regibus Comanorum, duxerat domnus Nargoldus balivus. Qui Nargoldus hoc anno decessit, et predicta uxor eius facta est monialis. Mortuus est hoc anno rex Ionas predictus nondum baptizatus, et idcirco sepultus est extra muros civitatis in altissimo tumulo, et octo armigeri appensi sunt vivi a dextris et a sinistris et ita voluntarie mortui, et 26 vivi equi similiter ibi fuerunt appensi' (Albericus Trium Fontium, *Chronicon*, in *MGH SS*, xxiii, p. 950, = Gombos, *Cat.*, i, p. 34).

CUMANS IN THE SERVICE OF JOHN BATATZES AND
THEODOROS II, 1241–1256

But it was not only the Latin Empire that employed the runaway Cuman masses that were roving around in the Balkans; the Greeks of the Nikaian Empire did so too. The main Byzantine authorities of the age, such as Georgios Akropolites, Georgios Pachymeres, Nikephoros Gregoras and Ioannes Kantakouzenos, report an important event. Emperor John III (Doukas Batatzes) of Nikaia settled a large group of Cumans as *stratiotes* in various frontier areas of the empire: in Thrace and Macedonia in the Balkans, and in the Maiandros valley and Phrygia in Anatolia. Let us take a closer look at this process of Cuman settlement, unanimously regarded as of immense importance by all Byzantine historiographers.

According to Gregoras, these Cumans were refugees who fled from the Tatars. Together with their wives and children, they crossed the Danube on sacks stuffed with straw. This description of the fugitive Cumans fits the first immigration wave of 1237, described by Akropolites and Ephraim (see above, p. 64). A large group of them, numbering at least 10,000 persons, were roving around in Thessaly when Emperor John Batatzes took some of them into his service, granting them lands in Thrace and Macedonia, while others were sent to the Maiandros region and Phrygia.[43] This policy of military settlement was much appreciated by his contemporaries, since it meant that the old Byzantine system of frontier defence was restored, especially in the east. In the encomium he addressed to his father, Theodoros II Laskaris, he praised his father's deeds in the following words: 'Having removed the Scyth [i.e. Cuman] from the west and the western lands, you led his race to the east as a subject people and, substituting [them] for the sons of Persians [i.e. the Turks], you have securely fettered their assaults toward the west.'[44] This settlement policy of John Batatzes was regarded by Pachymeres as the greatest achievement of the Nikaian state.[45] Akropolites also speaks about these events in a positive tone.[46]

In Kantakouzenos' narrative, one of the highest-born Cuman leaders was a certain Sytzigan (Συτζιγάν), who was baptised and given the Christian

---

[43] Greg. *Hist.*/Bekker, 1, pp. 36$_{16}$–37$_9$ (11.5), = Greg. *Hist.*/van Dieten, 1, p. 81.
[44] Bartusis, *Late Byz. Army*, p. 26. Cf. also Ostrogorsky, *Gesch.*, p. 316.
[45] Pachym. *Hist.*/Bekker, 1, pp. 16ff.
[46] Georg. Akr. *Chron.*/Bekker, pp. 53–4, 65. For the settlement policy of John Batatzes, cf. also Uspenskij, *Zemlevladenie*, p. 339; Mutafčiev, 'Vojniški zemi', p. 76, n. 2; Ostrogorski, 'Proniari Kumani', pp. 63–74; Bartusis, 'Smallholding soldiers', p. 12; Asdracha, *Rhodopes*, pp. 80–2.

name Syrgiannes (Συργιάννης) by his godfather. His 'son' was also called
Syrgiannes.[47] The name 'Sytzigan' is from the Cuman-Turkic *Sičğan*, meaning 'mouse',[48] while his new Christian name can be interpreted as *Sir
Yanni*.[49] The fate of the younger Syrgiannes, who must in fact have been
the grandson of Syrgiannes senior, and his role in Byzantine history, will be
dealt with in Chapter 7. But who was this older Syrgiannes, alias Sytzigan,
who entered into Byzantine service in the second half of 1241 or in 1242? I
suspect that he must be identical with the Cuman prince Saronius, co-
ruler of Jonah, mentioned in Albericus' *Chronicle*. The overlapping of
the two names and the chronology cannot be incidental. *Saroni*(us) is a
Latinized and slightly distorted form of the Greek name *Siryani* (written
as Συργιάννης). In addition, if our supposition holds true, the strange
description of Saronius as a traitor (*traditor*) in Albericus' text becomes
totally understandable: Saronius/Syrgiannes went over to Greek service
and embraced Byzantine Christianity. His daughters, however, who had
formerly been given as wives to two French knights of Constantinople,
were as a result baptised by the Catholic Church. This new interpretation
demonstrates that at least a part of the Cumans who went over to Byzantine
service in 1241 or 1242 were formerly allies of the Latin Empire.

---

[47] Kant. *Hist.*/Fatouros-Krischer, I, p. 22 (1.2) = Kant.*Hist*/Schopen, I, p. 18.
[48] Moravcsik (*Byz.-turc.*, I, p. 294) and others have been unable to identify the name with any Turkic
word.
[49] Parisot, *Cant.*, p. 37. Binon's statement that Syrgiannes was of Mongol descent (Binon, 'Prostagma',
p. 138) lacks any ground. This conjecture was taken over by Nicol, *Rel. Emp.*, p. 19 ('His curious
name betrayed his Mongol descent on his father's side').

CHAPTER FOUR

The first period of Tatar influence in the Balkans,
1242–1282

THE TATAR CONQUEST IN THE BALKANS

The age of Tatar influence in the Balkans lasted for over a hundred years, from the great Tatar campaign in 1242 till Jānibek Khan's reign (1342–57) in the Golden Horde. Then, owing to the growing anarchy within the Golden Horde, which led to total political confusion after Berdibek Khan's death (1259), the Tatar state lost all its influence and interest in the Balkans. This hundred-year period can be divided into three phases, the first characterised by the ever-growing power of Nogay, lord of the westernmost territories of the Golden Horde. The end of this phase can be marked by the deaths of three rulers of the area: the Bulgarian tsar Konstantin Tikh in 1277, the khan of the Golden Horde Mengü-Temür in 1280, and the Byzantine emperor, founder of the Palaiologos dynasty, Michael VIII, in 1282. The change of power in these countries led to the second phase, a period of weakening and decay in Bulgaria and Byzantium, while the power of the Tatar chief Nogay rose to unprecedented heights, such that very briefly his son was even able to occupy the Bulgarian throne. The heyday of Tatar influence in the Balkans ended with the deaths of Nogay (1300) and his son Čeke (1301). The last phase of the now fading Tatar presence in the Balkans fell between 1302 and the middle of the fourteenth century.

The storm of the Tatar invasion, which demolished the medieval Hungarian Kingdom, swept through the country in 1241, and only the news that the Great Khan Ögödey had died (on 11 December 1241) compelled Khan Batu's ferocious warriors to leave the devastated country for their Asiatic homeland. But, before returning to their Asiatic pastures, a contingent of the Tatar army under Qadan's commandership advanced to Dalmatia in pursuit of King Béla IV of Hungary. Meeting with no success, they left Dalmatia for Bulgaria, marching through Serbia and devastating the countryside as they went. In the meantime, the main forces of the Tatars under Khan Batu's commandership followed the course of the

Danube and also reached Bulgaria.[1] Tsar Ivan Asen II, the greatest ruler of medieval Bulgaria, had died in June 1241, but just before his death he had heard the shocking news of the Tatar invasion of Poland, Moravia and Hungary, so he must have closed his eyes with anxious forebodings about the imminent future of his country. Under the regencies that governed Bulgaria during the minority of his two sons (Coloman Asen I, 1241–6; Michael Asen, 1246–56), the country again sank to the rank of a third-rate power in the Balkans because of the Tatar invasion and the ensuing internal anarchy.[2]

In 1242 the Tatar armies began to ravage Bulgaria, and encountered no real resistance. Moreover, judging by the silence of the sources and the relatively small scale of the devastation, one has the impression that the enfeebled Bulgarian regency accepted Tatar suzerainty, thereby avoiding the same terrible destruction at Tatar hands that took place in Hungary as a result of King Béla IV's strong resistance.[3] Then the Tatars drew to the south of Bulgaria where they met resistance from Baldouin II, Latin Emperor of Byzantium. In the first clash the Byzantine army had the upper hand, but in the second the Tatars gained the victory and withdrew to the east. The locations of these encounters are unknown, the memory of this episode in the Tatar–Byzantine conflict being preserved only in the Austrian annals.[4] Thus, in 1242, Bulgaria escaped with a relatively small amount of Tatar destruction, but the price it paid was subjection to the Tatars in the form of paying tribute to the Tatar state. In 1253, eleven years after the Tatar subjugation of Bulgaria, Rubruc, in his famous travel account, clearly indicates that the Bulgars paid tribute to the Tatars.[5]

The first two decades of Bulgaro–Tatar relations are shrouded in obscurity, especially as far as the character of these relations is concerned.

[1] Hammer-Purgstall, *GH*, pp. 124–6; Spuler, *GH*, p. 24.   [2] Nikov, 'B''lg. i tat.', p. 103.
[3] For a good analysis of the Tatar invasion of 1242 in Bulgaria, see Pavlov, 'Preminavaneto'.
[4] *Chronicon Austriacum*, *sub anno* 1243: 'Tartari et Chumani nemine resistente et occurrente, recesserunt ab Vngaria cum infinita preda auri et argenti, vestium, animalium, multos et captivos utriusque sexus ducebant in obproprium christianorum. Qui intrantes Greciam totam terram illam depopulabant, exceptis castellis et civitatibus valde munitis. Rex vero Constantinopolitanus nomine Paldwinus, congressus est cum eis, a quo primo victi in secunda congressione victus est ab eis' (Rauch, *SS Austr.*, II, p. 245, = Gombos, *Cat.*, I, p. 507). The same text can be found in the *Chronicon Leobiense* (Pez, *SS Austr.*, I, p. 816, = Gombos, *Cat.*, I, p. 271) and in the *Continuatio Sancrucensis*, II. (*MGH SS*, IX, p. 641, = Gombos, *Cat.*, I, p. 778). The data of the Austrian annals were first referred to by Hammer-Purgstall, *GH*, p. 126.
[5] Rubruc, *Itinerarium*, I.5: 'Ab orificio Tanais versus occidentem usque ad Danubium totum est eorum [i.e. Tartarorum], etiam ultra Danubium versus Constantinopolim, Blakia que est terra Assani et minor Bulgaria usque in Sclavoniam omnes solvunt eis tributum; et etiam ultra tributum condictum sumpserunt annis nuper transactis de qualibet domo securim unam et totum ferrum quod invenerunt in massa' (*Sin. Franc.*, I, pp. 167–8). Or at another place, *Epilogus* 3: 'Filius Vastacii debilis est [Theodoros Lascaris II] et bellum habet cum filio Assani, qui similiter est garcio [Michael, Rex Bulgariae] et attritus servitute Tartarorum' (*Sin. Franc.*, I, p. 331).

Was there a regular yearly tribute, and if so, what was the amount and in what form was it collected? Were there any additional obligations, such as a requirement to send Bulgarian recruits as auxiliaries to the Tatar campaigns, as the Russians and other subjugated peoples were compelled to do? The sources are scarce and meagre, and in this respect they are silent. Yet one has the impression that the first twenty years of subjection to the Tatar rule must have had a merely formal and rather loose character. But the restoration of the Byzantine Empire in Constantinople in 1261 by Emperor Michael VIII Palaiologos gave rise to radically new power relations in the Middle East and the Balkans, and this impacted on the Tatars' relative indifference towards the Balkanic lands. Before proceeding to these stormy decades of Tatar and Balkanic history, we must look briefly at Prince Nogay of the Golden Horde, since it was he who determined the Tatar policy in the Balkans in the last four decades of the thirteenth century.

PRINCE NOGAY

Nogay was a key figure in Tatar history, and from the 1260s he played an increasingly important part in Balkanic events.[6] Nogay was a Chingisid, one of the great-grandsons of Joči (elder son of Chingis), founder of the Golden Horde.[7] Though all the sons of a Chingisid prince were considered legitimate in the Tatar-Turkic world, only those born to legal wives were given appanages (*ulus*) and could become khans. Probably that is why Nogay is mentioned in most sources only as commander-in-chief and 'head of ten thousand people' (Turkic *tümen begi*, Russian *tëmnik*). The young Chingisid prince began by excelling in the battle of Terek in 1255–6 (AH 653) where he lost an eye, which was pierced by a lance.[8] This was the first clash between Berke and Hülegü, which launched the centuries-long enmity and struggle between the Chingisid branches of the Golden Horde and Iran.

Nogay, like his great-uncle Berke Khan, embraced Islam.[9] There is no evidence to indicate when this event happened, but probably it came soon after Berke's conversion to Islam, which took place in the 1250s. When Berke's envoys notified the Mameluke Sultan al-Malik az-Zāhir of his

---

[6] For his life, the best monograph is still Veselovskij, 'Nogaj'. For his name (< Mong. *noqai*, 'dog'), see Pelliot, *Horde d'Or*, p. 73.

[7] His genealogy is as follows: Jingis → Joči → Moğul (or Bo'al) → Tatar → Nogay. For the genealogy and its different names in different sources, see Veselovskij, 'Nogaj', pp. 2–3; Pelliot, *Horde d'Or*, pp. 10–28, 52–4.

[8] Baybars: Tiz., I, pp. 96, 121, = İzm., pp. 230–1; Nuwayrī: Tiz., I, pp. 131, 152, = İzm., pp. 251, 253.

[9] Vásáry, *Berke*.

conversion in 1262/3 (AH 661), the name of Nogay was already included among the new converts.[10] Much later, in 1270/1 (AH 669), Nogay himself, in his letter to the Egyptian sultan, claimed that he had embraced Islam.[11]

From the 1260s Prince Nogay became the absolute master of the western-most territories of the Golden Horde, which stretched from the river Don as far as the Lower Danube. Though he was not a khan in these territories, he behaved as a real autocrat, so much so that the Russian annals often call him *tsar* (the Russian translation and equivalent of *khan*) and describe him as a ruler equal to the khans of the Golden Horde.[12] The region of the Lower Danube and Northern Bulgaria directly belonged to his sphere of influence, and, as will be seen, he often intervened in Balkanic power struggles, first on the Bulgarian side, then on the Byzantine.

THE TATARS RELEASE 'IZZADDĪN IN THRACE, 1264

To return to the restoration of Byzantine power in Constantinople in 1261 by Emperor Michael VIII Palaiologos, we may safely state that a new period had begun in Balkanic and broader power relations. Contacts between the newly founded Tatar states of the Golden Horde and Mameluke Egypt were possible only via the Black and Mediterranean Seas, and consequently only with the consent of Byzantium. Prior to 1261 Sultan Baybars' Egypt and the Latin Empire of Constantinople had no contact, but Berke Khan's conversion to Islam in the 1250s prompted Egypt's approach to the new Tatar state of the Golden Horde. In 1263 Baybars sent his envoys to Berke, khan of the Golden Horde, but they were detained at the Byzantine court. Behind this move of the Byzantine emperor one might suspect his fear of Hülegü, the Mongolian lord of Persia, who was on terms of enmity with the Golden Horde. Hülegü's friendship, however, was an effective tool of psychological pressure on the Seljuks of the Sultanate of Iconium, arch-enemies of the Byzantines.[13] The tension caused by captivity of the Egyptian envoys was aggravated by the fact that 'Izzaddīn, the former Sultan of Iconium, was also being held as a hostage; his release too was demanded by the Egyptians. These events formed the background to a military intervention against Byzantium launched by Berke in 1264, aimed at freeing 'Izzaddīn from captivity.

---

[10] Baybars: Tiz., I, pp. 77, 99, = İzm., p. 161. In Tizengauzen the corrupted form of the MS 'Yanšunuka' occurs, which was corrected by İzmirli to the well-known form 'Yisü-Nogay'.

[11] Baybars: Tiz., I, pp. 79, 80, 101, 102, = İzm., pp. 169–72.   [12] E.g. *PSRL*, VIII, p. 241.

[13] For these power relations of the 1260s see Vernadskij, 'ZO, Eg. i Viz.', pp. 77 ff.; Ostrogorsky, pp. 328–9 (378–80); Pavlov, 'B"lg. Viz. Eg'.

'Izzaddīn Kaykā'ūs was the eldest son of the Seljuk Sultan Kayḫusraw II and a Greek mother. After his father's death in 1245 he became the ruler. It was a confused historical period, two years after the Mongol victory at Köse Dağ, when the Seljuks were subjected to the Tatars. Baiju-noyon was the omnipotent Mongolian regent of Anatolia, and 'Izzaddīn and his minor half-brothers, Ruknaddīn Qïlïč Arslan and 'Alāaddīn Kaykubād, were often mere tools in the power games of the Mongol overlords, the Seljuk emirs, and the Byzantine emperors. In 1256, after a defeat at Baiju-noyon's hands, 'Izzaddīn took refuge with Emperor Theodoros Laskaris II in Nikaia, but soon the brothers 'Izzaddīn and Ruknaddīn divided the Seljuk land: the territories east of the Kïzïl Irmak (Halys) became Ruknaddīn's property, while those west of the river came into the hands of 'Izzaddīn. But after a few years 'Izzaddīn again brought the Mongols' wrath down on himself by seeking contacts with Mameluke Egypt, and he was compelled to escape, this time for good.[14] Together with his wife, sons and escort, he first hastened to Attaleia, whence he fled to the protection of Emperor Michael Palaiologos VIII. This must have happened some time prior to 1261, since the Byzantines reconquered Constantinople from the Latins on 25 July 1261.[15]

Before tracing the further fate of the Seljuk political émigré in Byzantium a word must be said about the sources. We are fortunate enough to have numerous and varied sources that report on these events, but their evidence is not always unanimous. Three main groups of sources must be distinguished: the Egyptian Mameluke sources (Baybars, 'Aynī, Nuwayrī, Maqrīzī, etc.), the Persian sources of Anatolian Seljuk history (Ibn Bībī, Aqsarāyī), and the Byzantine Greek sources (Georg. Akr. *Chron.*, Pachym. *Hist.*, Nik. Greg. *Hist.*). In addition, a later but important Turkish source from the first half of the fifteenth century, the *Oğuznāme* or *Seljuknāme* of Yazïcïoğlu 'Alī, also reports on these events.[16]

'Izzaddīn was heartily received by Michael Palaiologos, for three main reasons. First, 'Izzaddīn's maternal family was Greek. Secondly, Emperor Michael did not forget the hospitality 'Izzaddīn had shown him when he had been obliged to take refuge with him during his conflicts with the Laskaris house. Thirdly, Byzantium could profit politically from the presence of the illustrious Seljuk refugee. But the cordial relations between Michael Palaiologos and 'Izzaddīn soon became tense. According to Ibn

---

[14] On 'Izzaddīn's life see *EI*, II, pp. 682–3 (Cl. Huart); *İA*, VI, pp. 642–5 (O. Turan); *EI²*, III, pp. 846–7 (C. Cohen); for his 'pre-exile' life from 1249 to 1261, see Flemming, *Pamph. Pis. Lyk.*, pp. 19–27.
[15] Duda, 'Isl. Quellen', p. 135.
[16] For the works of Ibn Bībī, Aqsarāyī and Yazïcïoğlu 'Alī see Duda, 'Isl. Quellen', pp. 136–9.

Bībī and Aqsarāyī, 'Izzaddīn was incited by his people to devise a plot to
take over power in Byzantium. But 'Izzaddīn's maternal uncle, a certain
Kyr Kedīd (who, judging from his name, must have been a priest), revealed
the plot. The emperor's response was immediate: 'Izzaddīn's chief equerry
Uğurlu was blinded, his commander-in-chief 'Alī Bahādur was executed,
and his whole family, including his mother, was taken into custody.[17] The
Byzantine and Mameluke sources do not speak of the plot; only Dhahabī
mentions that the emperor became angry with 'Izzaddīn and had him jailed
in a fortress.[18]

But 'Izzaddīn seemingly did not give up his plan to return to power in
one way or another. Most sources agree that he turned to the Tatars of the
Golden Horde for help. Aqsarāyī says that 'Izzaddīn's paternal aunt was
one of Berke Khan's wives, and it was she who got 'Izzaddīn's message for
help.[19] But Pachymeres claims that it was one of 'Izzaddīn's kinsmen (later he
calls him an uncle), an illustrious person in the northern part of the Pontus
Euxinus (that is, in the Golden Horde), whom he encouraged to attack the
Byzantine emperor with Tatars and Bulgars of Tsar Konstantin in order to
free him from Byzantine captivity.[20] The other sources do not tell us who
this 'uncle' was, but it is quite possible that 'Izzaddīn had relatives in the
Crimea: contacts between the Seljuks and the opposite coast of the Black
Sea, especially the Crimea, are attested in sources well before the period of
Mongol invasion.[21] The Bulgarians too were also interested in mounting an
assault against Byzantium, since Tsar Konstantin Tikh's wife, Irene, was the
daughter of Theodoros Laskaris II, whose son John, the younger brother of
Irene, was blinded by Michael Palaiologos after their father's death in 1258.
Irene wanted to take revenge on Emperor Michael VIII, who had crushed
the house of Laskaris, and 'Izzaddīn's case seemed a good reason to launch
an attack against Michael VIII.[22] In addition to this personal element,
Bulgaria had been on terms of enmity with Byzantium since 1262, when
the Byzantines had taken the forts of Philippoupolis (Plovdiv), Stenimachos
(Stanimaka), Mesembria (Nesebăr) and Anchialos. So both the Tatars and
the Bulgars were equally motivated against Byzantium, but the sources
diverge on whether it was the Tatars or the Bulgarians who initiated the
attack. The Muslim sources and Pachymeres place the initiative on the

[17] Ibn Bībī/Houtsma, pp. 296–8; Aqsarāyī/Işıltan, pp. 55, 58–9. For more on 'Alī Bahādur and Uğurlu, see Flemming, *Pamph. Pis. Lyk.*, p. 29, esp. nn. 2 and 5.
[18] Dhahabī: Tiz., I, pp. 200, 203, = İzm., p. 351.   [19] Aqsarāyī/Işıltan, p. 55.
[20] 'διαμηνύεται τῶν τινι συγγενῶν, ἐπιδόξῳ γε ὄντι κατὰ τὰ πρὸς ἄρκτον μέρη τοῦ Εὐξείνου πόντου' (Georg. Pach. *Hist.*/Laurent, p. 301₁₇₋₁₉).
[21] Jakubovskij, *Pohod.*
[22] Nik. Greg./Schopen-Bekker, I, pp. 99₂₁–100₂ (IV.6), = Nik. Greg./van Dieten, I, pp. 113–14.

Tatar side, but Nikephoros Gregoras claims that 'Izzaddīn himself incited Konstantin Tikh and promised him much money for his liberation.[23] Be that as it may, the Tatar and Bulgar warriors soon appeared in the Balkans, the dominant element being the Tatar troops. According to Nikephoros Gregoras there were 2,000 Tatar warriors from the Paristrion region, that is, the Lower Danube.[24] It was wintertime and the Tatar troops crossed the frozen Danube.[25] It is not known who the commander-in-chief of the Tatar troops was, but Pachymeres gives interesting information about the Tatars who took part in the expedition. These Tatars were independent, or 'autonomous', as Pachymeres puts it, and not yet totally subjected to Nogay; they came like dogs to devastate the fertile and prosperous lands.[26] So these Danubian Tatars on the westernmost borders of the Golden Horde were rather beyond central control, and even Nogay could not impose his will on them at that time; as nomadic warriors they were always ready to be employed by anyone as mercenaries. Most probably, therefore, Nogay did not take part in this campaign, and the Tatars had no direct political goal like the Bulgarians, whose declared target was to take the Byzantine emperor captive. According to common opinion, the campaign clearly demonstrates Bulgaria's vassal dependence on the Tatars of the Golden Horde: it had to participate in a Tatar campaign with its own auxiliary troops.[27] But contrary to this generally accepted opinion of historians, it was not a Tatar 'state campaign' led by Nogay with the help of Bulgarian auxiliary troups of Tsar Konstantin Tikh against Byzantium,[28] but rather the reverse: the Bulgarians wanted an anti-Byzantine campaign, and the semi-independent Tatar groups of the Danube region readily joined the expedition in the hope of rich booty. The liberation of Sultan 'Izzaddīn was only a secondary goal of some leading Tatar families in the Golden Horde. Naturally enough, this interpretation of the facts does not question the vassal dependence of Bulgaria on the Tatar state of the Golden Horde. What I want to stress here is that the majority of the Tatars who freed 'Izzaddīn from prison were 'freelances' whose only concern was booty.

---

[23] Nik. Greg./Schopen-Bekker, i, p. 1008 (iv.6), = Nik. Greg./van Dieten, p. 114.

[24] 'Οἱ παρὰ τὸν Ἴστρον οἰκοῦντες Σκύθαι', 'πλείους ἢ δισμυρίους τῶν Παριστρίων Σκυθῶν' (Nik. Greg. *Hist.*/Schopen-Bekker, pp. 99₁₆, 100₁₁₋₁₂.

[25] Ibn Bībī/Houtsma, p. 297. Aqsarāyī's report that Berke Khan sent his commander Qutluq Malik (unknown from other sources) across the sea to Constantinople to free 'Izzaddīn, lacks any probability (Aqsarāyī/Işıltan, p. 58).

[26] Pachym. *Hist.*/Failler-Laurent, p. 303₂₃₋₉. – Pachymeres' comparison of the Tatars (in his work always the Τοχάροι) to dogs may refer to Nogay's name, meaning 'dog' in Mongolian.

[27] See e.g. Nik. Greg./van Dieten, i, p. 247, n. 176, with ample further literature.

[28] Nikov, 'B''lg. i tat,' pp. 109–10.

The Mameluke sources disagree on the date of 'Izzaddīn's liberation from Byzantine captivity. Some of them locate it in Berke's time in 1263/4, while others connect the event with the name of Mengü-Temür and date it to 1269/70 (AH 668).[29] Nuwayrī even relates that the Egyptian envoy then staying in Constantinople, a certain Fārisaddīn al-Mas'ūdī, dissuaded Mengü-Temür's troops from attacking the Byzantines since Byzantium was a good ally of Egypt. Later, when Fārisaddīn Al-Mas'ūdī was in the Golden Horde, Mengü-Temür rebuked him for his behaviour, and after his return to Egypt Fārisaddīn was arrested for his unauthorised deed.[30] 'Aynī combines the two traditions by claiming that 'Izzaddīn was arrested in the fortress in 1263/4 (AH 662) and freed in 1269/70 (AH 668) by Mengü-Temür.[31] The oldest and best tradition lies with the *Tārīḫ-i Baybars*; most of the other traditions seem unauthentic, and so do not compel us to alter the date of 'Izzaddīn's liberation: it took place in 1263/4, during Berke Khan's reign.

When the Tatars and Bulgars fell on the Balkans, Emperor Michael VIII was on his way back from Thessaly, with no significant military retinue. In Pachymeres' version, 'Izzaddīn, together with his wife and children, joined the emperor on his journey, and that was the sign for the Tatars and Bulgars to attack and free them. The Byzantines panicked at the Tatar assault and the emperor had a narrow escape. He made his way through the Ganos Mountains (north-west of Rhaidestos, now Tekirdağ) and reached the sea coast, where two Latin galleys bore him and his retinue to Constantinople. The other part of the Byzantine troops, together with the treasury and 'Izzaddīn's family, withdrew to the coastal fortress of Ainos (now Enez) on the estuary of the river Marica (Turkish Meriç). In Nikephoros Gregoras' version, the emperor, when leaving for the western countryside, shut 'Izzaddīn up in the fortress of Ainos so that he could not escape. The version of the well-informed Pachymeres, however, seems more likely. After the emperor's flight the Tataro-Bulgarian forces set out and laid siege to Ainos. After a fierce fight, those within the fortress were forced to surrender. The condition of their surrender was the release of 'Izzaddīn (without his family) to the Tatars. But the surrender was corroborated by an oath sworn by the Byzantine and the Bulgarian parties before the Metropolitan and clergy of Ainos. The Bulgarian tsar himself was present at the ceremony. (Later, Michael VIII apprehended and dismissed his metropolitan

---

[29] Berke Khan: Dhahabī (Tiz., I, pp. 200, 203, = İzm., p. 351); Baybars (Tiz., I, pp. 81, 103, = İzm., pp. 175–6). Mengü-Temür Khan in AH 668: 'Aynī (Tiz., I, pp. 482, 511); Nuwayrī (Tiz., I, pp. 133, 154, = İzm., pp. 259–62); Maqrīzī (Tiz., I, pp. 422, 434).

[30] Nuwayrī: Tiz., I, pp. 133, 154, = İzm., pp. 259–62.   [31] 'Aynī: Tiz., I, pp. 482, 511.

for this misdeed.) The second act of the drama was over: 'Izzaddīn was handed over to the Tatars, his family was deported again to Byzantium, his treasures were confiscated in the Byzantine treasury, and his soldiers were baptised and conscripted into the Byzantine army. The Tatars returned to their land north of the Danube, devastating and plundering the country-side as they went. According to Nikephoros Gregoras, innumerable people and draught animals of Thrace were pursued and killed.[32]

'Izzaddīn's further fate was not the concern of the Byzantine authors, but the Muslim sources supply us with some hints about his life in Tatar exile, where the third act of his life began. 'Izzaddīn was taken to the Crimea, where Berke Khan gave him the provinces of Solgat (Eski Qïrïm) and Sugdaq.[33] Moreover, he was given one of Berke's daughters, Urbay-ḫatun, as a wife.[34] He remained in the Golden Horde until his death in the capital city of Saray in 1278/9 (AH 677). Afterwards, Mengü-Temür Khan tried to persuade 'Izzaddīn's son Mas'ūd to marry his father's wife Urbay-ḫatun, in accordance with the old Mongolian custom. But Mas'ūd, as a good Muslim, was disgusted by this pagan custom, and instead escaped from the Crimea, together with his sons Malik and Qara-Murād.[35] This Mas'ūd, who is thereafter referred to simply as *Melik* ('king') by Nikephoros Gregoras,[36] became the last Seljuk Sultan of Iconium, under the name Ghiyāth ad-Dīn Mas'ūd II. He must have died in about 1306.[37]

The fate of 'Izzaddīn's Turkish people who remained in Byzantium and were baptised and conscripted into the Byzantine army, and later went over to serve the Serbs, lies outside the scope of our present investigation. But in connection with 'Izzaddīn's story a theory emerged concerning the possibility of a Seljuk (Oguz) settlement in Dobrudja in the thirteenth century. The theory was linked with J. Hammer-Purgstall, who obtained a copy of Seyyid Lokman's historical work (now in the Wiener National-bibliothek), which is a later (end of the sixteenth century) paraphrase of

---

[32] Nik. Greg./Schopen-Bekker, I, p. 108₋₁₂ (IV.6.), = Nik. Greg./van Dieten, I, p. 114.

[33] Ibn Bībī/Houtsma, p. 298; cf. also Duda, 'Isl. Quellen', p. 142.

[34] Baybars: Tiz., I, pp. 81, 103, = Izm., pp. 175–6; 'Aynī: Tiz., I, pp. 482, 511. We hear of this Urbay-ḫatun some time in 1276–8 when she pleaded with Abaqa Khan for the son of Gurǰi-ḫatun, the wife of the emir of Amasya, Sayf ad-Dīn Torumtay (Flemming, *Pamph. Pis. Lyk.*, p. 54).

[35] Baybars: Tiz., I, pp. 81, 103, = Izm., pp. 175–6; 'Aynī: Tiz., I, pp. 483, 512.

[36] Μελήκ: Nik. Greg./Schopen-Bekker, I, p. 825 (here erroneously as 'Izzaddīn's brother'), 1376, 8, 16, = Nik. Greg./van Dieten, I, pp. 103, 133. For the name *Melik* in the Byzantine sources, see Laurent, *Mélikès*, pp. 361, 368; *Byz.-turc.*, II, pp. 187–8. This Melik (= Mas'ūd II) must not be confused, as often happens, with Melik, the leader of the *Tourkopouloi* in the first decade of the fourteenth century.

[37] On Mas'ūd II, who returned to Anatolia, see Spuler, *GH*, p. 62; Flemming, *Pamph. Pis. Lyk.*, pp. 52–3; Nik. Greg./van Dieten, I, p. 239, n. 132, and pp. 260–1, nn. 240–3.

the *Oğuznāme*.[38] The *Oğuznāme* itself was the work of Yazïǰioğlu ʿAlī, who wrote his voluminous work in Ottoman Turkish during the reign of Sultan Murad II (1421–51).[39] Yazïǰioğlu ʿAlī drew on different written and oral sources of Oguz and Seljuk history, and his version of ʿIzzaddīn's story contains an episode that cannot be found in any other source. It runs as follows. ʿIzzaddīn and his commander-in-chief ʿAlī Bahādur turned to the Byzantine emperor asking him to grant them land to which they could withdraw with their Turks. Their argument is extremely interesting: 'We are Turks and cannot live in towns for long.' The emperor fulfilled their wish and gave them the land of Dobrudja (*Dobruca ilini*), to which they moved, together with the saintly Sarï Saltïq. Subsequently, two or three Muslim towns and thirty to forty divisions (*bölük*) of Turkish nomadic groups (*oba*) arose on that territory.[40] Later, Sarï Saltïq moved to the Crimea along with ʿIzzaddīn.

According to the analyses of Mutafčiev and Duda,[41] Yazïǰioğlu's, and hence Lokman's, account of a possible Oguz/Turk/Turkmen settlement in Dobrudja in the thirteenth century lacks all probability. P. Wittek,[42] however, tried to prove the reliability of Yazïǰioğlu's narrative, and hence the reality of a thirteenth-century Oguz settlement in Dobrudja. The later descendants of these Oguz immigrants would be the Gagauz Turks. Despite the great erudition and richness of data evident in Mutafčiev's work, however, Wittek's views found almost unanimous acceptance in scholarly literature. It is not the task of the present book to go into detail concerning this question, so I offer only a few remarks. Even if we disregard the clear anachronism of the Turkish appellation 'Dobruca' in the thirteenth century (it became the name of the territory only after the death of the Bulgarian prince Dobrotica in 1387),[43] Sarï Saltïq was a typical representative of popular mystical Islam among the Turkic peoples, just as Baba Tükles, for instance, was among the Central Asian and northern Turks. The figure of Sarï Saltïq, the *ghāzī* saint who propagated Islam, was especially well known within the one-time Ottoman Empire. He was particularly popular in the Balkans and the Crimea, where several holy sites and mausolea were linked with him.[44] By the first half of the fifteenth century, when Yazïǰioğlu wrote his work, the figure of Sarï Saltïq was already an organic part of the Anatolian Bektashi tradition. Similarly, the connection of Sarï Saltïq's alleged missionary activity with ʿIzzaddīn's flight to the Crimea and

---

[38] For editions and translations of Lokman's work, see Mutafčiev, 'Dobr.', p. 7ff.
[39] For the MSS of the work, see Duda, 'Isl. Quellen', p. 138.
[40] Duda, 'Isl. Quellen', pp. 143–4, 144, n. 1.   [41] Mutafčiev, 'Dobr.'; Duda, 'Isl. Quellen'.
[42] Wittek, 'Gagaouzes'; Wittek, 'Yazijioghlu'.   [43] Mutafčiev, 'Dobr.', pp. 26–7.
[44] Cf. Smith, 'Sarı Saltuq'; DeWeese, *Baba Tükles*, pp. 86, 250–5.

Dobrudja must have been part of the Anatolion *ṣūfī* tradition reflected in Yazïjïoǧlu's work.

NOGAY'S MARRIAGE TO A BYZANTINE PRINCESS, 1272

A few years later, after the united Tatar and Bulgarian troops had liberated 'Izzaddīn from Byzantine captivity, a new Tatar attack befell Byzantium in 1271. This time the Tatars were invited by Ioannes Sebastokrator, lord of Thessaly, and Andronikos Tarchaneiotes to make an assault on Byzantium.[45] These events prompted Emperor Michael VIII's decision to regulate his relationship with the new nomadic power of the Golden Horde. First he married off one of his daughters, Mary, to the Ilkhan Abaqa;[46] then, in 1272, he made peace with Prince Nogay, the Tatar commander-in-chief, and in confirmation of the alliance he married off another of his illegitimate daughters, Euphrosyne, to Nogay.[47] Thus the leaders of both Tatar states (Iran and the western half of the Golden Horde) became his sons-in-law and allies. The political goal and the importance of these marriages were perfectly obvious to his contemporaries; Pachymeres remarks in connection with the Tatar–Bulgarian campaign of 1264 that 'the matrimonial alliance was not yet contracted with Nogay. It was after these events that the sovereign had to contract it with him in the person of his natural daughter Euphrosyne'.[48] Thanks to Emperor Michael's masterly manoeuvres, Byzantium could rely on friendly allies that encircled the enemy powers surrounding Byzantium. Thus Hülegü's Iran controlled the Sultanate of Iconium, Nogay and his Tatars kept a tight rein on Bulgaria, and the Hungarian Kingdom kept a watchful eye on Serbia. From 1273 onward, Nogay had changed from an enemy to a close ally who, if need arose, would help Byzantium even against the Bulgars. And such an opportunity for intervention presented itself in no time.

THE TATARS' ROLE IN THE STRUGGLE FOR THE BULGARIAN THRONE, 1277–1280

In 1277, a new age of political instability dawned for Bulgaria. The final balance of Konstantin Tikh's rule was very unfavourable to almost all strata

---

[45] Ostrogorsky, *Gesch.*, p. 329 (379).   [46] Pachym. *Hist.*/Failler-Laurent, pp. 234–5 (III.3).

[47] Pachym. *Hist.*/Failler-Laurent, pp. 242–3 (III.5); Nik. Greg. *Hist.*/Schopen-Bekker, p. 149₁₇₋₁₉ (V.7). Nik. Greg. calls the emperor's daughter Irene.

[48] "Ἔτι δὲ καὶ τὸ κῆδος τὸ πρὸς Νογᾶν οὔπω ἦν συνεστός, ὅπερ μετὰ ταῦτα ἐπὶ νόθῳ θυγατρὶ τῇ Εὐφροσύνῃ ὁ κρατῶν πρὸς ἐκεῖνον ἔμελλε συνιστᾶν" (Pachym. *Hist.*/Failler-Laurent, p. 303).

of Bulgarian society. Feudal anarchy was raging in the country, and the central power was weak. Finally, the economic exploitation of the peasantry, and the boyars' inability and negligence when it came to defending the people of the countryside against the frequent Tatar raids and pillages, led to the outbreak of the great peasant uprising in the spring of 1277. This movement, combined with the struggle for the Bulgarian throne, lasted well into 1280.[49]

Our best source, is again Pachymeres, who recounts the events in a reliable manner, and Gregoras adds some details.[50] Tsar Konstantin Tikh, together with his wife Tsarica Maria and their minor son, were staying in the capital city of Tărnovo when the news arrived that in the countryside a strong pretender had arisen in the person of an illiterate swineherd called Ivaylo.[51] His name in the Greek sources, *Lachanas* (Λαχανᾶς), was simply a Greek translation of his Bulgarian nickname *B"rdokva*, λάχανον meaning 'cabbage' or 'lettuce'.[52] The centre of the uprising must have been somewhere in north-eastern Bulgaria, near the area later called Dobrudja. This was a territory of flat plains over which all the Tatar invading troops had marched, and the Bulgarian central power had always been weak. Peripheries are always apt and ready to revolt; the general truth was valid in Bulgaria's case too. Ivaylo's troops gained one victory after another, and by autumn 1277 the formidable and invincible Tatars were compelled to leave Bulgaria and draw back to the left bank of the Danube, their homeland proper. Hearing of Ivaylo's successes, more and more people deserted Konstantin and joined Ivaylo as he approached the capital, Tărnovo. Then, in an open battle (the location of which is unknown), Tsar Konstantin's army was defeated, and he himself perished at Ivaylo's hands.[53] By the beginning of 1278 the rebels were already near Tărnovo, a capital without a ruler.

This was the moment at which Emperor Michael of Byzantium unhesitatingly intervened in Bulgarian affairs – not because he was grief-stricken by Konstantin's death or distressed by the internal Bulgarian turmoil, but because of his fear that Bulgarian instability might pose a threat

---

[49] The history of these troubled years of Bulgarian history has often been subjected to enquiry; see Jireček, *Bulg.*; Zlatarski, *Ist.*, III.; Mutafčiev, *Ist.* A popular monograph on the theme, with a primitive Marxist bias, is Petrow, *Iwailo*.

[50] Pachym. *Hist.*/Failler-Laurent, pp. 549₁₅–569₂₁ (VI.3–9), 589₅–591₂₅ (VI.19); Nik. Greg. *Hist.*/Schopen-Bekker, I, pp. 130₁₆–133₁₈ (V.3), = Greg./van Dieten, I, p. 129–31.

[51] For Ivaylo, see Jireček, *Serb.*, pp. 328ff.; Zlatarski, *Ist.*, III, pp. 544ff.

[52] Pachym. *Hist.*/Failler-Laurent, p. 549₁₆–₁₈ (VI.3); Nik. Greg./Schopen-Bekker, I, p. 131 (V.3) = Nik. Greg./van Dieten, I, p. 130. The MSS of Pachym.'s Greek text contain *Kordokubas* (Κορδόκουβας), which must be corrected to *Bordokubas* (*Βορδόκουβας), see Nik. Greg./van Dieten, I, p. 130.

[53] Pachym. *Hist.*/Failler-Laurent, pp. 551₁₀–553₂₀ (VI.3).

to Byzantium and favour the anti-Byzantine Neapolitan coalition that was being brought together by Charles of Anjou at that time. A decision was promptly reached in Adrianople. First, Emperor Michael gave one of his daughters, Irene, as wife to Ivan, son of Mico, a Bulgarian refugee of noble descent then in Byzantine service. Mico was King Michael Asen's brother-in-law. His reliability was unquestioned since it was he who had handed over Mesembria to the emperor in about 1261, for which he was rewarded with a fief in Troy in Anatolia.[54] His son Ivan was the grandson of Ivan Asen II, so he had a legal right to the Bulgarian throne. Shortly after his marriage, this Ivan, son of Mico, was proclaimed Bulgarian tsar under the name Ivan Asen III. Having taken the oath of fealty to Emperor Michael VIII, he set out for Tărnovo with Byzantine troops to assert his imperial rights in Bulgaria.

The situation of the widow Tsarica Maria and the Bulgarian boyars in Tărnovo was very precarious. They were between a rock and a hard place: they could surrender either to the peasant rebels of Ivaylo or to the pretender Ivan Asen III, who was supported by the Byzantine army. The first option looked like an impossible solution, because of the social gap between the two parties, while the second would have meant Bulgaria's vassal dependence on Byzantium. Strangely enough, the first option was chosen: in the spring of 1278 Tsarica Maria surrendered and opened the gates of Tărnovo to the pretender Ivaylo on the condition that he acknowledged her son Michael as the lawful heir to the throne. Ivaylo immediately married her as a token of his legitimacy, and was crowned tsar.

At this juncture the Byzantine emperor turned to his other son-in-law, Prince Nogay, who sent his Tatar troops to Bulgaria. The appearance of Tatar troops in Dobrudja changed the course of events. From the autumn of 1278 Ivaylo's rebels had to fight on two fronts. Ivaylo himself withdrew to the fortress of Drăstăr (now Silistra) which was for three months besieged by the Tatars. In the meantime, in the beginning of 1279, the Byzantine forces, under the commandership of Protostrator Michael Glabas, embarked for Galata, near Varna, and launched an attack on the fortresses of Petrič and Provat (now Provadija). After the capture of Preslav the way was open to Tărnovo.

In the spring of 1279, when the united Byzantine and Tatar forces besieged Tărnovo, the Bulgarian boyars saw that their situation could no longer be defended. They devised a plot, captured Tsarica Maria and her son Michael, and delivered them to the Byzantines, who sent them to

---

[54] Nik. Greg./Schopen-Bekker, I, pp. 60–1, = Nik. Greg./van Dieten, I, p. 93.

Constantinople. Ivan Asen III was placed on the throne, and Ivaylo could not return to Tărnovo.

The role of the Tatar troops was instrumental in the surrender of Tărnovo. Had not the Tatar army distracted Ivaylo's attention in the north, the Byzantine troops would not have been able move from the southern fortresses of the Haimos Mountains to the northern Black Sea region, from where they could launch the final, victorious attack against the rebels. Emperor Michael VIII was well aware of the merits of the Tatars, which is why he rewarded the Tatar commander-in-chief Čavušbašï (Τζασίμπαξις) with the honorary title *protostrator*.[55]

But the Bulgarian boyars, just as they were reluctant to accept Ivaylo on the Bulgarian throne, were similarly suspicious of the new tsar, the Byzantine puppet Ivan Asen III. Neither of them was their man. Instead, the most popular figure in Tărnovo was George Terter, a boyar from their own ranks (who, a year later, in 1280, was elected the new tsar). The Terter family was of Cuman descent like the Asenids, and the Terterids shared ancestry with the Asenids on the maternal line.[56] The Byzantine emperor knew that Ivan Asen III had no backing among the Bulgarian aristocracy, so he wanted to ensure their support by linking Terter, the strongest boyar, to the new tsar and to Byzantium. In accordance with an agreement, Terter divorced his Bulgarian wife, who, together with their son Svetoslav (the later ruler Teodor Svetoslav, 1300–21), was exiled to Nikaia. Terter then married Ivan Asen III's sister. For all this he was given the title of 'despot' (δεσπότης).

The price of Terter's inclusion in the ruling power was that the Bulgarians and Byzantines lost Čavušbašï's support. He was ousted from his high post by George Terter, and the offended Tatar commander-in-chief went over to Ivaylo's side. But Terter's role was doubtful right from the start. He probably never gave up the idea of becoming tsar, and with the boyars' help he devised a plot. Ivan Asen III realised the hopelessness of his situation and, after a few months on the Bulgarian throne, left Tărnovo in secret and fled to Constantinople via Mesembria. All this happened towards the end of 1279. The next year, in 1280, George Terter was elected the new Bulgarian tsar.

---

[55] For Τζασίμπαξις see *Byz.-Turc.*, II, p. 310; Zachariadou, 'Turcica', pp. 265–6. Formerly the Greek form was erroneously read as Qāsim-beg (Jireček, *Bulg.*, p. 276; Spuler, *GH*, p. 61), but Zachariadou (*loc. cit.*) convincingly proved that it must be interpreted as *Čavušbašï*, 'head of the čavuš'. Τζάσις is a Greek variant of τζαούσιος (Turk. *čavuš*), often occurring in fourteenth- and fifteenth-century documents of southern Morea. For the title 'protostrator', see Guilland, *Recherches*, I, pp. 478–97.

[56] For George Terter, see Zlatarski, *Ist.*, pp. 570–5.

But before this final development, Ivaylo, together with his newly acquired Tatar commander Čavušbašï, caused the Byzantines a great deal of headache. Ivaylo did not acquiesce in his expulsion from power, and tried to recapture Tărnovo. On 17 July 1279 his troops clashed with 10,000 Byzantine soldiers under the command of protovestiarites Murinos. The battle took place at Diabaina (now Devina on the Kotlenski road, south-east of Tărnovo), and Ivaylo gained the victory. Later, on 5 August, Ivaylo's troops encountered 5,000 warriors of the Byzantine protovestiarites Aprenos somewhere in the outer Zygos Mountains (now Sredna Gora), and the Byzantines were similarly defeated, Aprenos himself being killed by Ivaylo.[57] But despite all his efforts, Ivaylo remained unsuccessful; in the end, he could not recapture Tărnovo. After Ivan Asen III's flight and George Terter's accession to the Bulgarian throne, some time in 1280 he decided to take refuge with the Tatar prince Nogay. Together with his Tatar commander Čavušbašï, he appeared at Nogay's court. Nogay received them cordially and promised aid. But the news of Ivaylo's lodging at Nogay's court caused anxiety in Byzantium. Emperor Michael sent his son-in-law, the fallen ex-tsar Ivan Asen III, to his other son-in-law Nogay, to ensure Nogay's support in regaining the Bulgarian throne. A very strange situation came about: two Bulgarian pretenders simultaneously strove to win the favour of the Tatar leader, who was benevolent enough to receive the gifts and homage of both. Pachymeres pointedly remarks that 'actually it was one embassy for both of them directed against Terter'.[58] This episode alone may be enough to illustrate the political and military importance of Nogay's Tatars in the politics of the Balkans in those days. Finally, Nogay made his choice, and, probably at the behest of Emperor Michael VIII, turned against Ivaylo. Nogay called all the 'actors' to a feast; Ivaylo, Čavušbašï and Ivan Asen III were all there. At a certain moment during the banquet he ordered Ivaylo and Čavušbašï to be killed. His case was very simple: 'This is the enemy of my father the Emperor; he is not worthy at all to live, but to be killed.'[59] Nogay's servants did not hesitate to fulfil their master's command. The life of Ivan Asen III was spared, mainly thanks to the intervention of Nogay's Greek wife, Euphrosyne.

With George Terter's accession to the throne and Ivaylo's death, both the Bulgarian peasant uprising and the struggle for the throne were ended.

---

[57] Pachym. *Hist.*/Failler-Laurent, p. 589$_{5-20}$ (VI.19).
[58] 'ἡ γὰρ πρεσβεία μία ἦν ἀμφοτέροις κατὰ τοῦ Τερτερῆ' (Pachym. *Hist.*/Failler-Laurent, pp. 591$_{5-6}$: (VI.19).
[59] 'Οὗτος ἐχθρός ἐστι τοῦ πατρός μου καὶ βασιλέως καὶ ζῆν ὅλως οὐκ ἄξιος, ἀλλὰ τέμνεσθαι' (Pachym. *Hist.*/Failler-Laurent, p. 591$_{17-18}$ (VI.19)).

Nogay and his Tatars were present at each decisive phase of the fight, and these phases proved to be decisive precisely because the Tatars were invited to decide disputed questions between the warring factions by military means. Nogay was firm in his allegiance to his father-in-law, the Byzantine emperor, which cannot be said of local Tatar commanders such as Čavušbašï, who went over to the rebel Ivaylo. Though the Tatars were not the chief protagonists in the Bulgarian–Byzantine fights, without their active participation events would have taken a fundamentally different course.

TATARS INVITED TO PUNISH SEBASTOKRATOR IOANNES OF THESSALY, 1282

Emperor Michael VIII encountered a great deal of trouble with John I, sebastokrator of Thessaly (1271–89), the illegitimate son of Michael II of Epeiros. These small Greek statelets, which had come into existence after the Fourth Crusade (1204), wanted to preserve their independence from Byzantium; while the main desire of the emperor Michael VIII, in accordance with his plans to restore Byzantine greatness, was to reunite them with the empire. John I of Thessaly rebelled against the Byzantine imperial power several times, and in 1282 he joined the Serbs in their move against Macedonia. The emperor, tired of John's animosity, decided to reprimand him. He called in Nogay's Tatars with the aim of sending them to Thessaly to plunder the country.[60] He found a favourable occasion in winter 1282, since the Tatars, so Pachymeres claims, preferred the winter time for their campaigns and military excursions.[61] Pachymeres even expresses mild criticism in connection with the emperor's plan: though it was convenient militarily, from another point of view it was something of a scandal that unbelievers and atheists were sent to punish Christians. But the emperor was resolute and in November 1282 he embarked on the military expedition. He marched with his troops to Selymbria (Silivri), and then went by boat to Rhaidestos (Tekirdağ). The 4,000 Tatar warriors[62] sent by Nogay must have already been in the vicinity. The emperor's army was encamped

---

[60] 'Τοχάρους ἐπαγαγών, πᾶσαν μὲν τὴν ἐκείνου λῃΐσεται' (Pachym. _Hist._/Failler-Laurent, p. 659₁₄: VI.35).

[61] 'Εὔκαιρον δ' εἶχε καὶ τὸν ἐφεστῶτα χειμῶνα – χειμῶνος γὰρ καὶ σύνηθες ἐκείνοις στρατεύειν – ὃν καὶ προκαταλαβεῖν ἠπείγετο, ὡς ἔξω πόλεως συμβαλεῖν Τοχάροις.' (Pachym. _Hist._/Failler-Laurent, p. 659₁₆₋₁₈ (VI.35)).

[62] 'Ἐκεῖθεν οὖν εἰληφὼς τετρακισχιλίους Σκυθῶν ἐπιλέκτους στρατιώτας ἔμελλε καὶ Ῥωμαίων ὁπλιτικήν τινα δύναμιν προσμίξας πέμπειν κατὰ τοῦ Θετταλοῦ Ἰωάννου τοῦ Σεβαστοκράτορος' (Nik. Greg./Schopen-Bekker, I, p. 149₁₉₋₂₂ (V.7), = Nik. Greg./van Dieten, I, p. 140).

near Lysimachia, between the villages of Pachomiou and Allage,[63] aiming to unite with the Tatars and march to Thessaly. But suddenly Michael VIII became ill with a heart condition, and shortly afterwards, on 11 December 1282, he passed away.[64] The military expedition against Thessaly was cancelled, but the Tatar troops, hungry for booty and ready to plunder, caused problems for the Byzantines. The deceased emperor's son, who, immediately upon his father's death, was declared emperor under the name Andronikos II, decided to postpone the attack against John of Thessaly and dispatched the Tatar warriors against the Serbs, enemies of Byzantium at that time. He ordered his famous military commander Michael Glabas, the great equerry, to lead the Tatars against the Serbs (Τριβαλλοί).[65] They could then have returned to their homes beyond the Danube (Ἴστρος) with their plunder, but the expedition ended unsuccessfully at the river Drim, where many Tatars perished.[66] (We shall look more closely at this event in Chapter 6.)

---

[63] The exact locations of these settlements are unknown. *Allage* means 'change', and probably refers to a place where horses were changed (Nik. Greg./van Dieten I, p. 264, n. 261). At this juncture Nik. Greg. recounts an interesting historical anecdote that sheds light on everyday beliefs and superstitions of the day. Having learnt the names of the settlements, the emperor gave up hope of survival. 'Only the end is left for me, *change* into another life is my fortune,' he said, evidently referring to Allage by this pun. Simultaneously, he began to accuse himself severely, for once he had ordered an honourable man called Pachomios to be blinded, because there was a popular prophecy that 'Upon the change of life Pachomios will take over the royal duty.' By blinding Pachomios the emperor wanted to make him incapable of ruling. Nik. Greg./Schopen-Bekker, I, p. 150₁₁₋₂₀, = Greg./van Dieten, I, pp. 140–1.

[64] For the whole history of this frustrated Thessalian expedition, see Pachym. *Hist.*/Failler-Laurent, pp. 659₈–663 (VI.35–6); Nik. Greg./Schopen-Bekker, pp. 149₅–150₂₀ (V.7), = Nik. Greg./van Dieten, I, pp. 140–1.

[65] Nik.Greg./Schopen-Bekker, pp. 158₁–159₁₇ (VI.1), = Nik. Greg./van Dieten, I, p. 144.

[66] For a short description of these events, with further literature, see Laiou, *Const. and the Latins*, p. 30.

CHAPTER FIVE

The heyday of Tatar influence in the Balkans, 1280–1301

GEORGE TERTER I (1280–1292) AND NOGAY

In 1280, with the conclusion of both the Bulgarian peasant uprising and the struggle for the throne, a new period began in Bulgaria's life. But it was not only in Bulgaria that, by the will of the boyars, a new ruler (and founder of a new dynasty) was seated on the throne. As was mentioned earlier, two leading powers of the area, the Golden Horde and Byzantium, also experienced a change of rulers. The khan of the Golden Horde, Mengü-Temür, died in 1280, and the Byzantine emperor Michael VIII, founder of the Palaiologos dynasty, passed away in 1282. The new rulers Tudā-Mengü (1280–7) in the Tatar state and Andronikos II (1282–1328) in Byzantium, though successors of the former imperial dynasties, proved much weaker than their predecessors, so the change of power in these countries led to a weakening of central power.

Until 1280 the traditional Balkanic lands, that is, the territories south of the Danube, belonged indisputably to the Byzantine sphere of interest. This statement is valid despite frequent nomadic incursions and the turbulance caused by them from time immemorial. Not even the Tatars of the Golden Horde questioned Byzantium's authority in Balkanic affairs. As we saw in the previous chapter, after a few years of uncertainty in Byzantium's northern policy, from 1272 onwards the western Tatar chief Nogay became tied to New Rome through firm matrimonial bonds. Nogay never hesitated to send his troops to help the emperor, his father-in-law and ally. His only concern was booty; he had no political interest in the Balkans. But the deaths of his powerful khan Mengü-Temür (1280) and of his father-in-law, Emperor Michael VIII (1282), opened new horizons for Nogay's dormant dreams for more power. In his own native Golden Horde he became the strong man, a real kingmaker, as Batu Khan had been earlier; all three successive khans, Tudā–Mengü (1280–7), Telebuğa (1287–91) and Toqta (1291–1312), owed their accession to the throne to Nogay's effective help and power. Soon his appetite grew, and his attention turned to Bulgaria, where he wanted to play the same kingmaking role.

During the twelve years of Terter's reign (1280–92), a relative peace dominated the troubled land of Bulgaria, soon to give way again to chaotic years loud with the tumult of battle. In the last decade of the thirteenth century the flame of Tatar influence flared up once more in Bulgaria, to such an extent that for a short period the country lost its independence and fell under direct Tatar rule. When George Terter I was elected tsar by the boyars of Tărnovo, Nogay was practically indifferent to the internal affairs of Bulgaria. He did what the Byzantines demanded from him. 'Do not support Ivaylo and his Tatar chief Čavušbašĭ,' said Michael VIII, so he made away with them. 'Do not kill our protégé Ivan Asen III,' said his wife Euphrosyne, so he pardoned and released him. 'We want Terter to be our tsar,' said the boyars in Tărnovo, so he let them have their wish. But from almost the first moment of Terter's accession to the throne, Nogay was not really satisfied with him. Terter was not his man. He began to behave as if he were really an independent ruler; he did not reckon with the realities of Byzantium and the Tatars.

In 1284 Terter sent his second wife, Ivan Asen III's sister, back to Byzantium, and recovered his first wife and their son, Svetoslav, who lived in Nikaia under Byzantine tutelage. Svetoslav was made co-ruler with his father, according to Byzantine custom. It was an internal political victory for Terter, whose second marriage was never acknowledged by the Bulgarian clergy. Andronikos II was willing to accede to this act of reconciliation with Terter, since there was no real chance of Ivan Asen III's return to the Bulgarian throne.[1]

But Terter's endeavours to achieve greater independence were soon frustrated by Nogay's campaigns in the following year. In 1285, the Tatars launched a campaign against Hungary, often referred to in Hungarian historiography as 'the second Tatar invasion',[2] and rumour had it that the Tatars also wanted to invade Thrace and Macedonia. Terter was well aware that he could not arrest a Tatar attack against Bulgaria. The Byzantines took

---

[1] Pachym. *Hist.*/Bekker, II, p. 573–17 (1.20). Cf. also Jireček, *Bulg.*, pp. 281–2.

[2] The Tatar campaign of Nogay and Telebuǧa took place in February–March 1285. The Tatars arrived from the north bringing with them auxiliary troops from Galič and Ladomer (Volhynia). The Tatar forces initially proceeded as far as Pest. They stopped at the Danube and did not cross the river, but turned to the east and pillaged the Transylvanian towns of Beszterce, Torda, and Torockó. The local Hungarian, Székely and Saxon population displayed strong resistance and caused much damage to the invading Tatars. For this Tatar campaign in Hungary, see Szabó, *Kun László*, pp. 117–20; Pauler, *Árp.*, II, pp. 386–8, 565–6, n. 271; Spuler, *GH*, pp. 66–7; and recently Székely, *Második tatárjárás*, pp. 68–81.

precautions to weaken such a potential attack by deporting the Vlakhs *en
masse*. The Vlahks, who pursued their nomadic, pastoral lifestyle in Thrace
between Constantinople and Bizye (Vize), were settled in Anatolia in order
to prevent their possible joining up with the Tatar invaders. At the same
time, Emperor Andronikos II had the corpse of his father Michael VIII
transported from Allage to Selymbria, fearing that in the event of a Tatar
incursion the Tatars would take the corpse and demand a high ransom for
it.[3] As a result, the Tatar campaign in the Balkans in 1285 never got beyond
the planning stage.[4] But soon after the Hungarian campaign, the Tatars
turned against Poland and in 1286–7 they ravaged Cracaw (Kraków) and
Lemberg (Lwów).[5]

NOGAY'S *ULUS* BECOMES INDEPENDENT

Prince Nogay, the kingmaker, must have been dissatisfied with his latest
choice. Telebuğa, who ascended to the throne in 1287, was headstrong and
seemingly did not want to play the role of an obedient puppet, so Nogay
soon decided to make away with him. He was ensnared and killed by Nogay
and his men, and Nogay's new protégé, Mengü-Tämür's son Toqta, was
given the khan's throne in 1291.[6]

The Tatar campaign against Hungary and the strengthening of Nogay's
power frustrated George Terter I's hopes, and in 1285 he was compelled
to send his son Svetoslav as a hostage to Nogay's court, and his daughter
(unknown by name; Svetoslav's sister or half-sister) to marry Čeke, elder
son of Nogay. But even this act of evident submission could not satisfy
Nogay's appetite. It was not only the tsardom of Tărnovo that fell under
stronger Tatar tutelage after 1285; so also did the two Bulgarian despotates of
Vidin and Braničevo. At that time these two principalities were practically
independent. The Šišman family, which was also of Cuman origin, ruled
in Vidin, and Braničevo was under the rule of Kudelin and Dorman, two
lords who were probably also of Cuman or Cumano-Slav extraction. In
the 1280s both principalities were subjected to the attacks of Dragutin, the
dethroned Serbian king whose aspiration was to create a new Serbian state
in the north, independent of his brother Milutin's Serbia. In 1291 the local
Cumano-Bulgarian power in Vidin and Braničevo turned to Nogay, whose

[3] Pachym. *Hist.*/Bekker, ii, pp. 6–7 (1.37).
[4] Jireček's statement (Jireček, *Bulg.*, p. 282) that the Tatars ravaged Thrace and Macedonia in 1285 cannot be corroborated by any source. The same was repeated by Nikov, 'B"lg. i tat.', p. 122.
[5] Spuler, *GH*, p. 67.
[6] Baybars: Tiz., i, pp. 84–6, 106–8; Nuwayrī: Tiz., i, pp. 136, 157; Ibn Ḫaldūn: Tiz., i, pp. 369, 382.

Tatars rapidly appeared on the scene and menaced Milutin's Serbia. In an attempt to forestall the danger, Milutin sent his own son Stefan Uroš (later the Serbian king Stefan Dečanski) to Nogay's court as a hostage. The Tatar invasion of the Balkans in 1291/2 overthrew Terter's rule in Bulgaria, and helped Smilec, the representative of another important Bulgarian clan, to power. All these events will be dealt with in more detail in Chapter 6.

In 1292 Terter escaped Nogay's threat by fleeing to Byzantium, and concealed himself near Hadrianoupolis. But the Byzantine emperor did not dare to give him political asylum.[7] It is clear that Terter fell into disgrace and was compelled to flee, but nothing is known of the course that led from 1285, the year of Terter's submission to Nogay, to 1292, when he was forced from the throne.[8] Smilec, the next ruler, came from one of the noblest Bulgarian boyar families and ruled for six years on the Bulgarian throne (1292–8). His family possessions were situated between Stara Planina and Sredna Gora.[9] He was placed on the Bulgarian throne as Nogay's obedient puppet, and behaved as he was expected.[10] After his death in 1298 a long period of chaos ensued in Bulgarian history.

But before proceeding to these extremely intriguing years (1298–1301), which even saw a descendant of the Chingisids on the Bulgarian throne, we must investigate Nogay's rule in the westernmost *ulus* of the Golden Horde. It was in the last decade of the thirteenth century that Nogay's power rose to unprecedented heights, and for a short time he became legally independent of the khan of the Golden Horde. As we saw in Chapter 4, from the 1270s onward Nogay and his sons had professed Islam, just as Berke and his circle had done since the 1250s. In the 1280s the influence of Nogay and his elder son Čeke began to grow rapidly in the Lower Danube region. This fact has received ample testimony in recent decades through the valuable archaeological (mainly numismatic) findings in Dobrudja. In Isaccea (the county of Tulcea, Romania) and its surroundings, coins with Greek inscriptions cropped up. The coins display the tamga of the Nogay clan on their obverse, while the reverses depict various Greek religious symbols and legends. Moreover, on one silver coin the names of Nogay and Čeke are

---

[7] Pachym. *Hist.*/Bekker, II, p. 264₈₋₁₀ (III.26).

[8] Nikov, 'B"lg. i tat.', p. 124.

[9] *Ibid.*, p. 128. Between Tatar-Pazardžik and Ikhtiman one can find the ruins of a *Smilcev monastir*, which had been built by Smilec in 1286, during the reign of George Terter I (Jireček, *Bulg.*, p. 283). For Smilec, cf. also *PLP*, no. 26295 (Σμίλτζος).

[10] Pavlov, 'Nogai', p. 126, claims that despite the generally accepted view, Bulgaria under Smilec had an independent (or at least relatively independent) foreign and internal policy. As far as foreign policy is concerned, this surely does not hold true.

rendered together in the Greek alphabet as ΝΟΓΑΗΣ/ΤΖΑΚΑΣ.[11] These findings obviously reflect the facts that in Dobrudja a Greek despotate existed with Isaccea (in Tatar, Saqčï) as its centre, and that from the 1280s onward this despotate acknowledged the suzerainty of Nogay and his son Čeke. According to the Romanian archaeologist E. Oberländer-Târnoveanu, the two-headed eagle became the symbol of despotic authority towards the end of the thirteenth century, and it is conspicuous that in the 1290s a great many rulers in the vicinity bore the title *despot*, including Šišman of Vidin, Svetoslav of Tărnovo (son of George Terter I) and Eltimir of Krăn (brother of George Terter II).[12] All of them, of course, like the unknown despot of Saqčï, were vassals of Nogay and his son Čeke. As far as the dating of the coins is concerned, Oberländer-Târnoveanu first suggested 1285–95, but then opted for the earlier date of 1271–85.[13]

During the last twenty years, new hoards of coins bearing Arabic inscriptions have emerged in and near Isaccea. All these findings testify to the existence of a significant Tatar mint in Saqčï.[14] These silver and copper coins were minted with Arabic inscriptions including the names of Nogay and Čeke and the Nogayid tamga, and the place of minting is always written as Saqčï. These hoards, whose interpretation we owe mainly to Oberländer-Târnoveanu, are of particular importance since they shed new light on the historical role of Nogay and his sons. The minting of Tatar coinage began in Saqčï in 1286 and lasted till 1351. Two types of coins were struck there: first, those bearing the names of legitimate khans of the Golden Horde (Tudā-Mängü, Telebuǧa, Toqta) and anonymous coins bearing the representation of the Jočid tamga; and secondly, coins struck in the name of Nogay and/or his son Čeke, and anonymous coins bearing the image of the tamga of Nogay's clan. Nogay and Čeke's coins were struck in the period between 1296 and 1301. The discovery of Nogay and Čeke's coins, I must stress again, was of crucial importance. They force us to interpret historical events of the last decade of the thirteenth century anew. Nogay really founded a new khanate; we may call it the Nogayid khanate. As a Chingisid he had full legal justification in doing so, for as a khan he could not be regarded as 'unlawful', only 'illegitimate' at the most. The later relentless struggle between Nogay and Toqta, the legitimate khan of the Golden Horde (1291–1312), can be

---

[11] Oberländer-Târnoveanu, 'Num. contr.', pp. 246–9. According to Konstantin Dočev, the same types of coins cropped up in the Tărnovo findings (Pavlov, 'Pandoleon', p. 183, n. 5).

[12] Oberländer-Târnoveanu, 'Num. contr.', p. 249.

[13] Oberländer-Târnoveanu, 'Isaccea', p. 294, n. 18. Cf. also Oberländer-Târnoveanu, 'Contr.'; Oberländer-Târnoveanu, *Doc. num.*; Oberländer-Târnoveanu, 'Noi descoperiri'.

[14] Oberländer-Târnoveanu, 'Isaccea', pp. 296–8.

explained by Nogay's separatist politics, which led to the creation of an independent *ulus* with Saqči (Isaccea) as its centre in the 1290s. The minting of coins in the ruler's name is an obvious sign of sovereignty in Islam. The official title of Nogay as reflected in the coins was *khan*, while his son Čeke is designated *sulṭān*; but during his father's lifetime, probably as early as AH 698 (1298/9), he also adopted the title of *khan*. Oberländer-Târnoveanu put forward the unproved though remarkable suggestion that this form of double reign may go back to a Byzantine model of 'associate reign', since in the Byzantium of the Palaiologos period imperial fathers on the throne often shared their rule with their sons.[15] But it may be pointless to turn to Byzantine models in cases where native examples are also at hand: double reign or double kingship is equally present in the Turco-Mongolian world, although one must admit that the joint presence of the names of father and son is extremely rare in Muslim-Turkic coinage.[16] As we evaluate these facts, it becomes increasingly clear why Toqta reacted so vehemently to Nogay's separatistic movement, which ended with Nogay's death on the battlefield of Kügenlik, near the Bug river towards the end of 1299.[17] The Byzantine emperor desired to maintain the friendly status of ally to the Tatars into the post-Nogay period. It was probably during Nogay's lifetime or just after his death that Andronikos II offered his illegitimate daughter Mary in marriage to Toqta, who accepted the offer. After the conclusion of the civil war, when all the Tatar factions had been subjected to Toqta, the Byzantine imperial bride was sent to Toqta Khan and the marriage ceremony was performed.[18] So the Byzantine–Tatar alliance remained secure after Nogay's disappearance from the historical scene.

ČEKE'S EMERGENCE AS KHAN

After the death of the Tatar protégé Smilec in November 1298, medieval Bulgaria faced a new period of total political chaos for some years. Common opinion has it that for more than two years there was an interregnum in Bulgaria, since the Bulgarian boyar clans could not reach agreement over the succession to the throne, nor could Nogay intervene in these struggles

---

[15] Oberländer-Târnoveanu, 'Num. contr.', pp. 254–5.
[16] For dual governance in the Chingisid realm, see Trepavlov, *Gos. stroj*, esp. ch. 4. I have not undertaken a systematic overview of Islamic coinage, but there are examples of coins struck in the names of two rulers of the Qara-qoyunlu dynasty, e.g. Qara-Yūsuf and his son Pīr Budaq have common coins from 1407 to 1411 (cf. Artuk, *Sikkeler*, II, p. 833).
[17] For the battle of Kügenlik, see Baybars: Tiz., I, pp. 90–1, 113–14, = İzm., pp. 210–13.
[18] Pachym. *Hist.*/Bekker, II, p. 268$_{1-14}$ (III.27).

because of his conflict with Toqta, khan of the Golden Horde. Be that as it may, the chaos in the country and the death of Nogay at the beginning of 1300 enabled Nogay's son Čeke to enter the forefront of Bulgarian events.

These events, subsequent to Nogay's death, are well represented in the Arabic and Byzantine sources. The double testimony of these sources, complemented by the evidence of numismatics, enables us to reconstruct the happenings of these decisive years. To gain a better understanding of the events to be related, we must first be acquainted with Nogay's relatives and surroundings. Nogay had three sons: Čeke and Teke were born to Alakke, and Turay to another woman whose name is unknown from the sources. Nogay also had a daughter called Tuğulǰa (her mother's identity is unknown), who married Taz, the son of Münǰük. Taz was one of the emirs who went over from Toqta to Nogay, who then rewarded him with his daughter's hand.[19] She had a son called Aqtaǰï (whether by Taz or another man cannot be decided from the sources).[20]

After Nogay's death in the devastating battle of Kügenlik, a terrible struggle for the inheritance broke out among his sons, the result of which was their total destruction within eighteen months. Čeke assumed power in all his father's possessions and left his younger brother Teke out of the inheritance, whereupon Teke was offended and endeavoured to go over to Toqta.[21] But the situation was less simple than suggested by Baybars; Teke was not an innocent party ignored and marginalised by his brother. Their enmity went back to earlier times, and according to Rašīd ad-Dīn it was Teke who dealt the first blow to their brotherly relationship. In AH 698 (9 October 1298 to 17 September 1299), Nogay sent his grandson Aqtaǰï to the Crimea to collect tribute from the Genoese of Kaffa. Aqtaǰï was

---

[19] Baybars: Tiz., I, pp. 86, 87, 109, 110, = İzm., pp. 195–6, 199–201.

[20] Baybars: Tiz., I, pp. 86, 109, = İzm., pp. 195–6 (*ǰka, tka, tray, tğlǰa, aqtaǰy, tz bn mnǰk*). The names of the brothers Čeke and Teke are tentative since there are several ways of reading their names. Rašīd ad-Dīn transcribes the first names with a *waw* (Raš./Blochet, pp. 122, 150, = Raš./Khetagurov, II, pp. 75, 86), so the following options for reading them exist: *Jöke, Jöge, Cöke, Cöge, Jeke, Jege, Čeke, Cege*. Similarly, for the second name the following possibilities are given: *Töke, Töge, Tüke, Tüge, Teke, Tege*. Pelliot, *Horde d'Or*, pp. 79–81, preferred the readings *Jögä* and *Tügä*, but I have not found his interpretations of the names convincing. I prefer to use *Čeke* and *Teke* (*Cege* and *Tege* are also possible variants). Both names are known in the Kipchak languages and in Hungarian names of Cuman/Turkic origin (cf. Rásonyi, 'Kuman özel ad.', pp. 99, 129). Regarding the massive stratum of Turkic names among the early Mongolian names, it is quite plausible to interpret the above names as of Turkic origin. In addition, the Byzantine Greek form Τζακᾶς ensures that the original form was with *ä* or *e*, and the form with *ö* or *ü* in Rašīd ad-Dīn, if it really reflected an existing form, must have been secondary (as e.g. *Börke* < *Berke* at Abūlğāzī). Čeke's mother, whose name is known only from Pachymeres as Ἀλάκκη (Pachym. *Hist.*/Bekker, II, p. 264; cf. also *PLP*, no. 536), can probably be identified with Yaylaq (Pelliot, *Horde d'Or*, pp. 73–9).

[21] Baybars: Tiz., I, pp. 91, 115, = İzm., pp. 214–16.

assassinated by the inhabitants of Kaffa, and Nogay's punitive expedition followed: the Tatars pillaged the Crimean towns and took many prisoners.[22] Later, when, in order to meet the demands of the Crimeans, Nogay returned the captives, some of his regiments became annoyed with their leader and planned to go over to Toqta. Some of them sent a message to Teke, promising to raise him to the position of khan if he would join them. When Teke approached them to negotiate, he was captured. Čeke then turned against the rebellious divisions, suppressed them, had one of their leaders decapitated, and sent the head to the troops as a deterrent. Teke, together with 300 men who had captured him, came back to Nogay and Čeke's side.[23] It is evident that after such an interlude the trust between the two brothers was permanently destroyed, and if Teke thought that he had suffered a slight at the hands of his brother it was only a consequence of his former disloyalty. Čeke decided to settle old scores and dispatched a few warriors to kill his brother. They surrounded Teke's tent and tried to stab him to death, but they did not succeed; Teke survived and Čeke was called in to investigate the case. He tried to feign innocence, but Teke uncovered his trick, whereupon Čeke made his man kill Teke – this time making sure that the deed was done. This went down very badly with Čeke's men – not because fratricide was an event unheard of in the Tatar world, but because the guile and cruelty of his deed appalled even the Tatars, and began a process of estrangement among his troops.[24] Soon an internal rebellion broke out against Čeke under the leadership of two of his emirs: Taz, son of Münjük, the husband of Nogay's daughter Tuǧulja; and Toñuz, son of Qačan,[25] who had been appointed regent by Čeke upon his coming to power. Taz and Toñuz had become allies and had launched a marauding expedition against the Bulgars[26] and the Russians. During the campaign they covenanted to turn against their lord Čeke lest he turn against them as he did against his brother Teke. But one of their soldiers overheard them and disclosed their plot to Čeke so that the latter could escape with a small troop of 150 warriors to the country of the Alans or Yas (called *As*

---

[22] Baybars: Tiz., I, pp. 88–9, 111–12, = İzm., pp. 204–05. Rašīd ad-Dīn (Raš./Blochet, p. 148) does not mention Kaffa, but according to him Nogay had devastated the town of Qïrïm (i.e. Solgat).

[23] Raš./Blochet, pp. 148–50.

[24] Baybars: Tiz., I, pp. 91–2, 115–16, = İzm., pp. 214–16.

[25] This name has generally been read as *Tunguz*, but the correct reading is *Toñuz*. For the latter name, known among the Pechenegs and Cumans, see Rásonyi, 'Kuman özel ad.', p. 133.

[26] *Ulaq* is the word used in the Arabic text that can be interpreted as Bulgaria. (For the use of the term *Vlakh* for Bulgaria and the Bulgars, see Chapter 2 of this book.) The interpretations Wallachia (Tiz., I, p. 116; Veselovskij, 'Nogaj', p. 55) or Moldavia (Spuler, *GH*, p. 77. n. 1) are out of place here, since a few lines further on the reference to Tǎrnovo in the same text makes it indisputable that *Ulaq* stands for Bulgaria.

in Baybars). These Yas were faithful allies of Nogay, their territory being at the Lower Danube in what was later known as Moldavia.[27] The Romanian town of *Iaşi* (in Hungarian *Jászvásár*) preserves the memory of their earlier presence in Moldavia.[28] The Yas, representing a military force of 10,000 men, joined Čeke and returned to his homeland, where they clashed with the Tatar troops led by Taz and Toñuz. According to the chronicler, Tuğulǰa herself, the sister of Čeke and wife of Taz, fought fiercely against her husband's army. Taz and Toñuz were beaten and had to turn to Toqta Khan, who sent his brother Bürlük with further troops to aid them. At this juncture in the life-and-death struggle of Čeke and his opponents, Čeke had to decide whether to withstand his enemies or flee. He chose the latter option and fled to Bulgaria.[29]

ČEKE AND TEODOR SVETOSLAV IN BULGARIA

Čeke must have arrived in Bulgaria in the spring of 1300.[30] According to the Arabic sources the king and ruler of Bulgaria (*wa kāna malikuhā wa'l-ḥākimu 'alayhā*)[31] married one of Čeke's relatives. Here the Arabic sources contain a faint and erroneous reminiscence of Čeke's marriage to Teodor Svetoslav's sister. Thus Teodor Svetoslav reappears in the picture.

Teodor Svetoslav, son of George Terter I by a Bulgarian woman, had a hard childhood.[32] Together with his mother he spent more than four years in Nikaia. But after the release of his mother in 1284, the small boy was retained as a hostage by the Byzantines. He was set free a little later when Patriarch Ioakeim was at Byzantium to negotiate a marriage,[33] and Svetoslav was raised to the rank of co-emperor. But a year later Terter was compelled to send his son to Nogay's court as a political hostage. Svetoslav's fate took a further turn for the worse when his father fled to Byzantium and Smilec occupied the Bulgarian throne in 1292. But after Smilec's death in 1298 his situation did not improve; only the marriage of his sister to Čeke safeguarded his political survival. Pachymeres relates some interesting details

---

[27] Brătianu, 'Commerce Génois', p. 43. [28] Iordan, *Toponimia*, pp. 169, 274.

[29] *Ulaq* in the Arabic texts: Baybars (Tiz., I, pp. 93, 117, = İzm., pp. 221, 219), Nuwayrī (Tiz., I, pp. 139, 161, = İzm., pp. 282, 280), Ibn Ḫaldūn (Tiz., I, pp. 370, 384). The reference to the wife of Ulaq's king as Čeke's relative, and the mention of the town of Tărnovo by name confirm that *Ulaq* stands here for Bulgaria.

[30] Oberländer-Tărnoveanu, 'Num. contr.', pp. 256–7.

[31] See Baybars: Tiz., I, pp. 93, 117, = İzm., pp. 221, 219.

[32] 'Svetoslav, being Bulgarian on his maternal side (his father Terter was of Cuman descent)' (Ὀσφεντίσθλαβος, Βούλγαρος ὢν ἐκ μητρὸς (ὁ γὰρ πατὴρ Τερτερῆς ἐκ Κομάνων ἦν)) (Pachym. *Hist.*/Bekker, II, p. 265₈₋₉).

[33] Pachym. *Hist.*/Bekker, II, p. 266 (III.26).

of his life in Tatar exile. Svetoslav became acquainted with a rich merchant called Pantoleon, and soon married his granddaughter, the daughter of a certain Mankousos (presumably Pantoleon's son-in-law).[34] Svetoslav's bride was the goddaughter of Euphrosyne, Nogay's wife and the daughter of Emperor Michael Palaiologos VIII.[35] Judging by their Greek names, Pantoleon and his family must have belonged to the Greek commercial elite of the Black Sea region, and that is why Euphrosyne, Michael Palaiologos' daughter, became the godmother of Pantoleon's granddaughter. Later, back in Bulgaria, Euphrosyne, daughter of Mankousos, was crowned queen as Svetoslav's wife.[36] In 1307 or 1308 Teodor Svetoslav married Theodora Palaiologina, granddaughter of Emperor Andronikos II. Since there is no account of any divorce or of her being sent to a monastery, it seems plausible that Euphrosyne had died between 1301 and 1307.[37]

As we have seen, according to the Arabic sources Čeke fled to his relative, the king and ruler of Bulgaria, and shut himself up in one of his fortresses. Again, however, Pachymeres is better informed, and has left us a more reliable and precise account of the events. Contrary to the Arabic sources, Pachymeres states that Čeke arrived in Tărnovo, together with his wife and his brother-in-law Teodor Svetoslav. So it was a joint venture from which each party benefited: Svetoslav, as son of the former king George Terter I, exploited his contacts with the Bulgarian boyars, while Čeke guaranteed the military power to enforce their will. But Pachymeres leaves us no doubt as to which of them was superior to the other. He writes: 'Having gained the good will of the Bulgars with gifts and recognising Čeke as his lord, together with him he [Svetoslav] took possession of Tărnovo.'[38] This indicates that Svetoslav was not yet ruler of Bulgaria, but only the regent or *locum tenens* of his brother-in-law Čeke. As is known from the evidence of the recently found coins, Čeke had taken the title of khan as early as 1296–7, during his father's lifetime; so now, when he marched to Tărnovo, he evidently regarded himself as the legitimate ruler of Bulgaria. For since the end of 1298 (Smilec's death) there had been no legitimate ruler of Bulgaria. The fact that he was married to George Terter's daughter could have been an equal factor in his acceptance by the Bulgarian boyars and

---

[34] In the former literature (also in Pachym. *Hist.*/Bekker, II, p. 266), Mankousos' daughter is referred to as Enkone, and she was supposedly adopted by the rich Pantoleon. It was Failler, *Euphrosyne*, pp. 92–3, who pointed out that the Greek name Ἐγκόνη is a corruption of the word ἐκγόνη 'granddaughter'; consequently the girl (whose name was probably Euphrosyne after her godmother) was Pantoleon's granddaughter, her mother being Pantoleon's daughter and Mankousos' wife.

[35] Pachym.*Hist.*/Bekker, II, p. 266 (III.26).

[36] She is mentioned in Boril's Sinodik (*Sinodik Borila*, p. 88, no. 120).

[37] Pavlov, 'Pandoleon', pp. 179, 182.   [38] Pachym. *Hist.*/Bekker, II, p. 265 (III.26).

his recognition as the legitimate ruler. Recent numismatic findings from Dobrudja also corroborate the fact that Čeke as self-proclaimed ruler of Bulgaria had his own coinage.[39] In the light of these events one must concur with Oberländer-Târnoveanu's opinion that north-eastern Bulgaria lost its political autonomy for two years after Smilec's death (1298).[40]

But, seemingly, Svetoslav did not forget that he was the son of the former Bulgarian tsar George Terter I. At the first opportunity, backed by Toqta, khan of the Golden Horde, he had Čeke seized and imprisoned in Tărnovo. With Toqta's consent, Svetoslav later made his Jewish servants strangle Čeke. Soon Patriarch Ioakeim also fell on hard times, and was thrown over a cliff, charged with treason.[41]

Thus, by the spring or summer of 1301, Teodor Svetoslav became the Bulgarian tsar. In his person the Cumano-Bulgarian oligarchy restored its power in Bulgaria, and for twenty years a period of relative peace and consolidation again blessed Bulgaria's troubled land. The long Tatar period of Bulgarian history had commenced with a milder form of subjection in 1242–77, which had given way to a period of ever-increasing and provocative Tatar pressure that concluded with the direct Tatar subjection of Bulgaria for two years. But the steep and rapid decline of Nogay and his son Čeke meant the end of the separatistic movement of the Nogayids. The Balkanic lands, especially Bulgaria, though bordering on the territory of the Golden Horde on the Lower Danube, was liberated from direct Tatar menace. The centre of gravity of Tatar power was now located in the Volga region, and the territories stretching to the west of the Bug gradually slipped from the direct control of the Golden Horde. But even later, in the first half of the fourteenth century, the Tatars were often invited by the Bulgarians and Byzantines to supply auxiliary troops to support one or another of the parties in their battles.

[39] Some extremely rare coins of Čeke have recently been found in Romania; for them see K. Khromov's website (www.hordecoins.folgat.net/egalGH-isaqchi.htm) and Bogdan C.'s notes (www.zeno.ru/showphoto.php.?photo=600) (both accessed 9 August 2004). This coin must have been struck in Saqči, during the short time between Nogay's death (AH 699) and Čeke's own death, i.e. some time between 28 September 1299 and 6 September 1301. The legend containing Čeke's name in Greek and the cross appearing on the obverse of the coin are evident signs that this issue was minted to meet the demands of Čeke Khan's new Christian subjects, the Bulgarians and Romanians. The extreme rarity of these coins is easy to explain. Both Nogay and his son Čeke were 'usurper' khans, who, after their defeat at the hands of the legitimate ruler Toqta, suffered a kind of *damnatio memoriae*, so any reminder of their rebellion, including their coinage, had to be annihilated – which meant melting the metal and remoulding it into new coinage.

[40] Oberländer-Târnoveanu, 'Num. contr.', p. 257.

[41] Pachym. *Hist.*/Bekker, ıı, p. 265₅₋₁₆ (ııı.26). The Arabic sources speak only of the fact of Čeke's execution in a Bulgarian prison, and stress that all this happened by Toqta's command; other details are not mentioned (Baybars: İzm., pp. 221, 219; Nuwayrī: İzm., pp. 282, 280–1).

THE FINAL DISAPPEARANCE OF THE NOGAYIDS

After Čeke's execution the Nogayid khanate collapsed. In Bulgaria Teodor Svetoslav fully restored the Terterids' power, while Čeke's *ulus* was given to the regency of Toqta's brother Saray-Buǧa. Toqta Khan's two sons Tükel-Buǧa and İlbasar were sent to Nogay's former country (*bilād Noghayya*). Tükel-Buǧa became the governor of Saqčï (Isaccea) and the region between the Danube and the Iron Gate (*bāb al-ḥadīd*),[42] while İlbasar was sent to the river Yayik (Ural).[43]

But Toqta could not be safe while Turay, the third son of Nogay, was still alive. And Turay really wanted to avenge his brothers' death. He insinuated himself into the confidence of the new regent, Saray-Buǧa, and systematically instigated him to wrest the khanal power from his brother Toqta. But this plot of Saray-Buǧa and Turay was soon exposed by Bürlük (brother of Toqta and Saray-Buǧa), whereupon Toqta put down their rebellion and had both the instigators killed. Saray-Buǧa's regency was taken over by Toqta's son, İlbasar.[44]

But the drama of Nogay and his sons was not yet completely over. Though all three sons of Nogay were dead, Čeke's son (Nogay's grandson), Qara-Kesek, was still alive. Together with two of his relatives, Čerik-Temir and Yol-Qutlu, he escaped to the south. Toqta sent his brother Bürlük to chase and capture them. Qara-Kesek and his team fled to the country of Šišman (*bilād Šišman*) to a place called Bdl, near Krk, together with 3,000 horsemen. Šišman settled them in his country, where they were still living in the time of the historiographer Baybars (d. 1325).[45] 'Šišman's country' evidently refers to Vidin and its surroundings, a semi-independent Bulgarian despotate in 1301–2 when Qara-kesek appeared in that country. The names Bdl and Krk must therefore be emended to Bdn near Krl, and read as Bdin, or Bodun, and Kerel. The former name evidently renders Vidin, and the latter is the Arabic-Persian name of the Hungarian and Polish kings in the Mongol period, and hence of their respective countries (Hungarian *király* and Polish *król*, 'king').[46] Earlier scholars, including Spuler, inter-

[42] This Iron Gate evidently refers to the Iron Gate at the Lower Danube and has nothing to do with the Iron Gate in Derbend on the Caspian Sea, as İzmirli claimed (İzm., p. 219, n. 1). Derbend is always called *Bāb al-abwāb* in the Arabic sources, cf. *İA*, III, pp. 532–9 (W. Barthold); *EI*, II, pp. 835–6 (M. Dunlop); *TDV İA*, IX, pp. 164–6 (S. M. Aliyev).
[43] Baybars: Tiz., I, pp. 93, 117, = İzm. pp. 221, 219; Nuwayrī: Tiz., I, pp. 138–9, 160–1, = İzm. pp. 282, 280–1.
[44] Baybars: Tiz., I, pp. 93–4, 118–19, = İzm., pp. 222–4; Nuwayrī: Tiz., I, pp. 139–40, 161–2, = İzm., pp. 283–4.
[45] Baybars: Tiz., I, pp. 94, 119, = İzm. pp. 225, 223; Nuwayrī: Tiz., I, pp. 140, 162, = İzm. pp. 283–4.
[46] Cf. Pelliot, *Horde d'Or*, pp. 116ff.; Ligeti, 'Magyar, baskír, király'.

preted the names erroneously as Budul (for Podolia) and Kerek (for Cracaw), and deduced that Qara-Kesek's Tatars settled in Podolia.[47] The fact is
that Nogay's grandson Qara-Kesek migrated to Vidin with 3,000 warriors
and, as we shall see in Chapter 8, this Tatar contingent made a considerable contribution to the military victories of both Šišman and his son, Tsar
Michael Šišman.

Parallel to the gradual dwindling of the once feared Tatar warriors from
the life of the Balkans, a new, even more powerful conqueror was in the
making. While Nogay was at the apogee of his powers in 1280–1300, over
in Söğüt and Bilecik, villages of western Anatolia, Osman the son of a small
tribal chief called Ertuğrul, was growing up to be a *ghāzī*, a valiant fighter
of the Muslim faith. Who could have foretold in Tărnovo, when the Tatar
rule ceased in 1301, that in less than a hundred years Osman's sons would
rule Bulgaria for more than five centuries?

---

[47] İzm., p. 223 (Budul and Kırakof); Spuler, *GH*, pp. 79, 297 (Budūl/Podolien, Krakau). Pelliot, *Horde d'Or*, pp. 116ff., corrected the reading 'Krk' to 'Krl', and read *Kerel* instead of *Krak*, but he did not recognise the name of Vidin in 'Bdl'. It was Schütz, 'Könige', p. 262, then Pavlov, 'Nogai', p. 127, who were the first rightly to identify the two names.

CHAPTER SIX

Cumans and Tatars on the Serbian scene

The Serbians, who belonged to the western branch of the southern Slavs, had long lived under their tribal chiefs, called *knezes*, between the political spheres of power of Byzantium and Bulgaria. After the fall of the First Bulgarian Empire in 1018, Serbia became an autonomous territorial unit (Serbian *župa*) within the Byzantine Empire, under the rule of a Serbian grand župan nominated by Byzantium. In respect of religion, the Serbian Orthodox Church was part of the autocephalous archbishopric of Ohrid. The power of an independent Serbia began to rise during the rule of Grand Župan Nemanja, at the end of the twelfth century. His son Stefan Nemanjić became the first independent Serbian ruler whose international recognition was assured by his coronation as king of Serbia by the legate of Pope Honorius III in 1217. (That is why he was later given the epithet *prvovenčani*, 'first crowned'.) The autonomous Serbian Church was established a few years later in 1219, when Stefan Prvovenčani's brother Sava Nemanjić created an autonomous Serbian archbishopric under the direct jurisdiction of the patriarchate of Constantinople, at that time exiled in Nikaia. Serbia emerged as a truly great power in the Balkans under the long reign of Stefan Uroš I (1243–76).[1]

CUMANS AT GACKO, 1276

The first appearance of Cumans on the Serbian scene came about as a result of their Serbo-Hungarian contacts. King Stephen V of Hungary (reigned 1270–2) gave his daughter Catherine, by his wife Elisabeth who was the daughter of the Cuman chief Seyhan, in marriage to Stefan Dragutin, elder son of King Stefan Uroš I.[2] According to Danilo's Chronicle,

---

[1] For all these events of early Serbian history see Jireček, *Serb.*, I, pp. 210–326; Jiriček, *Ist. Srba*, I, pp. 121–86.

[2] On this marriage see Danilo/Daničić, pp. 13–14 (Danilo/Mirković, p. 14; Danilo/Hafner, p. 63). Among other sources, only the *Chronicon Posoniense* mentions this event (*SRH*, II, p. 46), and the Byzantine Pachymeres (Pachym. *Hist.*/Bekker, I, p. 350).

Uroš promised both his son and the Hungarian king that he would make Dragutin king even during Uroš' own lifetime, but later declined to do so. His disappointed son then turned to his father-in-law, the Hungarian King Stephen V, who seemed ready to lend him his Hungarian and Cuman troops: '"I will give you my forces to your aid as much as you want." So he took great forces of Hungarians and Cumans, and set out hurriedly with his numerous troops.'[3] After a repeated refusal on the part of his father, in the autumn of 1276 Dragutin clashed with his father's forces in Gacko (an important commercial centre at that time, in Herce-govina on the Dubrovnik–Foča route, now known as Gacko or Gatačko Polje), and gained the upper hand. After this, Dragutin became king of Serbia. Though it seems evident that Hungarian and Cuman auxiliaries took part in Dragutin's battles, it is not certain whether they were present at the battle of Gacko. Since King Stephen V died on 6 August 1272, and the battle of Gacko took place more than four years later, a degree of chronological fuzziness can be observed in the Serbian source. But the fact that Cuman auxiliaries of the Hungarian king were sent to Dragutin's aid cannot be questioned. After King Stephen V's death, his son Ladislas IV, the Cuman (Kún László in Hungarian), became king, and continued to support Dragutin, his brother-in-law.

CUMANS IN ŽIČA

Cuman auxiliaries must have been present in Serbia on different sides of the fighting factions from the 1270s. Moreover, as often happened with nomadic warriors, they must have disregarded the orders of the party they were sup-posed to be fighting for, and acted on their own, looting and marauding the countryside. This can be corroborated by a remark of Danilo, Archbishop of Peć (Ipek) from 1323 to 1337. He tells of the renovation of Žiča, the former see of the archbishopric of the Serbian Church, the see having been transferred to Peć in 1253 by Archbishop Arsenije. According to Danilo, Žiča had been destroyed by the Cumans and had long lain in ruins before it was renovated. He writes as follows:

The holy place called House of the Saviour, which is the great and first-founded Serbian Archbishopric of Serbia in Žiča (*Zhid'cha*), formerly stood for a long time in desolation owing to the attack of the godless Cuman people (*ezyka kuman'ska*),

---

[3] 'Eliko khošteši, dam' ti sily von moikh' v' pomošt' tebe. I tako poem' sily mnogye ezyka ugr'skaago i kuman'skaago, i ide t'št'no vode s' soboju veliku pobedu' (Danilo/Daničić, p. 17; Danilo/Mirković, p. 16; see also Danilo/Hafner, p. 66).

and it was totally burnt with fire. Afterwards, during the reign of the God-fearing king Uroš and in the days of the holy archbishop Jevstatije II, that place was renovated, but not to such a degree as it was formerly.[4]

The name 'Uroš' refers here to King Stefan Uroš II (Milutin), since Archbishop Jevstatije II held the archbisopric from 1292 to 1309. Consequently, the *terminus ante quem* of the Cuman incursion is 1292; it must have taken place at any time between 1276 and 1292. Therefore a link with the marauding campaign of Šišman's Bulgar-Tatarian forces against Peć (see further below) is improbable, despite the opinion of Jireček.[5]

TATARS AT THE DRIM, 1282

In 1282 the short reign of King Stefan Dragutin came to an end when he was compelled to abdicate and hand over the throne to his younger brother Milutin, who assumed the name Stefan Uroš II. Milutin's long rule (1282–1321) was a period of conquest and further strengthening of the Serbian state. Immediately after seizing royal power he marched to the southern borders of the Serbian state, in present-day Kosovo-Metohija. The Byzantine sphere of power extended to the north as far as Lipljan in Kosovo Polje (Ulpiana, later Iustiniana Secunda of the Roman and Byzantine periods). Milutin proceeded southwards, to northern Macedonia, which was an integral part of Byzantium at that time, and conquered Gornji and Donji Polog (by the upper courses of the Vardar river), Skopje, Ovče Polje (a territory south of present-day Kumanovo, surrounded by the rivers Pčinja, Vardar, Zletovska reka and Bregalnica), Zletovo, and Pijanec (two territorial units in north-west Macedonia, the latter by the upper courses of Bregalnica, with Delčevo as its centre).[6] Consequently, a considerable part of northern Macedonia was conquered by the Serbs. It was just at this time that the Byzantine emperor, Michael Palaiologos VIII, decided to invite Nogay's Tatars to punish the unruly John I of Thessaly. The emperor himself set out hastily with a sizeable army of Byzantine warriors and, according to Archbishop Danilo, was accompanied by auxiliary troops of Tatars, Turks and Franks.[7] But at a distance of three days' march from Constantinople, in Allage, near Rhaidestos (Tekirdağ), the emperor died unexpectedly,

---

[4] Danilo/Daničić, pp. 371–2; see also Danilo/Mirković, p. 283.

[5] Jireček, *Serb.*, I, p. 335; Jiriček, *Ist Srba*, I, p. 192.

[6] 'Pr'vee priet' oba Pologa s' gradovy ikh' i s' oblastiju, i grad' slavnyi Skopie, po sikh' že Ov'če Pole i Zletovu i Pijan'c'' (Danilo/Daničić, pp. 108–9).

[7] 'Mnogy inoplemen'ny ezyky, tatary i tur'ky i frugy' (Danilo/Daničić, p. 110; see also Danilo/Hafner, p. 153).

without having shown any symptoms of illness, on 11 December 1282. His body was first sent to Selymbria (Silivri), and the military expedition against Thessaly was cancelled. The new emperor, Andronikos II, decided to send the Tatar warriors against the Serbs. They marched under the guidance of the Grand Constable Michael Glabas[8] to the Serbian–Byzantine frontier near Lipljan and Prizren. Then a contingent of the Tatar troops continued to the river Drim and tried to cross it by throwing themselves, together with their horses, into the fast-flowing torrent. But because the water was deep, most of them were drowned. Their chief, called *Čr'noglava*, 'Black Head', was first captured, and then his head, embellished with pearls, was severed from his body, stuck on a spear, and presented to King Milutin.[9] It is noteworthy that the name *Čr'noglava*, 'Black Head', must be a Slavic translation of a Tatar-Turkic name, *Qara-Baš*, with the same meaning.[10] (The Byzantine background to this event was set out more fully in Chapter 4.)

CUMANS AND TATARS IN THE BATTLES AT BRANIČEVO, 1284

When Dragutin was compelled to hand over his throne to his younger brother Milutin in 1282, the act of abdication took place in Deževo, one of the places inhabited by the Nemanjids in Rascia.[11] But Dragutin did not withdraw from the political scene; certain parts of northern Rascia, such as Rudnik and Arilje, remained in his possession, and he made a special effort to extend his power northwards to the buffer zone stretching along the south of the Hungarian Kingdom, between the Hungarian and Byzantine spheres of interest. This vast territory, lying south of the Danube, comprised different territorial administrative units organised into semi-independent provinces by the Hungarian kings during the thirteenth century. These provinces were called *bánság* in Hungarian (the territory of the *ban*, = banate), and had been created to defend the southern frontier of Hungary. Proceeding from west to east, we must first mention the northern parts of Bosnia. The territory called Usora (*Ozora* in Hungarian) lay between the rivers Sava, Vrbas and Drina, to the north of Bosnia proper. The heart of this territory was the Usora, a tributary of the river Bosna on the left. Soli (*Só* in Hungarian) was the area around the present-day Tuzla. Both Usora

---

[8] Nik. Greg. *Hist.*/Schoppen-Bekker, I, p. 159 (VI.1.), = Nik. Greg. *Hist.*/van Dieten, I, p. 144. For Michael Glabas' person and career, see Nik. Greg. *Hist.*/van Dieten, I, p. 265, n. 268.

[9] Danilo/Daničić, p. 112; see also Danilo/Hafner, p. 155.

[10] Rásonyi-Baski, p. 83. For further data of *qarabaš/qaravaš*, 'slave, servant', see Radloff, *USp.*, nos. 61, 73, 110; Clauson, *ED*, pp. 643–4.

[11] Danilo/Hafner, pp. 73, 75.

and Soli were donated by King Andrew II of Hungary to Ugrin, Archbishop of Kalocsa, in 1224, in order to purge these areas of heretics. Both territories became Hungarian banates some time after the Tatar invasion of Eastern and Southern Europe in 1241/2. In 1253, after the Bosnian campaign of King Béla IV, Usora and Soli fell under the jurisdiction of Rostislav Mihailovič, former Prince of Černigov, son-in-law of the Hungarian king Béla IV by marriage to his daughter Anna. The territory between the Sava, Drina and Kolubara rivers was called Mačva (*Macsó* in Hungarian). Its preponderantly Slavic population was first (in the ninth and tenth centuries) under Bulgarian suzerainty, and then from 1018 onwards under that of Byzantium. The ecclesiastical jurisdiction of Sirmium (Sremska Mitrovica) was extended to what was later to become Mačva, and was often called Sirmia Ulterior, as contrasted with Sirmia Citerior (*Szerém* or *Szerémség* within the Hungarian Kingdom). Prince Rostislav, who bore the title *dux de Macho*, had been given Mačva in 1247, before he gained Usora and Soli.[12] In 1280/4, all three banates were in the possession of Elizabeth, the Cuman queen dowager of King Béla IV; she was called 'Princess of Mačva and Bosnia'. After 1284, Usora, Soli and Mačva fell to Dragutin through his wife Catherine, the daughter of Elizabeth (the queen dowager herself died only later in 1290). He took up residence in Debrac, near the river Sava, between Šabac and Belgrade. According to Danilo, Mačva was originally given to Dragutin by his father-in-law King Stephen V.[13] Probably all three of the provinces that came to Dragutin from Elizabeth had been part of Catherine's dowry. This large area, ruled by Dragutin, was called *Srem* in the Serbian sources, and we must distinguish it carefully from the town and county in the Hungarian Kingdom (*Szerém* in Hungarian) that lay between the Danube and the Sava.[14]

By the acquisition of Usora, Soli and Mačva, Dragutin became lord of a large territory which he immediately tried to expand eastwards. His declared aim was to create a 'northern' Serbian state by uniting the provinces south of the Danube, thereby counterbalancing his brother Milutin's 'southern' Serbian state. East of the river Morava there were two territories named Braničevo and Kučevo (*Barancs* and *Kucsó* in Hungarian) after their central towns. Like Mačva, Braničevo was also originally (in the ninth and tenth centuries) under Bulgarian suzerainty, and then from 1018 onwards

---

[12] For a short overview of the history of Usora, Soli and Mačva, see *KMTL*, pp. 518, 603, 421–2 (s.vv. *Ozora, Só*, and *Macsó*).

[13] Danilo/Hafner, p. 76.

[14] For example, Milutin sent his brother Dragutin 'v' dr'žavu ego zemlju srem'skuju' (Danilo/Daničić, p. 113; see also Danilo/Hafner, p. 156). For the difference between the two Srems see Dinić, 'Odnos'.

under that of Byzantium. After Bulgaria regained its independence, from the beginning of the thirteenth century Braničevo fell alternately under Bulgarian and Hungarian rule. From 1272 onwards, Braničevo became a Hungarian banate, but soon its overlords, the brothers Dorman and Kudelin, became independent.[15] The unfaithfulness and separation of the two oligarchs in Braničevo must have irritated the Hungarian king Ladislas IV, while Dragutin, as indicated above, had his eye on the disobedient vassals of the Hungarian king. So the Hungarians and Serbs had a common interest in crushing the rebellious brothers of Braničevo. But we must not forget that after the turmoil of Ivaylo's rebellion and the ascension to the throne of the new Terter dynasty in 1280, the political dependence of the Bulgarian lands on the Tatars had loosened, so the Tatars had an interest in supporting Dorman and Kudelin against the Hungarian and Serbian attack.

But who were these brothers, born of one mother?[16] Their names are given by Archbishop Danilo as *Dr'man* and *Kudelin*.[17] In a Latin diploma of King Ladislas IV, issued in 1285, the first name appears as *Dorman(us)*.[18] The name *Kudelin* is of Slavic origin (from *kuděl'*, *kudělja*, 'oakum, tow'), while *Dorman* is a Turkic name widely used by the Pechenegs and the Cumans;[19] as a personal name it has been preserved both in Hungary and in Wallachia and Moldavia.[20] There are four occurrences of geographical names deriving from the personal name *Dorman*, two in Moldavia, one in Wallachia, and one in Hungary.[21] All these data amply demonstrate the Turkic (Cuman) origin of the name *Dorman*. The Cuman and Slavic names of the brothers in Braničevo clearly indicate the social and cultural

---

[15] 'Obretosta se dva neka vel'muža ukoreniv'ša se v' dr'žave zemle braničev'skye v' meste rekomem' Ždrele, i ot mnogyikh' vremen' tu utvr'div'ša se samovlastna sušta, i nikoegož' nasilija boešta se, brata edinye matere, iže glagolju Dr'mana i Kudelina' (Danilo/Daničić, p. 115). Ždrelo was a fortress in Gornjačka Klisura, near the Mlava river, now in ruins.

[16] 'Brata edinye matere' (Danilo/Daničić, p. 115).

[17] 'Dr'mana i Kudelina' (Danilo/Daničić, p. 115).

[18] 'Ad Dormanum', 'Dormani': Gyárfás, II, p. 451 (no. 79). For more on this diploma, see further below.

[19] The Turkic name is a derivative of the verb *tur-/dur-*, 'to stand', meaning 'steady, steadfast, persistent'; see Rásonyi, *Kuman özel ad.*, p. 103.

[20] Some of the data for the personal name are as follows: 1364: 'Johannis dicti Dorman vicecastellani de Crassofew' (Hurm., 1/2, p. 88); 1499: 'dočka Petra Dr"mana' (Bogdan, *DSM*, II, p. 166); etc. All these data were collected by Rásonyi, 'Val.-Turc.', p. 19.

[21] 1. *Dărmăneşti*, c. 15 km north-west of Suceava, on the left bank of the river Suceava. 2. *Dărmăneşti*, c. 25 km north of the Ojtoz Pass (Pas Oituz), near the Tatroş river, its old Hungarian name being *Dormánfalva*, 'Dorman's village'; in the middle of the nineteenth century 250 Hungarian Catholics inhabited the village (Jerney, *Kel. ut.*, I, p. 173). 3. *Dărmăneşti*, between Ploieşti and Tîrgovişte, c. 10 km from both. 4. *Dormánd*, a settlement in the county of Heves (Hungary), formerly (fourteenth and fifteenth centuries) called *Dormánháza*, 'Dorman's house' (*FNESz*, p. 185; Gyárfás, II, p. 358. Formerly, the original name of this village was *Bogorbesenyő* (Györffy, *Geogr. hist.*, III, p. 72) which also points in the direction of Pecheneg settlers.

background of the Bulgarian lands in the Second Bulgarian Empire. A considerable number of the Bulgarian political elite were of Cuman origin, and this must have been the case with the brothers of Braničevo. Dorman and Kudelin, then, were either Cuman warriors in Bulgarian service or Bulgarian boyars of Cuman origin, who became partly or totally Bulgarised.

Dragutin soon launched an attack against the brothers of Braničevo, but met with no success. Moreover, as might have been foreseen, Dorman and Kudelin turned to the Cumans and Tatars for help, hiring them as auxiliary troops.[22] In his position, hard pressed by the enemy, Dragutin turned to his brother King Milutin. They met in Mačkovci (today Mačkovac) on the river Morava in the župa Rasina, and with Milutin's help Dragutin was able to secure victory over Dorman and Kudelin.[23]

The Serbian sources do not mention the role of King Ladislas IV of Hungary, but it is obvious from Hungarian sources that the Hungarian king also intervened in the affair of Braničevo on the side of his brother-in-law Dragutin. In his diploma issued on 8 January 1285, King Ladislas IV donated the royal villages Sóvár, Sópatak and Delne (in County Sáros) to Master George, son of Simon (*Magister Georgius filius Symonis*) (the ancestor of the later Sóvári family) as a reward for services rendered to the king.[24] Among Magister Georgius' noble deeds that were worthy of remuneration, mention is made of his participation in the battles against Dorman and the Bulgars, together with the Transylvanian and Cuman contingents of the king (*cum nostros homines fideles Transilvanos una cum Comanis nostris contra Dormanum et Bulgaros misyssemus*).[25] So the Hungarian king continued to negotiate with the rebellious oligarchs of Braničevo, and when that strategy failed he sent his Transylvanian and Cuman troops against them. It seems that Cuman warriors took part in the fights on both the Bulgarian-Tatar and the Hungarian-Serbian sides; their light cavalry must have been indispensable for both.

---

[22] 'S'v'kupiše okolo sebe voisku mnogu ezyka tatar'ska i kumany, zlato dav'še im'; i s' simi edin-oduš'no istr'miše se na dr'žavu sego blagoč'stivaago kralja Stefana' (Danilo/Daničić, p. 115; see also Danilo/Hafner, p. 158).

[23] Danilo/Daničić, pp. 115–16; see also Danilo/Hafner, pp. 158–9.

[24] For the best edition of the diploma preserved in a later *vidimus* of King Louis the Great (2 October 1367) in the Hungarian National Archives, Budapest (Dl. 57357), see Györffy, 'Román állam', pp. 14–16. For the transmission of other copies and falsifications, and further literature, see *ibid.*, pp. 17–19.

[25] Györffy, 'Román állam', p. 15, = Gyárfás, II, 451 (no. 79). Györffy ('Román állam', p. 544 and p. 15, n. 67) failed to recognise that this Dorman was identical with the Dorman of the Serbian sources, and supposed, without any sound proof, that Dorman must have been a Cuman chief of Cumania east of the river Olt.

To clarify the chronology of these events in Braničevo is not an easy task. The *terminus ante quem* is fixed at 8 January 1285, the date of the charter of King Ladislas IV. The *terminus post quem* is also fixed by the same diploma; before recounting the event concerning Dorman, the king refers to his expedition against his rebellious Cumans.[26] But when did this Hungarian military action take place? There was much confusion in Hungarian historiography regarding the date of the expedition, until Györffy made it clear that there were two Hungarian clashes with the Cumans, one in 1280 and the other in 1282.[27] The first took place some time before 11 November 1280, when the king moved south in Hungary as far as Szalánkemén (Slankamen) in the county of Szerém, and was able to dissuade his rebellious Cumans from leaving the country. The second event was a decisive battle between the Cuman rebels and the king's forces, which took place at Lake Hód (in the county of Csanád, in southern Hungary).[28] The chronology of this battle perplexed Hungarian historians, and they wavered between 1280 and 1282, but recently A. Zsoldos succeeded in proving that the Battle of Hód must have taken place between 17 September and 21 October 1282.[29] The Hungarian king's Hungarian and Cuman troops must therefore have marched against Dorman and Kudelin some time between October 1282 and 1284, and the forces of Dragutin and Milutin must have fought against the rebellious brothers at the same time. This is corroborated by the fact that Dragutin abdicated the Serbian throne in favour of Milutin in 1282, so their fights against Braničevo probably took place later. The itinerary of King Ladislas IV enables us to give an even more precise date for the Hungarian king's unpleasant encounter with Dorman. The year 1283 can surely be excluded, as there is no hint in the documents of any journey by the king to the south of Hungary. But in April and May 1284 there are several references to the king's stay in southern Hungary, and in mid-May he was in the vicinity

---

[26] 'Item in expeditione nostra, quam contra infideles Comanos nostros habuimus, idem magister Georgius ante oculos nostre maiestatis in ipsos, tanquam leo fortis irruit, ubi equi subsidii destitutus, in ipsa area certaminis acerbissime preliavit et diversa ibidem vulnera recepit sagittarum atque lancearum' (Györffy, 'Román állam', p. 15, = Gyárfás, II, p. 451).

[27] Györffy, 'Román állam', p. 15, n. 65.

[28] For the exact location of *Hód*, see Györffy, *Geogr. hist*, I, pp. 858–9 (s.v. *Hódvásárhely*).

[29] According to the *Chronicon Pictum*, *Chronicon Budense* and *Chronicon Posoniense* (*SRH*, I, p. 471) the battle is placed under 1282 (cf. Karácsonyi, 'Hódtavi csata'); but, drawing on the evidence of King Ladislas IV's diplomas dated 1280, Szabó, *Kun László*, pp. 99–100, and in his wake Pauler, *Árp.*, II, p. 561 (n. 251), and Hóman-Szekfű, I, pp. 604–5, corrected the date 1282 to 1280. The decisive arguments in favour of the autumn of 1282 were put forward by Zsoldos, *Téténytől a Hód-tóig, passim*, esp. p. 96.

of the Serbian border, near Dorman's province in Braničevo.[30] Consequently, it is reasonable to suppose that King Ladislas IV's unsuccessful meeting with Dorman took place somewhere near the Hungarian–
Serbian border in mid-May 1284, and the subsequent punitive royal
expedition against Dorman, led by George Sóvári, followed in the second
half of 1284.

ŠIŠMAN'S TATARS AGAINST THE SERBS IN VIDIN, 1290–1300

Like Braničevo, Vidin too was the target of Serbian expansionist policies to
the east. At the end of the thirteenth century, Vidin was a semi-independent
Bulgarian principality under the political control of the Tatars. In 1280,
when the Bulgarian boyars raised Terter, the protégé of the Cuman lobby,
to the throne in Tărnovo, another Cuman boyar, Šišman, became sovereign
of the western Bulgarian principality of Vidin. The Serbian archbishop
Danilo reports on this as follows: 'At that time in the land of the Bulgars a
prince called Šišman emerged. He lived in the town of Vidin, and obtained
the adjacent countries and much of the Bulgarian land.'[31]

Šišman, together with his Tatar and other troops, invaded Milutin's
Serbia and advanced as far as Hvostno, a *župa* on the White Drim river
(now in Kosovo-Metohija). The Bulgars could not capture Ždrelo, and
drew back to Vidin.[32] But Milutin pursued them to Vidin and devastated
the town and the land, and Šišman fled to the woods on the opposite side
of the Danube. But having punished and reprimanded Šišman, Milutin
soon replaced him on his throne on the condition that he would become
Šišman's faithful ally. The political alliance was sealed by the marriage of
Šišman and the daughter of the Serbian grand župan Dragoš. Moreover,
Milutin later gave his daughter Anna as wife to Šišman's son Michael, who
later, in 1323, became Tsar of Bulgaria.[33]

---

[30] On 24 April 1284 the king's diploma was dated in Pankota in the county of Zaránd; on 3–4 May
1284 in Érdsomlyó in the county of Krassó (identical with today's Vršac in Serbia); on 18 May the
king was in Och in the county of Krassó (Györffy, *Geogr. hist.*, III, p. 477). I am grateful to P. Engel
for drawing my attention to these data.

[31] 'V'sta bo v' ta vremena v' zemli b"lgar'scei knjaz' nek'to glagolemyi Šišman', živy v' grade rekomem'
B'dini, predr'že okr'st'nye strany i mnogy zemle bl'gar'skye' (Danilo/Daničić, p. 117; see also
Danilo/Hafner, pp. 159–60). For the history of the principality of Vidin, see Nikov, *Vidin.
knjaž.*

[32] Danilo/Daničić, p. 117. The town of Ždrelo, mentioned here, is a place at Rugovska Klisura, near
Peć, the see of the Serbian archbishopric; not to be confused with another Ždrelo, in Braničevo (for
the latter see n. 15).

[33] Danilo/Daničić, pp. 118–19; see also Danilo/Hafner, pp. 160–2.

While the chronology of these events cannot be established exactly, the clashes between Šišman and Milutin must have taken place, in all probability, in the last decade of the thirteenth century.

STEFAN UROŠ AS A TATAR HOSTAGE

Since Prince Nogay's territory bordered on the Danube and his sphere of interest extended to the right bank of the Danube, to the principalities of Tărnovo, Vidin and Braničevo, it was only a question of time before he would engage in conflict with the Serbian power that was seeking expansion to the east. Some time between 1290 and 1300, Nogay launched a campaign against Milutin's Serbia, but this time the Serbian ruler succeeded in averting the imminent Tatar danger by offering Nogay his son Stefan (the future king Stefan Uroš III of Dečani) as a hostage. Milutin's son, together with his Serbian entourage, spent a long time in Nogay's court and returned only some years later.[34] In addition to its appearance in Archbishop Danilo's work, this event is also mentioned in a Serbian diploma (*hrisobul*) of King Milutin.[35] Archmandrite Leonid places this event in 1296, the year following Milutin's Greek campaign.[36] According to Jireček, Milutin's son Stefan Uroš was able to return from the Tatars only after Nogay's death in 1299.[37] Be that as it may, with Nogay's death the heavy pressure on the Balkanic lands was relieved. Though the sphere of interest of the Golden Horde extended to the Balkanic lands, after the crushing of Nogay's local power the Tatars were able to enforce their interest from the centre of the empire with less intensity than Nogay had done previously.

TATAR AND YAS TROOPS ON MOUNT ATHOS, 1307–1311

In the first decade of the thirteenth century, the Catalan Company played a key role in the history of Byzantium. After the unsuccessful fights of Byzantium's Alan (Yas) mercenaries against the Turks in Anatolia, the Catalan Company offered their services to the Byzantine emperor. In 1303 they liberated the town of Philadelphia, but soon the Catalonians began to plunder the countryside and captured the Byzantine town of Magnesia. Though they withdrew to the European coast in Kallioupolis by the end of 1304, they were dissatisfied and restless because of the irregularity of the Byzantine payments for their services. Following the assassination of Roger

---

[34] Danilo/Daničić, p. 122; see also Danilo/Hafner, pp. 164–5.
[35] Grigorovič, *Donesenie*, pp. 81–2.
[36] Leonid, 'Han Nagaj', p. 36. Cf. also Veselovskij, 'Nogaj', pp. 41–2; Spuler, *GH*, p. 74.
[37] Jireček, *Serb.*, I, p. 336; Jiriček, *Ist Srba*, I, p. 192.

de Flor, the chief of the Catalan Company, by the Byzantines in April 1305, the Catalans openly turned against their former Byzantine employers, and in Apros they defeated the Byzantine army, which was strongly supported by Turkish and Alan mercenaries. Afterwards, the Catalans began to loot and pillage Thrace; they then marched to the Rodope Mountains, where they settled in Kassandreia in the autumn of 1307.[38] They continued their raids as far as the monasteries of Athos.

It was during these troubled years that the future Serbian Archbishop Danilo II served as igumen of the Serbian Hilandar Monastery on Mount Athos, in 1306–11.[39] In his biography he describes the barbarian attacks on Mount Athos and the ensuing misery and famine. Comparing the events of his day to the sufferings of Jerusalem under the Emperor Titus, he writes:

Such a horror could be seen when the Holy Mountain was ravaged at the hand of the foe. The godless peoples, such as the Franks and Turks, Yas and Tatars, Mogovars and Catalans, and various other peoples, fell on the Holy Mountain. They set fire to many holy churches, stole all the riches piled up in them and took away the captives to work. Those who remained there died of famine. No one was there to bury them, and the beasts of earth and the birds of heaven were feeding on their flesh.[40]

The different names of the marauding troops may refer to different actions perpetrated by them in the years after 1307. The Tatars and Yas (Alans) could have participated in these actions either jointly or separately; the mention of ethnonyms in pairs is merely a stylistic device in Danilo's text (although the Tatars and the Yas, the two oriental mercenary groups, often took part together in many warlike actions of the fourteenth century).[41]

---

[38] For a short description of the Catalans' role in Byzantium, with further literature, see Ostrogorsky, *Gesch.*, pp. 353–6 (406–9).

[39] The events of his life (c. 1270–1337) are well known from his biography; see Danilo/Hafner, pp. 32–4, 48, n. 42; Cf. also Živojinović, 'Zitije Danila'.

[40] 'Takovyi bo užas' be videti togda suštee zapustenie Svetye Gory ot' ruky s'protiv'nyih'. Sim' bo bezbož'nyim' ezykom', eže frugy i turky, jasi že i tatari, mogovari že i katalani i pročii mnogoimen-ovanii ezyci priš'd'še togda na Svetuju Goru mnogye hramy svetye ognem' zažegoše i v'se s'branoe ih' bogat'stvo rashytiše i pl'n'niki vedoše v'rabotu, pročee že ostan'ky ih' ljutenčeju s'mr'tiju gladaa s'kon'čavaahu se. ne be že pogrebae ih', n' zverie zemnii i p'tice nebesnye pitaahu se ot' pl'ti ih" (Danilo/Daničić, pp. 341–2; see also Danilo/Mirković, p. 259). The Slavic plural form *Mogovari* comes from *Almugavar(es)*, the name of the Catalan infantry; cf. Novaković, *Srbi i turci*, p. 62, n. 1; Schlumberger, *Almugavares*. The *Yas* were erroneously identified as an Anatolian Turkic tribe by Novaković, *Srbi i turci*, p. 62, n. 1; Danilo/Mirković, p. 298; later corrected by M. Ćirković, in Novaković, *Srbi i turci*, p. 437.

[41] Consequently, the occurrence of the two ethnonyms does not entail that the Catalans and the Yas took part in joint actions. So Jireček's doubt (namely that the Yas could not be the Catalans' ally, because of their enmity going back to the time of the Anatolian campaign) is pointless: the text does not speak of their alliance (cf. M. Ćirković, in Novaković, *Srbi i turci*, p. 437).

TATAR AND YAS TROOPS IN MILUTIN'S SERVICE, 1311–1314

In 1311 King Dragutin launched a battle against his brother King Milutin to secure the Serbian throne for his son. (According to Guillaume Adam this son was Vladislav, while Danilo refers to Urošic as the possible heir to the throne).[42] Most of the Serbian nobility backed Dragutin, yet it was Milutin who gained the upper hand. Milutin's state treasury was housed in St Stephen's monastery in Banjska, and in 1311–14 the Bishop of Banjska was Milutin's confidant Danilo (the later Archbishop Danilo II). With the help of this money Milutin was able to hire Tatar, Yas and Turkish mercenaries (*mnogye voinsky ezyka tatar'ska i turs'ka i jaš'ska*), and thus win the fight against Dragutin.[43] After his victory, Nikodim, the igumen of Hilandar Monastery (Danilo's successor in this post) was sent to Constantinople to petition the Byzantine emperor to negotiate peace between the two feuding royal brothers of Serbia.[44]

TATARS AND YAS IN THE BATTLE OF VELBUŽD, 1330

As we have noted, Nogay's death eased the Tatar pressure on the Balkanic lands. It was Bulgaria that especially benefited from the extinction of the Nogayid clan, since George Terter's son, Teodor Svetoslav, was able to return from Nogay's court, and during his long reign (1300–21) Bulgaria began to recover from the political and economic vicissitudes of the previous stormy decades. Similarly, Serbia also profited from the decline of Tatar power in the western territories of the Golden Horde; apart from the misdeeds of independent Tatar troops on the Hilandar Monastery in Athos (see above), no Tatar incursions took place against Serbian targets in the first two decades of the fourteenth century. From the 1290s onwards, Byzantium followed the Bulgaro–Serbian reconciliation with growing concern, and did its utmost to hinder the friendship between the two parties. Emperor Andronikos II tried to attach Milutin to the Byzantine side through marriage, by offering him his daughter Eudokia, the widow of the Emperor of Trapezunt. Finally, after the expulsion of Milutin's Bulgarian wife, he married Simonis, another daughter of Emperor Andronikos II, and a minor. After the wedding ceremony, an occasion of great pomp that took place in Thessalonike in the spring of 1299, Milutin was given Ohrid,

---

[42] On these events see Jireček, *Serb.*, I, pp. 347–8; Jiriček, *Ist Srba*, I, p. 198.
[43] Danilo/Daničić, p. 359; see also Danilo/Mirković, p. 273.
[44] Jireček, *Serb.*, I, p. 348; Jiriček, *Ist Srba*, I, p. 198.

Prilep and Štip, places formerly conquered by him. Milutin's marriage was the beginning of Serbia's Byzantine orientation, which reached its climax during Stefan Dušan's reign (1331–55).[45]

After a long struggle for power between grandfather and grandson, in May 1328 Andronikos III marched to Constantinople with his victorious troops, led by Kantakouzenos, and dispatched his father, the aged Andronikos II, to be a monk. A new era began in the history of Byzantine decay. The Serbian king Stefan Uroš Dečanski supported the old emperor in his fight against his son, with the result that the relationship between the new Byzantine power and Serbia became tense. This was exacerbated by the loosening of the Bulgarian–Serbian alliance and the renewal of Byzantine–Bulgarian friendship; the Bulgarian tsar Michael Šišman dismissed his wife Anna, sister of Stefan Dečanski, and married the Byzantine princess Theodora, sister of Emperor Andronikos III and former wife of the late Bulgarian tsar Teodor Svetoslav. Thus a Byzantine–Bulgarian alliance against the Serbs was in the making, and the clash of arms seemed unavoidable. The Byzantines and the Bulgarians took the initiative and launched the aggression, but the Byzantine army set off late and failed to arrive in time.

The Bulgarian army moved from Vidin to Zemen on the river Struma, on the Bulgarian–Serbian border, while Stefan Dečanski set up his camp at the river Kamenča (now Sovolštica). The two armies were located north of Velbužd (now Kjustendil in Bulgaria).[46] Both armies hired mercenaries in large numbers: the Serbian king had Spanish and German armoured knights, while the Bulgarian Tsar employed Tatar, Yas and Wallachian light cavalry. Danilo speaks only of the presence of foreign mercenaries in Tsar Michael's army,[47] while in the Serbian chronicles mention is made of the participation of the Tatars and Wallachians in the fight.[48] According to Tsar Dušan, in his letter preserved in one of the manuscripts of his

[45] Ostrogorsky, *Gesch.*, pp. 350–1 (403–4).

[46] For a description of the battle of Velbužd, see Danilo/Daničić, pp. 178–96. For other sources (Gregoras, Kantakouzenos, etc.) and the analysis of the battle, see Jireček, *Serb.*, 1, pp. 361–3; Jireček, *Ist Srba*, 1, pp. 206–7; Jireček, *Bulg.*, pp. 292–6; Škrivanić, *Velbužd*.

[47] 'Cara bl'garom' priš'd'šaago s' mnogyimi silami ezyk' inoplemen'nyih'' Danilo/Daničić, p. 190.

[48] Cetinjski letopis': 'Izyde že i načelnik' skitskyi glagolemyi Mihail' car' s' siloju mnogoju i s' nim' okr'stni ezyci glagolju že i Tatare i Basarabe noet s' soboju' (Letopisi/Stojanović, p. 79). Practically the same text is repeated, with only minor textual changes, in the Koporinjski and the Pećki letopis' (pp. 78–9), in the Vrhobreznički letopis' (p. 103), the Berkovićev and Ostojićev letopis' (pp. 192–3) and the Sečenički letopis' (p. 199). It is noteworthy that the Bulgarian tsar Michael is called 'chieftain of the Scythians'; the use of this ethnonym for the Bulgarians displays Byzantine influence on the Serbian chronicles.

Zakonik, Yas troops also took part in the battle.[49] In both sources the Wallachians are connected with Basarab(a) (*Basarabe, Basarabu Ivan'ka*), evidently referring to Basarab, the leader of the Wallachian troops. Basarab was the first Wallachian voivode, or prince, who was able to loosen the vassal dependence on the Hungarian king Charles Robert of Anjou, so he is rightly considered the real founder of the Wallachian principality. It was in November 1330, half a year after the battle at Velbužd, that Basarab gained a victory over the Hungarian king in the southern Carpathians.[50] Since Basarab married the sister of the Bulgarian tsar Ivan Alexander, it was natural that he should hasten to his brother-in-law's help when he was in need at Velbužd. Apart from that, Basarab was also the descendant of a Cuman clan, and his brother-in-law the Bulgarian Ivan Alexander was the offspring of the Šišmanids, which too was a clan of Cuman origin in Vidin. As we have seen and will see several times in this book, the Bulgarian and Romanian (Wallachian and Moldavian) upper classes, the layer of the boyars and the *knezes*, were densely permeated by Cuman ethnic elements in the thirteenth and fourteenth centuries.[51] The Tatars in the Bulgarian Tsar's army are called 'black Tatars' (*čr'nyih' Tatar'*) in the letter of Tsar Dušan preserved in one of the manuscripts of his *Zakonik*.[52] The term *qara*, 'black', was frequently used in Turco-Mongolian ethnonyms,[53] as well as in connection with the Tatars. In the Chinese sources the Black Tatars (*Hei T'a-t'a*) were the real Tatars.[54]

The Bulgarian and the Serbian armies had approximately 15,000 warriors each. The Bulgarian army included 12,000 Bulgarian warriors and 3,000 Tatars; the number of Yas and Wallachian light cavalry is unknown. To start with, the two parties concluded an armistice for a day, but then the Bulgarian army entered the neighbouring villages to acquire provisions. At noon on 28 July 1330, the Serbian army launched an attack that found the Bulgarians unprepared, so that they could not form a battle line. The armoured

[49] In the Rakovački rukopis of the *Zakonik*: 'A pozavidev' zlonenavistnik' diavol našemu blagomu žitiju i zlon'raviem' v'zdviže na nas' 7 carev' v' lete 6838 meseca iunija 19. den', reku ž' i cara gr'časkago Mihaila i brata Belaura i Aleksandra, cara Bl'garom', i Basarabu Ivan'ka tasta Aleksandra cara, sumet' živuštih' čr'nyih' Tatar', i gospodstvo jaško, i pročiih' s' nim' gospoda . . . I siim' v'sem' priš'd'šim' v' zemlju našu rekomoe mesto Vel'bužd" (Novaković, *Zakonik Dušana*, pp.xxiii–xxiv).
[50] For the reports of the contemporary Latin and German chronicles, see the *Chronicon Pictum Vindobonense* (*SRH*, I, pp. 496–500), the *Chronicon Posoniense* (*SRH*, II, p. 50), the German chronicle of Heinrich von Mügeln (*SRH*, II, pp. 220–2), and the Saxon chronicle from Georgenberg (Hung. *Szepesszombat*, Slovakian *Spišská Sobota*, now in Slovakia) (*SRH*, II, p. 284). Cf. also Chapter 9 of this book.
[51] For Basarab's Cuman extraction and his name, see Chapter 9 of this book.
[52] Novaković, *Zakonik Dušana*, p. xxiv.   [53] See Pritsak, 'Qara'.
[54] For *qara* in ethnic names, and the term *Qara Tatar*, see Pritsak, 'Farbsymbolik', p. 378.

western mercenaries of the Serbian king decided the outcome of the battle.[55] The Bulgarian tsar Michael himself fell off his horse and died, and his body was interred in the monastery of St George in Nagoričin (Kumanovo). Those Tatar warriors who died were left unburied in the Bulgarian camp. Having learnt the news of the Bulgarian defeat at Velbužd, the Byzantine emperor Andronikos III turned against the enfeebled Bulgaria and captured the coastal towns of Mesembria (Nesebăr) and Diampolis (Jambol).[56]

---

[55] Kant. *Hist.*/Fatouros-Krischer, II, p. 78 (II.21.), = Kant. *Hist.*/Schopen, I, pp. 429–30; Nik. Greg. *Hist.*/van Dieten, II.2, p. 237 (IX.12), = Nik. Greg. *Hist.*/Schopen-Bekker, I, pp. 455–6.
[56] Jireček, *Serb.*, I, pp. 361–3; Jireček, *Ist Srba*, I, pp. 206–7.

CHAPTER SEVEN

Cumans in Byzantine service after the Tatar conquest, 1242–1333

THE CUMANS IN THE WARS OF THEODOROS II, MICHAEL VIII AND ANDRONIKOS II

As we saw in Chapter 3, on the eve of the Mongol invasion Cuman troops were settled in different parts of the Byzantine Empire, both in Thrace and Macedonia, and in Asia Minor. The Cumans were used by the Byzantines in two capacities: as reserve light cavalry and as standing troops. The emperor John III (Doukas Batatzes) called them to arms as light cavalry on every possible occasion, and his successors after 1254 followed him in their deal-ings with the Cumans. We shall now briefly review the Cumans' presence in Byzantine military actions after the Tatar invasion. In 1242 the Cumans came to Thessalonike to assist Batatzes in his siege of Thessalonike. In 1256 Theodore II Laskaris left a contingent of 300 Cumans and Paphlagonians with the governor of Thessalonike. In 1259, 2,000 Cuman light cavalry fought in the battle of Pelagonia. In 1261, the bulk of Alexios Strategopou-los' troop of 800 men who took part in Constantinople's recapture were Cumans. In 1263–4, 1270–2, and 1275 considerable Cuman contingents fought in Michael VIII's European campaigns. The last mention of the Cumans, when they were settled in Byzantium by Batatzes, occurs in 1292; during Andronikos II's abortive campaign in Epeiros the undisciplined forces of the Cumans and Turks withdrew without permission.[1] Hiring Cumans had great advantages for the Byzantines: the Cumans lived within the confines of the empire, but in return for the lands they had obtained from the emperor they could be obliged to fight – which they also did voluntarily, being warlike nomads.

Other elements of the Cumans were present as standing troops. When Michael VIII was elected as regent in 1258, the Cumans delivered their opinion on the matter in Greek, indicating that they were familiar with

---

[1] For all these events, see Bartusis, 'Smallholding soldiers', pp. 12–13; Bartusis, *Late Byz. Army*, pp. 26–7.

the Greek language. Their presence at the imperial court demonstrates that they were either part of the imperial guard or simply a light-cavalry squadron that could be mobilised more promptly than other military units outside the court. Their number could not have been more than a few hundred. As Bartusis remarks: 'The real importance of the group lay in its tendency to foster the Hellenization, assimilation, and eventually the social advancement of its members.'[2] A typical representative of this assimilating Cuman group was a certain Sytzigan, son of a Cuman tribal chief, who took the Christian name Syrgiannes. Later he married a woman from the Palaiologos family, and some time before 1290 he was granted the title of *megas domestikos*. His son was the famous Syrgiannes Palaiologos, *pinkernēs* (lit. 'cupbearer'), friend of two emperors, Andronikos III and Ioannes Kantakouzenos. (The life and career of this famous assimilated Cuman family will be traced separately at the end of this chapter.) It seems, then, that the majority of the Cumans who had settled in Byzantium before the Tatar invasion became assimilated in the 1290s and lost their Cuman identity. So Batatzes' policy of settling the Cumans was fully successful.

In 1259, the year following Theodoros Laskaris' death, Michael Palaiologos' Nikaian army marched to Kastoria, where they made a surprise attack on the anti-Nikaian coalition of Michael II Doukas, lord of Epeiros, King Manfred of Sicily, and William II Villehardouin, Prince of Achaia. The two armies met on the plain of Pelagonia (modern Bitola in West Macedonia). According to the Greek and French versions of the *Chronicle of Morea*, the Nikaian army consisted of 1,500 Hungarian and 300 German mercenaries, 600 Serbian cavalry and an unspecified number of Bulgarian cavalry. But the most important part of the army comprised a cavalry of 1,500 Turks and 2,000 Cumans, plus the Greek archers.[3] The Turks and the Cumans attacked the enemy with great force, and under their pressure Michael II fled to Prilep, while his son John the Bastard went over to the Nikaian side. The next day the Nikaian army gained the upper hand in the battlefield between Pelagonia and Kastoria, and the Turks and Cumans butchered the fleeing enemy.[4]

Early in 1261, a short while after the defeat at Pelagonia, Michael II of Epeiros regained some of his political strength, so Michael VIII sent an army against him under the command of his brother John Palaiologos.

---

[2] Bartusis, *Late Byz. Army*, p. 27.
[3] Nicol, *Despotate*, pp. 176, 179; Geanakoplos, *Pelagonia*, pp. 124–5.
[4] Schreiner, *Chron. brev.* II, pp. 199–200; Nicol, *Epiros*, pp. 174–82; Geanakoplos, *Emp. Michael*, pp. 67–73; Geanakoplos, 'Pelagonia', pp. 99–141; Bartusis, *Late Byz. Army*, pp. 37–8.

At the same time, Alexios Strategopoulos *kaisar*, together with a troop of 800 Greek and Cuman warriors, was dispatched to the Bulgarian frontier to secure that section of the border. While they were on their way to Constantinople, that city was unexpectedly recaptured.[5]

After this event, the ethnic composition of the Byzantine mercenary troops underwent substantial changes. Latin troops appear to have been absent from the Nikaian army in the battle of Pelagonia in 1259, and later, in the campaigns of Morea in 1263 and 1276, the Latins were again lacking. In accordance with the Western orientation of Michael VIII Palaiologos, the Turks and Cumans as foreign mercenaries became increasingly important to the emperor. They also filled the gap left by the Latins' diminishing military service during the reign of Andronikos II (1282–1328).[6]

In 1270 Emperor Michael VIII sent an army consisting of Greeks from Asia Minor together with Cumans and Turks, to engage William II of Achaia at Monembasia, under the command of Protostrator Alexios Philanthropenos. Despite the superiority of the Byzantine army, for almost two years there was no serious clash or casualty. Both forces contented themselves with plundering the countryside of Morea. Neither of the parties wished to fight; the obvious and sole aim of Emperor Michael VIII was simply to weaken William of Achaia and to demonstrate to Charles of Anjou (1266–85 in Sicily), William's supporter, that Byzantium was inaccessible to him through Morea, that is, the Peloponnesos.[7]

In 1275 Ioannes Sebastokrator, lord of Thessaly, broke the peace treaty that had been concluded with the emperor and made frequent incursions into Byzantine territory. The emperor Michael VIII soon lost patience and decided to reprimand his unruly vassal. He dispatched his own brother, the Despot John, to fight against the sebastokrator. John recruited a huge army: a cavalry from Paphlagonia and Bithynia, as well as contingents from the Cumans and the Tourkopouloi (τὰ Κομάνων καὶ Τουρκοπούλων τάγματα). Then he set out to enlist the infantry from Thrace and Macedonia. Ioannes Sebastokrator saw that he was in a hopeless position, and the Byzantines were expected to finish the campaign swiftly and subjugate the recalcitrant lord of Thessaly. The Byzantine troops penetrated Thessaly and proceeded without any substantial resistance against

[5] Pachym. *Hist.*/Failler-Laurent, I, p. 191; Nik. Greg. *Hist.*/van Dieten, I, p. 104, = Nik. Greg. *Hist.*/ Schopen-Bekker, I, 83 (here soldiers from Bithynia are mentioned); Georg. Akr. *Chron.*/Heisenberg, I, p. 181; Geanakoplos, *Emp. Michael*, pp. 92–3; Bartusis, *Late Byz. Army*, pp. 39–40.

[6] Bartusis, *Late Byz. Army*, pp. 50–1.

[7] *Chronicle of Morea*/Schmitt, vv. 6487–790; Geanakoplos, *Emp. Michael*, pp. 229–30.

the local forces when something unexpected happened. The Cumans began to plunder the churches and monasteries and set them on fire. They seized the nuns and made them their slaves, and desecrated the holy objects, using the icons as tables for eating. The sebastokrator shut himself up in his strongest fortress, that of Neai Patrai. The Byzantines surrounded the fort, which had been built in a very safe place on the top of a hill, though its provisioning was difficult. Then Ioannes tricked his pursuers; on a dark, moonless night he was lowered by a rope from the walls of his fortress, secretly made his way through the Byzantine camp, and reached a monastery. Here he revealed his identity and received five draught animals and five servants from the prior of the monastery. The next day he crossed the Thermopylai Mountains, and in two days he reached Boiotia. By the third day he was already in Attike. He succeeded in reaching an agreement with the Prince of Athens, who, in return for money and a favourable marriage offer, was willing to support Ioannes with 500 soldiers. (Pachymeres, who, for this period, is generally better informed than Gregoras, gives the number as 300.[8]) The sebastokrator quickly returned and, at the head of the Athenian military, surprised the unsuspecting Byzantine forces and forced them to escape. The sebastokrator's men then rushed out of the fortress and joined the Athenians. According to Gregoras, the Byzantines were defeated because of the godless and mischievous deeds of the Cumans.[9] The Prince of Athens mentioned in the narrative was John I de la Roche. The sebastokrator offered his own daughter Helena to the prince, who accepted the marriage offer not for himself but for his younger brother William.[10]

The last appearance of the Cumans can be placed in 1292. Since the struggle of the Angevin to conquer the empire was frustrated after the Sicilian Vespers, Nikephoros I Doukas of Thessaly had enjoyed friendly relations with the Byzantines. But the alliance between the Kingdom of Naples and the Despotate of Epeiros, concluded in 1291, alerted the Byzantines, who launched a preventative campaign against Epeiros in 1292. The sole source to report on the events of this campaign is the *Chronicle of Morea*, which gave the incredibly high figures of 30,000 infantry and 14,000 cavalry as constituting the Byzantine army. The main strength of the Byzantines were the Turks and the Cumans. They soon laid Ioannina under siege,

---

[8] For the whole episode, see Nik. Greg. *Hist.*/vanDieten, 1, pp. 120–2 (iv.9), = Nik. Greg. *Hist.*/Schopen-Bekker, 1, pp. 111–15.

[9] Nik. Greg. *Hist.*/vanDieten, 1, p. 253, n. 205.

[10] Pachym. *Hist.*/Failler-Laurent, 1, pp. 423ff. For this episode of 1275, see also Jireček, 'Überreste', pp. 112–13, and Bartusis, *Late Byz. Army*, pp. 60–1, who places the event in 1273.

while forty to sixty ships of the Genoese fleet, full of Byzantine warriors, anchored near Atra, the capital city of the province. After some military success in the initial stages of the campaign, the Byzantine army withdrew upon hearing that Florent of Hainault, Prince of Achaia, was an his way with some 400 to 500 men to help Nikephoros. The retreat of the Turkish and Cuman forces was rather undisciplined, and Florent pursued them to the south Macedonian border. Later the Byzantine-Genoese fleet also withdrew from Arta. Thus the Byzantine campaign against Epeiros ended in total frustration.[11]

THE CUMANS IN THE STRUGGLES FOR THE THRONE OF
THE TWO EMPERORS ANDRONIKOS, 1320–1328

The last decade of Andronikos II's reign was overshadowed by the unfortunate animosity that existed between him and his grandson Andronikos III. It is only natural that, in the internecine wars into which the country was often plunged, different armies, among them the Cuman contingents, also had their role. We know from Kantakouzenos' *Historia* that in 1320, while the young Andronikos and his friend Kantakouzenos were discussing where to move with their armies against the old emperor Andronikos II, an embassy arrived from the Serbian king Stefan II Uroš (Milutin). Milutin was the son-in-law of Andronikos II through marriage to Simonis, the emperor's daughter. The immediate reason for his sending the embassy to the Byzantines was that Andronikos II had borrowed some 2,000 Cuman warriors from the Serbian king. Later the Cumans were persuaded by the emperor to remain and not to return to Serbia. The leader of the Serbian embassy, a monk called Kallinikos, was well aware of the enmity between the two Andronikoses and desired to meet the young Andronikos and his friend Kantakouzenos. These two accepted Kallinikos and offered an alliance to the Serbian king. After Kallinikos' return, the Serbian king accepted the alliance and asked the young Andronikos to go to Macedonia.[12]

It is not clear from the sources when these 2,000 Cumans arrived to serve the Byzantines, though we know that in 1312 or 1313 the Serbian king Milutin sent a cavalry troop of 2,000 warriors to help the Byzantines. With

[11] *Chronicle of Morea*/Schmitt, vv. 8791–3, 9086; Nicol, *Epiros*, pp. 38–43; Laiou, *Const. and the Latins*, pp. 40–1; Nicol, *Last Centuries*, p. 123; Bartusis, *Late Byz. Army*, p. 70.
[12] Kant. *Hist.*/Fatouros-Krischer, I, pp. 33–4 (1.7–8), = Kant. *Hist.*/Schopen, I, 35–6.

their assistance the Byzantines succeeded in pushing the Turks of Ḥalīl to the peninsula of Gallipoli.[13] According to Danilo, the troop consisted of Milutin's relatives and friends.[14] It is not impossible that this troop sent by Milutin consisted of Cuman warriors.[15]

Kantakouzenos reports that at some time during the battles of the two Andronikoses the young emperor ordered his troops to be gathered in Didymotoichon. In a few days all the Thracian troops assembled, except the Cumans. These Cumans were the 2,000 men who came from Dalmatia and joined Emperor Michael IX (Andronikos II's son). Later, on the command of the older emperor, these Cumans were withdrawn from Thrace by Andronikes Tornikes and Manuel Laskaris and settled in the islands of Lemnos, Thasos and Lesbos. The precise background of the emperor's decision was not known, but presumably the older emperor had learnt that the Cumans had made a secret agreement with the chiefs of the Tatars (Skythai) that in the event of a Tatar campaign the Cumans would join them as allies and leave the country together with the booty and their families. But this supposition could not be verified (adds Kantakouzenos). The young emperor was annoyed when he was notified of the Cumans' removal to the islands, but hid his indignation in order to avoid speculation about his plans against the old emperor.[16] The removal of the Cumans to the islands, related by Kantakouzenos, must have taken place between 1322 and October 1327; Bartusis puts it in 1327.[17]

In sum, in 1312 the 2,000 Cuman warriors arrived from Serbia and entered Byzantium's service. First they were settled in Thrace, where they formed a defensive buffer against the Bulgars and Tatars. Later, by 1327, they were removed to three Greek islands. From then onwards they disappear from the sources. These 2,000 Cuman warriors, then, arrived as allied troops from the Serbian king, and after their settlement they became reserve troops who had strict military obligations.[18]

---

[13] Nik. Greg. *Hist.*/van Dieten, pp. 200, 203, = Nik. Greg. *Hist.*/Schopen-Bekker, pp. 263, 268.
[14] Danilo/Daničić, p. 145. Cf. also Laiou, *Const. and the Latins*, p. 233, n. 137. According to the *Chronicle of Morea*/Schmitt, vv. 3577–9, 3598–9, 3708, Michael VIII turned to Stefan Uroš I for help before the battle of Pelagonia, and the Serbian king sent him 600 horsemen. Since Michael and Uroš were on terms of enmity at that time, and there are no other data on this event, this evidence of the *Chronicle of Morea* appears to be unauthentic (Geanakoplos, 'Pelagonia', p. 124, n. 116).
[15] Mavromatis, *Milutin*, p. 70, nn. 212, 213; Bartusis, *Late Byz. Army*, p. 83.
[16] Kant. *Hist.*/Fatouros-Krischer, I, p. 177 (1.51) = Kant. *Hist.*/Schopen, I, p. 259.
[17] Kant. *Hist.*/Fatouros-Krischer, I, p. 294, n. 354; Bartusis, *Late Byz. Army*, p. 83.
[18] Bartusis, 'Smallholding soldiers', p. 13; Bartusis, *Late Byz. Army*, p. 83.

A BYZANTINE ADVENTURER OF CUMAN EXTRACTION:
SYRGIANNES

At the end of 1320, after the death of the co-emperor Michael IX, son of Andronikos II, all the leaders of the empire were convoked to renew their oath of fealty to Emperor Andronikos II. It was at that time that a plot began to be formed, which led to the enmities between the old emperor and his grandson, the future Andronikos III, and finally to a civil war that enfeebled the empire to such an extent that it could make no appropriate response to the Turkish and Serbian expansion. One of the leading figures among the the old emperor's opponents was a certain Syrgiannes, who was of Cuman descent on his father's side. It is this historical person to whom we now devote our attention.

Syrgiannes came of an elegant Cuman clan. The origin of his family goes back to Batatzes' time (1222–54), when a sizeable contingent of Cuman warriors, together with their families, came over to the Byzantine Empire and were settled in different parts of the country (see Chapter 3 above). One of the Cuman leaders, as we have seen, was a certain Sytzigan (Συτζιγάν), who was soon baptised and given the Christian name Syrgiannes (Συργιάννης) by his godfather. His son was also called Syrgiannes.[19] 'Sytzigan' is from a Cuman-Turkic name, *Sïčğan*, meaning 'mouse',[20] while the immigrant's new Christian name can be interpreted as *Sir Yanni*.[21] The mother of Syrgiannes junior was Eugenia Palaiologina, a niece of Michael VIII, so he acquired connections with the imperial family.[22] Syrgiannes senior (Sytzigan) could not have been the father of Syrgiannes junior, as stated by Kantakouzenos and Gregoras,[23] since he migrated to Byzantium in 1241 or 1242, and Syrgiannes junior must have been born around 1290. Most probably the word 'father' (πατρός) as applied to Syrgiannes senior has the meaning of 'forefather, ancestor'; he must have been the grandfather of Syrgiannes junior.[24]

Syrgiannes was an ambitious adventurer. In 1315 he participated in a rebellion as the Governor of Macedonia, and then he was imprisoned

---

[19] Kant. *Hist.*/Fatouros-Krischer, I, p. 22 (1.2), = Kant. *Hist*/Schopen, I, p. 18.

[20] Moravcsik (*Byz.-turc*, II, p. 294) and others could not identify the name with any Turkic word.

[21] Parisot, *Cant.*, p. 37. Binon's statement that Syrgiannes was of Mongol descent (Binon, 'Prostagma', p. 138) lacks any ground. This conjecture was taken over by Nicol, *Rel. Emp.*, p. 19 ('His curious name betrayed his Mongol descent on his father's side').

[22] Kant. *Hist.*/Fatouros-Krischer, I, p. 217, n. 29.

[23] Kant. *Hist.*/Fatouros-Krischer, I, p. 22, = Kant. *Hist.*/Schopen, I, 1; Nik. Greg. *Hist.*/Schopen-Bekker, I, p. 296.

[24] Kant. *Hist.*/Fatouros-Krischer, I, pp. 217–18, n. 29.

in Constantinople. In 1320 he was pardoned and, soon after his release in the same year, was appointed Governor of Thrace. It was in this capacity that he threw himself into the plot against the old Andronikos II. The three initiators of the plot were all good friends of the young Andronikos: Ioannes Kantakouzenos, the later emperor and historiographer; Syrgiannes Palaiologos, Governor of Thrace; and Protostrator Theodoros Synadenos. According to a treaty concluded at Rhegion on the shores of the river Melas (between Selymbria and Constantinople) in June 1321, the empire was divided between grandfather and grandson. The old emperor was in Constantinople, while the young one presided in Thrace. Within a few months Syrgiannes went over to the old emperor's side in Constantinople because his wife had allegedly been molested by the young Andronikos. In December 1321 the open conflict between the adherents of the two Andronikoses was renewed, and a new reconciliation followed only in June 1322, in Epibatai, near Selymbria.[25] Syrgiannes often changed sides and was imprisoned several times. Seemingly, both parties eventually lost confidence in this careerist adventurer. He was sent to Thessalonike, where Maria, the emperor's mother, adopted him as a son to keep an eye on him. After the empress' death in 1333 he was ordered to come to Constantinople for trial, but he fled to Serbia. Finally, he was killed by the emperor's men on 23 August 1334.[26]

---

[25] Nicol, *Rel. Emp.*, pp. 21–2.

[26] Schreiner, *Chron. brev.*, I, p. 351. For the various episodes of Syrgiannes' life, see Kant. *Hist.*/Fatouros-Krischer, II, pp. 13–17, 66–7, 82–96, = Kant. *Hist.*/Schopen, II, pp. 329–35, 411–12, 436–57; Nik. Greg. *Hist.*/van Dieten, II/2, pp. 224, 228, 255–62, = Nik. Greg. *Hist.*/Schopen-Bekker, I, pp. 432–3, 440, 488–501. For his life cf. also *PLP*, XI, no. 27167.

CHAPTER EIGHT

The Tatars fade away from Bulgaria and Byzantium, 1320–1354

TATAR RAIDS, 1320–1321

As we saw in Chapter 5, the fall of Nogay and his son Čeke in 1300–1 did not mean the end of Tatar rule in Dobrudja and Bessarabia. Tatar power simply shifted from Nogay (a local chief) to Toqta (the khan in the centre). Yet this shift from local to central power was enough to loosen the dependence on the Tatars of the Balkanic territories south of the Danube. Tatar power did not disappear from the region; it was just that the burdens of that power were lifted. Bulgaria, Serbia and Byzantium did not have to face an imminent and head-on collision with the Tatars of the Golden Horde. Rather, during Teodor Svetoslav's reign (1300–22), the Bulgarian–Tatar relationship was well balanced. The Bulgars recognised the Tatar suzerainty and paid tribute to the Tatars, and in return, the towns of the Danube and Dniestr deltas and possibly Bessarabia were under their actual control.[1] Bulgar dependence on the Tatars must have been much less than during Nogay's time, prior to 1300.

After the withdrawal of the Catalans from Macedonia in 1311, Andronikos II maintained friendly relations with the Serbian and Bulgarian rulers, both of whom were related to him by marital connections. His daughter Simonis was married to the Serbian Milutin, and his granddaughter Theodora to the Bulgarian Teodor Svetoslav. Thus, in the first twenty years of the four-teenth century, relative peace prevailed in Byzantine–Bulgarian–Serbian relations. This situation changed only after Teodor Svetoslav's death (1322), when semi-independent, scattered groups of Tatars who had settled in Dobrudja and Bujaq often involved themselves in the conflicts of Balkanic rulers as mercenaries, especially as auxiliary troops of the Bulgarians.[2] After 1323, the Bulgarian rulers Michael Šišman (1323–30) and Ivan Alexander (1330–71) often turned to the Tatars in their fights with Byzantium and

---

[1] See in detail Chapter 9, below. Cf. esp. Brătianu, *Recherches*; Nikov, 'B"lg. i tat', pp. 138–9.
[2] Laiou, *Const. and the Latins*, p. 281.

the Serbs. Together with the Tatars, Wallachian troops also frequently supported the Bulgarians in this period. In 1323, for example, Michael Šišman was supported by Wallachian and Tatar troops against Byzantium (see further below in this chapter), and in 1330, in the battle of Velbužd Wallachians, Tatars and Yas were fighting against the Serbs (see Chapter 6 above).

In the year of the death of the Co-emperor Michael IX, 1321, there was one Tatar raid through Bulgaria to Hadrianoupolis, but the Tatars caused little damage because their number was insignificant. But when the younger emperor Andronikos approached Constantinople against his grandfather in December 1321, a sizeable Tatar army entered Thrace. They too, however, were unable to cause much damage because the Thracian towns were notified of their coming in time, and people were transferred from the countryside to help defend the towns.[3]

TATAR INCURSIONS OF 1323 AND A NEW HALF-CUMAN
BULGARIAN TSAR

At the end of 1322, after a short reign of less than a year, the Bulgarian ruler George Terter II died. The Bulgarian towns lying between Nesebăr (Mesembria) and Sliven (Stilbnos) went over to the Byzantines. Vojsil (Boesilas), brother of the former Bulgarian king Smilec (1292–8) and a political émigré at that time in Byzantium, captured the towns between Sliven and Kopsis[4] without any resistance and offered them to the Byzantine emperor; in return, he was granted the title 'Despot of Mysia'. With his father's consent, the young emperor Andronikos moved with his troops to Plovdiv (Philippoupolis) and Vojsil joined him there. The united Byzantine forces surrounded the town, but could not take it by siege, for the numbers defending Plovdiv had been massively increased by George Terter II out of fear of Byzantine attacks. An elite troop of 1,000 Alanian (Yas) and Bulgarian horsemen and a light infantry of 2,000 men were stationed in the fortress, led by the Alanian Itiles and Temeres and the Hungarian Inas, but under the command of the Russian Ivan, an experienced strategist.

---

[3] Kant. *Hist.*/Fatouros-Krischer, 1, pp. 132–3 (1.39), = Kant. *Hist.*/Schopen, 1, pp. 188–9. The above two incursions are mentioned in Laiou, *Const. and the Latins*, p. 281, where she erroneously states that the Tatars did not cause much harm 'despite their substantial numbers'. On the contrary, Kantakouzenos clearly states that it was a small army: '... ʽκαὶ ἐζημίωσεν οὐ πολύ, ἅτε καὶ τῆς στρατιᾶς εὐαριθμήτου οὔσης' (Kant. *Hist.*/Schopen, 1, p. 188).

[4] *Kopsis* was a frontier fortress, presumably between Sopot and Karlovo, mentioned also by Pachymeres. The same name occurs in Macedonia as well (Kant. *Hist.*/Fatouros-Krischer, 1, p. 263, n. 221).

Ivan and the Alanian and Bulgarian mercenary troops defended the town against the Byzantines, who besieged the town for four months with no success.[5]

Before we discover the outcome of the siege, we should take a closer look at the commanders of the mercenary troops in Plovdiv. The two Alan commanders have typical Turkic names, *Itil* and *Temir*. This seems quite natural if one thinks of the close contacts between the Cumans and Alans (Yas) before and after the Tatar invasion.[6] The Hungarian commander *Inas* seems to bear a Hungarian name.[7] The name of the Russian, Ivan, causes no problem, but his identity is mysterious, for he was identified with different persons. An old, unfounded, idea seems to persist, which says that the 'Russian Ivan' may have been the same man as the later Grand Prince of Moscow, Ivan I Kalita (ruled 1328–41).[8] That this supposition is untenable can be seen from the fact that the Russian Ivan played an important role in the Byzantine–Bulgarian events in 1328,[9] whereas Ivan Kalita of Moscow acquired the title of 'grand prince' in the same year. To have been a military commander in Constantinople and a prince in Moscow at the same time, all without leaving the slightest trace in contemporary accounts, is unthinkable. Györffy put forward another supposition, which we must also reject. He claimed that the Russian Ivan of the Byzantine sources is identical with a person who first cropped up in a Hungarian diploma of 1288 as 'Iwan dicto Oroz'.[10] This latter Ivan was a brother-in-law of Theodore, Ban of Severin (on him, see Chapter 9), who, after the extinction of the Árpád House in 1301, played an important role as a semi-independent oligarch in southern Hungary and often leant on the assistance of the Despot of Vidin in his battles. After the fall of this Theodore in 1321 or 1322, his relative Ivan the Russian may have fled to Bulgaria and became the well-known actor on the Bulgarian–Byzantine scene in the 1320s.[11] This identification, however, lacks any written evidence and

---

[5] For a description of these events, see Kant. *Hist.*/Fatouros-Krischer, 1, pp. 122–3 (1.36.) = Kant. *Hist.*/Schopen, 1, pp. 172–3. For comments, see Burmov, 'Šišmanovci', pp. 228, 229.

[6] Moravcsik (*Byz.-turc.*, 11, p. 142) remarks that 'Da der Name *Itil* türkischen Charakter hat (s. Ἀτήλ), müssen wir entweder annehmen, daß hier unter dem Namen Ἀλανοί Tataren zu verstehen sind, oder daß diese Alanen Namen türkischer Herkunft führten.' The latter half of his statement is correct, but the Alans cannot be identified with the Tatars. For *Temir*, see also *PLP*, no. 27564.

[7] According to Gyóni, *Szórv.*, pp. 59–60, the name Ἰνᾶς can be identified with the Old Hungarian name *Ina*.

[8] Brun, *Černomor'e*, 11, pp. 359–62; Bosch, *Andronikos III*, p. 63, n. 3; Kant. *Hist.*/Fatouros-Krischer, 1, p. 263, n. 224.

[9] Kant. *Hist.*/Fatouros-Krischer, 1, p. 200, = Kant. *Hist.*/Schopen, 1, p. 295; for these events of 1328 see further below in this chapter.

[10] *ÁÚO*, IX, p. 420.   [11] Györffy, 'Román állam', p. 540.

is devoid of plausibility.[12] The time-span between the two persons is two wide to permit of their being the same individual, and the relatives of Russian Ivan (Ivan Orosz) seemingly remained in Hungary in their estates in the county of Arad; with Ivan's son John the family died out shortly before 1350.[13]

When George Terter II died in 1322 without leaving a successor to the throne, and the Byzantine forces launched their attacks against the southern Bulgarian towns, the Bulgarian boyars elected the ruler of Vidin to be their tsar. The Despot of Vidin, Michael Šišman, was half-Cuman and half-Bulgarian,[14] his father, Šišman, being a boyar of Cuman descent.[15] Kantakouzenos was misinformed in identifying his father as Stracimir, the father of Ivan Alexander, the next Bulgarian ruler (1331–71). Michael must have been born to Šišman's first Bulgarian wife before 1292.[16] The Bulgarian boyars apparently lost no time in deciding upon Michael Šišman as their ruler. The rapidity of their action can be explained by the imminent Byzantine danger. The Terterid line had died out, and Smilec's younger brother Vojsil was an agent of the Byzantine court. In Michael's person the house of the Vidin rulers offered several advantages: Michael was unaffected by the inner feuds of the Bulgarian boyars, had no contacts with pro-Byzantine circles, possessed a rather large territory, and, last but not least, like his father he had close contacts with the Tatars. This last point was especially important, since Michael's Tatar contacts ensured that there would always be a Tatar military contingent in his battles.[17]

The Bulgarian boyars handed Tărnovo over to Michael Šišman, their newly elected sovereign, who immediately marched on the capital of Bulgaria with his army and the allied Wallachian (Οὐγγροβλάχοι) and Tatar (Σκύθαι) forces. Michael knew that his army was not strong enough to take on the Byzantine emperor, who was besieging Plovdiv (Philippoupolis)

---

[12] First refuted by Holban, *Cronica rel.*, pp. 96–7.

[13] King Louis I of Hungary, in his diploma of 1350, recounts that John, son of Ivan the Russian (*Ioannis filii Iwanka Ruteni*), died without heir, and that the king now grants his possessions in the county of Arad and elsewhere to Nicholas and Paul, sons of the Master Ladislas in question (Györffy, 'Román állam', p. 540).

[14] 'τὸν τῆς Βιδύνης ἄρχοντα Μιχαὴλ τοῦ παρ' αὐτοῖς δεσπότου τοῦ Στρεαντζιμήρου υἱὸν ἐκ Μυσῶν καὶ Κομάνων τὰς τοῦ γένους ἕλκοντα σειρὰς' (Kant. *Hist.*/Fatouros-Krischer, I, p. 124, = Kant. *Hist.*/Schopen, I, pp. 175¹¹–14).

[15] For the Cuman name Šišman, see Rásonyi, 'Kuman özel ad.', p. 127.

[16] Nikov, *Vidin. knjaž.*, pp. 43, 84. Šišman's second wife was Anna (or Neda), second daughter of the Serbian king Milutin. Some time before 1313 Michael succeeded his father as ruler of Vidin, a vassal of the Serbian king. In a Venetian document he is called the Despot of Bulgaria (Theiner, *Mon. Slav. merid.*, I, p. 192), a title either inherited from his father or granted to him by his father-in-law, the Serbian king (Burmov, 'Šišmanovci', pp. 229, 230).

[17] Burmov, 'Šišmanovci', pp. 230–1.

at that time. Instead, he marched against the Bulgarian towns that had gone over to the Byzantine side after Terter's death. His troops ravaged the countryside and besieged these towns, but with little success, since the Tatar and Wallachian light cavalry were not at their most effective in the heavy, mountainous region. After a while the emperor stopped besieging Plovdiv and tried to engage Michael's forces.[18] Meanwhile, Michael sent part of his army to Plovdiv to relieve its faithful defenders. The Russian Ivan and the other commanders (Bulgarian, Yas and Hungarian) met them and agreed to hand over the town the next day. But when Georgios Bryennios, commander of the Byzantine army, was notified of these plans, he rushed back to the town and the inhabitants let the Byzantines enter without any force. When Russian Ivan and the commanders learnt that the town had fallen because of treason, they returned to their countries.[19]

In the autumn of 1323 a large-scale Tatar incursion was launched on Byzantine territory. Kantakouzenos is the sole authority to have reported these events in detail,[20] and we shall rely on his narrative in what follows. The Tatar army consisted of 120,000 warriors (probably an exaggerated figure) and had two commanders-in-chief, Taytaq and Toğlu-Torğan.[21] This Tatar incursion was particularly long-lasting, as the Tatar troops stayed in Thrace after forty days of plundering. They especially marauded the imperial lands in Thrace. The young emperor Andronikos tried to resist the Tatars by assembling his scattered troops from the Thracian towns, but his effort was rather unsuccessful. After fifteen days of incessant clashes with the Tatars, the young Andronikos withdrew with his soldiers to Hadrianoupolis and left his troops there while he himself, accompanied by the great domestikos Kantakouzenos, marched to Didymotichon. On their way to the town, at a village called Promosullu,[22] they met a Tatar troop bearing slaves and other booty. Though the Byzantines were much smaller in number, they made a surprise attack on the Tatars. Most of the Tatars were killed or thrown in the river Marica (Hebros), where they drowned. Only twenty-eight Tatars escaped by swimming across the river. The young

---

[18] Kant. *Hist.*/Fatouros-Krischer, I, p. 124 (1.36), = Kant. *Hist.*/Schopen, I, pp. 175–6.

[19] Kant. *Hist.*/Fatouros-Krischer, I, p. 126 (1.37), = Kant. *Hist.*/Schopen, I, pp. 178–9.

[20] Kant. *Hist.*/Fatouros-Krischer, I, pp. 133–6 (1.39), = Kant. *Hist.*/Schopen, I, pp. 189–93.

[21] Ταϊτάχ (Kant. *Hist.*/Schopen, I, p. 1899); cf. also *Byz.-turc.*, II, p. 296; Τογλοὺ Τοργάν (Kant. *Hist.*/Schopen, I, p. 1899), cf. also *Byz.-turc.*, II, p. 315. Hammer, *GH*, p. 293, emends the first name to *Kaitak* (Qaytaq) and the second one to *Toghlu Toghan* (Toğlu Toğan). The first name has no satisfactory etymology, whereas the first element of the second name can probably be connected with the Turkic name *Toq*, frequently used also in compounds such as *Toq-Buqa*, *Toq-Temür* (cf. Pelliot, *Horde d'Or*, p. 68, n. 1).

[22] For this name, see Kant. *Hist.*/Fatouros-Krischer, I, p. 268, n. 248.

emperor withdrew to Didymoteichon with the booty. Those who escaped with their lives reported the defeat to their chiefs, who came to the site of the battle with a larger Tatar troop and buried the dead warriors. The Tatars then moved on towards a place called Morrha,[23] at which point the young emperor set out from Didymoteichon to pursue them. But the Tatars crossed the river Marica (Hebros) in the town of Tzernomianon,[24] where the Byzantine military contingent that had been left in Hadrianoupolis joined the emperor's troops and continued the hunt for the Tatars. Meanwhile the Tatars crossed the river Tundža.[25] They knew that the Byzantines were following them, but did not attack, since there was an early spring flood (1324) and the size of the Byzantine army was unknown to them. The Byzantines did not attack either, as they were fewer in number than the Tatars. The two armies stood on opposite sides of the river, and the two commanders began to shout across the river, the young emperor Andronikos on the one side, and a Tatar chief called Taš-Buğa[26] on the other. The dialogue was conducted by an interpreter on the emperor's side. The Tatar asked him who they were. The emperor's evasive answer was that they were men who wanted to hunt. Then the emperor accused the Tatars of being, not honest and brave men, but bandits who were overrunning the country and making unarmed peasants their slaves. In his response, Taš-Buğa, the Tatar chief, defended himself with typical military logic: they were subordinates who attacked or withdrew on the orders of their superior. He asked the emperor whether his was the troop that had defeated a Tatar troop earlier. The emperor denied it, and the Tatars withdrew and eventually left Byzantine soil. There was a strong rumour, Kantakouzenos adds in his narrative, that the Tatars were invited by the old emperor to ravage Thrace, which was under the control of his grandson, the young emperor. Though Kantakouzenos flatly denies the rumour, the fact that he mentions it in his

---

[23] *Morrha* is the late Byzantine name of a province round the Arda valley in the Middle Rodope; its earlier name was Achrido (Kant. *Hist.*/Fatouros-Krischer, I, p. 268, n. 249).

[24] *Tzernomianon* (Černomen, Čirmen, Zeirinia) lay on the right bank of the southern reaches of the Marica (Hebros), to the north of the mouth of the river Arda, between Hadrianoupolis and Neutzikon. At that place a stone bridge already spanned the Hebros in antiquity (Kant. *Hist.*/Fatouros-Krischer, I, p. 268, n. 250).

[25] The Tunca (Tonzos), the largest tributary of the Marica (Hebros). There are numerous small islands in the river before it flows into the Hebros at Hadrianoupolis (Kant. *Hist.*/Fatouros-Krischer, I, p. 268, n. 251).

[26] Τασπουγᾶς (Kant. *Hist.*/Schopen, I, p. 192₉, ₂₁). According to Rásonyi's correct interpretation, *Taš-buğa* 'Stone Bull' (*Byz.-turc.*, II, p. 300). Parisot, *Cant.*, p. 10, interpreted the name as Tašbu-ḫan; Hammer-Purgstall, *GH*, p. 293, identified Taš-Buğa with Taš-beg, son of Čoban, governor of Özbek Khan. Both ideas are groundless.

work demonstrates his ambiguous attitude and suspicion towards the old Andronikos II.[27]

The death of a monarch in the Middle Ages often caused political instability, activating both internal opposition and foreign enemies. The events to be discussed in this section aptly illustrate the first of these well-known historical patterns.

The Byzantine emperor Andronikos II died in 1328 and the Bulgarian tsar Michael Šišman two years later in 1330. Both events caused tension and some turbulence in Byzantine–Bulgarian relations. The Tatar auxiliaries, as ever, meddled in these events.

Towards the end of the civil war the co-emperor, young Andronikos, and Ioannes Kantakouzenos were staying in Thessalonike, when an envoy arrived from the governor of Skopelos[28] and reported that the Bulgarian tsar had moved to the Byzantine–Bulgarian border at the town of Jambol (Diampolis),[29] together with an allied Tatar (Skythai) army, which had set up camp at Rhosokastron.[30] The Byzantines decided to withdraw to a mountain fortress called Logus.[31] When they reached the river Melas, a Bulgarian cavalry force of 3,000 men was reported to have arrived in Constantinople under the command of the Russian Ivan (known from the events of 1321; see above). The Bulgarians were sent to Constantinople as guards of the imperial palace, but the young Andronikos entertained the suspicion that the Bulgarians, as guards, could easily capture the palace, and that the Bulgarian tsar Michael would then invade Byzantium. His suspicion was corroborated by the presence of the Tatars in Michael's army in Rhosokastron. The young Andronikos decided to test the Russian Ivan by sending an envoy who was to announce to him, 'The Bulgarian tsar is an ally of Andronikos, but the latter does not need Ivan's help now, so return to your country; or, if you came to fight, do not hide, but do so!' In his letter of reply, Ivan swore that he came as the Bulgarian

---

[27] For the Thracian Tatar incursion of 1323–4, see also Bosch, *Andronikos III*, pp. 64ff.

[28] A small Thracian town near Hadrianoupolis (Kant. *Hist.*/Fatouros-Krischer, i, p. 307, n. 422).

[29] At the river Tunca (Tonzos), on the site of former Diospolis (Kant. *Hist.*/Fatouros-Krischer, i, p. 307, n. 423).

[30] On the southern side of the Small Balkans, not far from Ajtos (Kant. *Hist.*/Fatouros-Krischer, i, p. 307, n. 424).

[31] An unidentified settlement, cf. Kant. *Hist.*/Fatouros-Krischer, i, p. 307, n. 425.

tsar's man and Andronikos' friend, but this letter did not allay the young emperor's suspicions. He warned his grandfather that the Bulgarians wanted to start a palace rebellion and that the Bulgarian and Tatar troops stationed on the Bulgarian–Byzantine border were ready to back it up.[32]

Not long after Andronikos III had captured Constantinople on 24 May 1328, Michael Šišman of Bulgaria made an incursion into Byzantium, presumably in July of the same year. He brought his Tatar auxiliaries with him, and the allied Bulgarian and Tatar forces spent many days marauding the towns of northern Thrace. Having heard the bad news of this Bulgarian-Tatar incursion, Andronikos III marched to Bizye[33] and prepared his troops for an encounter with the Bulgarians. But Michael Šišman did not wish to lead his army into action, and withdrew to his own country. The emperor pursued the Bulgarians and in a few days he entered Bulgarian territory. The Byzantine army took, Diampolis (Jambol), pillaged the town, and returned home.[34] In September 1328, more than sixty days after the emperor's incursion into Bulgaria, Tsar Michael invaded Thrace for the second time and took the town of Bukelon, near Adrianople. This time there is no explicit mention of the Tatar auxiliaries, but their presence in Michael's military force is probable.[35]

The power politics of Byzantium, Bulgaria and Serbia in 1328–30, which led to an open clash and to the battle of Velbužd on 28 July 1330, were discussed in detail in Chapter 6 above. As we saw there, the Bulgarian–Tatar–Yas alliance suffered a severe blow at the Serbian king's hand. The Bulgarian ruler Michael Šišman himself was captured and died of his wounds after a few days. The Serbian king Stefan Uroš III (Dečanski) was content with his victory and did not want to turn against Byzantium. After Michael's death the Bulgarian boyars expelled his wife Theodora, sister of Andronikos III, and recalled Michael's former wife Neda (Anna), the Serbian king's sister, and her children.[36] Obviously enough, the pro-Serbian faction of the Bulgarian boyars gained the upper hand over the pro-Byzantine one. The Byzantine emperor then gave up his plan to conduct a war against the Serbs, and decided to discipline the unruly Bulgarians.

[32] Kant. *Hist.*/Fatouros-Krischer, I, pp. 199–202, = Kant. *Hist.*/Schopen, I, pp. 294–7.
[33] Bizye was a town in Thrace (today *Vize* in Turkey), c. 120 km NW of Constantinople and 25 km from the Black Sea.
[34] Kant. *Hist.*/Fatouros-Krischer, II, pp. 9–10 (II.3), = Kant. *Hist.*/Schopen, I, pp. 323–4. Gregoras also reports on these events, and stresses that the Bulgarian tsar arrived with a huge army of Tatar mercenary troops who came from the Danube region (Nik. Greg. *Hist.*/van Dieten, II.2, pp. 222–3 (XI.8) = Nik. Greg. *Hist.*/Schopen-Bekker, I, pp. 430–1).
[35] For these incursions, see Kant. *Hist.*/Fatouros-Krischer, II, p. 167, nn.16–18.
[36] Kant. *Hist.*/Fatouros-Krischer, II, p. 78 (II.21), = Kant. *Hist.*/Schopen, I, p. 430.

The Byzantine emperor was supported and assisted by the Bulgarian inner opposition. In the spring of 1331, two Bulgarian boyars, the Pro-tovestiarios Raksin and the Logothetes Philip, revolted against the recalling of Neda. The Serbian woman was compelled to escape to her brother the Serbian king.[37] Then the rebels placed Alexander, son of Stracimir and cousin of the late Tsar Michael, on the throne. Immediately after his enthronement Tsar Ivan Alexander launched an attack against the unfaith-ful towns that had gone over to the Byzantine side, and repossessed them as far as Mesembria on the Black Sea coast. Tatar auxiliaries took part in Alexander's army in great numbers, as usual. On hearing this news, the Byzantine Emperor Andronikos III left Constantinople for Thessalonike and openly prepared his troops for war.[38]

The emperor marched to Bulgaria, then crossed the Haimos Mountains and reclaimed the towns that had gone over to the Bulgars. He proceeded as far as Anchialos, which was held by the Bulgars. Finally, the emperor and the Bulgarian ruler agreed that the Bulgars would return Anchialos to the Byzantines, who would hand over Diampolis. The agreement took place on 17 July 1331, and the ceremony of oath-taking and the surrender of each other's towns was planned for the next day.[39]

During the night preceding the oath, however, an allied Tatar force reached the Bulgarian Tsar Alexander. He had summoned them to come and assist him in punishing his uncle Belaur, who had revolted against him. Now Alexander planned to misuse the Tatars' assistance, and told them instead to attack those who were present alongside his own army. Thus he deliberately deceived the Tatars, who, having just made an agreement with the Byzantines, had no intention of attacking them. Next day, the Tatars launched their attack. The emperor, who in the expectation of peace, had dismissed most of his troops, now felt bitterly let down. At first he thought that it was the Bulgars who were attacking him, but soon he recognised the Tatars by the typical sharp sound of their trumpets. He could hardly believe that the Tatars had come against him, since he had just made peace with them. He thought rather that the Wallachians had arrived as allies of the Bulgarians. They lived on the other side of the Danube and were very similar in appearance to the Tatar archers. After a long fight, in which the emperor and his friend Kantakouzenos also participated, the Tatars won the

---

[37] Kantakouzenos, who reports on these events, is wrong in stating that Neda-Anna escaped to his nephew the Serbian king, namely Stefan Uroš IV (Dušan). The latter ascended the throne only on 8 September 1331, so Neda must have gone over to his brother Stefan Uroš III (Dečanski) (Kant. *Hist.*/Fatouros-Krischer, II, p. 213, nn. 198, 198a).

[38] Kant. *Hist.*/Fatouros-Krischer, II, p. 97 (II.26), = Kant. *Hist.*/Schopen, I, pp. 458–9.

[39] Kant. *Hist.*/Fatouros-Krischer, II, pp. 98–100 (II.26), = Kant. *Hist.*/Schopen, I, pp. 460–4.

battle and the Byzantine army withdrew to Rhosokastron. Tsar Alexander quickly sent an envoy, who proposed the conclusion of the peace treaty formerly agreed, and also demanded the emperor's daughter as Alexander's son's wife. This demand was refused, but all the other conditions were accepted and the treaty was concluded.[40]

In the summer of 1332 the emperor launched a new campaign against the Bulgarians with the aim of repossessing the fortresses in the Haimos Mountains that had been occupied by Tsar Alexander. His grandfather Andronikos II had forced Michael Glabas, governor of Thrace, to build or renovate these fifteen fortresses in order to prevent the Tatars from crossing the borders and raiding the countryside. After the emperor had succeeded in capturing a few of the fortresses, Alexander sent his envoys to negotiate, but they were turned away by the emperor. Alexander therefore gathered his army of 8,000 Bulgarian warriors and 2,000 Tatar mercenaries. Having left Tărnovo, on the fifth day they arrived in Rhosokastron, where they set up their camp. The emperor's army was much smaller than the Bulgarian-Tatar troops, numbering at most 3,000 men. The two armies clashed and struggled valiantly, with Kantakouzenos excelling on the Byzantine side (so Gregoras claims). The Byzantines had to withdraw to the fortress. Finally, they were unable to attain their goal, and returned home.[41]

THE LAST APPEARANCES OF THE TATARS IN BYZANTIUM, 1337, 1341

Andronikos III (1328–41) tried to maintain friendly relations with the Tatars. In the early years of his reign (prior to July 1331) he concluded a peace treaty with the Tatars,[42] and the friendly state relations between the Byzantines and the Tatars were further strengthened when the emperor Andronikos II gave his daughter in marriage to Özbek Khan.[43] Notwithstanding the

---

[40] Kant. *Hist.*/Fatouros-Krischer, II, pp. 100–4 (II.27), = Kant. *Hist.*/Schopen, I, pp. 464–70.

[41] Nik. Greg. *Hist.*/van Dieten II.2, pp. 252–5 (x.4), = Nik. Greg. *Hist.*/Schopen-Bekker, I, pp. 483–8. The dating of events between 1330 and 1334 is different in Kantakouzenos and Gregoras. For a precise analysis of these chronological questions, see Nik. Greg. *Hist.*/van Dieten, II.2, pp. 339–41, n. 370.

[42] Kant. *Hist.*/Fatouros-Krischer, II, p. 101 (II.27), = Kant. *Hist.*/Schopen, I, p. 465.

[43] Bayalun was the third wife (*ḫatun*) of Özbek Khan. She was the daughter of the Byzantine emperor Andronikos II; Ibn Baṭṭūṭa met her personally and travelled with her to Constantinople. Bayalun went to the Byzantine capital to give birth to her child but never returned to the Golden Horde (Ibn Baṭṭūṭa/Gibb, II, pp. 483, 488, 497–8; Tiz., I, pp. 290, 294, 301–2). The marriage of a daughter of the emperor is confirmed by a letter of Gregory Akindynos from 1341 (Lemerle, *Aydin*, p. 265). For the name *Bayalun*, which is a Mongolian feminine name formed from *bayan*, 'rich', see Pelliot, *Horde d'Or*, pp. 83–5. Cf. also Laurent, 'L'assaut', pp. 154, 157, 160.

relatively balanced official relations between Byzantium and the Golden Horde in these years, however, in 1337 a serious 'unofficial' Tatar incursion shook the empire, probably the last of its sort. Only Gregoras reports this event; Kantakouzenos is silent. According to Gregoras, the main cause of the incursion was that Byzantium had forgotten to send the regular gifts (i.e. tribute) to the Tatar ruler and nobility. So in early spring a troop of Tatars crossed the Danube and plundered the whole of Thrace as far as the Hellespontos. There they came across a few Turks who made a habit of crossing the Hellespontos to plunder the Thracian coast. These Turks were either taken captive, or killed if they tried to resist. This incursion was quite different from earlier ones in that formerly the Tatars were accustomed to appearing suddenly, plundering the place and leaving in a day or two. Now they did not leave, and instead spent fifty days plundering the country-side. On leaving Thrace it is reported that they took 300,000 captives with them,[44] but Gregoras' figure is clearly wrong; either he exagerrated or it was a scribal error. The story of this incursion, though absent from Kantakouzenos' narrative, however, can be regarded as authentic.[45] It is the last Tatar incursion into Byzantium mentioned in the sources.

A special element in the story is the encounter between the Tatar and Turkish troops near the Hellespontos. One could regard this episode as symbolic: the northern nomadic warriors and old conquerors of the Balkans were passing the baton to the new, ambitious, nomadic warriors coming from the south. In a few decades the Turks were to set foot in the Balkans, more firmly than the Tatars could ever have dreamt of for themselves.

Though the last Tatar incursion occurred in 1337, the Tatar danger was not over for some years. In 1341 the emperor sought to rebuild and repopulate the old ruined town of Arkadioupolis,[46] since it was still an important strategic point in the defence system against the Tatars.[47] This precaution on the Byzantine side was not unfounded. In spring 1341 a Byzantine embassy under the leadership of Demetrios Kydones set out to Özbek Khan in order to avert an alleged Tatar attack against Byzantium. This information comes from Byzantine documents concerning the hesychast movement.[48]

---

[44] Nik. Greg. *Hist.*/van Dieten, II.2, p. 280 (XI.3), = Nik. Greg. *Hist.*/Schopen-Bekker, I, pp. 535–6.

[45] Spinei's assertion (Spinei, *Moldavia*, p. 127) that the incursion of 1337 was 'probably the most ravaging invasion that affected the Empire after that of Nogai' is a gross exaggeration. This incursion did not substantially exceed in number and character any of the former Tatar incursions in the fourteenth century.

[46] Arkadioupolis (today Turkish Lüleburgaz) was founded by Arkadios, son of Theodosios the Great in 403, and built on the site of ancient Bergule, situated c. 50 km south-west of Bizye (Kant. *Hist*/Fatouros-Krischer, II, p. 251, n. 360).

[47] Kant. *Hist.*/Fatouros-Krischer, II, pp. 150–1 (II.38), = Kant. *Hist.*/Schopen, I, pp. 541–2.

[48] Laurent, 'L'assaut', pp. 145–62; Kant. *Hist.*/Fatouros-Krischer, II, p. 251, n. 359.

The Tatars had apparently given up their plan to penetrate the Balkans because of their internal troubles. The greatest khan of the Golden Horde, Özbek, died in 1341, and from that time onwards the Golden Horde was involved in other theatres of war and lost its interest in the Balkanic region. The independent Tatar groups in Dobrudja and Buǰaq became separated from the central power of the Tatars and lost their political importance in Balkanic events.[49]

I conclude this chapter on Byzantine–Tatar relations with a curious story presented by Gregoras in his historical work.[50] It sheds interesting light on everyday Tatar–Byzantine contacts. I would tentatively entitle Gregoras' narrative 'The story of the brave Scythian (i.e. Tatar) woman'.

A Tatar woman living north of the Danube saw the Thracian captives march before her dwelling. This woman had long planned to embrace Christianity, so she purchased a Christian captive, married him, and made him swear not to leave her even if circumstances should change fundamentally. Before long she gave birth to a child, and was pregnant with another when the first wife of her husband appeared as a captive. On seeing her husband's sorrow, she bought the first wife, who became their servant. The Tatar woman eventualy embraced Christianity and settled with her family in Constantinople. There the first wife lodged a complaint against her Tatar rival, telling the patriarch that she had been deprived of her husband and treated badly. But nothing could be done, because of the Tatar woman's superior social position. Then the Tatar woman made a magnanimous decision: she would pay the ransom for her husband out of gratitude to him, and make it possible for the first wife to redeem herself. If they could get enough money, the 'original' couple could go, while the Tatar wife would remain with her children. The patriarch and everyone admired the Tatar woman's honesty. So the Byzantine woman went to Thrace to get the ransom for herself, but in a new Tatar raid she was captured again. So the Tatar woman could go on living with her husband.

Whether the 'moving' story reflects a historical kernel later embellished in a literary way, or is merely an example of Byzantine fiction, seems to matter little now. What is really interesting is the fact that Tatars were part of everyday life in Byzantium in the first half of the fourteenth century.

---

[49] Spinei, *Moldavia*, p. 127.
[50] Nik. Greg./van Dieten, II.2, pp. 284–5 (XI.5), = Greg./Schopen-Bekker, I, pp. 542–4.

CHAPTER NINE

The emergence of two Romanian principalities in Cumania, 1330, 1364

CUMANS AND TATARS IN ROMANIAN HISTORY

The territories stretching east and south of the Carpathian ranges met a peculiar historical fate in the second millennium. Now, for the most part, these territories are within the boundaries of present-day Romania, which was founded in 1859 by the union of the two Danubian principalities of Wallachia and Moldavia. The territory between the rivers Prut and Dniestr, called Bessarabia after its Russian conquest in 1812, lay for a long time under Russian, then Romanian, then Soviet suzerainty, but gained independence as the state of Moldoa in 1991. The Principality of Wallachia (1330–1859) comprised two geographical units: *Oltenia* is the territory between the Carpathian Mountains, the Danube and the river Olt (it was the medieval Banate of Severin/Szörény in the thirteenth and fourteenth centuries under the tutelage of the Hungarian kings), while *Muntenia* comprised the territory east of the Olt. The north-eastern borders of Wallachia, separating it from Moldavia, stretched along the river Buzău. The Principality of Moldavia lay between the Carpathian ranges, the rivers Dniester and Danube, and the Black Sea. The plain region north of the Danube delta, favourable for nomadic cattle-breeders, was called *Bujak* (now *Bugeac* in Romanian), a Turkic term meaning 'corner'. Finally, Dobrudja (now *Dobrogea* in Romanian), the territory south of the Danube delta, historically always part of Bulgaria, became part of Romania after the First World War.

These territories, so diverse in both geographical and historical respects, share at least one common feature: they have always been at the borders and crossroads of various civilisations. The Danube was the real dividing line between the Roman Empire and the *barbaricum*. Dacia's Roman subjugation in Trajan's time (101–6) and its existence as a Roman province till 257 did not basically alter this situation. The territories of the German, Iranian, Turkic and Slavic peoples and confederacies constantly underwent rapid fluctuations in the fourth to ninth centuries, and only the final settlement of the Hungarians in the Carpathian Basin and the foundation of the Hungarian state brought about fundamental historical changes in the area. With their conversion to Christianity and the coronation of King Stephen I in AD 1000, medieval Hungary became part of contemporary Christian Europe, while the territories east and south of the Carpathians remained the most westerly region still to experience waves of nomadic migration. After AD 1000 it was not only Byzantium and Bulgaria by the Lower Danube but also the Hungarian Kingdom near the Carpathians that put a stop to the nomadic influxes from the East. It is in these territories of nomadic turbulence that the two Romanian principalities emerged in the fourteenth century, thereby connecting the territories between the Danube and Dniester to European historical development. Geographically, it is doubtful whether these territories of Eastern Europe could be considered as belonging to the Balkans. At any rate, the genesis and historical destinies of the Romanian states understandably connect them to Balkanic historical development, though a considerable Western influence through Hungary and Poland has also been a factor in their history. The important role of the Turco-Tatar nomadic peoples in the historical fate of this area in the thirteenth and fourteenth centuries has always been evident, and it is this theme that I shall endeavour to investigate in this chapter.

The importance of the settlement of Turkic and Mongol peoples in the north Danubian plains, their cohabitation with the local Slavic and later Romanian population, and their role in the creation of the forms of political organisation of the area, have all been recognised by the greatest of Romanian historians, N. Iorga.[1] After the foundation of the Wallacho-Bulgarian Kingdom in 1185 (for details see Chapter 2 above), the Cumans provided rulers and dynasties for a number of states along both banks of the Danube: Asenids (1185–1280), Terterids (1280–1323), and Šišmanids (1323–98), and the Basarabids in Wallachia (1330 to the seventeenth century).[2]

During the 300 years between the advent of the Hungarians in the Carpathian Basin (896) and the foundation of the Second Bulgarian Kingdom (1185), it was mainly Slavic and Turkic peoples that inhabited the north Danubian lands, which later became the Romanian principalities. There is no compelling historical evidence that any serious Vlakhian settlement existed north of the Danube in this period, though the possibility cannot be excluded. As I explained in Chapter 2, the first mention of the Vlakhs north of the Danube is dated to 1222, and their massive migration to the area must have begun after the foundation of the Second Bulgarian

---

[1] Iorga, *Hist.*, III, *passim*.   [2] Lăzărescu-Zobian, 'Cumania', p. 267.

Kingdom in 1185. As we saw in Chapter 3, it was the land of *Cumania* that they reached, that is, the territory of later Wallachia and southern Moldavia. There was no state organisation in this territory, though the Cumans had been the decisive ethnic element for the past 150 years.[3] It was the Cuman tribal chiefs who gave this land any political shape that it had, so it was no wonder that the Hungarian king and the Pope turned to the Cumans in their desire to spread Christianity and founded the Cuman episcopate in Milcov (southern Moldavia). The first decades of the thirteenth century, prior to the great Tatar invasion in 1241, must have witnessed intensive contact between the Vlakh immigrants and the Cuman and other Turkic inhabitants of the area (Pecheneg and Oguz splinter groups). The Vlakhs, who were Christianised by the Bulgarians and to a lesser extent by the Greeks, encountered a strong Turkic influence in Cumania. As so often, it was the stratum of Turkic tribal leaders and their retinue that gave political shape to the new conglomerate of Turks and Vlakhs. Just as, in the case of contacts between the Bulgaro-Turks and Southern Slavs, the Bulgars organised a state, gave it political stability, and were assimilated into the numerically stronger Slavic population, so the Cumans organised the Vlakh settlers and within a few generations had become culturally assimilated into them. But the traces of Cuman–Romanian contacts can be detected in Romanian vocabulary, personal and geographical names, ethnography and folklore.[4]

In parallel with the emergence of the Second Bulgarian Kingdom, from the end of the twelfth century onwards the Hungarian Kingdom pursued an active expansionist policy in the Balkans. It had to defend its southern and eastern borders against the Cumans and the new Bulgarian power. To that end the most effective tool was the establishment of the Cuman episcopate and the organisation of the Banate of Szörény in 1227. The first territorial units, the small voivodates or kenezates of the Vlakhs in Cumania, testify to Hungarian initiatives: among others, the territory of Litvoy, the Cîmpulung area, and the Moldva valley are all counterparts of

---

[3] See Diaconu, *Coumans*, passim.
[4] Giurescu, *Ist. Rom.*, 1, pp. 284–7. There is no good monograph on the pre-Ottoman Turkic elements of Romanian. The fullest collection of material is in Şăineanu, *Infl. orient.*, 1–11; a very poor modern representation of the question is Wendt, *Türk. Elem.* For a historical survey of research, see Lăzărescu-Zobian, 'Cumania'. The latest monograph on the question is unpublished at the time of writing: Lăzărescu-Zobian, *Kipch. Rum.* Until now the best and sometimes pioneering works on Romanian personal and geographical names of Kipchak origin are those of Rásonyi; see especially Rásonyi, 'Val.-Turc.'; Rásonyi, 'Contr.'; Rásonyi, 'Kuman özel ad'.

certain important settlements in Transylvania.[5] The Hungarian expansion in the thirteenth century and the Tatar invasion in 1241 crushed the political preponderance of the Cumans. It is from this point that we shall trace Cumania's further historical fate: what happened after the withdrawal of the Tatars in 1242?

FROM CUMANIA VIA TARTARIA TO WALLACHIA AND MOLDAVIA

The journey indicated in the subtitle is not geographical but chronological. All the terms refer to virtually the same territory. We must remember that the territory bordered by the southern Carpathian Mountains, the Danube, the Black Sea and the Dniestr was designated by different names in the tenth to fourteenth centuries before the names *Wallachia* and *Moldavia* became firmly rooted in the second half of the fourteenth century. These names were formed from those of the peoples that actually exerted political control over the area. Thus, in the tenth century, Constantine Porphyrogenitus calls it Patzinakia (Πατζινακία), the land of the Pechenegs.[6] By the time of the appearance of the Kipchak/Cuman confederacy in the second half of the eleventh century, the steppe region between the Dnieper and the Lower Danube fell under Cuman suzerainty for almost 200 years. The general term to designate the vast empire of the Cumans stretching from the Aral Sea in the east as far as the Lower Danube in the west was *Dašt-i Qipčaq* in the Muslim sources, and *Pole Poloveckoe* in the Russian sources.[7]

It is interesting that the geographical name *Cumania* was not used prior to the thirteenth century in either the Byzantine Greek or Latin sources, and even afterwards it is hardly ever used in the Greek sources.[8] The term appears in Latin sources only in the 1220s, in connection with the Cuman mission, and does not refer to the full extent of *Dašt-i Qipčaq*, but only to the territory of the future Moldavia and eastern Wallachia. Thus, in Albericus Trium Fontium's *Chronicle* (*sub anno* 1221), we read, '. . . to

---

[5] Elekes, 'Román fejl.', pp. 284, 289.
[6] Konst. Porph. *DAI*/Moravcsik, p. 182 (§42).   [7] For more on this see Chapter 1, above.
[8] For the occurrences of *Cumania/Comania* in the Latin sources, see Gombos, *Cat.*, iv, p. 47. There are only two occurrences of the term prior to 1200, once under the year 1161 in the *Chronica regia Coloniensis* (*Comanie: MGH SS*, xvii, p. 774, = Gombos, *Cat.*, i, p. 481) and once under the year 1189 in Iacobus Moratinus' *Chronicon de rebus Foroliviensibus* (*Cumaram*, correctly *Cumaniam*: Iac. Morat. *Chron.*, p. 786, = Gombos, *Cat.*, ii, p. 1223). Both works were compiled at a later date, so the names used for events in the twelfth century have no direct source value. There are only *three* occurrences of the name in Byzantine sources; see *Byz.-turc.*, ii, p. 167 (Κουμανία).

Cumania which is beyond Hungary and at the borders of Russia'.⁹ In the
titulature of the Hungarian king the title *rex Cumaniae* appears for the
first time in 1233: 'Béla, by the grace of God the firstborn son of the King
of Hungary . . . Bulgaria and *Cumania*'.¹⁰ The territory lying west of the
river Olt, later called Oltenia, was not part of this *Cumania*, since this
important border area of the Hungarian Kingdom was organised, simultaneously with the Cuman mission, as the Banate of Szörény (Severin). Again,
from Pope Gregory IX's diploma addressed to the Archbishop of Esztergom
(*Archiepiscopo Strigoniensi*) on 31 July 1227, it becomes clear that *Cumania*
comprised Moldavia and the eastern part of Wallachia.¹¹ Rogerius in his
Carmen miserabile also makes it evident that *Cumania* was partly identical with what was later to become Moldavia. In March 1241, the Tatar
chief Qadan arrived to attack the Transylvanian Saxon town of Radna from
the direction of Cumania (i.e. Moldavia): 'King Qadan took a three days'
journey through the forests between Russia and *Cumania* and arrived in
Radna, a rich town of the Germans lying among high mountains, a place
of the royal silver mines, where innumerable people lived.'¹² Another Tatar
chief, Bochetor, crossed the river Seret and came to the land overseen
by the Cumans' bishop.¹³ In the following year, when the Tatars left
Hungary, they first arrived in *Cumania*.¹⁴ All these data testify to the fact that
Cumania was a term used in Latin documents of the Hungarian king and
the papal court from the 1220s onward to designate the territory bordered
by the Olt, the Danube, the Black Sea, the Dnieper and the Carpathian
ranges.

The Tatar invasion in 1241–2 put an end to the Cuman mission in
Cumania and fundamentally changed the balance of power in the area.
Cumania as a political entity ceased to exist, and some of the Cumans
(maybe most of them) fled to Hungary while others were dispersed in Bulgaria. The territories east and south of the Carpathians fell under Tatar

⁹ 'In Cumaniam, que est ultra Hungariam et in partibus Russie' (*MGH SS*, XXIII, p, 911, = Gombos,
   Cat., I, p. 31).
¹⁰ 'Bela dei gratia primogenitus Regis Hungariae . . . Bulgariae Comanieque' (Hurm., I, p. 127
   (no. 99), = Fejér, *CD*, VII/4, 81; XI, 502 (regesta transsilvana)). But it has to be mentioned that
   the authenticity of this diploma of Béla, the junior king of Hungary in 1233, was seriously questioned by Jakó, *Erd. Okm.*, I, no. 169.
¹¹ Theiner, *Mon. Hung.*, I, p. 86 (no. 154), = Hurm., I, p. 102 (no. 77).
¹² 'Rex Cadan inter Rusciam et Camoniam, [*var.*: Comaniam] per silvas trium dierum habens iter
   sive viam pervenit ad divitem Rudanam inter magnos montes positam Theutonicorum villam regis
   argentifodinam, in qua morabatur innumera populi multitudo' (*SRH*, II, p. 564).
¹³ 'Bochetor autem cum aliis regibus fluvium, qui Zerech dicitur, transeuntes pervenerunt ad terram
   episcopi Comanorum' (*SRH*, II, p. 564). The person and name of Bochetor are not correctly
   identified; cf. Pelliot, *Horde d'Or*, p. 132, n. 2.
¹⁴ 'Iam, cum exirent Hungariam, Comaniam intrare ceperunt' (*SRH*, II, p. 586).

overlordship. But the geographical term *Cumania* survived for many centuries in Latin chronicles and diplomas of European chancelleries. It became a name used by learned circles 'who had a marked propensity towards archaic toponyms'.[15] The name *Tatar* only gradually became part of the geographical definitions applied to the former *Cumania*. One of these terms, *Tartaria*, was used much less than *Cumania* had been, and forms such as *terra/confines/metae Tartarorum* were preferred. By the middle of the fourteenth century the terms containing the name *Tatar* gained the upper hand, yet the name *Cumania* was persistently used even much later than Tatar rule, when the Wallachian and Moldavian Principalities occupied the territory of the former Cumania. Bishop John of Sultaniyye, for example, speaks of *Thartaria sive Comania* in 1404 (!),[16] and the Hungarian kings went on using the term *Cumania* in their royal titulature long after the foundation of the two Romanian principalities, and practically till the fall of the Austro-Hungarian monarchy in 1918. At the end of the fourteenth century, for instance, King Sigismund of Hungary had the following titulature cited in his diploma issued on 29 March 1390: 'Sigismundus dei gratia Hungariae, Dalmaciae, Croaciae, Ramae, Seruiae, Galliciae, Lodomeriae, *Comaniae* Bulgariaeque rex . . .'[17]

There is an inveterate commonplace in modern historiography that goes back to the alleged statements of Kézai and Thuróczy that Moldavia was called *Nigra Cumania*, 'Black Cumania'.[18] Kézai, in his combined Hun–Hungarian history, when describing the migration of the Hungarians from their eastern abodes to the new homeland in the Carpathian Basin, claims that they 'crossed the land of the Pechenegs and the *White Cumans*. Then entering Suzdal, Ruthenia and the land of the *Black Cumans*, finally they arrived as far as the river Tisza.'[19] The chronicles of the fourteenth century contain the same information, deriving from Kézai.[20] Thuróczy, in narrating the story of the Huns' (i.e. Hungarians') exodus from Scythia, repeats the earlier chronicles and says that 'they arrived in *Black Cumania*,

---

[15] Spinei, *Moldavia*, p. 28.   [16] Kern, *Libellus*, p. 106.

[17] Zimm.-Werner-Müller, II, p. 644 (no. 1247).

[18] For example, Spinei (*Moldavia*, p. 28) asserts that the term *terra nigrorum Cumanorum* was used by the Hungarian chroniclers, beginning with Kézai, to designate the eastern Carpathian region in order to avoid confusion between Cumania in the broader sense (the land between the Aral Sea and the Lower Danube) and Cumania in the stricter sense (Moldavia + Wallachia).

[19] 'Bessorum et Cumanorum Alborum terras transirent. Deinde Sosdaliam, Rutheniam et Nigrorum Cumanorum terras ingressi tandem usque Tize fluvium . . . pervenerunt' (Kézai, §8: *SRH*, I, p. 148).

[20] 'Tunc omnes capitanei . . . egressi de Scythia, intrantes tandem Bissos et Cumanos Albos, deinde Susdalos, Ruthenos terramque Nigrorum Cumanorum intravere. Abinde egressi usque ad Tysciam pervenerunt' (Chronici saeculi XIV, §8: *SRH*, I, p. 257). Practically the same text is in Chronicon Posoniense: *SRH*, II, p. 18 = Chronicon Monacense: *SRH*, II, p. 58.

which is now supposed to be Moldavia'.[21] These are the texts at our disposal, which encouraged most researchers to equate *Black Cumania* with *Moldavia*. But are they right, and do they have sufficient evidence to prove that the two are one and the same? I think not. *Nigra Cumania* as the name of a country crops up only in Thuróczy, and its timid identification (*forte*, 'perhaps') with *Moldavia* can be found only in Thuróczy's chronicle. Since Thuróczy's work was finished and published in 1488 in Brünn (Brno), and the above data can be found in his Hun–Magyar historical narrative taken over from Kézai's Chronicle (1288), the source value of his remark concerning the location of Black Cumania is nil. I think I may risk the conjecture that Moldavia's name in Turkish, *Kara Boğdan*, 'Black Bogdan (= Moldavia)',[22] may have given Thuróczy the idea of identifying the Black Cumania of the Hungarian chronicles with Moldavia, since the texts of earlier chronicles gave no hint as to the location of *Black Cumania*. B. Kossányi was the first to attempt to determine the real meaning of the terms 'white Cumans' and 'black Cumans' in the Hungarian chronicles. According to his convincing arguments, the term 'white Cuman' refers to the Cumans proper (the *Polovcy* of the Russian annals), while the term 'black Cuman' stands for the mixed Kipchak tribes that are called *Černye Klobuky*, 'black hats', in the Russian sources.[23] Thuróczy's haphazard identification of Black Cumania with Moldavia thus lacks any sound basis, and despite its persistence in modern scholarship it must be abandoned.[24]

To return to the term *Tartaria*: by the middle of the fourteenth century definitions such as *terra Tartarorum* gradually ousted the archaic and by then obsolete term *Cumania*. Even the papal documents, which are

[21] 'In nigram Cumaniam, quae nunc Moldavia forte creditur, devenerunt' (Thuróczy's *Chronicle*, 1.x, in Schwandtner, 1, p. 70).
[22] *ÍA*, 11, p. 697 (A. Decei); *TDV ÍA*, vi, p. 269 (A. Özcan).
[23] Kossányi, 'Úzok és kománok', pp. 534–5.
[24] To answer the question 'Why was Moldavia called *(Kara) Boğdan* by the Ottomans?' is another task the result of which does not affect our opinion on the Black Cumania of Kézai and Thuróczy. It is interesting, however, to notice that the adjective 'black' seems to have been attached to the territory of later Moldavia well before the Ottoman *Kara Boğdan* was formed. The Byzantine term *Maurovlachia* was attested for the first time in 1386 (see further below), and Rašíd-ad-Dīn, in describing the Tatar campaign against Hungary in 1241, mentions that Böjek traversed the mountains through *Qara Ulağ* and crushed the *Ulağ* tribes there (Raš./Blochet, p. 55; translations: d'Ohsson, *Hist.*, 11, p. 628; Bretschneider, *Med. Res.*, 1, p. 330; Pelliot, *Horde d'Or*, p. 153; Raš./Ali-zade, 11, p. 45; Decei, 'L'invasion', p. 103). The whole narrative of Rašíd-ad-Dīn is rather obscure, and his geographical terms are loose. That is why d'Ohsson and Bretschneider thought that Qara Ulağ and Ulağ must mean Transylvania and Wallachia, while Pelliot preferred the interpretation Moldavia and Wallachia. But none of these interpretations can be convincingly proved by the Persian author's text. The most plausible conjecture is that of Spinei (*Moldavia*, p. 113), who identified Qara Ulağ with Moldavia, and the Ulağ tribes or people with 'the Romanians in the sub-Carpathian zones in Wallachia or those in the south of Transylvania'.

most conservative in this respect, abandoned the fictive term *Cumania*, and in their geographical terminology they followed the political reality of Tatar presence. In his letter of 29 January 1345, addressed to the Christians of Transylvania, Pope Clement VI speaks of them as 'the Transylvanian Church formed at the borderland of Christianity and near the Tatars and other infidels'.[25] In a letter of 13 October 1374, addressed to the archbishops of Esztergom and Kalocsa (*archiepiscopis Strigoniensi et Colociensi*), Pope Gregory IX mentions the Vlakhs who live on the border of Hungary towards the Tatars.[26] Definitions such as *iuxta Tartaros*, 'near the Tatars', *versus Tartaros*, 'towards the Tatars' and *in confinibus Tartarorum*, 'at the borderland of the Tatars', became common; the vagueness of these terms clearly demonstrates that Tatar control over the former Cumania was loosened and then totally disappeared after 1345, when the reality of the new Romanian state structures began to gain acceptance.

The equivalence of *Tartaria* and *Cumania* was preserved by European cartography well into the middle of the sixteenth century. *Tartaria Cumania* or *Tartaria Cumaniae* were used as alternative terms, seemingly without any exact distinction, for the region lying between the Azov and the Caspian Seas.[27]

It was only from the 1370s that the Vlakh lands, that is, the two new Romanian principalities of Wallachia and Moldavia, which had emerged on the territory of the former Cumania and Tartaria, began to be regularly designated by new names. It is not my task here to explain all the intricacies of the different names used for the two Romanian states;[28] I shall briefly summarise them only in so far as they are relevant to our theme. It is quite evident that, after the Cumans and the Tatars, it was the Vlakhs who succeeded in organising the Transcarpathian region; consequently, they lent their name to the new states: *Vlakhia*. But the term *Vlakhia* was not unambiguous. The reader may remember (see Chapter 1) that there were several *Vlakhia*s, that is, Vlakh lands, in the Balkans in the twelfth and thirteenth centuries. (Even Bulgaria was referred to under that name long after the foundation of the Second Bulgarian Kingdom.) Consequently, the new

---

[25] 'Ecclesia Transilvana in finibus Christianitatis et iuxta Tartaros et infideles alios constituta' (Theiner, *Mon. Hung.*, I, p. 679, no. 1023).

[26] 'Certa pars multitudinis nationis Wlachonum, qui circa metas Regni tui [Ungarie] versus Tartaros commorantes' (Theiner, *Mon. Hung.*, II, p. 152, no. 303, = Hurm., 1/2, p. 217, no. 165, = Mihályi, *Máramaros*, p. 72, no. 40).

[27] For example, in Gregorius Reisch's *Margarita Philosophica nova* (Strasbourg, 1515), in *Mappa mundi auctoris incerti* (Nuremberg, c. 1540) and in Robert Thorne's map of 1527 (for all these see Nordenskiöld, *Atlas*, tables XXXVIII, XL, XLI).

[28] For a good overview of these terms, see Spinei, *Moldavia*, pp. 29–34.

state on the left bank of the Danube had to be distinguished from the
Vlakhias in the Balkans. No wonder that, at first, the Byzantine chancelleries found this problem a source of confusion, since different Balkanic
*Vlakhia*s were known in their literature. They therefore began to distinguish the Vlakhs on the left bank of the Danube from other Balkanic
Vlakh groups by denoting them as Ungrovlakhs (Οὐγγροβλάχοι) and
their country as Ungrovlakhia (Οὐγγροβλαχία). The term Οὐγγροβλάχοι is first mentioned in Ioannes Kantakouzenos' historical work. In
1323, after his election to the Bulgarian throne, Michael Šišman, the former
Despot of Vidin, marched into the capital city of Tărnovo accompanied by
his allied troops of Tatars and *Ungrovlakh*s.[29] The name of the country as
Οὐγγροβλαχία is first encountered in a Greek diploma issued by the
synod of the Constantinople patriarchate, in which the ruler of the young
Vlakh state is titled 'grand voivode and sovereign of all Ungrovlakhia' (μέγας
βοϊβόδας καὶ αὐθέντης πάσης Οὐγγροβλαχίας).[30] There has been much
debate whether this term had its origin in the usage of the Byzantine chan-
cellery. Many Hungarian scholars saw it as proof of Hungarian overlordship
in Wallachia, while some Romanian historians of a strongly nationalistic
bias tried to turn the argument round and prove the obviously impossible
case that the Wallachian voivodes had a claim on Hungary.[31] There is no
dispute among serious historical scholars that the Hungarian kings had a
claim on the former Cumania even after the Tatar invasion in 1241–2, and
that the first Vlakh socio-political organisations, the kenezates and voivodates, were in vassal dependence on the Hungarian kings. The birth of the
first Vlakh principalities on the left bank of the Danube, as we shall see
below in our narrative, was nothing but a process of secession from this
dependence. As far as the Byzantine terms *Ungrovlakh* and *Ungrovlakhia* are
concerned, they are simply expressions of the fact that these *Vlakhia*s on the
left bank of the Danube were adjacent to and bordering on the Hungarian
Kingdom (*Ungria*), and their proximity to Hungary and the Hungarians
was their distinguishing feature in comparison with Great Vlakhia, Upper
Vlakhia, and other possible Vlakhias in the Balkans. But *Ungrovlakhia* was
a term occurring only in the Greek and Slavic documents, and it survived
in Romanian only in the title of the head of the Romanian autocephalous
church as 'archiepiscopu şi metropolit *Ungro-Vlachiei*'.[32] One must add that
the term *Ungrovlachia* does not occur in medieval Latin documents that

---

[29] Kant. *Hist.*/Schopen, I, p. 175 (1.36), = Kant. *Hist.*/Fatouros-Krischer, I, p. 124.
[30] Acta Patr. Const., I, no. 171. For further occurences of Οὐγγροβλαχία and Οὐγγροβλάχοι, see
Byz.-turc., II, pp. 224–5.
[31] For example, Haşdeu's claims and their refutation; see Hunfalvy, *Oláhok tört.*, I, pp. 444–8.
[32] Hunfalvy, *Oláhok tört.*, I, p. 448.

used the term *Wallachia*, or *Wallachia maior* for Muntenia and *Wallachia minor* for Oltenia. The former appears first in 1373, the latter in 1377. But the Latin documents of Hungary have never used the term *Wallachia*, but rather *terra transalpina, partes transalpinae* and *voivoda transalpinus* for the land or ruler of Wallachia. These names originated on Hungarian soil and reflect the fact that Wallachia lay beyond the snowy peaks of the southern Carpathian Mountains, called *Havasok* in Hungarian and *Alpes* in Latin – the old Hungarian name of Wallachia was *Havaselve* '(territory) beyond the Alps' – so the Latin term is simply a translation of a Hungarian geographical term. The Hungarian terminology was taken over by and used in the Latin documents of the Wallachian voivodes.[33]

The terminology for the designation of the second Romanian state of Moldavia, founded in 1359, displays a more uniform picture. From 1360 onwards the geographical name *Moldova, Moldava, Moldavia*, taking its origin from the river Moldva, spread strongly in both the Latin and Slavic documents (1360: *terra Moldauana*; 1365: *terra Molduana*; Ioannes de Küküllő: *terra Moldaviae*, etc.).[34] But the Byzantine terminology again departed from the general rule: Moldavia, since it was another *Vlakhia*, was called Μαυροβλαχία, 'Black Vlakhia' (first mention in 1386), Ῥωσοβλαχία, 'Russian Vlakhia', that is, 'Vlakhia near Russia' (first mention 1395) and Μολδοβλαχία, 'Moldavian Vlakhia' (first mention 1401).[35]

Finally, mention must be made of the designation of certain parts of the Romanian principalities after the name of Basarab, the founder of the Wallachian Principality. *Basarab* appears in Serbian, Hungarian, Moldavian and Polish sources from the mid-fourteenth century onwards as the name of Wallachia, and from the fifteenth century as a name for the territory between the lower reaches of the Prut and the Dniestr. *Bessarabia* became the name of the whole land between the Prut and the Dniester (i.e. today's Republic of Moldoa) only after the Russian conquest of the area in 1812.[36]

CUMANIA AND SEVERIN AFTER 1242

As the Tatars withdrew to their eastern homelands in 1242 they left Hungary and the adjacent territories in ruins.[37] Since no Tatar military contingent

---

[33] *FNESz*, p. 267; *KMTL*, pp. 257–8 (L. Makkai).
[34] For these and more data, see Spinei, *Moldavia*, pp. 33–4.   [35] Spinei, *Moldavia*, pp. 32, 34.
[36] *İA*, II, p. 743 (A. Decei, *sub voce* Bucak); Spinei, *Moldavia*, p. 30.
[37] King Béla IV in his letter of 11 November 1247, addressed to Pope Innocent III, writes as follows: 'When the Hungarian kingdom was for the most part turned into desert by the infliction of the Tatars, and became surrounded, as a sheepfold is by fences, by different infidel peoples, such as the Rutens, Brodniks in the east, and the Bulgarian and Bosnian heretics in the south . . . ' ('Cum

remained in Hungary and Cumania, the status of the conquered territories
remained open. In Hungary, King Béla IV returned and the rebuilding of
the Hungarian Kingdom began, but the imminent danger of a possible
Tatar return did not fade away for decades. Cumania was in a much worse
situation; though it fell within the sphere of interest of the Hungarian
Kingdom and, as we have seen, the Hungarians and the papacy made significant efforts to draw the eastern Carpathian region into the framework
of European religious and social development, it had no serious state traditions. Prior to the Tatar invasion, the most important factor in the region
were the Cumans, but after the invasion a great many (if not most) of the
Cuman population were dispersed and left Cumania for Hungary and the
Balkans. The Vlakh population remained there under the leadership of
their local chiefs, called *knezes* and *voivodes*. (Both terms clearly display the
Slavic origins of these institutions.) But these 'mini-states', which one may
call *knezates* or *voivodates*, were far from being real states.

The reawakening Hungarian Kingdom tried to press on with the extension of its jurisdiction in the former Cumania,[38] but the balance of power
was substantially different from the pre-1241 situation; Hungary was weaker
and the young, robust power of the Tatar Empire was present. Until the
1260s, during the first twenty years of the formative period of the Golden
Horde (the reigns of Batu and Berke), the most westerly part of the Tatar
world empire, the status of Cumania must have been obscure; but from
then onwards it became, and remained for many decades, an integral part
of the Tatar Empire as Prince Nogay's appanage (*ulus*). But, immediately
after the Tatar invasion of Eastern Europe, some Tatar contingents probably remained in the southern, littoral part of the region between the Prut
and the Dniester, called *Bujaq* in Turkic and *Pruto-Dnestrovskoe mežduree'e*
in Russian. The archaeological findings testify to an early Tatar presence
there.[39] The Western travellers give a contradictory picture of the western

regnum Hungarie per pestem Tartharorum pro maiori parte in solitudinem sit redactum, et quasi
ovile sepibus sit diversis infidelium generibus circumseptum, utpote Ruthenorum, Brodnicorum a
parte orientis; Bulgarorum et Boznensium hereticorum a parte meridiei . . .') (Theiner, *Mon. Hung.*,
I, p. 230, no. 440, = Hurm., I, p. 259, no. 199). This letter of the Hungarian king, traditionally
allocated to 1254, has now been convincingly redated to 1247 by Senga, 'IV. Béla tatár levele'.
[38] King Béla IV, in the same letter of 11 November 1247, addressed to Pope Innocent III, asked for help
against the Tatars, Bulgarians, Rutens and other 'heretics and pagans'. In this letter the king made
mention of the territories that were subjected to the Hungarian throne before the Tatar invasion:
'regions that border on our kingdom from the east, such as Russia, *Cumania*, Brodniks, Bulgaria, for
the most part formerly subjected to our dominion' ('regiones, que ex parte orientis cum regno nostro
conterminantur, sicut Ruscia, Cumania, Brodnici, Bulgaria, que in magna parte nostro dominio
antea subiacebant') (Theiner, *Mon. Hung.*, I, p. 231, no. 440, = Hurm., I, p. 260, no. 199).
[39] Egorov, *Ist. geogr.*, p. 12.

extension of the Golden Horde. In 1247, Plano Carpini locates the western borders of the Tatar state on the right bank of the river Dnieper, where the Tatar chief Corenza (Qurumši) had wandered. He states that he had traversed through the whole land of the Cumans (*per totam terram Comanorum*), beginning with the Dnieper and ending with the Yayik (Ural).[40] But Plano Carpini gave an account only of the territories he personally went through, that is why he ignored the region west of the Dnieper. But Rubruc, travelling in Cumania eight years later, in 1255, expressly stated that the borders of the land of the Kipchak Cumans were along the Danube (*a Danubio*).[41] Some scholars, referring to Plano Carpini's account, have tried to draw the western borders of the Tatar power along the Dnieper,[42] but, as was stated above, the Danube delta was the real dividing line from the first.

Nogay was a key figure in Tatar history, and from the 1260s he became the absolute master of the westernmost territories of the Golden Horde, which stretched from the river Don as far as the Lower Danube. Nogay's constant presence in the area must be ascribed to his mission in 1264 to free the Seljuk sultan 'Izzaddīn from Byzantine captivity.[43] The region south of the Lower Danube, that is, Dobrudja and Northern Bulgaria, was not under the direct jurisdiction of the Golden Horde, but did fall under its sphere of influence; and, as we have seen, Nogay often intervened in the Balkanic power struggles, first on the Bulgarian side, then on the Byzantine. Discoveries of Tatar coins on the right bank of the Danube at Isaccea and in other places do not prove the contrary, since Tatar coins were in circulation in, and could easily reach, the adjacent Dobrudja.[44] Incidentally, throughout history Dobrudja has been a typical border country, belonging to the Romans, then the Byzantines, the first to repel all nomadic influxes. After the Tatar invasion it continued in the same vein; it remained under Bulgarian jurisdiction with palpable signs of strong Tatar influence. I would describe Dobrudja as a strange counterpart of Buǰak: the latter has always been the first recipient of nomadic immigrants and settlers coming from the north, while the former was an outpost of Rome and Byzantium and a place where these nomadic waves were quelled and pacified.

If the southern borders of the Tatar power can be placed along the Lower Danube, the south-western and western borders followed the river

---

[40] *Sin. Franc.*, I, pp. 107–8 (IX.13).   [41] *Sin. Franc.*, I, p. 195 (XII.6).
[42] Grekov.-Jakubovskij, *ZO*, p. 84; Paraska, 'ZO i Mold.', p. 182.
[43] For Nogay and these events, see above, Chapter 4.
[44] Oberländer-Târnoveanu, 'Isaccea', pp. 292ff.

Olt before proceeding along the foothills of the Carpathian ranges. The territory of Oltenia has never been an integral part of Cumania; in the 1230s, a few years after the foundation of the Cuman episcopate in 1227, it was separated from it as the Banate of Severin (Hungarian *Szörény*). The first *ban*, Luke, was mentioned in 1233.[45] Severin had Hungarian, Cuman and Romanian inhabitants prior to 1241. West of the Olt river there are practically no geographical names of Turkic origin, while there are Hungarian and Romanian ones. The Hungarian settlers seem to have preceded the Turkic inhabitants here, but in the fourteenth century these early Hungarian colonies disappeared because of the cessation of waves of migration.[46] The Tatar invasion swept away all the organisational and ecclesiastical successes of the Hungarian king, and Severin was left devastated and depopulated by the Tatars. It seems that the oriental conquerors did not establish themselves in the region, so King Béla IV could rightly decide to validate his former jurisdiction over the territories of Severin and Cumania by reorganising them. In 1247 he invited Prior Rembaldus and the knights of the Hospitallers of St John in Jerusalem to settle in Severin and defend the southern borders of Hungary against the oriental invaders. In his diploma of 2 July 1247 he set out arrangements concerning this grant, and this diploma gives us a clear insight into the political and ethnic relations of that time and area.[47] The king gives the Hospitallers 'the whole land of Severin together with the mountains pertaining to it and all other possessions, like the *kenazates* of John and Farkas extending to the river Olt, with the exception of the land of the *kenazate* of Voivode Litvoy, which we leave to the Vlakhs as they had held it until now'.[48] Half of the income from the above resources would belong to the king, the other half to the Order. Then the king also gives the territories east of the Olt, called *Cumania*, to the knights, with the exception of the territory of the Vlakh voivode Seneslav, who would enjoy the same rights as

---

[45] The best history so far of the Banate of Szörény, with an ample list of geographical names and editions of documents, seems to be Pesty, *Szörény*, I–III. For a short overview, see *KMTL*, p. 657 (L. Makkai).

[46] Elekes, 'Román fejl.', p. 291.

[47] The original of the document is lost, but had been preserved in a transcription and confirmation of Pope Innocent III from 1250. This document was first edited in 1775 by Pray, *Diss.*, pp. 134–7, and has appeared in several editions since then, the latest being Zimm.-Werner-Müller, I, pp. 73–6 (no. 82). For a regesta with good annotations, see *Doc. hist. Valach.*, pp. 20–2 (no. 9); for a detailed analysis of the document, see Pesty, *Szörény*, I, 16–22.

[48] 'totam terram de Zeurino cum alpibus ad ipsam pertinentibus et aliis attinentiis omnibus, pariter cum kenazatibus Joannis et Farcasii usque ad fluvium Olth, excepta terra kenazatus Lynioy [correctly, Litvoy] vaivodae quam Olatis reliquimus, prout iidem hactenus tenuerunt' (Zimm.-Werner-Müller, I, p. 73).

Voivode Litvoy.[49] But the knights' mission proved to be a total failure. We have no report of whether they occupied their posts or not, and in a few years even their name disappeared from the sources relating to Severin and Cumania.

This diploma of Béla IV is of the utmost importance for our understanding of the ethnic and political relations of the area. The most striking fact in it is the appearance of autonomous territorial-administrative units of the Vlakhs (Romanians), called *kenazatus* in the Latin text. The *knez*s were local chiefs; the origins of both the institution and the name are Slavic (South Slavic *knez*, 'chief, prince' > Romanian *kneaz, knez*; Hungarian *kenéz*).[50] There are four *kenazates* mentioned in the territory of Severin (Oltenia) and Cumania (Muntenia), that is, the future Wallachia. Those of Johannes and Farkas are given to the Hospitallers, while the territories of the voivodes Litvoy (in Severin) and Seneslav (in Cumania) are exempted from the grant. There are three further differences between the first two and the second two *kenazates*. First, one of the first two names (*Johannes*) is given in its Latin form, and so contains no hint of the nationality of its bearer; but the second name (*Farkas*) is a typical Hungarian name meaning 'wolf'; *Litvoy* and *Seneslav*, however, are Slavic names well attested and in frequent use by the Vlakhs. Secondly, the ethnicity of Johannes and Farkas is not given, while Litvoy and Seneslav are expressly said to be Vlakhs (*Olati*). Thirdly, Litvoy and Seneslav are *voivodes* who have a territorial unit under their jurisdiction (*terra* (kenazatus) *Lynioy vaivodae* and *terra Szeneslai vaivodae Olatorum*), while Johannes and Farkas are *knez*s who have *kenazates*. That is why, I think, the term *kenazate* associated with Litvoy's name is an error and must be put in brackets.[51] These fine distinctions in the text show that voivodes were chiefs of larger territorial units than those of knezes, and Johannes and Farkas were either Hungarians, or Vlakhs with Hungarian names. The latter supposition is less probable, since *Lupu*, the Romanian equivalent of Hungarian *Farkas*, was used by the Vlakhs.

After the failure and disappearance of the Hospitallers, the history of the region is shrouded in obscurity for decades. Not even the names of the

---

[49] 'Ad haec contulimus praeceptori ante dicto [i.e. Rembaldo] et per ipsum domui hospitalis a fluvio Olth et alpibus Ultrasilvanis totam Cumaniam sub eisdem conditionibus, quae de terra Zeurino superius sunt expressae, excepta terra Szeneslai vaivodae Olatorum, quam eisdem relinquimus, prout iidem hactenus tenuerunt sub eisdem etiam conditionibus per omnia, quae de terra Lytua sunt superius ordinatae' (Zimm.-Werner-Müller, 1, p. 74).

[50] See Kniezsa, *Szláv jöv.*, 1/1, pp. 262–3. For the *knez*es in Hungarian sources of the thirteenth and fourteenth centuries, see Györffy, 'Román állam', p. 8, n. 29.

[51] F. Pesty was the first to notice the contradiction in that Litvoy is called voivode, but his land is designated as a *kenazate*. ('Valóban különös, hogy Lyrtioy – ki Linioy és Lithennek is iratik – vajdának neveztetik, földje pedig kenézségnek'; Pesty, *Szörény*, 1, p. 17).

Bans of Severin are known, and the Romanian voivode Litvoy must have gained increasing influence there. The Hungarian king's rule was rather nominal, but he insisted on his jurisdiction in the Banate of Severin. When Voivode Litvoy disputed the Hungarian jurisdiction and rebelled against King Ladislas IV in 1272, the king sent George, son of Simon, against Litvoy, who was killed in the battle; his brother Barbat was captured and sent to the royal court. This event is recounted in King Ladislas' letter of grant of 8 January 1285, in which he donated the villages of Sóvár, Sópatak and Delne, in the county of Sáros (now in Slovakia) to this Master George.[52]

The centre of the Banate of Severin was Fort Severin (*Szörényvár* in Hungarian, *Turnu Severin* in Romanian), on the left bank of the Danube, in the vicinity of the Iron Gate, at a place where, in Roman times, the stone bridge of Drobeta crossed the Danube.[53] It was of the utmost strategic importance, and served as the starting point for military actions against the Bulgarians of Vidin, the Tatars and the rebellious Romanian voivodes. Obviously, the Hungarian kings had no desire to relinquish this strategic point, and equally obviously the Romanians wished to take it. The Romanians in Muntenia (the south-western part of Cumania) were harassed by the Tatars of the Golden Horde, inasmuch they had to pay tribute to the Tatars; and in Oltenia they were oppressed by the bans put in place by the Hungarian kings. The future Wallachia was a typical frontier area, and the process of unifying the small Romanian voivodates took place in the course of constant conflict between two great powers, the Hungarian Kingdom and the Golden Horde. Seemingly, neither of these powers had enough energy and resources fully to annex and organise the territories of Oltenia and Muntenia. The Hungarian kings were occupied with the internal rebuilding of Hungary after the Tatar invasion, and from the viewpoint of the Golden Horde these territories constituted a faraway western province. So it was not by chance that the first Romanian state, founded by Basarab in 1330, was able to emerge in this area.

---

[52] 'Demum etiam cum nos in etate puerili post obitum karissimi patris nostri regnare cepissemus, Lythway wayuoda una cum fratribus suis per suam infidelitatem aliquam partem de regno nostro ultra alpes existentem pro se occuparet, et proventus illius partis nobis pertinentes nullis amonitionibus reddere curabat, sepedictum magistrum Georgium contra ipsum misimus, qui cum sumpmo fidelitatis opere pugnando cum eodem ipsum interfecit, et fratrem suum nomine Barbath captivavit et nobis adduxit; super quo nos non modicam quantitatem pecunie fecimus extorquere; et sic per eiusdem magistri Georgii servitium tributum nostrum in partibus eisdem nobis fuit restauratum' (Györffy, 'Román állam', p. 15). The best edition of the whole diploma, with a detailed description of the variants, copies and falsifications, and a diplomatic analysis, is in Györffy, 'Román állam', pp. 14–19.

[53] For *Szörényvár*, see *KMTL*, p. 657 (I. Petrovics).

BASARAB AND THE EMERGENCE OF WALLACHIA, 1330

Like his predecessors, Basarab was a Romanian voivode in Muntenia, the western half of the former Cumania, linked by vassal ties to the King of Hungary. In a diploma of King Charles I of Hungary, dated 26 July 1324, the king mentions him as *woyuodam nostrum Transalpinum*,[54] indicating that Basarab was a faithful vassal of the king at that time. In the sources, there is no direct clue to the date of his taking office as voivode of Wallachia, but it must have been between 1314 and 1322. These years were connected with the active presence of the Hungarian king in the region. During the turbulent years following the extinction of the House of the Árpáds (1301), the Banate of Severin also fell away from the jurisdiction of the Hungarian crown. The provincial lord (*tartományúr* in Hungarian) who gained the upper hand in Severin was Ban Theodore of Vejteh, along with his son John.[55] Theodore and John enjoyed the support of Michael Šišman, Despot of Vidin (*cum potentia domini dozpoth de Budinio*),[56] who later, in 1323, also occupied the throne of Tărnovo. Charles I dispatched his army under the command of Paul Széchy to bring the rebels to heel. In a grant given to the Széchy family on 23 October 1317, these events (which seem to relate to a time prior to 1315, most probably to 1314) are recounted in full detail.[57] Theodore of Vejteh was captured by the king's men, while his son John found refuge in the castle of Miháld (now Mehadia in Romania). Ban Theodore was tied to a horse's tail and dragged to the castle, but his son John, in Miháld, resisted the King's forces. On this occasion, then, King Charles I was not yet able to restore his suzerainty in the region. A few years later, towards the end of 1321 or the beginning of 1322 Charles I personally led a campaign to South Hungary that resulted in his recapture of the castle of Miháld from the rebel Vejteh family.[58] It was probably after 1321, therefore, that Basarab became the Hungarian king's faithful vassal as the voivode of Wallachia (*woyvoda Transalpinus*).

The question now emerges of when Basarab turned against his lord the Hungarian king. The date can be ascertained quite precisely; it must have

[54] Györffy, 'Román állam', p. 549. Earlier edition: Hurm., I/1, pp. 591–2.
[55] Theodore of Vejteh, coming from the Csanád clan, was the wealthiest landowner in the county of Temes. His name is known from diplomas from 1285 onwards; see Györffy, 'Román állam', pp. 538–9.
[56] Charles I's diploma of 23 October 1317: Györffy, 'Román állam', p. 548.
[57] Györffy, 'Román állam', p. 548.
[58] Holban, *Cronica rel.*, pp. 90–6; Engel, 'I. Károly', pp. 104, 130. The two campaigns against Miháld (1314 and 1321–2) were erroneously coalesced into one and dated to 1316 by Györffy, 'Román állam', p. 540.

happened between 26 July 1324 and 18 June 1325, the dates of two diplomas. In the first, Basarab is mentioned as *Woiuodam nostrum Transalpinum*, while in the second he is referred to as *Bazarab Transalpinum sancte regie corone infidelem*.[59] The date is very significant. After the death of George Terter II in 1323, Michael Šišman, the Despot of Vidin, himself half-Cuman, had been elected to the throne of Tărnovo. The new Bulgarian tsar succeeded in gaining the support of the Tatars (Σκύθαι) and the Vlakhs (Ούγγροβλά-χοι) in his struggle against the Byzantines.[60] He had also strengthened his alliance with the Vlakhs by giving his cousin Alexander, the future tsar, in marriage to Basarab's daughter. It was not by chance that a few years later, in 1330, the same Bulgarian–Tatar–Vlakh alliance confronted the Serbian force on the battlefield of Velbužd. Taking a stand with Michael of Bulgaria, Basarab supported an enemy of the Hungarian king, and it was only a question of time before the enmity became open; by 1325 at the latest, Basarab was considered an infidel vassal of the Hungarian king.

Between 1324 and 1330 we find no reference in the sources to any Ban of Severin, so it must have been during these years that the rebellious Basarab seized Fort Severin and the province.[61] On 1 February 1327, Pope John XXII sent identical letters to Solomon, Count of Brassó, Mikch, Ban of Slavonia, Thomas, Voivode of Transylvania, and Basarab, Voivode of Wallachia (*Comiti Salomoni de Brasso, Mikth* [correctly, *Mikch*] *bano totius Sclavonie, Thome woyvode Transilvano, Bazaras woyvode Transalpino*), in which he asked them to assist and support the Dominicans (*Inquisitores*) in their work against the heretics.[62] In his letter to Basarab, the Pope speaks of territories of the Hungarian Kingdom subjected to Basarab: *in terris tibi subiectis in regno Ungarie consistentibus*. This location is capable of different interpretations: according to Lupaş what is meant here is the territory of Severin that had been seized by Basarab a year earlier.[63] Contrary to this view, Pataki thinks that Basarab's original land, Muntenia (Wallachia without Severin = Oltenia) is the territory in question, which was acknowledged as belonging to the Hungarian crown.[64] I think that the Latin text itself and the whole situation favour Lupaş' interpretation: Severin was really

---

[59] Györffy, 'Román állam', pp. 549, 550.
[60] In Ioannes Kantakouzenos, 1.36.: Kant. *Hist.*/Schopen, I, pp. 175–6, = Kant. *Hist.*/Fatouros-Krischer, I, p. 124.
[61] Pesty, *Szörény*, I, p. 27. Without giving his source, Pesty mentions that the title of the Ban of Severin in 1324 was borne by Paul, Count of the counties of Szerém, Valkó and Bodrog. According to information kindly supplied by P. Engel, Pesty made a gross error in attributing the title of the Ban of Severin to this Paul (Paul Garai was his full name), since he was really the chief dignitary of these counties in 1323–8 but in his capacity as the Ban of *Mačva* (not *Severin*).
[62] Theiner, *Mon. Hung.*, I, p. 513 (no. 790), = Hurm., I, pp. 600–1 (no. 476).
[63] Lupaş, *Posada*, p. 125.   [64] Pataki, *Anjou*, pp. 31–2.

considered part of the Hungarian Kingdom, while the original territory of Basarab's Wallachia, that is, Muntenia, though in a vassal relationship with Hungary, had never been an integral part of the Hungarian Kingdom. Moreover, Severin's capture must have been the main cause of Basarab's becoming unfaithful to the Hungarian king and the object of King Charles I's punitive campaign in 1330. But before analysing the events and consequences of this campaign, the question of Basarab's ethnic extraction will be discussed here.

To his credit, it was Iorga who first called attention to the Cumans' role in the formation of the first Romanian state (he speaks of the Cuman–Romanian symbiosis as *colaboraţia româno-barbară*); moreover, he succeeded in identifying the second element of Basarab's name with the Turkic honorary title *aba, oba*, 'father, uncle, elder brother'.[65] He draws an interesting historical parallel: just as Muscovite Russia was the political successor to the Tatar state of the Golden Horde, so the Romanian state grew out of the Cumans' khanate.[66] Iorga's productive thinking concerning the Cuman origins of Basarab and his dynasty was more or less accepted even by Romanian researchers.[67] The best and most convincing solution was presented by Rásonyi, who derived the Romanian name from a well-attested Cuman-Kipchak personal name, *Basar-aba*. The second element, as had been stated by Iorga, is an honorary title (cf. the Cuman names *Arslanapa, Urusoba, Terteraba, Qutluba*, etc.; Pecheneg *Tonuzoba*, etc.), while the first element is a present participle from the verb *bas-*, 'to press, supress, rule, govern'. The name *Basar*, and other derivatives such as *Basan, Basmïš*, and *Bastï*, are well attested in old and modern Kipchak languages, both standing alone and as parts of compound names (e.g. *Ïz-basar, jol-basar, jaw-basar, Ïl-basar, Ïl-basan, Ïl-basmïš; Basar-oğul*, etc.).[68] The forms without a final *-a* appeared in Romanian (cf. the analogous development: Romanian *Catlapug* < Turkic *Qutlubuğa*).[69] The name *Basarab(a)* occurs dozens of times in Latin (Hungarian) and Slavic (Serbian and Romanian) sources of the fourteenth and fifteenth centuries.[70] The Slavic sources render the name as *Basaraba* and *Basarab*, but the Hungarian equivalents, in addition to the predominant forms of *Bazarab, Bozorab* (read *Basarab, Bosorab*), sometimes take forms such as *Bazarad, Bozorad, Bozarad, Basarat* (all read

[65] Iorga, 'Basaraba'.

[66] 'De même que la Russie moscovite succède au Khanat des Tartares, celui des Coumans passe à Ţara Românească' (Iorga, 'Basaraba', p. 101).

[67] Densuşianu, 'Originea'; Veress, 'Originea'; Popa-Lisseanu, *Izvoarele*, p. 28; Drăganu, 'Românii', pp. 520–5. Maybe Brătianu, 'Originea', p. 238, is the sole scholar to be rather sceptical about the origins of the name *Basarab*.

[68] Rásonyi, 'Contr.', esp. pp. 27–31 (247–51).   [69] *Ibid.*, p. 24 (244).

[70] For a comprehesive list of all forms, see Györffy, 'Román állam', pp. 543–4.

with -*s*-). Rásonyi and the Romanian researchers paid no attention to these strange forms. It is obvious that the original name ended with *b*, and the forms ending in *d* are secondary and must be explained by reference to the Hungarian language.[71] I think that the Hungarian forms *Baszarad*, *Baszarád*, can be explained the following way. Names ending in *b* were unusual in Old Hungarian, while personal and geographical names ending in *d* were common. The diminutive suffix +*d* was one of the most useful suffixes in the Old Hungarian period; any name could be used with or without it. (Two of the best-known Hungarian names ending in *d* during the Árpád period were *Árpád* and *Csanád*.) Consequently, when a Cuman and/or Romanian name such as *Basarab* entered Hungarian, in addition to the forms *Baszarab* > *Baszaráb* (well attested in the Hungarian sources), a secondary form such as *Baszarád* would also come into usage by analogy.[72]

In addition to explaining the name *Basarab(a)*, Rásonyi also explained the name of his father on Turkic grounds. But by contrast with the convincing etymology given for Basarab's name, the explanation of his father's name as being Cumano-Tatar is somewhat doubtful. The name of Basarab's father is known only from a diploma issued by King Charles I on 26 November 1332: *in terra Transalpina per Bazarab, filium* Thocomerii *scismaticum*.[73] Rásonyi derives this name from a well-known Cuman and Tatar name, *Toq-tämir*, gives ample data, and refers also to a Chingisid prince, *Toktomer*, mentioned in the Russian annals in 1295 as abiding in the Crimea.[74] The Turkic names are really convincing: the name *Toq-tämir* was especially in vogue in the Turco-Mongol steppe at the end of the thirteenth century. My doubts were raised by a remark of Györffy, who saw the original diploma and suggested an alternative reading, *Thotomerii*.[75] If that is correct, the possibility cannot be excluded that the name is identical with *Totomer* or *Tatamer*, frequently used in Hungary at that time.[76] But even if Basarab's father bore the Turkic name, his person can by no means by identified with a Chingisid prince. To

---

[71] Györffy's adventurous attempt to explain the form *Basarad* as deriving from an alleged Muslim name, *Başārat*, is totally unacceptable (Györffy, 'Román állam', pp. 543–4). He contents himself with the assertion that the (evidently original) form *Basarab* is secondary and leaves it without explanation.

[72] Two place-names in present-day Hungary, *Boszorád* (in the county of Nógrád) and *Bozorát* (in the county of Szabolcs) testify to the fact that *Baszarád* was a name that existed in old Hungary (see Györffy, 'Román állam', p. 544).

[73] Fejér, *CD*, VIII/3, p. 625, = Hurm., I, p. 625, = Györffy, 'Román állam', p. 555.

[74] Rásonyi, 'Contr.', pp. 251–3. For the same view cf. also Elekes, 'Basaraba'.

[75] Györffy, 'Román állam', p. 555, n. 103.

[76] For example, one of the well-known persons of the period was *Tatamer*, praepositus of Gyulafehérvár (Alba Iulia in Transylvania) and vice-chancellor of the court . In 1335, *Tatameri* (*Anjou Okm.*, III, p. 207, = Hurm., I, pp. 638–9, no. 51); in 1336, *Thatamerius* (*Anjou Okm.*, III, p. 290, = Hurm., I , pp. 645–7, no. 515); in 1342: *Thatamerii* (Fejér, *CD*, IX, p. 55, = Hurm., I, pp. 672–3, no. 535).

be a descendant of Chingis was a matter of such significance in the world
of the Turco-Mongol steppes that it could not have remained unknown in
the sources: no one could, or could have wanted to, conceal his Chingisid
descent.

Be that as it may, Basarab obviously bore a name of Turkic origin, and
possibly so also did his father. Though it cannot be definitely proved, they
were probably of Cuman extraction. But Basarab himself is expressly stated
to be a Vlakh; King Charles I speaks of him as *Bazarab infidelis* Olacus
noster.[77] The situation must have been very similar to that described in
connection with the Asen family a hundred years before. Like Asen and
his family, who were of Cuman extraction, and who founded a dynasty,
and became Bulgarians, Basarab and his family were also presumably of
Cuman extraction, founded a dynasty, and became Romanians. The figure
of an eagle on a helmet in the early coat of arms of the Basarabs seems to
point in the same direction: it must have been of totemistic origin, like
similar representations in Hungarian coats of arms of the Árpád period.[78]
Finally, an interesting episode from 1325 also seems to offer evidence that
the Basarab family had very strong Cuman contacts. In a diploma issued
on 18 June 1325 by Master Ladislaus, count of the royal chapel (*comes capelle
domini regis*), it is recounted that an injury befell a certain Paul of Ugal
at the hands of Stephen, son of Parabuh, a Cuman count in Hungary
(*Stephanus filius comitis Parabuh Comani*). This Stephen almost killed Paul
during a dispute, in the course of which the Cuman lord stated that the
strength of the Wallachian Basarab, recalcitrant subject of the Hungarian
king (*Bazarab Transalpinum sancte regie corone infidelem*) exceeded that of
the Hungarian king himself.[79] The evidence of this diploma is extremely
important, since it sheds light on the intimate connections which may have
existed between the Cumans of Hungary and the Cumans living east of
the Carpathians. The latter must have lived partly under the jurisdiction
of the Golden Horde and partly in subjection to the emerging Wallachian
state of Basarab.

After Basarab's secession from the Hungarian crown some time in 1324–5,
King Charles I probably wanted to chastise his faithless Wallachian vassal
Basarab, but he was compelled to wait some years to fulfil his plans. In
1326 the Hungarian king had to confront a severe Tatar attack somewhere

---

[77] See Györffy, 'Román állam', p. 555.

[78] According to E. Veress, the original emblem of the Basarabs was the eagle, venerated in the same way
as the bird *turul* (< Turkic *toğrul*) was by the Árpáds (Veress, 'Originea', p. 230). This supposition
was refuted by Brătianu ('Originea', p. 238), and accepted by Györffy, 'Román állam', p. 545, n. 37.
For the coat of arms of Wallachia, and the possible Byzantine and Hungarian connections of the
figure of the eagle, see Elekes, 'Havaselvi címer', p. 21.

[79] Györffy, 'Román állam', p. 550.

in Severin, which he repulsed successfuly.[80] Basarab was again in the camp inimical to the Hungarian king; he must have been among the direct or indirect supporters of the Tatars. In a later document, dated 27 March 1329, Basarab was mentioned among the king's enemies alongside the Bulgars, the Serbs and the Tatars. These enemies constantly attacked the Hungarian confines, but the king's castellan Dionysius Széchy, in Miháld (or Nagymiháld) in Severin (now Mehadia in Romania), sucessfully repelled them.[81]

As related in Chapter 6, on 28 July 1330 the Bulgars and their Wallachian, Tatar and Yas allies sustained a heavy defeat in the battle of Velbužd. Evidently King Charles I of Hungary considered this moment the most appropriate to launch a punitive expedition against Basarab and the rebellious Wallachians. The Hungarian chronicles (*Chronicon Pictum* fourteenth century; Thuróczy, fifteenth century) preserve a detailed account of the campaign.[82] Its first phase was accomplished quickly; in September 1330, King Charles marched to Severin, took it from Basarab and appointed Dionysius Széchy as Ban of Severin. Basarab surrendered to the king, offered to refund 7,000 silver marks for the costs of the army, and showed himself ready to continue paying tribute to the king and to send his son as hostage to the king's court. Some of the king's men such as Dancs, Count of Zólyom, and Liptó (*fidelis baro, Donch nomine, comes de Zolio et de Liptou*) advised acceptance of this reasonable offer, but Charles was unyielding; he wanted to punish the infidel vassal, so the campaign went on. The Hungarian army proceeded through Severin towards Argeş (today Curtea de Argeş) in Wallachia. Because of the low density of population, difficulties rose in the provision of food supplies; so the king was compelled to conclude an armistice with Basarab, and began to draw back. But the Wallachian chief had not intended to adhere to it, and barricaded the Hungarian army in a narrow pass. From the cliffs above, the Wallachians crushed the Hungarian troops by raining down arrows and lances and hurling rocks on the Hungarian warriors. The defeat was devastating, and the king was able to escape with his life only by exchanging his royal coat of arms for those of Desiderius Hédervári, who was killed

[80] *SS Pruss.*, I, p. 213, where an exaggerated number of 30,000 Tatar dead is mentioned.
[81] 'Cum nos ipsum magistrum Dionisium ad nostri regiminis augmentationem fideliter ab experto ferventem in castro nostro Nogmyhald vocato in confinio existente, contra Bulgaros, Bazarab woyuodam Transalpinum, regem Rascie scismaticum, ymo et Tartaros fines regni nostri ubi et unitatem ortodoxe fidei continue hostiliter invadentes constituissemus' (Györffy, 'Román állam', p. 552).
[82] *Chronici saeculi* XIV, §209: *SRH*, I, pp. 496–500; Thuróczy's *Chronicle*, II. xcvii, in Schwandtner, I, pp. 202–5.

later in the course of the battle.[83] According to Thuróczy, the king fled back to his royal residence in Visegrád through the town of Temesvár.

According to the formerly generally accepted view, the battle took place in the valley of Posada, between today's Cîmpulung and Bran (Törcsvár).[84] But Giurescu and others think that a place to the north-west of Argeş is more probable.[85] Various oriental auxiliary troops took part on both sides in the battle. Most of the Cumans who fought with the Hungarians perished in the fight (*Cumanorum denique corruit inestimabilis et plurima multitudo*).[86] The Wallachians were assisted by the Tatars (who may also have also been Cumans).[87] Charles I's defeat at Basarab's hands was a turning point in Hungarian–Wallachian relations; though the Hungarian kings tried to regulate the Wallachian voivodes again later in the course of the fourteenth century, they were successful only temporarily, and Basarab's victory irretrievably opened the way to independence for the Wallachian Principality.[88]

MOLDAVIA CASTS ASIDE TATAR AND HUNGARIAN TUTELAGE, 1359–1364

The formation of another 'Wallachian' state in Moldavia can be dated to a few decades later than that of Basarab's state. The territories between the eastern Carpathian ranges and the Dniester were also under direct Tatar control after 1242, but the ethnic map of this region in the century following the Tatar invasion is even more obscure than that of Oltenia and Muntenia. In addition to the Cuman and Tatar element present mainly in the region between the Prut and the Dniester, that is, the eastern half of later Moldavia, one must reckon with the ever-increasing immigration of Romanian ethnic elements both from the south (Muntenia, Bulgaria) and from Transylvania. The Romanians settled rather in the

---

[83] For a long time in the nineteenth century this Desiderius was erroneously identified in Hungarian scholarly literature as the (non-existent) son of Dionysius Széchy, the newly appointed Ban of Severin (courtesy of P. Engel).

[84] Lupaş, *Posada*, and others. Törcsvár (Bran) was a fortress in the Carpathians, not far from Brassó (Braşov); it was built by King Louis the Great in 1377 to defend the Hungarian borders against the Wallachians (Z. Kordé, in *KMTL*, p. 682).

[85] Giurescu, *Ist. Rom.*, I, p. 356; Györffy, 'Román állam', p. 546.

[86] *Chronici saeculi* XIV, §209: *SRH*, I, p. 499.

[87] In a diploma of Louis I of Hungary, dated April 24, 1351: 'predictusque Bozorab . . . cum tota sua potentia et vicinorum paganorum' (Fejér, *CD*, VII/3, p. 124, = Hurm., I/2, p. 14, = Györffy, 'Román állam', p. 562). The expression 'adjacent pagans' evidently refers to the Tatars.

[88] For a good summary of the events of 1320–30, see Kristó, *Anjou-kor*, pp. 78–85. Cf. also Minea, 'Războiul', p. 338; Lăzărescu, 'Lupta din 1330', p. 244.

hilly and wooded western and northern parts, and Hungarian and German (Saxon) ethnic elements also immigrated to the slopes of the eastern
Carpathians. It was precisely in these north-western parts, especially the
valley of the Moldva river, that the nucleus of another Romanian state
emerged.

The first significant rift in the monolithic Tatar power east of the
Carpathians resulted from the Hungarian campaign against the Tatars in
1345, and the ensuing power vacuum paved the way for the formation
of a new Romanian power centre in this region. The Tatars often raided
Transylvania, so it was not by chance that in 1345 King Louis I of Hungary
sent his Transylvanian voivode Andrew Lackfi and his Székely warriors
against the Tatars. Two contemporary Hungarian narrative sources provide
us with a detailed description of the campaign. The first is in Part 6 of the
Chronicle of John of Küküllő,[89] while the other is the Minorite Anonymous.[90] The event took place at Candlemas (Minorite Anonymous, 'circa
festum Purificationis beate virginis Marie'), that is, 2 February 1345. The
Voivode of Transylvania and the Székelys (John of Küküllő, 'cum siculis
nobilibus') penetrated the land of the Tatars and defeated them. The Tatar
prince Atlamïš,[91] who was brother-in-law to the khan and second in rank
to him, was captured, then decapitated in prison (John of Küküllő, 'cum
principe eorum nomine Athlamos'; Minorite Anonymous, 'princeps eorum
valde potens nomine Othlamus, secundus post Kanum, qui habebat in
uxorem sororem ipsius Kani, vivus captus est, sed postea decollatus'). The
remnants of the Tatars fled to their kinsmen in the coastal regions (John of
Küküllő, 'ad partes maritimas longe distantes ad alios tartaros fugerunt'). It
must have been a major blow to the Tatars. Their military defeat followed
by years of severe plague must have greatly reduced their number between
the Carpathians and the Dniester. After the Hungarian victory in 1345 the
Hungarian sphere of influence again stretched eastwards as far as the
Dniester, but the imminent danger of Tatar incursions was not over for
good; in the 1350s King Louis I of Hungary had several further clashes with
the Tatars.[92]

---

[89] *Font. dom.*, III, pp. 167–8. The above-mentioned Part 6 was taken over verbatim by the Chronicle
of Dubnic, the Chronicon Budense and Thuróczy. For the latter, see Schwandtner, I, p. 221.

[90] *Font. dom.*, III, pp. 151–2.

[91] The name as applied to this Tatar chief is unknown from other sources, but is itself a well-known
Turkic name: *Atlamïš* < *atla-*, 'to step, cross, pass' (Houtsma, p. 30; *MESz*, I, p. 171; Gombocz,
ÁTSz, p. 27). It also occurs later, in 1495 as *Athlamos*, the name of a Hungarian royal man (Csánki, I,
p. 685), probably of Cuman descent, and in 1515 as the name of a Székely (Bartholomeo Athlamos:
Szék. Okl., p. 248).

[92] Spuler, *GH*, p. 105.

At any rate, the event of 1345 was of utmost significance for the further history of Moldavia. Seeing the new power relations, Pope Clement VI considered it an appropriate moment to restore the Catholic Church hierarchy east of the Carpathians, which had been disrupted after the Tatar invasion. In his letter dated 29 January 1347 and addressed to the Hungarian Archbishop of Kalocsa (*archiepiscopo Colociensi*) he ordered the restoration of the episcopate of Milcov (*Episcopatus Milchovensis in regno Ungarie, in finibus Tartarorum*) and appointed as the new bishop one Thomas of Nympti, an Augustinian hermit and lector.[93]

It may seem paradoxical, but the spread of Hungarian influence in Moldavia after 1345 contributed to an increasing Romanian presence in the country. This is because the Romanian elements that organised the first Romanian state in Moldavia after 1345 had migrated from Hungary, from the county of Máramaros. This county, at the north-eastern corner within the Carpathian Mountains, was rather sparsely populated, and, as in all frontier regions of medieval Hungary, the Hungarian kings and nobility had tried to colonise the uninhabited territories by attracting foreign settlers. After the Tatar invasion in 1241–2, when half of the Hungarian Plain became depopulated, this colonising tendency spread over the whole country. Vlakh groups were settled in Hungary in greater numbers from the reign of Ladislaus IV (1272–90) onwards, and in the fourteenth century this tendency became more pronounced. Vlakh groups flocked to medieval Hungary from the Balkans, attracted by the possibility of a lighter tax burden and other favourable conditions. They arrived mainly from Greater Vlakhia (now in Central Macedonia), from the ecclesiastical jurisdiction of the bishopric of Vranje. The first Vlakhs must have appeared in Máramaros (Romanian *Maramureş*) at the end of the thirteenth century, but the first written evidence of the colonising activity of Vlakh *knezes* can be dated to 1326.[94] It is disputed whether the Romanians of Máramaros took part in Lackfi's Tatar campaign in 1345, but it seems plausible to reckon with their participation.[95]

The social and political organisation of the Romanian populations in north-west Moldavia and in Máramaros followed similar lines. The basic elements of this system had been taken over from the Slavs of the Balkans much earlier: *knezes* were the chiefs of villages, and several *knezes* would choose the voivode from among their number. With the progress

---

[93] Theiner, *Mon. Hung.*, I, pp. 737–8 (no. 1107), = Hurm., I/2, pp. 4–5 (no. 4).
[94] For a good summary of the history of Máramaros until the mid-fourteenth century, see Györffy, *Geogr. hist.*, IV, pp. 111–21.
[95] Spinei, *Moldavia*, p. 177.

of feudalisation, these elected positions became increasingly hereditary, and a Romanian elite of boyars began to be formed. The major difference between north-west Moldavia and Máramaros lay in the political loyalties of the two groups. The latter always fell within the confines of medieval Hungary under the Hungarian king's jurisdiction, whereas the former belonged to the khans of the Golden Horde. After 1345, Moldavia's political dependence on the Tatars was loosened, which created favourable circumstances for the Hungarian king to assert his old political claim to 'Cumania', especially as the southern part of the former Cumania had been transformed by Basarab into the new state of Wallachia. It was Dragoş, voivode of Máramaros, who, as an agent of the Hungarian king, was sent to north-west Moldavia to enforce the Hungarian king's rule.[96] The arrival of Dragoş in Moldavia is traditionally dated to 1359, which is considered by the Romano-Slavic chronicles to be the year of the birth of the Moldavian Principality. But we must not forget that King Louis I of Hungary had sent his Romanian voivode to assert his rights in Moldavia, and not to found a state, as was thought afterwards. King Louis always speaks of Moldavia as his property; in a famous diploma of 1365 (to be discussed below) he mentions Moldavia four times as *terra nostra Molduana*.[97] So Spinei and others are quite right to call Dragoş and the Romanians of Máramaros tools of the Hungarian king's policy.[98] Moreover, the timing of Dragoş' arrival in Moldavia (often referred to in native Romanian historiography as the *descălecat*, 'dismounting', meaning 'founding of land') was well chosen; it was in 1359, after the death of Berdibek Khan, that the twenty-year period of anarchy and struggles for the throne began in the Golden Horde, and this diverted the Tatar state's attention from their faraway western *uluses* and prevented them from directly influencing events in Moldavia. But it must be stressed that the south-eastern part of what was later to become the Principality of Moldavia, especially the coastal areas, remained unquestionably under Tatar suzerainty. The centre of Dragoş' Moldavian voivodeship must have been in the north-western parts, round the Moldva river and in Bukovina. But the new Romanian vassal state of Hungary did not last long. Soon Bogdan, another Romanian voivode of Máramaros, appeared, expelled Dragoş' successors, and laid the foundation of an independent Moldavian principality.

---

[96] This Dragoş, who is identified as Dragoş of Bedő (Bedeu), has often been falsely identified with another Dragoş, son of Gyula (Giula) (Spinei, *Moldavia*, p. 199).
[97] *Doc. hist. Valach.*, pp. 178–80.   [98] Spinei, *Moldavia*, p. 203.

Bogdan, son of Mikola, first appeared in Máramaros in 1334–5 when, together with his people, he migrated from the Balkans to Máramaros and settled there. The centre of the area he occupied was Konyha (now Cuhea) on the Iza river.[99] Soon after Louis I's enthronement (1342) Bogdan's relations with the Hungarian king deteriorated, and in a diploma of 21 October 1343 he is mentioned as the former Voivode of Máramaros who became unfaithful to the king ('Quondam woyvoda de Maramarosio, noster infidelis').[100] The direct causes and time of Bogdan's exodus from Máramaros are not precisely known, but it must have resulted from the disgrace Bogdan suffered at the king's hands, in consequence of which he lost even his voivodeship. According to the narrative sources, he secretly left Máramaros with his people and made for Moldavia, which was quite destitute at that time because of the proximity of the Tatars.[101] This fact of Bogdan's exodus from Máramaros to Moldavia is corroborated by King Louis I's diploma of 2 February 1365, given to Balk, son of Sas, Voivode of Máramaros. This Balk fled Moldavia for Hungary, leaving his parents, acquaintances, and property behind him.[102] For his services, the King gave him Konyha (Cuhea) and other possessions in Máramaros. These possessions had formerly belonged to Bogdan.[103]

The historical events can therefore be reconstructed as follows. Bogdan, a disgraced voivode of Máramaros, secretly fled to Moldavia and expelled Sas, voivode of Moldavia. Judging by the diploma just mentioned, this must have happened prior to its issue, that is, some time in 1364. The new voivode Bogdan declared himself independent and did not accept Hungarian vassalage. So Bogdan can rightly be regarded the first ruler of the independent Principality of Moldavia, though its foundation can be linked

---

[99] Györffy, *Geogr. hist.*, IV, p. 118. The attempts of Romanian historiography (Spinei, *Moldavia*, p. 204) to disconnect Bogdan, Voivode of Máramaros, and Bogdan, son of Mikola, who migrated from the south to Máramaros, and make them two persons, lack any evidence. The apparent objective of these attempts is to prove the groundless hypothesis that the Romanians are very old settlers, even indigenous to Máramaros.

[100] Mihályi, *Máramaros*, p. 17.

[101] Thuróczy's *Chronicle*, III.xlix: 'Huius etiam tempore, Bogdan, Wayvoda Olachorum de Maramorosio, coadunatis sibi Olachis ejusdem districtus, in terram Moldaviae, coronae Regni Hungariae subiectam, sed a multo tempore, propter vicinitatem Tartarorum habitatoribus destitutam, clandestine recessit' (in Schwandtner, I, p. 245).

[102] 'De terra nostra Molduana suis caris parentibus et quam plurimis cognatis nec non bonis universis in eadem terra nostra post tergum relictis et postpositis, in regnum nostrum Hungarie advenit' (*Doc. hist. Valach.*, pp. 178–9, no. 141).

[103] 'Quandam possessionem Kuhnya vocatam . . . a Bokdan voyvoda et suis filiis, nostris videlicet infidelibus notoriis ob ipsorum detestandam infidelitatis notam, eo quod idem Bokdan et filii sui de dicto regno nostro Hungarie in pretactam terram nostram Molduanam clandestine recedentes eandem in nostre maiestatis contumeliam moliuntur conservare' (*Doc. hist. Valach.*, p. 180, no. 141).

to the name of Dragoş and his son Sas, agents of the Hungarian king.[104]
This is also corroborated by the fact that the Turkish name for Moldavia
is *Kara Boğdan*, which evidently refers to Bogdan, founder of the principality.[105] Romanian tradition preserved in the Slavo-Romanian chronicles,
however, lists Dragoş and Sas as the first voivodes of Moldavia. The two
traditions appear to conflict, but both are true. Dragoş founded a principality as vassal and agent of the Hungarian king, whereas Bogdan seized
the new voivodeship and withdrew it from the tutelage of the Hungarian
king. One might say that Bogdan stole the show from the Hungarian king.
So the Moldavian Principality was born amid the struggles between the
Golden Horde and the Hungarian Kingdom. With the decay of Tatar
power, Hungary tried to infiltrate the power vacuum by founding a new
vassal state in Moldavia. But Bogdan and his men skilfully expropriated
the Hungarian initiative and made their own state. It is quite natural that
Romanian national historiography should put Bogdan on a pedestal, but
to say that Louis I of Hungary found him an opponent worthy of him is an
exaggeration.[106] Louis was the greatest king of the region in his age, worthily
called *Great* by posterity, whereas Bogdan was a provincial Romanian
chief of Máramaros, who made the Moldavian state independent of the
Hungarian crown. He may be a Romanian national hero, but the two
persons are not of the same stature.

The Moldavian state founded in 1359–64 comprised no more than two-
thirds of the territory of the later Principality of Moldavia. The south-
eastern third remained under Tatar rule, and these territories fell under
the jurisdiction of the Voivode of Moldavia only towards the end of the
fourteenth century. In what follows we shall trace the fate of these coastal
regions of the later Moldavian Principality.

TATAR CONTOL OVER THE TOWNS OF THE DANUBE
AND DNIESTER DELTAS

The region of the Danube delta has always been a typical frontier zone
between Byzantium and the northern *barbaricum*. As we saw earlier, the
territories north of the Danube delta became directly subjected to the
Tatars, and towards the end of the thirteenth century it was one of

---

[104] For the genealogy and later fate of the Dragoş family, see *Doc. hist. Valach.*, pp. 179–80.
[105] First used by Yazıcıoğlu ʿAlī at the end of the fourteenth century; cf. Decei, 'Turcs Seldjoucides',
      pp. 98–9, = Decei, *Rel. rom.-or.*, pp. 180–1.
[106] 'A reconciliation between Louis and Bogdan cannot be conceived, the Hungarian monarch finding
      an opponent worthy of him' (Spinei, *Moldavia*, p. 211).

the centres of Nogay's power. The towns of the Danube delta were mostly founded by the Byzantines prior to the Tatar invasion, when they fell under Tatar control. But despite their Byzantine foundation and their Tatar control, it was the Genoese who became the real actors on the scene in these towns.

The ascension of the maritime and commercial power of the Genoese within the Byzantine Empire began in the second half of the thirteenth century, when Michael VIII, then Emperor of Nikaia, concluded the famous Treaty of Nymphaion with Genoa on 13 March 1261. The Genoese pledged themselves to place fifty ships at the Byzantines' disposal to fight against the Venetians in Constantinople, while the commercial privileges of the Venetians would be transferred to the Genoese. These privileges included tax-free commerce within the empire and free passage to the ports of the Black Sea. In addition, the Genoese were given Smyrna, and they established their own quarters in Constantinople, Thessalonike and other ports. The Treaty of Nymphaion secured the commercial power of Genoa in the Black Sea and the eastern Mediterranean for the coming two centuries.[107] Finally, Emperor Michael succeeded in reconquering Constantinople from the Latins without Genoese aid in August 1261. The Genoese entered Constantinople, and in 1267 a new treaty secured them a settlement in Galata, on the other side of the Golden Horn. The Genoese possessed the most important ports on the Black Sea: Sinop and Trabzon on the southern shores; Kaffa and others in the Crimea; Vicina, Kilia and Licostomo on the Danube; and Maurocastro on the Dniester. We need to take a closer look at the latter four towns.

Vicina was in the territory of today's Isaccea, on the right side of the Danube. It was under Byzantine jurisdiction, but by the end of the thirteenth century a flourishing Genoese community was present in the town under the leadership of a consul.[108] After the fall of Nogay and his son, Teodor Svetoslav, the new Bulgarian ruler (1300–21), took over the jurisdiction of the Danube delta. The Genoese refused to undertake commercial activities in the towns under Bulgarian rule, probably because of the newly introduced Byzantine customs duty imposed on them. After Teodor Svetoslav's death (1321), the control of the area between the Lower Danube and Dniester returned to Tatar hands. This supposition about Bulgaria's temporary control over the Danube and Dniester deltas was put forward

[107] Geanakoplos, *Emp. Michael*, pp. 89–91. For an overall picture of the Black Sea trade prior to the Ottoman conquest, see Brătianu, *Mer Noire*.
[108] Giurescu, 'Lower Danube', p. 589, n. 7; Balard, 'Bas-Danube', pp. 2–3.

by Brătianu and others,[109] but has not been shared by all. Spinei,[110] for example, asserts that there is insufficient evidence, and thinks that, even if the Bulgars were there in the towns, they would have had to pay tribute continuously to the Tatars. Deletant is right in stating that the debate may have arisen from the ambiguity of the terms 'control', 'rule' and 'sway'.[111] Bujak and Dobrudja were typical frontier areas, and power was exercised through gathering taxes and applied mainly to the ports and towns, traditional centres of trade, while the sparsely populated province remained untouched by the power relations of the towns. Be that as it may, in 1331/2 Vicina was still under Byzantine control, but by 1337 or 1338 it had fallen directly into the hands of the Tatars. At that time Makarios, the newly consecrated Metropolitan of Vicina, promised the Patriarch of Constantinople that he would not desert his flock now that it was under pagan rule.[112] The Tatar capture of Vicina may be seen in the context of a broader Tatar plan to launch an overall attack against Byzantium. This attack was averted by a Byzantine legate sent to the Tatar khan's court.[113] The Genoese did not leave Vicina after the Tatar takeover, but the town declined in importance, as was clearly marked by the transfer of the Metropolitan see of Vicina to Wallachia in 1359.

The town of Kilia, like Vicina, was founded by the Byzantines (cf. the Greek etymology of its name: τὰ κελλία, 'granaries, warehouses, cellars'). It was situated on the right-hand shore of the northern branch of the Danube delta, some 20 km from the former Lykostomion and 3–4 km south-west of today's Chilia Veche. An early occurrence of the name can be found in Rašīd ad-Dīn's historical work, which records that in 1241/2, on his way back from Dalmatia, the Mongolian warlord Qadan occupied Tărnovo and Kilia.[114] After the Tatar invasion it must have remained in Byzantine jurisdiction. In 1318–23 it is mentioned in a church document as belonging to the Patriarchate of Constantinople.[115] By 1340 it must have slipped into the hands of the Tatars.[116] Probably in 1337 or 1338, Umur's Turks from Aydın launched a sea campaign at Kilia against the Tatars and their Romanian allies.[117] They must have raided the area of the Danube delta with Byzantine consent, since they passed the Dardanelles, and Umur himself stayed in

[109] Brătianu, 'Bulgares', pp. 153–68. For further literature, see Spinei, *Moldavia*, p. 124, n. 89.
[110] Spinei, *Moldavia*, pp. 123–5.   [111] Deletant, 'Gen., Tat., Rum.', p. 516.
[112] Laurent, 'Macaire de Vicina', pp. 230–1.
[113] Papacostea, 'De Vicina à Kilia', p. 70; and in Chapter 8 of this book.
[114] Cf. Decei, 'L'invasion', p. 120.   [115] *Acta Patr. Const.*, I, no. 95.
[116] Laurent, 'Macaire de Vicina', p. 230.   [117] Enverī/Mélikoff, vv. 1209–1306.

Constantinople for a while before they went on their way.[118] The Genoese appeared in Kilia only during 1350–60. For this period some wonderful source material stands at our disposal: the records of Antonio di Ponzò, a Genoese notary of Kilia.[119] In 1360, then, Kilia was a frontier town at the westernmost point of Tatar influence. It is not known from any source when the Tatar jurisdiction ceased, but it must have been soon after 1360, during the troubled years of the Golden Horde. First it went over to the Wallachian prince. There are numerous conjectures as to the date of this event (1361, 1388–90, 1394–5, 1402, 1403, 1404), but none of the evidence is conclusive.[120] At any rate, at the beginning of the fifteenth century it must already have belonged to the Moldavian Principality. In a treaty of King Sigismund of Hungary and King Władysław Jagiełło of Poland, concluded in Lubló in Upper Hungary (now L'ubovňa in Slovakia), Kilia is mentioned as Moldavian property.[121]

The third town on the Danube, Lykostomion (or Licostomo), was a fortified settlement on an island of the Danube (now on the mainland), near today's Periprava. Not far from Periprava, on the left side of the Danube, there is a settlement called Vîlcov(o) in Moldavia. The latter name (< Slavic *v"lk*, 'wolf') corroborates the Greek etymology of Lykostomion ('wolf's throat'). Lykostomion was first mentioned in the ninth century as a town founded by the Byzantines. By the 1350s it had become an important port from which mainly grain and cereals were exported.[122]

At the Dniester delta the most important town was Cetatea Albă (Romanian), Belgorod Dnestrovskij (Russian), Maurocastro (Greek, Italian) or Moncastro (Italian), Ak-kerman (Turkish-Tatar), or Nyeszterfehérvár (Hungarian). Each nation called it 'white town/castle' in its own language, but the Greek name means 'black town/castle'.[123] It had been built on the right side of the bay of the Dniester (*Dnestrovskij liman* in Russian), on the ruins of Greek Tyras. In the thirteenth century Akkerman soon fell under Tatar rule. Though the Genoese used it as a port, it never became a colony of Genoa. If Brătianu's assertion holds true, during the first two decades

---

[118] Lemerle, *Aydin*, pp. 129–43, puts this event in 1341 (after Emperor Andronikos III's death) and erroneously identifies Umur's enemies with the Bulgarians. Alexandrescu-Dersca (*Umur*, pp. 3–23) prefers the date 1337 or 1338, which seems the right solution. Cf. also Zachariadou, *Trade and Crus.*, p. 40, n. 158; Diaconu, *Kili.*

[119] Edited in Pistarino, *Notai.*   [120] See Deletant, 'Gen., Tat., Rum.', p. 528, n. 94.

[121] *Cod. dipl. Pol.*, I, pp. 46–8.   [122] Deletant, 'Gen., Tat., Rum.', pp. 522–3.

[123] For the history of *Akkirman*, see *TDV İA*, II, pp. 269–70 (M. L. Bilge). I could not find any explanation for the seeming contradiction between *Maurocastro*, 'black town', and other names of the town meaning 'white town'.

of the fourteenth century the towns of Bessarabia, including Akkerman, fell under Bulgarian jurisdiction.[124] The Bulgars' presence is indicated in 1314 by an incident in the course of which a Franciscan friar, Angelus de Spoleto, was killed by the Bulgars.[125] But the Tatars had not left the city, and the martyrdom of St John the New in 1330 at the Tatars' hands testifies to their presence and power in the town.[126] The Tatar presence can also be attested by the coins of the Golden Horde up to the 1360s. In the Tatar period Akkerman was an important trading port of the Black Sea, having close contact with the Genoese colonies in the Crimea. Its main export was cereals. According to the evidence of the excavations in Akkerman (L. Polevoj, A. Kravčenko, and others) a sizable community of Central Asian people engaged in handicraft and trade must also have inhabited the town.[127] The Tatars must have abandoned the town, like other towns in the region between the Prut and the Dniester,[128] in the critical decades following 1360, but their political control faded away only gradually.

We must remember that, after the Hungarian-Székely victory over Atlamïš in 1345, the erosion of the Tatars' power east of the Carpathians began. The process was further accelerated by the years of anarchy following Berdibek Khan's death in 1359. Finally, in 1363 a severe blow was dealt to the united Tatar army of Qutlu-beg (or Qutlu-buǧa?), Ḥājjï-beg, and Dmitriy, by Olgerd, the Grand Prince of Lithuania, at Sinie Vody, near the mouth of the Dnieper.[129] According to Górka,[130] the Lithuanians went as far as the Danube and must have captured Maurocastro on their way. At any rate, the Tatar influence did not fade away completely, since a part of the territory between the Danube delta and the Bug remained under the jurisdiction of the Tatar prince Dmitriy.[131] Tatar control over Maurocastro and its hinterland lasted well into the last quarter of the fourteenth century. There is an important Genoese source that sheds light on the question of jurisdiction at that time. In 1386 two Genoese envoys arrived in Maurocastro from Kaffa. They were accredited to the Moldavian princes Petru Muşat (c. 1377–c. 1391) and Costea (c. 1377–c. 1390), at a time when enmities cast a shadow over the Tatar–Genoese connections. The two Genoese were

[124] Nikov, 'B"lg. i tat.', pp. 138–9.   [125] Wadding, *Annales*, VII, p. 714.
[126] Heppell, *Camblak*, p. 21.   [127] Egorov, *Ist. geogr.*, pp. 79–80.
[128] Polevoj, *Ist. geogr. Mold.*, p. 69.
[129] Cf. Kuczyński, 'Sine Wody', pp. 157–77; Spuler, *GH*, pp. 116–17; Batūra, *Lietuva*, pp. 271–82.
[130] Górka, 'Zagadnienie', pp. 325–91.
[131] King Louis I of Hungary, in his diploma of 22 June 1368, granted tax exemption to the merchants of Dmitriy, Prince of the Tatars (*Domini Demetry Principis Tartarorum*) when they came to Hungary, in return for the same privileges as were enjoyed by the merchants of Brassó, subjects of the Hungarian king in Dmitriy's land (*in terra ipsius Demetry*) (Hurm., 1/2, p. 144).

ambaxiatores euntes Constantino et Petro vayvoda, and so exercised power in Maurocastro and its surroundings.[132] The date of 1386 gives us the *terminus ante quem* of the loss of the Tatar power in Maurocastro. In the following year Prince Petru Muşat became the vassal of Władysław Jagiełło, King of Poland. Polish power spread towards Moldavia and sought to control Maurocastro because of the commercial significance of this area for Poland; Maurocastro lay at the southern end of the commercial route connecting the Baltic region and Poland to the Black Sea. The following fifteenth century then saw an unprecedented boom of commerce in Maurocastro, but that period lies outside the scope of this work.

Just as the Polish king wished to possess an access route to the Black Sea, and by 1387 had gained control over Maurocastro, so it was in the interest of the Hungarian kings to have direct access to the Danube delta, especially to the port of Kilia. It is generally supposed that in the mid-fourteenth century there existed a so-called 'Hungarian corridor' between Wallachia and Moldavia.[133] But, while the port of Brăila was within this corridor and the stations of the Brassó–Brăila route are well-known, Kilia did not belong to this corridor. The records of the notary Di Ponzò, mentioned above, clearly demonstrate that in 1360 Kilia was still a Genoese colony under Tatar jurisdiction; and even later, Hungarian control never reached Kilia.

---

[132] See Papacostea, 'Aux débuts', pp. 141–2.
[133] The idea was first put forward by Iorga, *Hist.*, III, p. 161.

Conclusion

Many of the results of this investigation have been presented as isolated conclusions, especially when I have summarised sections or chapters of this book. It is now time to offer an overview of the main lessons drawn from the Cumans' and Tatars' presence in the Balkans. The most enduring impact of these nomadic peoples and empires on the history of the Balkans in the twelfth to fourteenth centuries affects three areas; first, political history; secondly, military history, and thirdly, ethnic history.

First, the Cumans' role in the political history of the Balkans was decisive in the period from 1185 to the 1330s. Cumans were the founders of three successive Bulgarian dynasties (the Asenids, the Terterids and the Šišmanids) and of the Wallachian dynasty (the Basarabids). Thus, apart from a few years of interregnum under the illegitimate pretenders Ivaylo (1277–80) and later Smilec (1292–7), all the dynasties of the Second Bulgarian Kingdom were of Cuman origin. They also played a considerable role in the political history of contemporary Byzantium, Hungary, and Serbia, and certain members of Cuman immigrant communities became integral members of the recipient country's elite (cf. Köten's relatives in Hungary, or Syrgiannes/Saronius and his family in Byzantium). The infiltration and rise to power of the immigrant Cuman elites in the Balkanic countries in 1242–1330 proceeded under the control and approval of the Tatar state of the Golden Horde. By all accounts, in that period the Cumans and the Tatars took an active part in writing the political history of the Balkans.

Secondly, the Cumans and Tatars also played a special role in the military history of the Balkans in the twelfth to fourteenth centuries. Their ubiquitous presence in the wars and battles of the Balkan Peninsula was well known to their contemporaries, who were well aware that without their military aid no warring party could claim victory over its opponents. Their decisive role in the Balkanic wars can be ascribed mainly to their use of nomadic light cavalry, which was practically invincible in those centuries.

Thirdly, the political and military role of the Cuman and Tatar warriors in the Balkanic lands made their settlement in different parts of the Balkanic countries necessary. It was not only a considerable part of the Bulgarian and Romanian (Wallachian and Moldavian) upper classes, the layer of the boyars and the *knezs*, that became thoroughly permeated by Cuman ethnic elements in the thirteenth and fourteenth centuries, but masses of the Cuman common people, too, must have settled in different parts of the Balkans. Systematic research into the former Cuman and Tatar settlements of the Balkans, drawing on the evidence of historical geography, place-names and linguistic data, remains to be carried out.

Finally, in addition to these general lessons, this book will, I hope, facilitate a better understanding of the pre-Ottoman Balkans in that it emphasises the idea that the Ottoman conquest was not an accidental and uniquely tragic event in the Balkans. The Balkans were ripe for the Ottoman conquest in the second half of the fourteenth century. The internal anarchy and the helplessness of the Balkanic local elites hastened Ottoman progress, and neither decadent Byzantium nor the enfeebled Serbian and Bulgarian states could defend their populations from the conquest of the most organised and ideologically motivated army of the age, that of the Ottomans. Within the framework of the Ottoman Empire the Balkans remained at peace for 500 years. The Balkanic nationalisms, the devastating local and world wars, the mass murders and ethnic cleansings of the nineteenth and twentieth centuries, have demonstrated that small nation states can create more complex problems and inflict deeper wounds than an imperialism like that of the Ottomans in the sixteenth to nineteenth centuries or the feudal anarchy dominating the Balkans in the thirteenth and fourteenth centuries could ever produce. At the same time, the lessons of this book may disperse the rosy clouds of nostalgia that hang over the medieval golden age of the pre-Ottoman Balkans, depicted with so much zeal by the historiographies of the Balkanic nation states. For the Balkans in the thirteenth and fourteenth centuries were the same grieving and afflicted lands as during Ottoman rule or at the end of the twentieth century. The Balkans have yet to find the key and meaning of their historical existence and to decide whether they want to belong to the mainstream of European development or to insist on their Byzantine and Ottoman autocratic traditions. This process of clarification will be the chief task of the third millennium.

APPENDIX I

Geographical names

This list contains only those geographical names that have different forms in different languages. Languages are designated by abbreviations: Bulgarian (Bu), Greek (Gr), Hungarian (Hu), Latin (La), Polish (Po), Romanian (Ro), Russian (Ru), Serbian (Se), Ukrainian (Uk).

Adrianople: Hadrianoupolis (Gr), Drinápoly (Hu), Edirne (Tu)
Agathopolis (Gr), Ahtopol (Bu)
Ainos (Gr), Enez (Tu)
Amaseia (Gr), Amasya (Tu)
Arkadioupolis (Gr), earlier Bergule (Gr), Lüleburgaz (Tu)
Athyras (Gr), Büyük Çekmece (Tu)
Balkans: Haimos (Gr)
Barcaság (Hu), Burzenland (Ge), Ţara Bîrsei (Ro)
Belgrade: Beograd (Se)
Beroe (Gr), Stara Zagora (Bu)
Bizye (Gr), Vize (Tu)
Braničevo (Se, Bu), Barancs (Hu)
Brassó (Hu), Braşov (Ro), Kronstadt (Ge)
Cracaw: Kraków (Po)
Danube: Istros (Gr), Ister, Danubius (La), Dunav (Bu), Duna (Hu), Dunărea (Ro), Donau (Ge)
Esztergom (Hu), Gran (Ge)
Fogaras (Hu), Făgăraş (Ro)
Gallipoli: Kallioupolis (Gr), Gelibolu (Tu)
Gyulafehérvár (Hu), Alba Iulia (Ro)
Halys (Gr), Kızıl Irmak (Tu)
Haram (Hu), later Palánka (Hu), Bačka Palanka (Se)
Iaşi (Ro), Jászvásár (Hu)
Ikonion (Gr), Iconium (La), Konya (Tu)
Jambol (Bu), Diampolis (Gr)
Kamenča (Bu), Sovolštica (Bu)

Kilia: Chilia (Ro), Kili (Tu)
Konyha (Hu), Cuhea (Ro)
Krassó (Hu), Karaš (Se), Caraş (Ro)
Kučevo (Se), Kucsó (Hu)
Kypsella (Gr), İpsala (Tu)
Lwów (Po), L'vov (Ru), L'viv (Uk), Lemberg (Ge)
Mačva (Se), Macsó (Hu)
Magnesia (Gr), Manisa (Tu)
Maiandros (Gr), Menderes (Tu)
Máramaros (Hu), Maramureş (Ro)
Marica (Bu), Hebros (Gr), Meriç (Tu)
Maros (Hu), Mureş (Ro)
Mesembria (Gr), Nesebăr (Bu)
Miháld (Hu), Mehadia (Ro)
Nagyolaszi (Hu), Franca Villa (La), Mandjelos (Se)
Nikaia (Gr), Nicaea (La), İznik (Tu)
Nikopol (Bu), Nikopolis (Gr), Nikápoly (Hu)
Niš (Se), Naissos, Nisos (Gr)
Ojtoz (Hu), Oituz (Ro)
Plovdiv (Bu), Philippoupolis (Gr)
Rasa (Se), Rascia (La), Rácország (Hu)
Rhaidestos (Gr), Tekirdağ (Tu)
Rousion (Gr), Keşan (Tu)
Šabac (Se), Szabács (Hu)
Saqči (Ta), Isaccea (Ro)
Selymbria (Gr), Silivri (Tu)
Severin (Bu, Se, Ro), Szörény (Hu)
Silistra (Bu), earlier Drăstăr (Bu)
Sliven (Bu), Stilbnos (Gr)
Soli (Se), Só (Hu), later Tuzla (Se)
Sofia (Bu), earlier Sredec (Bu), Sardike (Gr), Triaditza (Gr), Serdica (La)
Stanimaka (Bu), Stenimachos (Gr), modern Asenovgrad (Bu)
Szalánkemén (Hu), Slankamen (Se)
Szávaszentdemeter (Hu), Sremska Mitrovica (Se)
Szeben (Hu), Sibiu (Ro), Hermanstadt (Ge)
Székesfehérvár (Hu), Alba Regia (La)
Szerém, Szerémség (Hu), Srem (Se), Sirmion (Gr), Sirmium (La)
Temes (Hu), Timiş (Ro)
Temesvár (Hu), Timişoara (Ro)
Thessalonike (Gr), Selanik (Tu)

Tonzos (Gr), Tundža (Bu), Tunca (Tu)
Törcsvár (Hu), Bran (Ro)
Torda (Hu), Turda (Ru)
Torockó (Hu), Rimetea (Ro)
Turnu Severin (Ro), Szörényvár (Hu)
Tzurulon (Gr), Çorlu (Tu)
Usora (Se), Ozora (Hu)
Velbužd (Bu, Se), Kjustendil (Bu)
Vidin (Bu, Se), earlier Bdin' (Bu), Bodony (Hu)

Chronological table of dynasties

GOLDEN HORDE

	(CHINGIS KHAN)
1227	Batu
1256	Berke
1267	Mengü-Temür
1280	Tuda-Mengü
	Telebuga
1287 / 1291	Toqta
1312	Özbek
1341	Tinibek
1342	Jänibek
1357	Berdibek
1359	ANARCHY

BULGARIA

1186	Ivan Asen I
1196	Peter Asen
1197	Kaloyan
1207	Boril
1218	Ivan Asen II
1241	Kaliman Asen I
1246	Michael Asen
1256	Kaliman Asen II
1257	Konstantin Tikh
1277	Ivaylo
1279	Ivan Asen III
1280	George Terter I
1292	Smilec
1299	Teodor Svetoslav
1322	George Terter II
1323	Michael Šišman
1330	Ivan Stefan
1331	Ivan Alexander
1371	

BYZANTIUM

1185	Isaakios II Angelos
1195	Alexios III Angelos
1203	Theodoros I Laskaris
1222	Ioannes III Doukas Batatzes
1254	Theodoros II Laskaris
1258	Ioannes IV Laskaris
1261	Michael VIII Palaiologos
1282	Andronikos II Palaiologos
1328	Andronikos III Palaiologos
1341	Ioannes V Palaiologos
1346	Ioannes VI Kantakouzenos
1351	Ioannes V Palaiologos
1391	

SERBIA

	(GRAND ŽUPANS)
1217	Stefan Nemanja
1227	Stefan Radoslav
1234	Stefan Vladislav
1243	Stefan Uroš I
1276	Stefan Dragutin
1282	Stefan Uroš II Milutin
1321	Stefan Uroš III Dečanski
1331	Stefan Uroš IV Dušan
1355	Stefan Uroš V
1371	

HUNGARY

1173	Béla III
1196	Imre
1204	Ladislas III
1205	Andrew II
1235	Béla IV
1270	
1272	Ladislas IV (Kun László)
1290	Andrew III
1301	Charles I Robert of Anjou
1342	Louis I, the Great of Anjou
1382	

Maps

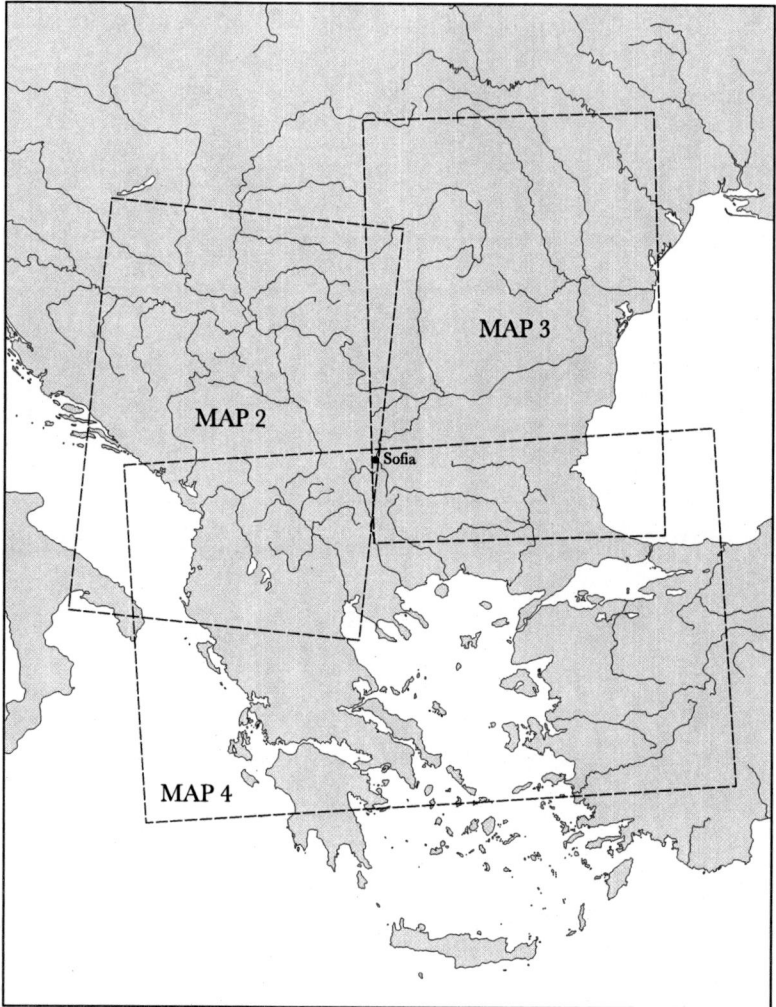

Map 1 The Balkans and adjacent territories

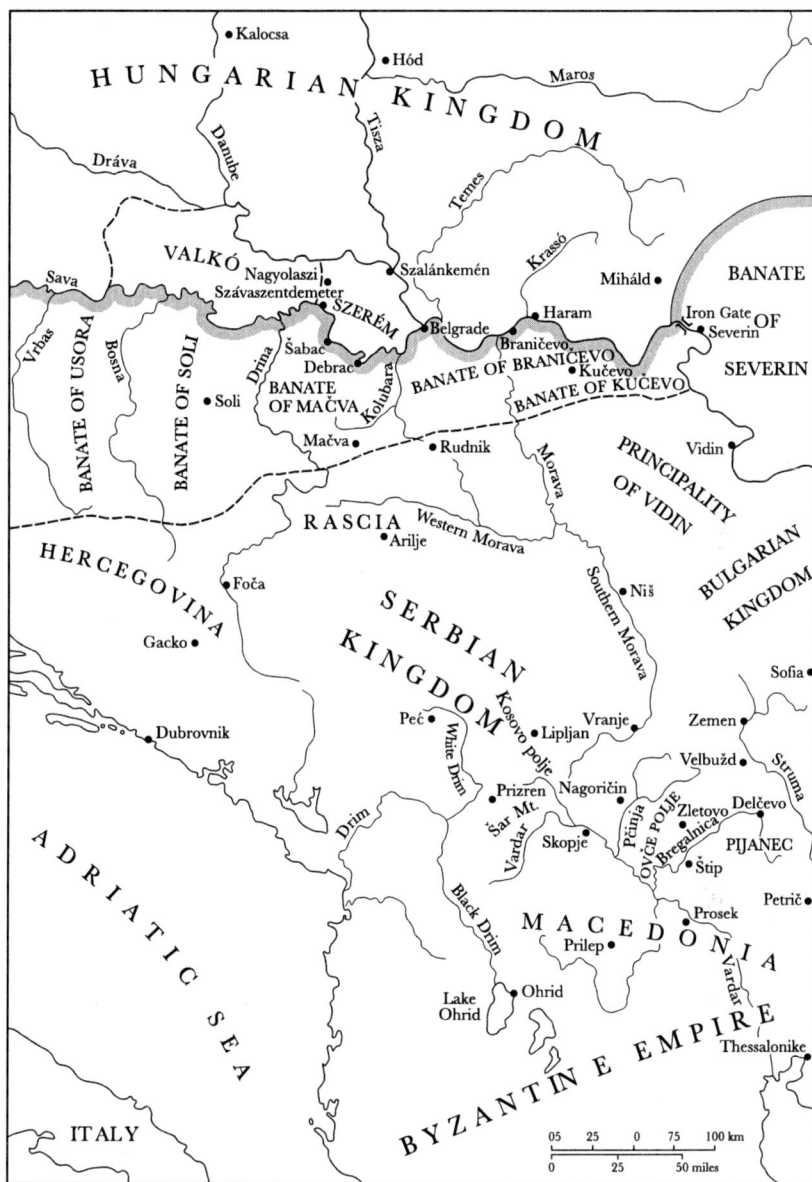

Map 2   The northwestern Balkanic lands

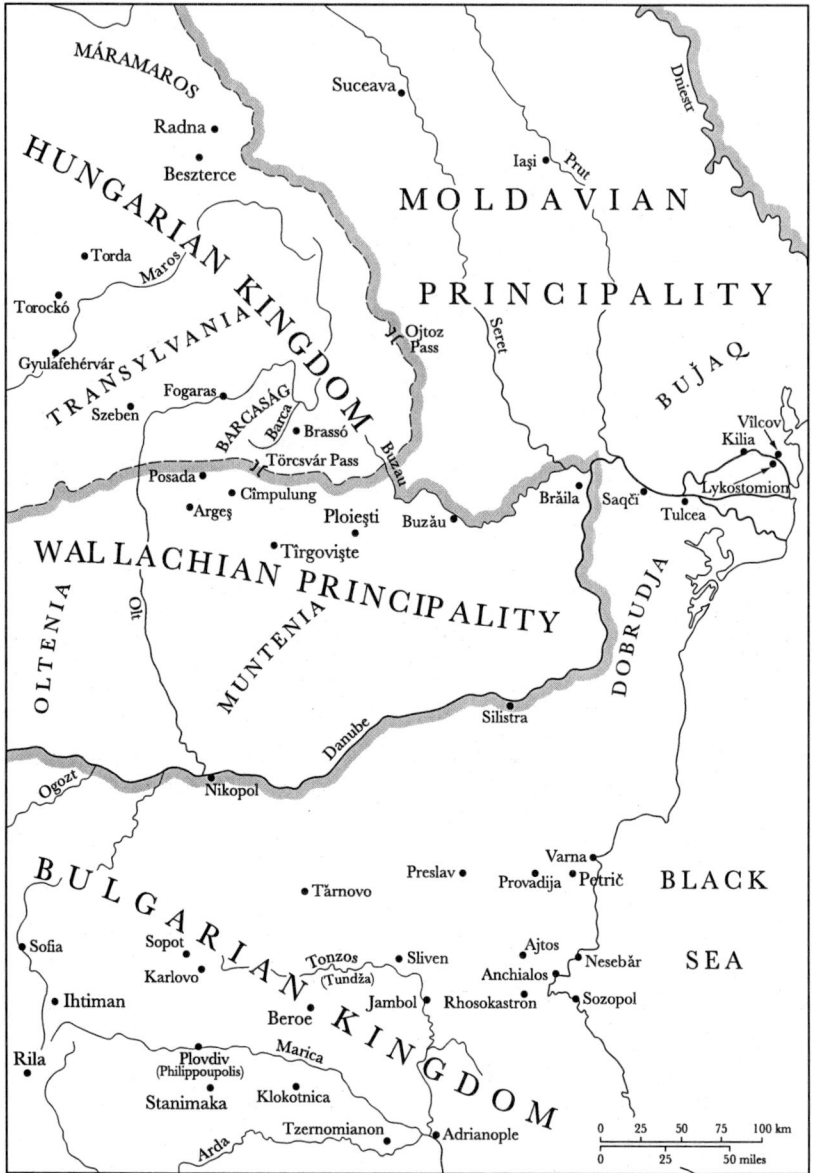

Map 3 The northeastern Balkanic lands

Map 4 The central and southern Balkanic lands

Abbreviations

ACIEB

Actes du XIVe Congrès International des études byzantines (Bucarest 6–12 septembre 1971), I–II. Bucharest, 1975.

Acta Patr. Const.

Acta Patriarchatus Constantinopolitani . . ., Fr. Miklosich and Ios. Müller (eds.)

Actes de Lavra

Lemerle, P., Guillou, A., and Svoronos, N., *Actes de Lavra.*

AECO

Archivum Europae Centro-Orientalis (Budapest)

AEMAe

Archivum Eurasiae Medii Aevi

Alemany, *Alans*

Alemany, A., *Sources on the Alans.*

Alexandrescu-Dersca, 'Umur'

Alexandrescu-Dersca, M., 'L'expédition d'Umur beg . . .'

Altaner, *Dominikaner*

Altaner, B., *Die Dominikanermission des XIII. Jahrhunderts.*

Amitai-Preiss, *Mongols and Mamluks.*

Amitai-Preiss, R., *Mongols and Mamluks.*

Anastasijević-Ostrogorsky

Anastasijević, D., and Ostrogorsky, G., 'Les Koumanes pronoiaires'.

And. Dand. *Chron.*/Muratori

Andreas Dandulus, *Chronicon Venetum.*

Anjou Okm.

Anjoukori Okmánytár.

Anna Komn. *Alex.*/Reiffersch.

Annae Comnenae porphyrogenitae *Alexias.*

Ann. Frol./Muratori

Annales Frolovienses.

Ansbert/Chroust

Quellen zur Geschichte des Kreuzzuges Kaiser Friedrichs I. A. Chroust (ed.), pp. I–II5.

AOH	*Acta Orientalia Academiae Scientiarum Hungaricae* (Budapest).
Aqsarāyī/Işıltan	Işıltan, F., *Die Seldschukengeschichte des Aqsarâyî*
Aristov, 'Zemlja polov.'	Aristov, N., 'O zemle poloveckoj'.
Artuk, *Sikkeler*	Artuk, İ., and Artuk, C., *İstanbul . . . islâmî sikkeler kataloğu.*
Asdracha, *Rhodopes*	Asdracha, C., *La région des Rhodopes aux* xiiie *et* xive *siècles.*
ASPh	*Archiv für slavische Philologie.*
Atanasov	See Pavlov-Atanasov, *Preminavaneto.*
ÁÚO	*Árpádkori új okmánytár.*
Balard, 'Bas-Danube'	G. Balard, M., 'Notes sur les ports du Bas-Danube au* xve *siècle'.
Bănescu, *L'ancien état*	Bănescu, N., *L'ancien état bulgare et les pays roumains.*
Bănescu, *Sec. emp. bulg.*	Bănescu, N., *Un problème d'histoire médiévale.*
Bartol'd, *Soč.* v.	Bartol'd, V. V., *Sočinenija,* v.
Bartusis, *Late Byz. Army*	Bartusis, M. C., *The Late Byzantine Army.*
Bartusis, 'Smallholding soldiers'	Bartusis, M., 'On the problem of smallholding soldiers in late Byzantium'.
Baski	See Rásonyi-Baski.
Batūra, *Lietuva*	Batūra, R., *Lietuva tautų kovoje prieš Aukso Ordą.*
Bekker	See Schopen-Bekker.
Bendefy, *Gyeretyán*	Bendefy, L., *A magyarság kaukázusi őshazája.*
Binon, 'Prostagma'	Binon, S., 'A propos d'un prostagma inédit d'Andronic III Paléologue'.
Bödey, 'Rilai Szent Iván'	Bödey, J., 'Rilai Szent Iván legendájának magyar vonatkozásai'.
Bogdan, *DŞM*	Bogdan, J., *Documente lui Ştefan cel Mare,* i–ii.
Boissonade, *Anec. Graeca*	Boissonade, J. F. (ed.), *Anecdota Graeca.*
Bosch, *Andronikos III.*	Bosch, U. V., *Kaiser Andronikos III. Palaiologos.*

Boutouras, *Kyria onom.*	Boutouras, A. Ch., *Ta neoellēnika kyria onomata.*
Božilov, *Asenevci*	Božilov, I., *Familijata na Asenevci.*
Brătianu, 'Bulgares'	Brătianu, G. I., 'Les Bulgares à Cetatea Albă (Akkerman) au début du xive siécle'.
Brătianu, 'Commerce Génois'	Brătianu, G. I., *Recherches sur le commerce génois dans la mer Noire au xiiie siècle.*
Brătianu, *Mer Noire*	Brătianu, G. I., *La mer Noire: des origines à la conquête ottomane.*
Brătianu, 'Originea'	Brătianu, G., 'În jurul originei stemelor Principatelor Române'.
Brătianu, *Recherches*	Brătianu, G. I., *Recherches sur Vicina et Cetatea Albă.*
Bretschneider, *Med. Res.*	Bretschneider, E., *Mediæval Researches from Eastern Asiatic Sources.*
Brun, *Černomor'e*	Brun, F., *Černomor'e: sbornik issledovanij.*
BSOAS	*Bulletin of the School of Oriental and African Studies* (London).
Burmov, 'Šišmanovci'	Burmov, A., 'Istorija na B"lgarija prez vremeto na Šišmanovci (1323–1396 g.)'.
Byz.-slav.	*Byzantinoslavica.*
Byz.-turc.	Moravcsik, Gy., *Byzantinoturcica,* I–II.
BZ	*Byzantinische Zeitschrift* (Munich).
CAJ	*Central Asiatic Journal* (Leiden).
Cankova-Petkova, *Asenevci*	Cankova-Petkova, G., *B"lgarija pri Asenevci.*
CFHB	*Corpus Fontium Historiae Byzantinae.*
Chron. *Morea*/Schmitt	Schmitt, J. (ed.), *The Chronicle of Morea.*
Chroust	See Ansbert/Chroust and *Hist. peregr.*/Chroust.
Clari/Pauphilet	*Historiens et chroniqueurs du Moyen Age.* Robert de Clari: pp. 17–91.

Clauson, *ED*	Clauson, G., *An Etymological Dictionary of Pre-Thirteenth-Century Turkish.*
Clauson, 'Uyğur'	Clauson, G., 'The name Uyğur'.
Cod. Dipl. Pol.	Dogiel, Matthaeus [Maciej] (ed.), *Codex diplomaticus regni Poloniae . . .*
Constantinidi-Bibicou, 'Yolande'	Constantinidi-Bibicou, H., 'Yolande de Montferrat'.
Const. Porph., *DAI*/Moravcsik	Constantine Porphyrogenitus: *De administrando imperio*, ed. Gy. Moravcsik, trans. R. J. H. Jenkins.
Csapodi, *Anonymus*	Csapodi, Cs., *Az Anonymus-kérdés története.*
Csánki	Csánki, D., *Magyarország történelmi földrajza a Hunyadiak korában*, I–V.
CSHB	*Corpus Scriptorum Historiae Byzantinae.*
Dančeva-Vasileva, *Lat. imp.*	Dančeva-Vasileva, A., *B"lgarija i Latinskata imperija (1204–1261).*
Daničić	See Danilo/Daničić.
Danilo/Daničić	*Životi kraljeva i arhiepiskopa srprskih.*
Danilo/Hafner	*Serbisches Mittelalter: altserbische Herrscher-biographien.*
Danilo/Mirković	Danilo, Arhiep., *Životi kraljeva i arhiepiskopa srpskih.*
Decei, 'La Horde d'Or'	Decei, A., 'La Horde d'Or et les pays roumains'.
Decei, 'L'invasion'	Decei, A., 'L'invasion des Tatars de 1241/1242'.
Decei, *Rel. rom.-or.*	Decei, A., *Relaţii româno-orientale.*
Decei, 'Turcs Seldjoucides'	Decei, A., 'Le problème de la colonisation des Turcs Seldjoucides'.
Deletant, 'Gen., Tat., Rum.'	Deletant, D., 'Genoese, Tatars and Rumanians at the mouth of the Danube in the fourteenth century'.
Densuşianu, 'Originea'	Densuşianu, O., 'Originea Basarabilor'.
DeWeese, *Baba Tükles*	DeWeese, D., *Islamization and Native Religion.*

Diaconu, *Coumans*	Diaconu, P., *Les Coumans au Bas-Danube aux* XIe *et* XIIe *siècles.*
Diaconu, 'Kili'	Diaconu, P., 'Kili et l'expédition d'Umur Beg'.
Dimashqī/Mehren	*Cosmographie de Chems-ed-Din Abou Abdallah Mohammed ed-Dimichqui.*
Dinić, 'Odnos'	Dinić, M., 'Odnos izmedju kralja Milutina i Dragutina'.
Doc. hist. Valach.	*Documenta historiam Valachorum in Hungaria illustrantia.*
Doc. Ital.	*Documenti di storia Italiana.*
d'Ohsson, *Hist.*	d'Ohsson, A. C. M., *Histoire des Mongols.*
Dölger, *Regesten*	Dölger, F., *Regesten der Kaiserurkunden des oströmischen Reiches.*
DOP	*Dumbarton Oaks Papers* (Washington, DC).
Drăganu, 'Românii'	Drăganu, N., 'Românii în veacurile IX–XIV'.
Duda, 'Isl. Quellen'	Duda, H. W., 'Zeitgenössische islamische Quellen'.
Dujčev, 'Conquête turque'	Dujčev, I., 'La conquête turque et la prise de Constantinople dans la littérature contemporaine'.
Dujčev, 'V"stanieto'	Dujčev, I., 'V"stanieto v 1185 g. i negovata hronologija'.
EEBS	*Epetēris Hetaireias Byzantinōn Spoudōn.*
Egorov, *Ist. geogr.*	Egorov, V. L., *Istoričeskaja geografija Zolotoj Ordy v* XIII–XIV *vv.*
EI	*Enzyklopaedie des Islam*, I–IV.
EI²	*Encyclopedia of Islam*, I–.
Elekes, 'Basaraba'	Elekes, L., 'Basaraba családja'.
Elekes, 'Havaselvi címer'	Elekes, L., 'A havaselvi vajdák címere a középkorban'.
Elekes, 'Román fejl.'	Elekes, L., 'A román fejlődés alapvetése'.
Engel, 'I. Károly'	Engel, P., 'Az ország újraegyesítése: I. Károly küzdelmei az oligarchák ellen (1310–1323)'.

Enverī/Mélikoff	*Le Destān d'Umūr Pacha (Düstūrnāme-i Enveri) . . .* I. Mélikoff-Sayar (trans. and ed.).
EphK	*Egyetemes Philologiai Közlöny* (Budapest).
Ephraim/Bekker-Mai	*Ephraemius* ex recognitione Immanuelis Bekkeri.
Érszegi, 'Neue Quelle'	Érszegi, G., 'Eine neue Quelle zur Geschichte der bulgarisch-ungarischen Beziehungen während der Herrschaft Borils'.
Failler	See also Pachym. *Hist.*/Failler-Laurent.
Failler, 'Euphrosyne'	Failler, A., 'Euphrosyne l'épouse du tsar Théodore Svetoslav'.
Fasmer	Fasmer, M., *Étimologičeskij slovar' russkogo jazyka*, I–IV.
Fejér, *CD*	Fejér, G., *Codex Diplomaticus Hungariae*.
Ferenţ, *Kunok*	Ferenţ, I., *A kunok és püspökségük*.
Flemming, *Pamph. Pis. Lyk.*	Flemming, B., *Landschaftsgeschichte von Pamphylien, Pisidien und Lykien im Spätmittelalter*.
FNESz	Kiss, L., *Földrajzi nevek etimológiai szótára*.
Font. dom.	*Fontes domestici*, I–III. M. Florianus (ed.).
Gáldi-Makkai, *Gesch. Rum.*	Gáldi, L., and Makkai, L., *Geschichte der Rumänen*.
Gardīzī/Martinez	Martinez, A. P., 'Gardīzī's two chapters on the Turks'.
Geanakoplos, *Emp. Michael*	Geanakoplos, D. J., *The Emperor Michael Palaeologus and the West, 1258–1282*.
Geanakoplos, 'Pelagonia'	Geanakoplos, D. J., 'Greco-Latin relations on the eve of the Byzantine restoration: the Battle of Pelagonia, 1259'.
Georg. Akr. *Chron.*	Georgios Akropolites, *Chronike syngraphé*
Georg. Akr. *Chron.*/Bekker	*Georgii Acropolitae Annales*.

Georg. Akr. *Chron.*/Heisenberg	*Georgii Acropolitae opera*, A. Heisenberg (ed.).
Giurescu, *Ist. Rom.*	Giurescu, Constantin C., *Istoria Românilor*, i.
Giurescu, 'Lower Danube'	Giurescu, C. C., 'The Genoese and the Lower Danube in the xiiith and xivth centuries'.
Golden, 'Cumanica'	Golden, P. B., 'Cumanica ii: The Ölberli (Ölperli).'
Golden, 'Tribes'	Golden, P. B., 'The tribes of the Cuman-Qipchaqs'.
Golubovskij, *PTP*	Golubovskij, P., *Pečenegi, torki i polovcy do našestvija tatar.*
Gombocz, *ÁTSz*	Gombocz, Z., *Árpádkori török személy-neveink.*
Gombos, *Cat.*	Gombos, A. F., *Catalogus fontium historiae Hungaricae.*
Górka, 'Zagadnienie'	Górka, O., 'Zagadnienie czarnomorske w polityce polskiego średniowiecza'.
Gorovei, 'Moldavie'	Gorovei, Şt., 'L'état roumain de l'est des Carpates . . .'
Grabler, *Abenteuer*	*Abenteuer auf dem Kaiserthron.*
Grabler, *Kreuzfahrer*	*Die Kreuzfahrer erobern Konstantinopel.*
Grekov-Jakubovskij, *ZO*	Grekov, V. D., and Jakubovskij, A. Ju., *Zolotaja Orda i ee padenie.*
Grigorevič, *Donesenie*	Grigorevič, V. I., *Donesenie putešestvij po slavjanskim zemljam.*
GSU	*Godišnik na Sofijskija Universitet.*
Guilland, *Recherches*	Guilland, R., *Recherches sur les institutions byzantines.*
Gyárfás	Gyárfás, I., *A jász-kúnok története.*
Gyóni, *Kékaumenos*	Gyóni, M., *A legrégibb vélemény a román nép eredetéről.*
Gyóni, *Paristrion*	Gyóni, M., *Zur Frage der rumänischen Staatsbildungen.*
Gyóni, *Szórv.*	Gyóni, M., *A magyar nyelv görög feljegyzéses szórványemlékei.*

Györffy, 'Besenyők' Györffy, Gy., 'Besenyők és magyarok'.

Györffy, *Geogr. hist.* Györffy, Gy., *Az Árpád-kori Magyarország történeti földrajza.*

Györffy, 'Kun és komán' Györffy, Gy.,'A kun és komán népnév eredetének kérdéséhez'.

Györffy, 'Román állam' Györffy, Gy., 'Adatok a románok XIII. századi történetéhez és a román állam kezdeteihez'.

Hambis See Pelliot-Hambis.

Hafner See Danilo/Hafner.

Hammer-Purgstall, *GH* Hammer-Purgstall, J. von, *Geschichte der Goldenen Horde in Kiptschak.*

Heisenberg See Georg. Akr. *Chron.*/Heisenberg.

Heppell, *Camblak* Heppell, M., *The Ecclesiastical Career of Gregory Camblak.*

Hist. peregr./Chroust *Quellen zur Geschichte des Kreuzzuges Kaiser Friedrichs I.* A. Chroust (ed.), pp. 116–72.

Höfler, 'Walachen' Höfler, C. R. von, 'Die Walachen als Begründer des zweiten bulgarischen Reiches . . .'

Holban, *Cronica rel.* Holban, M., *Din cronica relațiilor româno-ungare în secolele* XIII–XIV.

Hóman-Szekfű Hóman, B., and Szekfű Gy., *Magyar történet*, I–V.

Horváth, 'Török int.' Horváth, J., ifj., 'Török politikai intézmények nyomai a középkori magyar állam életében'.

Houtsma Houtsma, M. Th., *Ein türkisch-arabisches Glossar.*

Howorth, *History* Howorth, H. H., *History of the Mongols from the 9th to the 19th Century.*

Hruševskyj, *Ist.* Hruševskyj, M., *Istorija Ukrainy-Rusi*, I–IX.

Hunfalvy, *Oláhok tört.* Hunfalvy, P., *Az oláhok története*, I–II.

Hurm. Hurmuzaki, Eudoxiu, and de-Densușianu, Nic., *Documente privitóre la istoria Românilor.*

İA	*İslâm Ansiklopedisi*
Iac. Morat. *Chron.*	Iacobus Moratinus, *Chronicon de rebus Foroliviensibus.* In *Doc. Ital.*, VI.
Ibn Battuta/Gibb	Gibb, Hamilton A. R. (trans.), *The Travels of Ibn Battuta A.D. 1325–1354.*
Ibn Bībī/Houtsma	Houtsma, Th., *Histoire des Seldjoucides d'Asie Mineure.*
Idrīsī/Jaubert	Jaubert, A., *Géographie d'Edrisi.*
Iliev, 'Car Boril'	Iliev, N., 'Otnosno vremeto na potušavane bunta sreštu car Boril v"v Vidin'.
Iliev, 'Šišm. pohod'	Iliev, N., 'Šišmanovijat pohod sreštu S"rbija prez 1292 g.'.
Iordan, *Toponimia*	Iordan, I., *Toponimia Romînească.*
Iorga, 'Basaraba'	Iorga, N., 'Imperiul Cumanilor şi domnia lui Basaraba'.
Iorga, *Hist.*	Iorga, N., *Histoire des Roumains.*
İzm.	*Altınordu devleti tarihine ait metinler.*
JA	*Journal Asiatique* (Paris).
Jagić, 'Beitrag'	Jagić, V., 'Ein Beitrag zur serbischen Annalistik . . .'
Jakó, *Erd. Okm.*	*Erdélyi Okmánytár*, I. (1028–1300).
Jakubovskij, 'Pohod'	Jakubovskij, A. Ju., 'Rasskaz Ibn-al-Bibi o pohode maloazijskih turok na Sudak'.
Jaubert	See Idrīsī/Jaubert.
JEEH	*Journal of European Economic History* (Rome).
Jerney, *Kel. ut.*	Jerney, J., *Keleti utazása.*
Jireček, *Bulg.*	Jireček, C. J., *Geschichte der Bulgaren.*
Jireček, *Ist. Srba*	Jireček, K., *Istorija Srba*, I–II.
Jireček, *Serb.*	Jireček, K., *Geschichte der Serben.*
Jireček, *Staat u. Ges.*	Jireček, K., *Staat und Gesellschaft in mittelalterlichem Servien.*
Jireček, 'Überreste'	Jireček, C., 'Einige Bemerkungen über die Überreste der Petschenegen und Kumanen'.
Joinville/Wailly	Jean Sire de Joinville, *Histoire de Saint Louis.*

JRAS	*Journal of the Royal Asiatic Society* (London).
Kafalı, *AO*	Kafalı, M., *Altın Orda Hanlığının kuruluş ve yükseliş devirleri.*
Káldy-Nagy, 'Kleinasien'	Káldy-Nagy, Gy., 'Kleinasien im Spannungsfeld von vier neuen Machtzentren um 1260'.
Kant. *Hist.*	Ioannes Kantakouzenos, *Historia.*
Kant. *Hist.*/Fatouros-Krischer	Johannes Kantakuzenos, *Geschichte*, Georgios Fatouros and Tilman Krischer (trans. and eds.).
Kant. *Hist.*/Schopen	*Ioannis Cantacuzeni imperatoris historiarum libri* IV.
Karácsonyi, 'Hódtavi csata'	Karácsonyi J., 'A hódtavi csata éve. 1282'.
Karácsonyi, 'Székelyek'	Karácsonyi J., 'Az erdélyi székelyek első hadjárata 1210-ben'.
Karayan.-Weiss	Karayannopulos, J., and Weiss, G., *Quellenkunde zur Geschichte von Byzanz (324–1453).*
KCsA	*Kőrösi Csoma Archivum* (Budapest).
Kekaum. *Strat.*/Litavrin	*Sovety i rasskazy Kekavmena.*
Kekaum. *Strat.*/Wassil.-Jern.	*Cecaumeni strategikon et incerti scriptoris de officiis regiis libellus.* B. Wassiliewsky and V. Jernstedt (eds.).
Kern, 'Libellus'	Kern, A., 'Der "Libellus de Notitia Orbis"'.
Kljaštornyj, 'Das Reich der Tataren'	Kljaštornyj, S. G., 'Das Reich der Tataren in der Zeit vor Činggis Khan'.
KMTL	*Korai magyar történeti lexikon (9–14. század).*
Kniezsa, *Szláv jöv.*	Kniezsa, I., *A magyar nyelv szláv jövevényszavai.*
Kossányi, 'Úzok és kománok'	Kossányi, B., 'Az úzok és kománok történetéhez a XI–XII. században'.
Középk. hist. okl.	*Középkori históriák oklevelekben (1002–1410).*

Kristó, *Anjou-kor*	Kristó, Gy., *Az Anjou-kor háborúi.*
Kuczyński, 'Sine Wody'	Kuczyński, St. M., 'Sine Wody'.
Laiou, *Const. and the Latins*	Laiou, Angeliki E., *Constantinople and the Latins.*
Laurent	See Pachym. *Hist.*/Failler-Laurent.
Laurent, 'L'assaut'	Laurent, V., 'L'assaut avorté de la Horde d'Or'.
Laurent, 'Bardariōtōn'	Laurent, G., '*Ho Bardariōtōn ētoi Tourkon*: Perses, Turcs asiatiques ou Turcs hongrois?'
Laurent, 'Macaire de Vicina'	Laurent, V., 'Le Métropolite de Vicina Macaire et la prise de la ville par les Tartares'.
Laurent, 'Mélikès'	Laurent, V., 'Une famille turque au service de Byzance, les Mélikès'.
Lăzărescu, 'Lupta din 1330'	Lăzărescu, E. C., 'Despre lupta din 1330 a lui Basarab Voevod cu Carol Robert'.
Lăzărescu-Zobian, 'Cumania'	Lăzărescu-Zobian, M., 'Cumania as the name of thirteenth century Moldavia'.
Lăzărescu-Zobian, *Kipch. Rum.*	Lăzărescu-Zobian, M., *Kipchak Turkic Loanwords in Rumanian.*
Lemerle, *Aydin*	Lemerle, P., *L'Émirat d'Aydin.*
Lemerle, 'Recherches'	Lemerle, P., 'Recherches sur le régime agraire à Byzance'.
Leonid, 'Han Nagaj'	Leonid, Arhimandrit, 'Han Nagaj i ego vlijanie na Rossiju i južnyh slavjan',
Letopis/Stojanović	*Stari srpski rodoslovi i letopisi.*
Ligeti, 'Magyar, baskír, király'	Ligeti, L., 'A magyar nép mongol kori nevei (magyar, baskír, király)'.
Ludewig, *Reliquiae*	*Reliquiae manuscriptorum omnis aevi . . . Ex museo Io. Petri Ludewig.*
Lupaş, *Posada*	Lupaş, I., 'Lupta de la Posada 1330'.
Makk, 'II. István'	Makk F., 'Feljegyzések II. István történetéhez'.
Makkai	See Gáldi-Makkai, *Gesch. Rum.*

Makkai, *Milkói püspökség*	Makkai, L., *A milkói (kún) püspökség és népei.*
Malingoudis, 'Zweit. bulg. Staat'	Malingoudis, Ph., 'Die Nachrichten des Niketas Choniates . . .'
Mándoky, *Hantos*	Mándoky, K. I., 'A Hantos-széki kunok'.
Marquart, *Komanen*	Marquart, J., *Über das Volkstum der Komanen.*
Martene-Durand, *Vet. SS.*	*Veterum scriptorum et monumentorum . . . collectio.*
Marvazī/Minorsky	Minorsky, V., *Sharaf al-Zaman Tahir Marvazī.*
Mavromatis, *Miloutin*	Mavromatis, L., *La fondation de l'empire serbe: le kralj Miloutin.*
Melich, 'Barcza'	Melich, J., 'Barcza, Barczaság, Bárcza'.
Melich, *Honf. Magy.*	Melich, J., *A honfoglaláskori Magyarország.*
Mélikoff	See Enverī/Mélikoff.
Menges, *Vost. èl.*	Menges, K. G., *Vostočnye èlementy v Slovo o polku Igoreve.*
MESz	Gombocz, Z., and Melich, J., *Magyar etymologiai szótár.*
MGH SS	*Monumenta Germaniae Historica: Scriptores.*
Migne, *PG*	*Patrologiae cursus completus.* Series Graeca.
Migne, *PL*	*Patrologiae cursus completus.* Series Latina.
Mihályi, *Máramaros*	Mihályi, J., *Máramarosi diplomák a XIV. és XV. századból.*
Miklosich, *Mon. Serb.*	*Monumenta Serbica . . .* Fr. Miklosich (ed.).
Minea, 'Războiul'	Minea, I., 'Războiul lui Basarab cel Mare cu regele Carol Robert (Noemvre 1330)'.
Minorsky	See Marvazī/Minorsky.
Mirković	See Danilo/Mirković.

Mladenov, 'Belgun'   Mladenov, St., 'Potekloto i s"stav"t
                                      na srednob"lg. Belgun', prekor na
                                      car' Asenja I.'
Mon. Pol. hist.   Monumenta Poloniae historica.
Moravcsik, Árpád-kor   Moravcsik, Gy., Az Árpád-kori
                                      magyar történet bizánci forrásai.
Muratori, SS Ital.   Muratori, L. A., Rerum Italicarum
                                      scriptores.
Murnu, Ist. Rom. Pind   Murnu, G., Istoria Românilor din
                                      Pind.
Mutafčiev, 'Dobr.'   Mutafčiev, P., 'Die angebliche
                                      Einwanderung von Seldschuk-
                                      Türken'.
Mutafčiev, Ist.   Mutafčiev, P., Istorija na b"lgarskija
                                      narod.
Mutafčiev, 'Proiz. Asen.'   Mutafčiev, P., 'Proizhod"t na
                                      Asenevci'.
Mutafčiev, 'Vojniški zemi'   Mutafčiev, P., 'Vojniški zemi i vojnici
                                      v Vizantija prez XIII–XIV v.'
NEH   Nouvelles études d'histoire
Németh, HMK   Németh, Gy., A honfoglaló magyarság
                                      kialakulása.
Németh, 'quman und qūn'   Németh, J., 'Die Volksnamen quman
                                      und qūn'.
Nicol, Epiros   Nicol, Donald M., The Despotate of
                                      Epiros, 1267–1479.
Nicol, Last Centuries   Nicol, D. M., The Last Centuries of
                                      Byzantium, 1261–1453.
Nicol, Rel. Emp.   Nicol, D. M., The Reluctant Emperor.
Nik. Chon. Hist.   Niketas Choniates, Chronike diegesis.
Nik. Chon. Hist./van Dieten   Nicetae Choniatae Historia, I–II.
Nik. Greg. Hist.   Nikephoros Gregoras, Historia.
Nik. Greg. Hist./Schopen-Bekker   Nicephori Gregorae Byzantina
                                      historia.
Nik. Greg. Hist./van Dieten   Nikephoros Gregoras: Rhomäische
                                      Geschichte. Historia Rhomaike.
Nikov, 'B"lg. i tat.'   Nikov, P., 'B"lgari i tatari v srednite
                                      vekove'.
Nikov, 'Car Boril'   Nikov, P., 'Car Boril i svetlinata na
                                      edin nov pametnik'.

Nikov, *Vidin. knjaž.*	Nikov, P., *Istorija na Vidinskoto knjažestvo do 1323 g.*
Nikov, *Vtoro b"lg. carstvo*	Nikov, P., *Vtoro b"lgarsko carstvo 1186–1236.*
Nordenskiöld, *Atlas*	Nordenskiöld, A. N., *Facsimile-Atlas to the Early History of Cartography.*
Novaković, *Srbi i turci*	Novaković, St., *Srbi i turci* XIV *i* XIV *veka.*
Novaković, *Zakonik Dušana*	*Zakonik Stefana Dušana cara srpskog. 1349 i 1345.*
Oberländer, 'Doc. num.'	Oberländer-Târnoveanu, E., 'Documente numismatice . . .'
Oberländer-Târnoveanu, 'Contr.'	Oberländer-Târnoveanu, E. and I., 'Contribuţii la studiul emisiunilor monetare . . .'
Oberländer-Târnoveanu, 'Isaccea'	Oberländer-Târnoveanu, E., 'Un atelier monétaire inconnu de la Horde d'or . . .'
Oberländer-Târnoveanu, 'Noi descoperiri'	Oberländer-Târnoveanu, E. and I., 'Noi descoperiri de monede . . .'
Oberländer-Târnoveanu, 'Num. contr.'	Oberländer-Târnoveanu, E., 'Numismatical contributions . . .'
Orkun, *ETY*	Orkun, H. N., *Eski Türk yazıtları.*
Ostrogorski, 'Proniari Kumani'	Ostrogorski, G., 'Još jednom o proniarima Kumanima'.
Ostrogorski, *Pronija*	Ostrogorski, G., *Pronija. Prilog istoriji feudalizma u Vizantii . . .*
Ostrogorsky	See Anastasijević-Ostrogorsky.
Ostrogorsky, *Gesch.*	Ostrogorsky, G., *Geschichte des Byzantinischen Staates.*
Pachym. *Hist.*	Georgios Pachymeres, *Syngraphikai historiai*
Pachym. *Hist.*/Bekker	*Georgii Pachymeris de Michaele et Andronico Palaeologis libri* XIII.
Pachym. *Hist.*/Failler-Laurent	Georges Pachymérès, *Relations historiques*, I–II.
Papacostea, 'Aux débuts'	Papacostea, Ş., 'Aux débuts de l'état moldave'.
Papacostea, 'De Vicina à Kilia'	Papacostea, Ş., 'De Vicina à Kilia'.

Paraska, 'Obr. Mold. gos.'	Paraska, P. F., 'Politika Vengerskogo korolevstva v Vostošnom Prikarpat'e i obrazovanie Moldavskogo feodal'nogo gosudarstva'.
Paraska, 'ZO i Mold.'	Paraska, P. F., 'Zolotaja Orda i obrazovanie Moldavskogo feodal'nogo gosudarstva'.
Parisot, *Cant.*	Parisot, V., *Cantacuzène, homme d'état et historien.*
Pašuto, 'Polov. epis.'	Pašuto, V. T., 'Poloveckoe episkopstvo'.
Pataki, *Anjou*	Pataki, József, *Anjou királyaink és a két román vajdaság.*
Pauler, *Árp.*	Pauler, Gy., *A magyar nemzet története az Árpádházi királyok alatt.*
Pavlov, 'B"lg. Viz. Eg.'	Pavlov, P., 'B"lgarija, Vizantija i mamljukski Egipet prez 60-te–70-te godini na XIII v."
Pavlov, 'Brodnici'	Pavlov, P., 'Drevneruskite brodnici v b"lgarskata istorija (XII–XIII v.)'.
Pavlov, 'Kumanite'	Pavlov, P., 'Srednovekovna B"lgarija i kumanite'.
Pavlov, 'Nogai'	Pavlov, P., 'Tatarite na Nogaj, B"lgarija i Vizantija (okolo 1270–1302)'.
Pavlov, 'Pandoleon'	Pavlov, P., 'Teodor Svetoslav, Nogaj i t"rgovec"t Pandoleon'.
Pavlov, 'Zaselvanijata'	Pavlov, P., 'Po v"prosa za zaselvanijata na kumani v B"lgarija prez XIII v.'
Pavlov-Atanasov, 'Preminavaneto'	Pavlov, P., and Atanasov, D., 'Preminavaneto na tatarskata armija prez B"lgarija (1241–1242)'.
Pelenski, *Russia and Kazan*	Pelenski, J., *Russia and Kazan.*
Pelliot, 'Comans'	Pelliot, P., 'A propos des Comans'.
Pelliot, *Horde d'Or*	Pelliot, P., *Notes sur l'histoire de la Horde d'Or.*
Pelliot-Hambis	Pelliot, P., and Hambis, L., *Histoire des campagnes de Gengis khan*, 1.
Pesty, *Szörény*	Pesty, F., *A szörényi bánság és Szörény vármegye története.*

Petrow, *Iwailo* — Petrow, P., *Der Aufstand des Iwailo.*

Pez, *SS Austr.* — Pez, H. (ed.), *Scriptores rerum Austriacarum* ... I–III.

Pfeiffer, *Dominikaner* — Pfeiffer, N., *Die ungarische Dominikanerordensprovinz* ...

Pistarino, *Notai* — Pistarino, G., *Notai genovesi in Oltremare.*

PLP — Trapp, E., *Prosopographisches Lexikon der Palaiologenzeit.*

Polevoj, *Ist. geogr. Mold.* — Polevoj, L. L., *Očerki istoričeskoj geografii Moldavii* XIII–XIV *vv.*

Popa-Lisseanu, *Izvoarele* — Popa-Lisseanu, G., *Izvoarele Istoriei Românilor.*

Pray, *Diss.* — Pray, G., *Dissertationes historico-criticae.*

Primov, 'S"zdavaneto' — Primov, B., 'S"zdavaneto na Vtorata b"lgarska d"ržava i učastieto na Vlasite'.

Pritsak, 'Farbsymbolik' — Pritsak, O., 'Orientierung und Farbsymbolik'.

Pritsak, 'Polovcians' — Pritsak, O., 'The Polovcians and Rus''.

Pritsak, 'Qara' — Pritsak, O., 'Qara. Studie zur türkischen Rechtssymbolik'.

Pritsak, 'Two migratory movements' — Pritsak, O., 'Two migratory movements in the Eurasian steppe in the 9th–11th centuries'.

PSRL — *Polnoe sobranie russkih letopisej.*

Radloff, *USp.* — Radloff, W., *Uigurische Sprachdenkmäler.*

Raš./Ali-zade — Fazlallah Rašid ad-Din, *Džami at-tavarih,* I/1, II/1.

Raš./Blochet — *Djami el-tévarikh. Histoire générale du monde par Fadl Allah Rashid ed-Din* ... E. Blochet (ed.).

Raš./Tehran — Rawšan, M., and Mūsawī, M. (eds.), *Jāmiʿ at-tawārīḫ.*

Rásonyi, 'Anthrop.' — Rásonyi, L., 'Les anthroponymes Comans de Hongrie'.

Rásonyi, 'Bulaqs'	Rásonyi, L., 'Bulaqs and Oγuzs in mediaeval Transylvania'.
Rásonyi, 'Contr.'	Rásonyi, L., 'Contributions à l'histoire des premières cristallisations d'état des Roumains. L'origine des Basaraba'.
Rásonyi, 'Kuman özel ad.'	Rásonyi, L., 'Kuman özel adları'.
Rásonyi, *Tar. Türklük*	Rásonyi, L., *Tarihte Türklük.*
Rásonyi, 'Turcs non-isl.'	Rásonyi, L., 'Les Turcs non-islamisés en Occident (Péçénegves, Ouzes et Qiptchaqs)'.
Rásonyi, 'Val.-Turc.'	Rásonyi-Nagy, L., 'Valacho-Turcica'.
Rásonyi-Baski	Baski, I., *A Preliminary Index to Rásonyi's Onomasticon Turcicum.*
Rasovskij, 'Polovcy'	Rasovskij, D. A., 'Polovcy'.
Rasovskij, 'Rol' polovcev'	Rasovskij, D. A., 'Rol' polovcev v vojnah Asenej . . .'
Rauch, *SS Austr.*	Rauch, Adrianus (ed.), *Rerum Austriacarum scriptores . . .* I–III.
Raynaldus, *Ann. eccl.*	Raynaldus, O., *Annales ecclesiastici.*
REB	*Revue des Etudes Byzantines (Paris).*
Reifferscheid	See Anna Komn. *Alex.*/Reiffersch.
RESEE	*Revue des études sud-est européens* (Bucharest).
RHSEE	*Revue historique du sud-est européen* (Bucharest).
RO	*Rocznik Orientalistyczny* (Cracaw, Warsaw).
RRH	*Revue roumaine d'histoire* (Bucharest).
Safargaliev, *Raspad*	Safargaliev, M. G., *Raspad Zolotoj Ordy.*
Şăineanu, *Infl. orient.*	Şaineanu, L., *Influenţa orientală asupra limbei şi culturei română.*
SAO	*Studia et Acta Orientalia* (Bucharest).
Schlumberger, *Almugavares*	Schlumberger, G., *Expédition des Almugavares.*
Schopen	See Kant. *Hist.*/Schopen.
Schopen-Bekker	See Greg.*Hist.*/Schopen-Bekker.

Schreiner, *Chron. brev.*	Schreiner, P., *Die byzantinischen Kleinchroniken.*
Schütz, 'Könige'	Schütz, E., 'Könige und Eidechsen'.
Schwandtner	*Scriptores Rerum Hungaric. veteres ac genuini*, Johannes Georgius Schwandtner (ed.).
SCN	*Studii şi Cercetări de Numismatică* (Bucharest).
SEER	*Slavonic and East European Review* (London).
Senga, 'IV. Béla tatár levele'	Senga Toru, 'IV. Béla külpolitikája és IV. Ince pápához intézett "tatár" levele'.
SHM/Ligeti	Ligeti, L., *Histoire secrète des Mongols.*
Sibiescu, 'Milcova'	Sibiescu, V. G., 'Episcopatul cuman de la Milcova (1227–1241)'.
Sin. Franc.	Wyngaert, A. van den, *Sinica Franciscana*, I.
Sinodik Borila	Popruženko, M. G., *Sinodik carja Borila.*
SKBG	*Sitzungsberichte der Königlichen Böhmischen Gesellschaft der Wissenschaften* (Prague).
Škrivanić, 'Velbužd'	Škrivanić, G., 'Bitka kod Velbužda 28 VII 1330'.
Smith, 'Sarı Saltuq'	Smith, G. M., 'Some *türbes/maqāms*'.
Spinei, *Moldavia*	Spinei, V., *Moldavia in the 11th–14th centuries.*
Spuler, *GH*	Spuler, B., *Die Goldene Horde.*
SRH	*Scriptores Rerum Hungaricarum tempore ducum regumque stirpis Arpadianae gestarum*, I–II.
SS Pruss.	Hirsch, T., Töppen, M., and Strehlke, E. (eds.), *Scriptores rerum Prussicarum*, I–V.
Stritter	*Memoriae populorum, olim ad Danubium, Pontum Euxinum, . . . incolentium, e scriptoribus historiae Byzantinae . . . a Ioanne Gotthilf G. Strittero.*

Szabó, *Kun László*	Szabó, K., *Kun László 1272–1290*.
Szentpétery, *Reg. Arp.*	*Regesta regum stirpis Arpadianae critico-diplomatica.*
Szék. Okl.	*Székely Oklevéltár 1219–1776.*
Székely, 'Második tatárjárás'	Székely, Gy., 'Egy elfeledett rettegés: a második tatárjárás'.
TAD	*Tarih Araştırmaları Dergisi* (Ankara).
TDV İA	*Türkiye Diyanet Vakfı İslam Ansiklopedisi.*
Theiner, *Mon. Hung.*	*Vetera monumenta historica Hungariam Sacram illustrantia* . . . ab Augustino Theiner.
Theiner, *Mon. Slav. merid.*	Theiner, A., *Vetera monumenta Slavorum meridionalium.*
Theod. Skut. *Syn.*/Sathas	Theodoros Skutariotes, *Synopsis chronike.*
Thomsen, *Inscr.*	Thomsen, V., *Inscriptions de l'Orkhon déchiffrées.*
Thuróczy/Gal. -Kristó	Johannes de Thurocz: *Chronica Hungarorum*, I: Textus.
Tiz.	Tizengauzen, V. G., *Sbornik materialov, otnosjaščihsja k istorii Zolotoj Ordy*, I–II.
Trepavlov, *Gos. stroj*	Trepavlov, V. V., *Gosudarstvennyj stroj mongol'skoj imperii* XIII *v.*
UJb	*Ungarische Jahrbücher* (Berlin).
Uspenskij, 'Asen. viz. služ.'	Uspenskij, F. I., 'Bolgarskie Asenevici na Vizantijskoj službe'.
Uspenskij, 'Pronija'	Uspenskij, F. I., 'Značenie vizantijskoj i južnoslavjanskoj pronii'.
Uspenskij, *Vtor. bolg. carstvo*	Uspenskij, F. I., *Obrazovanie vtorogo bolgarskogo carstva.*
Uspenskij, *Zemlevladenie*	Uspenskij, F. I., 'K istorii krestjanskogo zemlevladenija'.
Valenciennes/Longnon	Valenciennes, H., *Histoire de l'empereur Henri de Constantinople.*
van Dieten	See Nik. Chon. *Hist.*/van Dieten; and Nik. Greg. *Hist.*/van Dieten.

van Dieten, *Erläuterungen*	van Dieten, J. A., *Niketas Choniates; Erläuterungen zu den Reden und Briefen.*
Vásáry, *AH*	Vásáry, I., *Az Arany Horda.*
Vásáry, *Berke*	Vásáry, I., 'History and Legend in Berke Khan's Conversion to Islam'.
Vásáry, 'Med. theories'	Vásáry, I., 'Mediaeval theories concerning the primordial homeland of the Hungarians'.
Vasiliev, *Hist. Byz.*	Vasiliev, A. A., *History of the Byzantine Empire*, I–II.
Veress, 'Originea'	Veress, E., 'Originea stemelor Ţărilor Române'.
Vernadskij, 'ZO, Eg. i Viz.'	Vernadskij, G., 'Zolotaja Orda, Egipet i Vizantija . . .'
Veselovskij, 'Nogaj'	Veselovskij, N. I., 'Han iz temnikov Zolotoj Ordy. Nogaj i ego vremja'.
Villani/Racheli	*Chroniche di Giovanni, Matteo e Filippo Villani.* A. Racheli (ed.).
Villehardouin/Pauphilet	*Historiens et chroniqueurs du Moyen Age.* Villehardouin: pp. 97–202.
Wadding, *Annales*	Waddingus, Luca, *Annales Minorum.*
Wendt, *Türk. Elem.*	Wendt, Heinz F., *Die türkischen Elemente im Rumänischen.*
Wittek, 'Gagaouzes'	Wittek, P., 'Les Gagaouzes: les gens de Kaykaus'.
Wittek, 'Yazijioghlu'	Wittek, P., 'Yazijioghlu Ali on the Christian Turks of Dobruja'.
Wolff, 'Sec. Bulg. Emp.'	Wolff, R. L., 'The Second Bulgarian Empire: origin and history to 1204'.
WZKM	*Wiener Zeitschrift für die Kunde des Morgenlandes* (Vienna).
Zachariadou, *Trade and Crus.*	Zachariadou, Elizabeth A., *Trade and Crusade.*
Zachariadou, 'Turcica'	Zachariadou, Elizabeth A., 'Observations on some Turcica of Pachymeres'.
Zimm.-Werner-Müller	*Urkundenbuch zur Geschichte der Deutschen in Siebenbürgen.*

Zlatarski, *Ist.*   Zlatarski, V. N., *Istorija na*
                                     b"lgarskata d"ržava prez srednite
                                     vekove, I–III.
Zlatarski, 'Potekloto'   Zlatarski, V. N., 'Potekloto na Petra i
                                     Asenja, vodačite na v"zstanieto v 1185
                                     god'.
Zsoldos, 'Téténytől a Hód-tóig'   Zsoldos A., 'Téténytől a
                                     Hód-tóig . . .'
Živojinović, 'Žitije Danila'   Živojinović, M., 'Žitije arhiepiskopa
                                     Danila II . . .'.
Žuglev, 'Blaquie'   Žuglev, K., 'Kakvo razbira Valensien
                                     pod "Blaquie" i "Blakie le Grant"'.

Bibliography

Abenteuer auf dem Kaiserthron: Die Regierungszeit der Kaiser Alexios II, Andronikos und Isaak Angelos (1180–1195) aus dem Geschichtswerk des Niketas Choniates. Franz Grabler (ed. and trans.). Graz, Vienna and Cologne, 1958. (*Byzantinische Geschichtsschreiber,* VIII.)

Acta Patriarchatus Constantinopolitani MCCCXV–MCCCCII e codicibus manu scriptis Bibliothecae Palatinae Vindobonensis . . . , I–II. Fr. Miklosich and Ios. Müller (eds.). Vienna, 1860–2. (*Acta et diplomata graeca medii aevi sacra et profana,* I–II.)

Alemany, A., *Sources on the Alans: A Critical Compilation.* Leiden, Boston and Cologne, 2000. (*Handbuch der Orientalistik,* VIII/5.)

Alexandrescu-Dersca, M., 'L'expédition d'Umur beg d'Aydin aux bouches du Danube (1337 ou 1338)', *SAO* 2 (1959), pp. 3–23.

Alexandrescu-Dersca Bulgaru, M. M., 'La Seigneurie de Dobrotici, fief de Byzance', *ACIEB,* II (1975), pp. 17–18.

Altaner, B., *Die Dominikanermission des XIII. Jahrhunderts.* Habelschwerdt, 1924.

Altınordu devleti tarihine ait metinler. W. de Tiesenhausen (ed.). İ. H. İzmirli (trans.). Istanbul, 1941. (*Türk Tarihi Kaynakları 2.*)

Amitai-Preiss, R., *Mongols and Mamluks.* Cambridge, 1995.

Anastasijević, D., and Ostrogorsky, G., 'Les Koumanes pronoïaires', *Annuaire de l'Institut de philologie et d'histoire orientales et slaves 6* (1951), pp. 19–29.

Andreas Dandulus, *Chronicon Venetum a pontificatu sancti Marci ad annum usque 1339–1342.* Libri X. In Muratori, *SS Ital.,* XII, pp. 13–416.

Andreev, J., *B"lgarskite hanove i care VII–XIV vek. Istoriko-hronologičen spravočnik.* Sofia, 1988.

Andreev, J., Lazarov, Iv., and Pavlov, Pl., *Koj koj e v srednovekovna B"lgarija.* Sofia, 1993.

Anjoukori Okmánytár. Codex Diplomaticus Hungaricus Andegavensis, I–VII. Budapest, 1878–1920.

Annae Comnenae porphyrogenitae *Alexias,* I–II. A. Reifferscheid (ed.). Leipzig, 1884.

Annales Frolovienses ab origine urbis usque ad a. 1473 auctore anonymo. In Muratori, *SS Ital.,* XXII/2, pp. 1–109.

Aristov, N., 'O zemle poloveckoj', *Izvestija ist.-fil. Instituta kn. Bezborodko v Nežine.* Kiev, 1877.

Bibliography

Árpádkori új okmánytár. Wenzel, G. (ed.), Pest, later Budapest, I–XII (1860–74). (*Monumenta Hungariae Historica*.)

Artuk, İ., and Artuk, C., *İstanbul Arkeoloji Müzeleri teşhirdeki islâmî sikkeler kataloğu*, II. Istanbul, 1974. VIII, pp. 453–972, tables LIX–CVII A.

Asdracha, C., *La région des Rhodopes aux XIIIe et XIVe siècles: étude de géographie historique*. Athens, 1976. (*Texte und Forschungen zur Byzantinisch-Neugriechischen Philologie* 49.)

Balard, M., 'Un document génois sur la langue roumaine en 1360', *RESEE* 18 (1980), pp. 234–6.

'Notes sur les ports du Bas-Danube au XIVe siècle', *Südostforschungen* 38 (1979), pp. 2–3.

La Romanie génoise (XIIe–début du siècle), I–II. Rome and Genoa, 1978.

Bănescu, N., *L'ancien état bulgare et les pays roumains*. Bucharest, 1947. (*Institut Roumain d'Etudes Byzantines*, new series 5.)

Un problème d'histoire médiévale: Création et caractère du second empire bulgare (1185). Bucharest, 1943. (*Institut Roumain d'Etudes Byzantines*, new series 2.)

Barker, J. W., 'The question of ethnic antagonisms among Balkan states of the fourteenth century', in T. S. Miller and J. Nesbitt (eds.), *Peace and War in Byzantium: Essays in Honor of George T. Dennis, SJ*. Washington, DC, 1995, pp. 165–77.

Bartol'd, V. V., *Sočinenija*, v. Moscow, 1968.

Bartusis, M., 'On the problem of smallholding soldiers in late Byzantium', *DOP* 44 (1990), pp. 1–26.

The Late Byzantine Army: Arms and Society, 1204–1453. Philadelphia, 1992.

Baski, I., *A Preliminary Index to Rásonyi's Onomasticon Turcicum*. Budapest, 1986. (*Debter. Deb-ther. Debtelin* 6.)

Batūra, R., *Lietuva tautų kovoje prieš Aukso Ordą: Nuo Batu antplūdžio iki mūšio prie Mėlynųjų Vandenų*. [Lithuania in the popular struggle against the Golden Horde. From the invasion of Batu's hordes to the Battle of Sinie Vody.] Vilnius, 1975.

Beljaeva, S. A., *Južnorusskie zemli vo vtoroj polovine XIII–XIV vv*. Kiev, 1982.

Bendefy L., *A magyarság kaukázusi őshazája: Gyeretyán országa*. Budapest, 1942.

Bíborbanszületett Konstantín A birodalom kormányzása. Moravcsik Gyula (ed. and trans.). Budapest, 1950.

Binon, S., 'A propos d'un prostagma inédit d'Andronic III Paléologue', *BZ* 38 (1938), pp. 133–55, 377–407.

Bödey J., 'Rilai Szent Iván legendájának magyar vonatkozásai', *EPhK* 64 (1940), pp. 217–21.

Bogdan, J., *Documentele lui Ștefan cel Mare*, I–II. Bucharest, 1913.

Boissonade, J. F. (ed.), *Anecdota Graeca e codicibus regiis* II. Paris, 1830.

Bosch, U. V., *Kaiser Andronikos III. Palaiologos: Versuch einer Darstellung der byzantinischen Geschichte in den Jahren 1321–1341*. Amsterdam, 1965.

Boutouras, A. C., *Ta neoellēnika kyria onomata historikōs kai glōssikōs hermēneuomena*. Athens, 1912.

Božilov, I., *Familijata na Asenevci (1186–1460). Genealogija i prosopografija*. Sofia, 1985.

Brătianu, G. I., 'Deux études historiques: II. Demetrius princeps Tartarorum (ca. 1360–1380)', *Revue des études roumaines* 9–10 (1965), p. 45.

'Les Bulgares à Cetatea Albă (Akkerman) au début du XIVe siècle', *Byzantion* 2 (1925), pp. 153–68.

'În jurul originei stemelor Principatelor Române', *Revista Istorică Română* (1931), p. 238.

La mer Noire: Des origines à la conquête ottomane. Munich, 1969.

Recherches sur le commerce génois dans la mer Noire au XIIIe siècle. Paris, 1929.

Recherches sur Vicina et Cetatea Albă. Bucharest, 1935.

'Vicina I: Contributions à l'histoire de la domination byzantine et du commerce génois en Dobrogea', *Académie Roumaine, Bulletin de la Section Historique* 10 (1928), pp. 113–89.

Bretschneider, E., *Mediæval Researches from Eastern Asiatic Sources: Fragments towards the Knowledge of the Geography and History of Central and Western Asia from the 13th to the 17th century*, I–II. London, 1910.

Brincken, A.-D. v. den, *Die 'Nationes Christianorum Orientalium' im Verständnis der lateinischen Historiographie von der Mitte des 12. bis in die zweite Hälfte des 14. Jahrhunderts*. Cologne and Vienna, 1973.

Brun, F., *Černomor'e: sbornik issledovanij po istoričeskoj geografii Južnoj Rossii*, I–II. Odessa, 1879–80.

Bryer, A., 'Greek historians on the Turks: the case of the first Byzantine-Ottoman marriage', in R. H. C. Davis and J. M. Wallace-Hadrill (eds.), *The Writing of History in the Middle Ages: Essays Presented to Richard William Southern*. Oxford, 1981, pp. 471–93.

Burmov, A., 'Istorija na B"lgarija prez vremeto na Šišmanovci (1323–1396 g.)', in A. Burmov, *Izbrani proizvedenija*, I. Sofia, 1968, pp. 220–78. (First published in *GSU* 43 (1947), pp. 1–56; 1–20.)

Cankova-Petkova, G., *B"lgarija pri Asenevci*. Sofia, 1978.

Cecaumeni strategikon et incerti scriptoris de officiis regiis libellus. B. Wassiliewsky and V. Jernstedt (eds.). St Petersburg, 1896. (*Zapiski istoriko-filologičeskogo fakul'teta imp. S.-Peterburgskogo Universiteta*, XXXVIII.)

Chroniche di Giovanni, Matteo e Filippo Villani secondo le migliori stampe e corredate di note filologiche e storiche, I–II. A. Racheli (ed.). Trieste, 1857.

Clauson, G., *An Etymological Dictionary of Pre-Thirteenth-Century Turkish*. Oxford, 1972.

'The name Uyğur', *JRAS* 1963.

Constantine Porphyrogenitus, *De administrando imperio*. Gy. Moravcsik (ed.). R. J. H. Jenkins (trans.). Budapest, 1949. (2nd edition, Washington, DC, 1967. Dumbarton Oaks Texts, I.)

Constantinidi-Bibicou, H., 'Yolande de Montferrat, Impératrice de Byzance', *L'Hellénisme Contemporain*, 2nd series, 4 (1950), pp. 425–42.

Cosmographie de Chems-ed-Din Abou Abdallah Mohammed ed-Dimichqui. Arabic text. M. A. F. Mehren (ed.). St Petersburg, 1864.

Csánki, D., *Magyarország történelmi földrajza a Hunyadiak korában*, i–v. Budapest, 1890–1913.

Csapodi, Cs., *Az Anonymus-kérdés története*. Budapest, 1978.

Dančeva-Vasileva, A., *B"lgarija i Latinskata imperija (1204–1261)*. Sofia, 1985.

Danilo, Arhiep., *Životi kraljeva i arhiepiskopa srpskih*. Lazar Mirković (trans.). Nikola Radojčić (introd.). Belgrade, 1935 (*Srpska Književna Zadruga*, series xxxviii, no. 257).

Decei, A., 'La Horde d'Or et les pays roumains aux xiiie et xive siècles selon les historiens arabes contemporains', *Romano-Arabica*, ii (Bucharest, 1976), pp. 61–3.

'L'invasion des Tatars de 1241/1242 dans nos régions selon la Djāmi ot-Tevārīkh de Fäzl ol-lāh Räšīd od-Dīn', *RRH* 12 (1973), pp. 101–21, = Decei, *Rel. rom.-or.*, pp. 193–208.

'Le problème de la colonisation des Turcs Seldjoucides dans la Dobrogea au xiiième siècle', *TAD* 6 (1968), pp. 85–111, = Decei, *Rel. rom.-or.*, pp. 169–92.

Relatii româno-orientale. Bucharest, 1978.

Deletant, D., 'Genoese, Tatars and Rumanians at the mouth of the Danube in the fourteenth century', *SEER* 62 (1984), pp. 511–30.

Densuşianu, O., 'Originea Basarabilor', *Grai şi suflet* 4 (1929), pp. 147–9.

Le Destān d'Umūr Pacha (Düstūrnāme-i Enverī). Irène Mélikoff-Sayar (trans. and ed.). Paris, 1954. (*Bibliothèque Byzantine*, Documents 2.)

DeWeese, D., *Islamization and Native Religion in the Golden Horde: Baba Tükles and Conversion to Islam in Historical and Epic Tradition*. University Park, Pa., 1994.

Diaconu, P., *Les Coumans au Bas-Danube aux IXe et XIIe siècles*. Bucharest, 1978. (*Bibliotheca Historica Romaniae. Etudes* lvi.)

'Kili et l'expédition d'Umur Beg', *RESEE* 31 (1983), pp. 23–9.

Dieten, J. A. van, *Niketas Choniates: Erläuterungen zu den Reden und Briefen. Nebst einer Biographie*. Berlin and New York, 1971.

Dimitrov, S., 'Gagauzskijat problem', *B"lgarite i Severnoto Pričernomorie: Izsledvanija i materiali*, iv. Veliko Tărnovo, 1995, pp. 147–68.

Dinić, M., 'Odnos izmedju kralja Milutina i Dragutina', *Zbornik Radova Vizantinološkog Instituta* 3 (1955), pp. 49–82.

Djami el-tévarikh: Histoire générale du monde par Fadl Allah Rashid ed-Din. Tarikh-i Moubarek-i Ghazani. Histoire des Mongols. ii: Contenant l'histoire des empereurs mongols successeurs de Tchinkkiz Khagan. E. Blochet (ed.). Leiden and London, 1911. (*E. J. W. Gibb Memorial Series*, xviii, 2.)

Documenta historiam Valachorum in Hungaria illustrantia usque ad annum 1400 p. Christum. Curante E. Lukinich et adiuvante L. Gáldi, A. Fekete Nagy and L. Makkai (eds.). Budapest, 1941.

Documenti di storia Italiana, i–ix. Florence, 1867–89.

Dogiel, M. (ed.), *Codex diplomaticus regni poloniae et Magni Ducatus Lithuaniae*, i, ii, v (no vols. iii and iv). Wilna, 1758–64.

d'Ohsson, A. C. M., *Histoire des Mongols depuis Tchinguiz-Khan jusqu'à Timour Bey ou Tamerlan*, i–iv. Amsterdam, 1852.

Dölger, F., *Regesten der Kaiserurkunden des Oströmischen Reiches*, I–V. Munich and Berlin, 1924–1965.

Drăganu, N., 'Românii în veacurile IX–XIV. pe baza toponimiei şi a onomasticei", *Studii şi Cercetări Akad. Rom.* 21 (1933), pp. 520ff.

Ducas, *Istoria Turco-Bizantină (1341–1462)*. Vasile Grecu (ed.). Bucharest, 1958. (*Scriptores Byzantini*, I).

Duda, H. W., 'Zeitgenössische islamische Quellen und das Oğuznāme des Jazyğyoğlu 'Alī zur angeblichen türkischen Besiedlung der Dobrudscha im 13. Jhd. n. Chr.', *B"lgarska Akademija na naukite i izkustvata 66/2* (1943), pp. 131–45.

Dujčev, I., 'La conquête turque et la prise de Constantinople dans la littérature contemporaine', *Byz-slav.* 16 (1955), pp. 321–2.

'La date de la révolte des Asénides', *Byz.-slav.* 13 (1952–3), pp. 227–32.

'V"stanieto v 1185 g. i negovata hronologija', *Izvestija na Instituta za b"lgarska istorija* 6 (1956), pp. 327–56.

Egorov, V. L., *Istoričeskaja geografija Zolotoj Ordy v XIII–XIV vv.* Moscow, 1985.

Elekes, L., 'Basaraba családja', *Turul* 58–60 (1944–6), pp. 19–28.

'A havaselvi vajdák címere a középkorban', *Turul* 56 (1942), pp. 12–21.

'A román fejlődés alapvetése', *Századok* (1940), pp. 278–313, 361–404.

Encyclopedia of Islam, I–. New edition in English, in progress. Leiden, 1954–.

Engel, P., 'Az ország újraegyesítése. I. Károly küzdelmei az oligarchák ellen (1310–1323)', *Századok* 122 (1988), pp. 89–144.

Enzyklopaedie des Islam, I–IV + Supplement. Leiden and Leipzig, 1913–38.

Ephraemius ex recognitione Immanuelis Bekkeri. Ephraemii monachi imperatorum et patriarcharum recensus. A. Maio (trans.). Bonn, 1840. (*CSHB*.)

Erdélyi Okmánytár, I (1028–1300). Zs. Jakó (ed.). Budapest, 1997.

Érszegi, G., 'Eine neue Quelle zur Geschichte der bulgarisch-ungarischen Beziehungen während der Herrschaft Borils', *Bulgarian Historical Review* 3 (1975), pp. 91–7.

Eskenasy, V., 'Din istoria litoralului vest-pontic: Dobrotici şi relaţiile sale cu Genova', *Revista de istorie* 34 (1981), pp. 2047–63.

Failler, A., 'Euphrosyne l'épouse du tsar Théodore Svetoslav', *BZ* 78/1 (1985), pp. 92–3.

Fasmer, M., *Ètimologičeskij slovar' russkogo jazyka*, I–IV. 2nd edition. Moscow, 1986–7.

Fazlallah Rašid ad-Din, *Džami at-tavarih*, I/I. A. A. Romaskevič, A. A. Hetagurov, A. A. Ali-zade (eds.). Moscow, 1965; II/I: A. A. Ali-zade (ed.). Moscow, 1980.

Fedorov, G. B., and Polevoj, L. L., *Arheologija Rumynii*. Moscow, 1973.

Fejér, G., *Codex Diplomaticus Hungariae Ecclesiasticus ac Civilis*, I–XLIII. Buda, 1829–44.

Ferenţ, I. *A kunok és püspökségük*. Pál Péter Domokos (trans.). Budapest, 1981. (Hungarian translation of Ferenţ, I., *Cumanii şi episcopia lor*. Blaj, 1931.)

Flemming, B., *Landschaftsgeschichte von Pamphylien, Pisidien und Lykien im Spätmittelalter*. Wiesbaden, 1964. (*Abhandlungen für die Kunde des Morgenlandes*, XXXV, I.)

Fine, J. G. A., *The Late Medieval Balkans: A Critical Survey from the Late Twelfth Century to the Ottoman Conquest*. Ann Arbor, 1987.

Fontes domestici, I–III. M. Florianus (ed.). Budapest, 1881–5.

Gáldi, L., and Makkai, L., *Geschichte der Rumänen*. Budapest, 1942. (*Ostmitteleuropäische Bibliothek* 36.)

Geanakoplos, D. J., *Emperor Michael Palaeologus and the West, 1258–1282: A Study in Byzantine–Latin Relations*. Cambridge, Mass., 1959.

'Greco–Latin relations on the eve of the Byzantine restoration: the Battle of Pelagonia, 1259', *DOP* 7 (1953), pp. 99–141.

Georges Pachymérès, *Relations historiques*, I–II. Albert Failler (ed.), Vitalien Laurent (trans.). Paris, 1984. (*CFHB*, Series Parisiensis XXIV/1, 2.)

Georgii Acropolitae Annales. Collected by Immanuel Bekker. Bonn, 1836. (*CSHB*.)

Georgii Pachymeris de Michaele et Andronico Palaeologis libri XIII, I–II. I. Bekker (ed.). Bonn, 1835.

Georgii Acropolitae opera. A. Heisenberg (ed.). Leipzig, 1903. I, pp. 1–189.

Gibb, H. A. R. (trans.), *The travels of Ibn Battuta A. D. 1325–1354*, I–III. Cambridge, 1958–71.

Giurescu, C. C., 'The Genoese and the Lower Danube in the XIIIth and XIVth centuries', *JEEH* 5 (1976), pp. 583–98.

Istoria Românilor, I: *Din cele mai vechi timpuri până la moartea lui Alexandru cel Bun (1432)*. Bucharest, 1935.

Golden, P. B., 'Cumanica, II: The Ölberli (Ölperli). The fortunes and misfortunes of an Inner Asian nomadic clan', *AEMAe* 5 (1985), pp. 5–29.

'The Tribes of the Cuman-Qipchaqs', *AEMAe* 9 (1995–7), pp. 99–122.

Golubovskij, P., *Pečenegi, torki i polovcy do našestvija tatar: istorija južno-russkih stepej IX–XIII vv.* Kiev, 1884.

Gombocz, Z., *Árpádkori török személyneveink*. Budapest, 1915. (*A Magyar Nyelvtudományi Társaság Kiadványai* 16.)

Gombocz, Z., and Melich J., *Magyar etymologiai szótár*. Budapest, I: 1914–44. II: 1934–44.

Gombos, A. F., *Catalogus fontium historiae Hungaricae aevo ducum et regum ex stirpe Arpad descendentium ab anno Christi DCCC usque ad annum MCCCI*, I–IV. Budapest, 1937–43.

Górka, O., 'Zagadnienie czarnomorske w polityce polskiego średniowiecza: I, 1359–1450', *Przegląd historyczny* 30 (1932–3), pp. 325–90.

Gorovei, Ştefan S., 'L'état roumain de l'est des Carpates: la succession et la chronologie des princes de Moldavie au XIVe siècle', *RRH* 18 (1979), pp. 473–506.

Grabler, Franz, *Die Krone der Komnenen*, I–III. Graz, Vienna and Cologne, 1958. (*Byzantinische Geschichtsschreiber*, VIII.)

Grekov, V. D., and Jakubovskij, A. Ju., *Zolotaja Orda i ee padenie*. Moscow and Leningrad, 1950.

Grigorevič, V. I., *Donesenie putešestvij po slavjanskim zemljam*. Kazan, 1915.

Guilland, R., *Recherches sur les institutions byzantines*, I–II. Berlin and Amsterdam 1967. (*Berliner Byzantinische Arbeiten* 35.)

Gyárfás, I., *A jász–kúnok története*, I: Kecskemét, 1870; II: Kecskemét, 1873; III: Szolnok, 1883; IV: Budapest, 1885.

Gyóni, M., *A legrégibb vélemény a román nép eredetéről: Kekaumenos művei mint a román történet forrásai*. Budapest, 1944. = 'L'oeuvre de Kékaumenos source de l'histoire roumaine', *Revue d'histoire comparée* 23 (1945), pp. 96–180.

A magyar nyelv görög feljegyzéses szórványemlékei. Budapest, 1943. (*Magyar-Görög Tanulmányok* 24.)

Zur Frage der rumänischen Staatsbildungen im XI. Jahrhundert in Paristrion (Archaisierende Volksnamen und ethnische Wirklichkeit in der 'Alexias' von Anna Komnene). Budapest, 1944. (*Osteuropäische Bibliothek* 48.)

Györffy, Gy., 'Adatok a románok XIII. századi történetéhez és a román állam kezdeteihez', *Történelmi Szemle* 7 (1964), pp. 1–25, 537–68.

'A kun és komán népnév eredetének kérdéséhez', in *idem, A magyarság keleti elemei*. Budapest, 1990, pp. 200–19. (First published in *Antiquitas Hungarica* 2 (Budapest, 1948), pp. 158–76; also as separate offprint.)

Az Árpád-kori Magyarország történeti földrajza, I–IV. Budapest, 1966–98 (not yet completed.)

'Besenyők és magyarok', in *idem, A magyarság keleti elemei*. Budapest, 1990, pp. 94–191. (A fundamentally revised version of the first edition in *KCsA* 1. Supplementary volume (1935–9), pp. 397–500.)

Hafner, S., *Studien zur altserbischen dynastischen Historiographie*. Munich, 1964. (*Südosteuropäische Arbeiten* 62.)

Hammer-Purgstall, J. von, *Geschichte der Goldenen Horde in Kiptschak, das ist: der Mongolen in Russland*. Pest, 1840.

Heppell, M., *The Ecclesiastical Career of Gregory Camblak*. London, 1979.

Heyd, W., *Histoire du commerce du Levant au moyen âge*, I–II. Revised edition, Amsterdam, 1959. Anastatic reprint of Leipzig edition, Harrassowitz, 1885–6.

Hintner, D., *Die Ungarn und das byzantinische Christentum der Bulgaren im Spiegel der Register Papst Innozenz' III*. Leipzig, 1976.

Hirsch, T., Töppen, M., and Strehlke, E. (eds.), *Scriptores rerum Prussicarum*, I–V. Leipzig, 1861–74.

Historiens et chroniqueurs du Moyen Age: Robert de Clari, Villehardouin, Joinville, Froissart, Commynes. A. Pauphilet (ed.). Paris, 1952.

Höfler, C. R. von, 'Die Walachen als Begründer des zweiten bulgarischen Reiches, der Asaniden, 1186–1257', *Sitzungsberichte der philosophisch-historischen Classe der kaiserlichen Akademie der Wissenschaften* 95 (1879), pp. 229–45. (Also separately as *Abhandlungen aus dem Gebiete der slavischen Geschichte*, 1. Vienna, 1879, pp. 1–19.)

Holban, M., *Din cronica relaţiilor româno-ungare în secolele XIII–XIV*. Bucharest, 1981.

Hóman, B., and Szekfű Gy., *Magyar történet*, I–V. Budapest, 1941–3. (7th edition.)

Hopf, Ch., *Chroniques gréco-romanes inédites ou peu connues*. Berlin, 1873. Robert de Clary: pp. 1–85; Cronaca di Morea: pp. 414–68.

Horváth, J., ifj., 'Török politikai intézmények nyomai a középkori magyar állam életében', *Ethnographia* 81 (1970), pp. 265–75.

Houtsma, Th., *Histoire des Seldjoucides d'Asie Mineure d'après l'Abrégé du Seld-jouknameh d'Ibn Bibi*. Leiden, 1902. (*Recueil de textes relatifs à l'histoire des Seldjoucides*, IV.)

Ein türkisch-arabisches Glossar. Leiden, 1894.

Howorth, H. H., *History of the Mongols from the 9th to the 19th Century*. Parts I, II/1, II/2, III, London, 1876–88; Part IV, London, 1927.

Hrušev'skyj, M., *Istorija Ukrainy-Rusi*, I–IX. Kiev and L'vov, 1903–31.

Hunfalvy, P., *Az oláhok története*, I–II. Budapest, 1894.

Hurmuzaki, E. de, and Densuşianu, N., *Documente privitóre la istoria Românilor*. I/1: 1199–1345. I/2: 1346–1450. Bucharest, 1887–90.

Iacobus Moratinus, *Chronicon de rebus Foroliviensibus*. In *Doc. Ital.*, VI.

Iliev, N., 'Otnosno vremeto na potušavane bunta sreštu car Boril v''v Vidin', *Izvestija na Muzeite ot Severozapadna B''lgarija* 9 (1984), pp. 85–94.

'Šišmanovijat pohod sreštu S''rbija prez 1292 g.', *Istoričeski pregled* 44/11 (1988), pp. 50–9.

İnalcık, H., 'The conquest of Edirne (1361)', *Archivum Ottomanicum* 3 (1971), pp. 185–209.

Ioannis Cantacuzeni imperatoris historiarum libri IV. L. Schopen (ed.). I–III. Bonn, 1828–32.

Iordan, I., *Toponimia Romînească*. Bucharest, 1963.

Iorga, N., *Histoire des Roumains et de la Romanité Orientale*, III. Paris, 1937.

'Imperiul Cumanilor şi domnia lui Basaraba. Un capitol din colaboraţia româno-barbară în evul mediu', *Analele Academiei Română*. Historical section, III/8 (1928), pp. 97–103.

Işıltan, F., *Die Seldschukengeschichte des Aksarâyî*. Leipzig, 1943.

İslâm Ansiklopedisi, I–XIII. Istanbul, 1988.

Ivanov, J., 'Pomenici na b''lgarskite care i carici', *Izbrani proizvedenija*, I, Sofia, 1982.

Izeddin, M., 'Notes sur les mariages princiers en Orient au moyen âge', *JA* 257 (1969), pp. 139–56.

Jagić, V., 'Ein Beitrag zur serbischen Annalistik mit literaturgeschichtlicher Ein-leitung', *ASPh* 2 (1877), pp. 1–109.

Jakubovskij, A. Ju., 'Rasskaz Ibn-al-Bibi o pohode maloazijskih turok na Sudak, polovcev i russkih v načale XIII v.' *Vizantijskij Vremennik* 25, pp. 59–70.

János minorita Nagy Lajosról szóló krónikatöredéke (Liber De Rebus Gestis Ludovici Regis Hungariae). Dékáni Kálmán (trans. and comm.). Budapest, 1910. (*Középkori krónikások* II.)

Jaubert, A., *Géographie d'Edrisi*, I–II. Paris, 1836–40.

Jean Sire de Joinville, *Histoire de Saint Louis, Credo et Lettre à Louis X*. Original text with trans. by M. Natalis de Wailly. Paris, 1874 (2nd edition.)

Jerney János, *Keleti utazása a' magyarok' őshelyeinek kinyomozása végett 1844 és 1845*, I–II. Budapest, 1851.

Jireček, C., 'Einige Bemerkungen über die Überreste der Petschenegen und Kuma-nen sowie über die Völkerschaften der sogenannten Gagauzi und Surguči im heutigen Bulgarien', *SKBG* (1889), pp. 3–30.

Geschichte der Bulgaren. Prague, 1876.

Geschichte der Serben, I–II. Gotha, 1911–18. (*Geschichte der europäischen Staaten.*)

Istorija Srba, I–II. J. Radonić (trans.). Belgrade, 1952. 2nd, enlarged edition.

Staat und Gesellschaft in mittelalterlichem Servien. Vienna, 1914. (*Denkschriften der Kaiserlichen Akademie der Wissenschaften.*)

Johannes Kantakuzenos, *Geschichte.* Georgios Fatouros and Tilman Krischer (trans. and eds.). I/I, Stuttgart, 1982. I/2, Stuttgart, 1986. (*Bibliothek der Griechischen Literatur* 17, 21.)

Johannes de Thurocz, *Chronica Hungarorum,* I. Textus. E. Galántai and J. Kristó. Budapest, 1985. (*Bibliotheca Scriptorum Medii Recentisque Aevorum,* new series, VII.)

Jurgevič, V., 'Ustav dlja genuèzskih kolonij v Černom more izdannyj v Genue v 1449 godu', *Zapiski Odesskogo obščestva istorii i drevnostej* 5 (1863), pp. 629–837.

Kafalı, M., *Altın Orda Hanlığının kuruluş ve yükseliş devirleri.* Istanbul, 1976.

Kaisertaten und Menschenschicksale im Spiegel der schönen Rede: Reden und Briefe des Niketas Choniates. Franz Grabler (trans. and com.). Graz, Vienna and Cologne, 1966. (*Byzantinische Geschichtsschreiber* IX.)

Káldy-Nagy, Gy., 'Kleinasien im Spannungsfeld von vier neuen Machtzentren um 1260', *WZKM* 85 (1995), pp. 117–46.

Karácsonyi, J., 'A hódtavi csata éve. 1282', *Századok* 35 (1901), pp. 626–9.

'Az erdélyi székelyek első hadjárata 1210-ben', *Századok* 46 (1912), pp. 292–4.

Karayannopulos, J., and Weiss, G., *Quellenkunde zur Geschichte von Byzanz (324–1453),* I–II. Wiesbaden, 1982.

Karpov, S. P., *Ital'janskie morskie respubliki i južnoe Pričernomor'e v XIII–XIV vv. (Problemy torgovli).* Moscow, 1990, pp. 276–91.

Každan, A. P., 'La date de la rupture entre Pierre et Asen (vers 1193)', *Byzantion* 35 (1965), pp. 167–74.

Kern, A., 'Der "Libellus de Notitia Orbis" Ioannes' III. (*De Galonifontibus?*), O. P. Erzbischofs von Sulthanyeh, *Archivum Fratrum Praedicatorum* 8 (1938), pp. 82–123.

Kiss, L., *Földrajzi nevek etimológiai szótára,* I–II. Budapest, 1988. 4th edition. (First edition in one volume, 1978.)

Kljaštornyj, S. G., 'Das Reich der Tataren in der Zeit vor Činggis Khan', *CAJ* 36 (1992), pp. 72–83.

Kniezsa, I., *A magyar nyelv szláv jövevényszavai,* I/I, 2. Budapest, 1955. (vol. II remained unpublished.)

Koledarov, P., 'B"lgarskata srednovekovna d"ržava i Černomorskijat brjag', *Srednovekovna B"lgarija i Černomorieto (sbornik dokladi ot naučnata konferencija) Varna-1980.* Varna, 1982, pp. 19–38.

Korai magyar történeti lexikon (9–14. század). Gy. Kristó (editor-in-chief). P. Engel and F. Makk (eds.). Budapest, 1994.

Kossányi, B., 'Az úzok és kománok történetéhez a XI–XII. században', *Századok* 57–8 (1924), pp. 519–37.

Középkori históriák oklevelekben (1002–1410). Gy. Kristó (ed.). Szeged, 1992. (*Szegedi Középkortörténeti Könyvtár* 1.)

Kretschmer, K., *Die italienischen Portolane des Mittelalters: Ein Beitrag zur Geschichte der Kartographie und Nautik*. Berlin, 1909. Reprint: Hildesheim, 1962.

Die Kreuzfahrer erobern Konstantinopel: Aus dem Geschichtswerk des Niketas Choniates. F. Grabler (trans.). Graz, Vienna and Cologne, 1958. (*Byzantinische Geschichtsschreiber* IX.)

Kristó, Gy., *Az Anjou-kor háborúi*. Budapest, 1988.

Kuczyński, S. M., 'Sine Wody', *Studia z dziejów Europy wschodniej* X–XVIII w., Warsaw, 1965, pp. 175–7.

Laiou, A. E., 'Byzantium and the Black Sea, 13th–15th centuries', *Bulgaria Pontica medii aevi* 2 (Sofia, 1988), pp. 164–201.

Constantinople and the Latins: The Foreign Policy of Andronicus II, 1282–1328. Cambridge, Mass., 1972.

'The provisioning of Constantinople during the winter of 1306–1307', *Byzantion* 38 (1968), pp. 386–410.

Lampros, S., '*To Hagion Oros kai hoi Katalōnioi*', *Neos Hellēnomnēmōn* 6 (1909), pp. 319–21.

Langdon, J., *John III Ducas Vatatzes' Byzantine Imperium in Anatolian exile, 1222–54: The Legacy of His Diplomatic, Military and Internal Program for the restitutio orbis*. Dissertation, University of California. Ann Arbor, Mich.: University Microfilms, 1979.

Laurent, G., '*Ho Bardariōtōn ētoi Tourkon*: Perses, Turcs asiatiques ou Turcs hongrois?', *Izvestija na B"lgarsko istoričesko družestvo* 16–18 (1940), pp. 275–89.

Laurent, V., 'L'assaut avorté de la Horde d'Or contre l'empire byzantin', *REB* 18 (1960), pp. 145–162.

'La domination byzantine aux bouches du Danube sous Michel VIII Paléologue', *RHSEE* 22 (1945), pp. 184–98.

'Une famille turque au service de Byzance, les Mélikès', *BZ* 49 (1956), pp. 349–68.

'Le Métropolite de Vicina Macaire et la prise de la ville par les Tartares', *RHSEE* 23 (1946), pp. 230–1.

Lăzărescu, E. C., 'Despre lupta din 1330 a lui Basarab Voevod cu Carol Robert', *Revista Istorică* 21 (1935), pp. 244ff.

Lăzărescu-Zobian, M., 'Cumania as the name of thirteenth century Moldavia and Eastern Wallachia: some aspects of Kipchak–Rumanian relations', *Journal of Turkish Studies* 8 (1984), pp. 265–72.

Kipchak Turkic Loanwords in Rumanian. PhD dissertation, Columbia University, 1982.

Leonid, Arhimandrit, 'Han Nagaj i ego vlijanie na Rossiju i južnyh slavjan', *Čtenija v Imperatorskom obščestve istorii i drevnostej rossijskih* 1868/III.

Lemerle, P., *L'Émirat d'Aydin: Byzance et l'Occident. Recherches sur 'La geste d'Umur Pacha'*. Paris, 1957. (*Bibliothèque Byzantine*, Études 2.)

'Recherches sur le régime agraire à Byzance: la terre militaire à l'époque des Comnènes', *Cahiers de civilisation médiévale xe–xIIe siècles* 2 (1959), pp. 265–81.

Lemerle, P., Guillou, A., and Svoronos, N., *Actes de Lavra*. I: *Des origines à 1204*. Paris, 1970. (*Archives de l'Athos* v.)

Ligeti, L., *Histoire secrète des Mongols*. Budapest, 1971. (*Monumenta Linguae Mongolicae Collecta* I.)

'A magyar nép mongol kori nevei (magyar, baskír, király)', *Magyar Nyelv* 60 (1964), pp. 384–404.

Litavrin, G. G., *Bolgarija i Vizantija v xI–xII vv*. Moscow, 1960.

'Novoe issledovanie o vosstanii v Paristrione i obrazovanii Vtorogo bolgarskogo carstva', *Vizantijskij Vremennik* 41 (1980), pp. 105–32.

'Vosstanie bolgar i vlahov v Fessalii v 1066 g.', *Vizantijskij Vremennik* 11 (1956), pp. 123–34.

Lupaş, I., 'Lupta de la Posada 1330', *Anuarul Comisiunei Monumentelor Istorice*. Transylvanian section. Cluj, 1932, pp. 125ff.

Makk, F., *The Árpáds and the Comneni: Political Relations between Hungary and Byzantium in the 12th Century*. Budapest, 1989.

'Feljegyzések II. István történetéhez', in J. Horváth and Gy. Székely (eds.). *Középkori kútfőink kritikus kérdései*. Budapest, 1974, pp. 253–9.

Makkai, L., *A milkói (kún) püspökség és népei*. Debrecen, 1936.

Malingoudis, Ph., 'Die Nachrichten des Niketas Choniates über die Entstehung des Zweiten Bulgarischen Staates', *Byzantina* 10 (1979), pp. 51–147.

Mándoky, K. I., 'A Hantos-széki kunok', *Székesfehérvár évszázadai* 2 (1972), pp. 73–82.

Marquart, J., *Über das Volkstum der Komanen*. In W. Bang and J. Marquart, *Osttürkische Dialektstudien*. Berlin, 1914, pp. 25–238.

Martinez, A. P., 'Gardīzī's two chapters on the Turks', *AEMAe* 2 (1982), pp. 109–217.

Mavromatis, L., *La fondation de l'empire serbe: le kralj Miloutin*. Thessalonica, 1978.

Melich, J., 'Barcza, Barczaság, Bárcza', *Magyar Nyelv* 11 (1915), pp. 241–5.

A honfoglaláskori Magyarország. Budapest, 1929. (A Magyar Nyelvtudomány Kézikönyve, I/6.)

Mélikoff, I., 'Qui était Sari Saltuk? Quelques remarques sur les manuscrits du Saltukname', in Colin Heywood and Colin Imber (eds.), *Studies in Ottoman History in Honour of Professor V. L. Ménage*. Istanbul, 1994, pp. 231–8.

Memoriae populorum, olim ad Danubium, Pontum Euxinum, Paludem Maeotidem, Caucasum, Mare Caspium, et inde magis ad septemtriones incolentium, e scriptoribus historiae Byzantinae erutae et digestae a Ioanne Gotthilf G. Strittero, gymnasii Academiae Scientiarum Imperialis Petropolitanae conrectore. St Petersburg. I: Gothica, Vandalica, Gepaedica, Longobardica, Herulica, Hunnica et Avarica complectens. 1771. II/I, 2: Slavica, Servica, Chrovatica, Zachlumica, Terbunica, Paganica, Diocleica, Moravica, Bosnica, Bulgarica, Valachica, Russica, Polonica, Lithuanica, Prussica, Samotica, Permica et Boemica complectens. 1774. III/I, 2: Turcica, Chazarica, Ungarica,

Patzinacica, Uzica, Comanica et Tatarica complectens. 1778. iv: Lazica, Avas-
    gica, Misimianica, Apsilica, Tzanica, Suanica, Mesehica, Zicchica, Iberica,
    Alanica; Iuthungica, Carpica, Varnica, Chamavica, Varangica, Nemitzica,
    Dacica, Pannonica, Sarmatica, Scythica, Massagetica, et genealogias gentium
    complectens (+ index). 1779.
Menges, K. G., *Vostočnye èlementy v Slovo o polku Igoreve*. Leningrad, 1979.
Mihályi, J., *Máramarosi diplomák a xiv. és xv. századból*. Máramaros-sziget, 1900.
Miletič, L., *Edna b"lgarska Aleksandrija ot 1810 god*. Sofia, 1936. (*B"lgarski starini*
    13.)
Miller, K., *Mappaemundi: die ältesten Weltkarten*, vi. (Concluding volume: redrawn
    maps.) Stuttgart, 1898.
Miller, T. S., *The History of John Cantacuzenus (Book iv): Text, Translation, and
    Commentary*. unpublished PhD thesis, Catholic University of America, 1975.
Minea, I., 'Războiul lui Basarab cel Mare cu regele Carol Robert (Noemvre 1330)',
    Cercetări Istorice 5–7 (1929–31), pp. 338ff.
Minorsky, V., *Sharaf al-Zaman Tahir Marvazī on China, the Turks and India: Arabic
    Text (circa AD 1120) with an English Translation and Commentary*. London,
    1942. (*James G. Forlong Fund*, xxii.)
Mladenov, St., 'Potekloto i s"stav"t na srednob"lg. Belgun', prekor na car' Asenja
    I.', *Spisanie na B"lgarskata Akademija na Naukite* 45 (1933), pp. 49–66.
Monumenta Poloniae historica: Pomniki dziejowe Polski, i–vi. L'vov and Cracaw,
    1864–93.
Monumenta Serbica spectantia historiam Serbiae, Bosniae, Ragusii. Fr. Miklosich
    (ed.). Vienna, 1858.
Moravcsik, Gy., *Az Árpád-kori magyar történet bizánci forrásai*. Budapest, 1984.
    Byzantinoturcica, i–ii. 2nd edition. Berlin, 1958.
Muratori, Ludovicus A., *Rerum Italicarum scriptores . . .* i–xxv. Milan, 1723–51.
Murnu, G., *Istoria Românilor din Pind: Valahia Mare 980–1259. Studiu istoric după
    izvoare bizantine*. Bucharest, 1913.
Mutafčiev, P., 'Die angebliche Einwanderung von Seldschuk-Türken in die
    Dobrudscha im xiii. Jahrhundert', *B"lgarska Akademija na Naukite i Izkust-
    vata* 66/1 (1943), pp. 1–128.
    Bulgares et Roumains dans l'histoire des pays danubiens. Sofia, 1932.
    Istorija na b"lgarskija narod. i–ii: Sofia, 1943–4.
    'Proizhod"t na Asenevci', *Makedonski Pregled* 4/4 (1928), pp. 1–42; French
    summary, pp. 149–52.
    'Vojniški zemi i vojnici v Vizantija prez xiii–xiv v.', *Spisanie na B"lgarskata
    Akademija na Naukite* 27 (1923), pp. 1–113.
Németh, Gy., *A honfoglaló magyarság kialakulása*. 2nd, enlarged, edition. Budapest,
    1991. (1st edition, Budapest, 1930.)
Németh, J., 'Die Volksnamen *quman* und *qūn*', *KCsA* 3 (1940), pp. 95–109.
Nicephori Gregorae Byzantina historia Graece et Latine. L. Schopen (ed.). i–ii: Bonn,
    1829–30. *Nicephori Gregorae historiae Byzantinae libri postremi*, I. Bekker (ed.)
    [iii]. Bonn, 1855.

Nicetae Choniatae Historia, i–ii. A. van Dieten (ed.). Berlin and New York, 1975. (*CFHB*, Series Berolinensis xi/1, 2.)

Nicol, D. M., *The Despotate of Epiros, 1267–1479: A Contribution to the History of Greece in the Middle Ages.* Cambridge, 1984.

The Last Centuries of Byzantium, 1261–1453. London, 1972.

The Reluctant Emperor: A Biography of John Cantacuzene, Byzantine Emperor and Monk, c. 1295–1383. Cambridge, 1996.

Nikephoros Gregoras: *Rhomäische Geschichte. Historia Rhomaike.* Jan Louis van Dieten (trans. and ed.). Part 1 (chs. 1–7), Stuttgart, 1973. Part 2 (chs. 8–11), Stuttgart, 1979. Part 3 (chs. 12–17), Stuttgart, 1988. (*Bibliothek der Griechischen Literatur* 4, 9, 24.)

Nikov, P., 'B"lgari i tatari v srednite vekove', *B"lgarska istoričeska biblioteka* 3/2 (Sofia, 1929), pp. 97–141.

'Car Boril i svetlinata na edin nov pametnik', *Spisanie na B"lgarskata Akademija na Naukite* 27 (1912), pp. 121–34.

Istorija na Vidinskoto knjažestvo do 1323 g. Sofia, 1922.

Vtoro b"lgarsko carstvo 1186–1236. Sofia, 1937.

Nordenskiöld, A. N., *Facsimile-Atlas to the Early History of Cartography with Reproductions of the Most Important Maps Printed in the xv and xvi Centuries.* Johan Adolf Ekelöf Roy and Clements R. Markham (trans.). Stockholm, 1889. Reprint, New York, 1961.

Novaković, St., *Srbi i turci xiv i xv veka.* Belgrade, 1960. (*Srpska Književna Zadruga*, ciii, nos. 356–7.) (4th edition, with a preface and addenda by S. M. Ćirković. First edition, Belgrade, 1893.)

Oberländer-Târnoveanu, E., 'Un atelier monétaire inconnu de la Horde d'Or sur le Danube: Sāqčy-Isaccea (xiiie–xive siècles)', *Actes du XIe Congrès International du Numismatique.* Louvain-la-Neuve, 1993, pp. 291–304.

'Documente numismatice privind relaţiile spaţiului est-carpatic cu zona gurilor Dunării în secolele xiii–xiv', *Anuarul Institutului de Istorie şi Arheologie 'A. D. Xenopol'* (Iaşi), 22/2 (1985), pp. 585–90.

'Numismatical contributions to the history of south-eastern Europe at the end of the 13th century', *RRH* 26 (1987), pp. 245–58.

Oberländer-Târnoveanu, E. and I., 'Contribuţii la studiul emisiunilor monetare şi al formaţiunilor politice din zona gurilor Dunării în secolele xiii–xiv', *Studii şi Cercetări de Istorie Veche şi Arheologie* 32 (1981), pp. 89–109.

'Noi descoperiri de monede emise în zona gurilor Dunării în secolele xiii–xiv', *SCN* 9 (1989), pp. 121–9.

Oikonomides, N., 'From soldiers of fortune to gazi warriors: the Tzympe affair', in C. Heywood and C. Imber (eds.), *Studies in Ottoman History in Honour of Professor V. L. Ménage.* Istanbul, 1994, pp. 239–47.

Orkun, H. N., *Eski Türk yazıtları*, i–iv. Istanbul, 1936–41.

Ostrogorsky, G., *Geschichte des Byzantinischen Staates.* 3rd, revised, edition. Munich 1963. (1st edition; Munich, 1940; in English, *History of the Byzantine State.* Joan Hussey (trans.). Oxford, 1956.)

'Još jednom o proniarima Kumanima', in D. Bogdanović, B. Jovanović-Štipčević, Dj. Trifunović (eds.), *Zbornik Vladimira Mošina*. Belgrade, 1977, pp. 63–74.

Pronija: Prilog istoriji feudalizma u Vizantii i u južnoslovenski zemljama. Belgrade, 1951, = *Sabrana dela* G. Ostrogorskog, 1. Belgrade, 1969, pp. 119–342.

Papacostea, Ş., 'Aux débuts de l'état moldave: considérations en marge d'une nouvelle source', *RRH* 12 (1973), pp. 139–58.

'De Vicina à Kilia: Byzantines et Génois aux bouches du Danube au XIVe siècle', *RESEE* 16 (1978), pp. 65–79.

Papadatos, S. I., '*Hē dioikētikē anexartēsia tou Hagiou Orous epi Byzantinōn*', *EEBS* 32 (1963), pp. 427–83.

Paraska, P. F., 'Politika Vengerskogo korolevstva v Vostočnom Prikarpat'e i obrazovanie Moldavskogo feodal'nogo gosudarstva', in *Karpato-dunajskie zemli v srednie veka*. Kishinev, 1975, pp. 33–52.

Vnešnepolitičeskie uslovija obrazovanija Moldavskogo feodal'nogo gosudarstva. Kisinev, 1981.

'Zolotaja Orda i obrazovanie Moldavskogo feodal'nogo gosudarstva', in *Jugovostočnaja Evropa v srednie veka*. 1. Kishinev, 1972, pp. 175–90.

Parisot, V., *Cantacuzène, homme d'état et historien, ou examen critique comparatif des mémoires de l'empereur Jean Cantacuzène*. Paris, 1845.

Pašuto, V. T., 'Poloveckoe episkopstvo', in *Ost und West in der Geschichte des Denkens und der kulturellen Beziehungen: Festschrift für Eduard Winter zum 70. Geburtstag*. W. Steinitz, P. N. Berkov, B. Suchodolski and J. Dolanský (eds.). Berlin, 1966, pp. 33–40.

Pataki, J., *Anjou királyaink és a két román vajdaság*. Kolozsvar, 1944. (*Erdélyi Tudományos Intézet*.)

Patriologiae cursus completus. Series Graeca, 1–CCXLVII. J. P. Migne (ed.). Paris, 1856–66.

Patrologiae cursus completus. Series Latina, 1–CCXXI. J. P. Migne (ed.). Paris, 1844–64.

Pauler, Gy., *A magyar nemzet története az Árpádházi királyok alatt*, 1–11. Budapest, 1899.

Pavlov, P., 'Beležki za njakoi ličnosti ot b"lgarskoto srednovekovie s ogled istorijata na Dobrudža prez XI–XIII v.', *Dobrudža*, 9 (1992), pp. 169–77.

'B"lgarija, Vizantija i mamljukski Egipet prez 60-te–70-te godini na XIII v.', *Istoričeski Pregled* 3 (1989), pp. 15–24.

'Drevneruskite brodnici v b"lgarskata istorija (XII–XIII v.)', in *B"lgaro-ukrainski vr"zki prez vekovete*. Sofia, 1983, pp. 226–8.

'Kumanite v obštestveno-političeskija život na srednovekovna B"lgarija (1186 g.–načaloto na XIV v.)', *Istoričeski Pregled* 7 (1990), pp. 16–26.

'Kumanite v"v voennata istorija na srednovekovna B"lgarija (1186 g.–krajat na XIII v.)', *Naučni trudove na VNVU 'V. Levski'*, 11: *Voenna istorija i istorija na B"lgarija*. Veliko Tărnovo, 1988, pp. 180–5.

'Po v"prosa za zaselvanijata na kumani v B"lgarija prez XIII v.', in *Vtori Meždunaroden kongres po b"lgaristika. Dokladi*. Sofia, 1987, pp. 629–37.

'Srednovekovna B"lgarija i kumanite: voennopolitičeski otnošenija (1186–1241)', in *Trudove na Velikot"rnovskija Universitet 'Sv. Sv. Kiril i Metodij'*, xxvii/3. Tărnovo, 1992, pp. 9–16.

'Tatarite na Nogaj, B"lgarija i Vizantija (okolo 1270–1302)', in *B"lgarite v Severnoto Pričernomorie: Izsledvanija i materiali*, iv. Veliko Tărnovo, 1995, pp. 121–130.

'Teodor Svetoslav, Nogaj i t"rgovec"t Pandoleon', in *Istoriko-arheologičeski izsledvanija. V pamet na prof. d-r Stančo Vaklinov*. Veliko Tărnovo, 1991, pp. 177–85.

Pavlov, P., and Atanasov, D., 'Preminavaneto na tatarskata armija prez B"lgarija (1241–1242)', *Voennoistoričeski Sbornik* 63 (1994), pp. 6–20.

Pelenski, J., *Russia and Kazan: Conquest and Imperial Ideology (1438–1560s)*. The Hague, 1974.

Pelliot, P., 'A propos des Comans', *Journal Asiatique*, 11/15 (1920), pp. 125–85.

Notes sur l'histoire de la Horde d'Or. Paris, 1949.

Pelliot, P., and Hambis, L., *Histoire des campagnes de Gengis khan*, i. Leiden, 1951.

Pesty, F., *A szörényi bánság és Szörény vármegye története*, i–iii. Budapest, 1878.

Petrow, P., *Der Aufstand des Iwailo: der Bauernkrieg in Bulgarien 1277–1280*. Berlin, 1988.

Pez, H., *Scriptores rerum Austriacarum . . .* i–iii. Leipzig and Regensburg, 1721–45.

Pfeiffer, N., *Die ungarische Dominikanerordensprovinz von ihrer Gründung 1221 bis zur Tatarenverwüstung 1241–1242*. Zurich, 1913.

Pistarino, G., *Notai genovesi in Oltremare: atti rogati a Chilia da Antonio di Ponzò (1360–61)*. Genoa, 1971. (*Collana Storica di Fonti e Studi* 13.)

Polevoj, L. L., *Očerki istoričeskoj geografii Moldavii* xiii–xv vv. Kishinev, 1979.

Polnoe sobranie russkih letopisej. 31 vols. St Petersburg and Moscow, 1846–1968.

Popa, R., *Ţara Maramureşului în veacul al XIV-lea*. Bucharest, 1970.

Popa-Lisseanu, G., *Izvoarele Istoriei Românilor*, vii. Cronica lui Nestor. Bucharest, 1935.

Popruženko, M. G., *Sinodik carja Borila*. Sofia, 1928.

Pray, G., *Dissertationes historico-criticae in Annales Veteres Hunnorum, Avarum et Hungarorum*. Vienna, 1775.

Primov, B., 'S"zdavaneto na Vtorata b"lgarska d"ržava i učastieto na Vlasite', in *B"lgarsko-rum"nski vr"zki i otnošenija prez vekovete*, i. Sofia, 1965, pp. 9–35.

Pritsak, O., 'Orientierung und Farbsymbolik: zu den Farbenbezeichnungen in den altaischen Völkernamen', *Saeculum* 5 (1954), pp. 376–83.

'The Polovcians and Rus', *AEMAe* 2 (1982), pp. 321–80.

'Qara: Studie zur türkischen Rechtssymbolik', in *Zeki Velidi Togan'a Armağan*. Istanbul, 1955, pp. 239–63.

'Two migratory movements in the Eurasian steppe in the 9th–11th centuries', *Proceedings of the 26th International Congress of Orientalists, New Delhi, 4th–10th January, 1964*, ii. New Delhi, 1968, pp. 157–63. Reprinted in Pritsak, O., *Studies in Medieval Eurasian History*. London, 1981.

Quellen zur Geschichte des Kreuzzuges Kaiser Friedrichs I. A. Chroust (ed.). Berlin, 1928. Reprinted, 1964. (*MGH SS*, new series, v). i: Ansbert, *Historia de expeditione Friderici imperatoris*, pp. 1–115; ii: *Historia peregrinorum*, pp. 116–72; *Epistola de morte Friderici imperatoris*, pp. 173–8; IV: *Narratio itineris navalis ad terram sanctam*, pp. 179–96.

Radloff, W., *Uigurische Sprachdenkmäler*. S. Malov (ed.). Leningrad, 1928.

Rakintzakis, G. E., *Orthodox–Muslim Mixed Marriages, ca. 1297–1453*. University of Birmingham, unpublished MA thesis, 1975.

Rásonyi, L., 'Les anthroponymes Comans de Hongrie', *AOH* 20 (1967), pp. 135–49.

'Bulaqs and Oγuzs in mediaeval Transylvania', *AOH* 33 (1979), pp. 129–51.

'Contributions à l'histoire des premières cristallisations d'état des Roumains: L'Origine des Basaraba', *AECO* I (1935), pp. 221–53. Also separately: Budapest, 1936. (*Etudes sur l'Europe Centre-Orientale*, no. 3).

'Kuman özel adları', *Türk Kültürü Araştırmaları* 3–6 (1966–9), pp. 71–144.

Tarihte Türklük. Ankara, 1971.

'Les Turcs non-islamisés en Occident (Péçénegves, Ouzes et Qiptchaqs, et leurs rapports avec les Hongrois)', *Philologiae Turcicae Fundamenta*, III. Wiesbaden, 1970, pp. 1–26.

Rásonyi-Nagy, L., 'Valacho-Turcica', in *Aus den Forschungsarbeiten der Mitglieder des Ungarischen Instituts und des Collegium Hungaricum in Berlin. Dem Andenken Robert Graggers gewidmet*. Berlin and Leipzig, 1927, pp. 68–96.

Rasovsky, D. A., 'Les Comans et Byzance', Actes du IVe Congrès International des Etudes Byzantines. *Bulletin de l'Institut Archéologique Bulgare* 9 (1935), pp. 346–54.

Rasovskij, D. A., 'Polovcy', *Seminarium Kondakovianum* 7 (1935), pp. 1–18; 8 (1936), pp. 19–40; 9 (1937), pp. 41–55; 10 (1938), pp. 57–80; 11 (1939), pp. 81–114.

'Rol' polovcev v vojnah Asenej s Vizantijskoj i Latinskoj imperijami v 1186–1207 godah', *Spisanie na B"lgarskata Akademija na Naukite* 58 (1939), pp. 203–11.

Rauch, A., *Rerum Austriacarum scriptores . . .* I–III. Vienna, 1793–4.

Rawšan, M., and Mūsawī, M. (eds.), *Jāmi' at-tawārīḫ-i Rašīd ad-Dīn Faḍlullāh Hamadānī*, I–IV. Tehran, 1373 [1994–5].

Raynaldus, O., *Annales ecclesiastici ab anno* MCX VIII. 21 vols. Lucca, 1747–.

Regesta regum stirpis Arpadianae critico-diplomatica: az Árpádházi királyok okleveleinek kritikai jegyzéke, I. E. Szentpétery (ed.). II/1, II/2–3, II/4, E. Szentpétery and I. Borsa (eds.). Budapest, 1923–87.

Reliquiae manuscriptorum omnis aevi, . . . Ex museo Io. Petri Ludewig. I–XII. Frankfurt, 1720–31.

Rowell, S. C., *Lithuania Ascending: A Pagan Empire within East-Central Europe, 1295–1345*. Cambridge, 1994.

Sacerdoţeanu, A., 'Guillaume de Rubrouk et les Roumains au milieu du XIIIe siècle', *Mélanges de l'École Roumaine en France*, part 2. Paris, 1929, pp. 335ff.

Safargaliev, M. G., *Raspad Zolotoj Ordy*. Saransk, 1960. (New edition: *Na styke kontinentov i civilizacij . . . Iz opyta obrazovanija i raspada imperij* XV–XVI *vv.* Moscow, 1996, pp. 277–526.)

Şaineanu, L., *Influenţa orientală asupra limbei şi culturei română*, I–III. Bucharest, 1900.

Salaville, S., 'Un peuple de race turque christianisé au XIIIe siècle: les Comans', *Echos d'Orient* 17 (1914), pp. 193–209.

Saltukname: The Legend of Sarı Saltuk from Oral Tradition by Ebu'l-Hayr Rûmî. Text in facsimile with critical and stylistic analysis and index by Fahir İz. Şinasi Tekin (ed.). Cambridge, Mass., 1974–6.

Savvides, A. G. K., 'Hoi Komanoi (Koumanoi) kai to Byzantio 110s–130s ai. m. Ch.', *Byzantina* 13 (1985), pp. 939–55.

'Late Byzantine and Western historiographers on Turkish mercenaries in Greek and Latin armies: the Turcoples/Tourkopouloi', in R. Beaton and Ch. Roueché (eds.), *The Making of Byzantine History: Studies Dedicated to Donald M. Nicol.* Aldershot, 1993, pp. 122–36.

Schlumberger, G., *Expédition des 'Almugavares' ou routiers Catalans en Orient de l'an 1302 à l'an 1311.* Paris, 1902.

Schmitt, J. (ed.), *The Chronicle of Morea.* London, 1904.

Schreiner, P., *Die byzantinischen Kleinchroniken*, I–III. Vienna, 1975–9. (*CFHB*, XIII.)

Schünemann, K., 'Ungarische Hilfsvölker in der Literatur des deutschen Mittelalters', *UJb* 4 (1924), pp. 99–115.

Schütz, E., 'Könige und Eidechsen (Bemerkungen zum Fortleben des ungarischen Wortes *király* "König" in kiptschakischen Sprachen)', *Proceedings of the IXth Meeting of the Permanent International Altaistic Conference, Ravello, 20–30 September 1966.* Naples, 1970, pp. 259–67. (Reprinted in E. Schütz, *Armeno-Turcica. Selected Studies.* Bloomington, 1998.)

Scriptores Rerum Hungaricarum tempore ducum regumque stirpis Arpadianae gestarum, I–II. E. Szentpétery (ed.). Budapest, 1937–8.

Scriptores Rerum Hungaricarum veteres ac genuini . . . Part I. Johannes Georgius Schwandtner (ed.). Vienna, 1766.

Senga Toru, 'IV. Béla külpolitikája és IV. Ince pápához intézett "tatár" levele', *Századok* 121 (1987), pp. 583–612.

Serbisches Mittelalter: Altserbische Herrscherbiographien, II: *Danilo II. und sein Schüler: Die Königsbiographien.* Stanislaus Hafner (ed.). Graz, Vienna and Cologne, 1976. (*Slavische Geschichtsschreiber*, IX.)

Sibiescu, V. G., 'Episcopatul cuman de la Milcova (1227–1241): Împrejurările înfiinţării; Rezistenţa băştinaşilor români-ortodocşi', *Spiritualitate şi Istorie la Întorsătura Carpaţilor* I (Buzău, 1983), pp. 296–308.

Škrivanić, G., 'Bitka kod Velbužda 28 VII 1330', *Vesnik vojnog muzeja* 16 (Belgrade, 1970), pp. 67–77.

Smith, G. M., 'Some *türbes/maqāms* of Sarı Saltuq, an early Anatolian Turkish gāzī-saint', *Turcica* 14 (1982), pp. 216–25.

Sovety i rasskazy Kekavmena: Sočinenie vizantijskogo polkovodca XI veka. G. G. Litavrina (ed.). Moscow, 1972.

Spinei, V., *Moldavia in the 11th–14th centuries.* Bucharest, 1986. (*Bibliotheca Historica Romaniae*, Monographs, XX).

Realităţi etnice şi politice în Moldova meridională în secolele X–XIII. Români şi Turanici. Iaşi, 1985.

Spuler, B., *Die Goldene Horde: die Mongolen in Rußland 1223–1502*. Leipzig, 1943; 2nd edition, Wiesbaden, 1965.

Stari srpski rodoslovi i letopisi. Ljub. Stojanović (ed.). Beograd–Sr. Karlovci 1927.

(Zbornik za istoriju, jezik i književnost srpskog naroda. I/XVI.)

Szabó, K., *Kun László 1272–1290*. Budapest, 1886. (*Magyar Történeti Életrajzok* II/5.)

Székely, Gy., 'Egy elfeledett rettegés: a második tatárjárás a magyar történeti hagyományokban és az egyetemes összefüggésekben', *Századok* 122 (1988), pp. 52–85.

Székely Oklevéltár 1219–1776. Barabás Samu (ed.). Budapest, 1934.

Thallóczy, L., 'Nagy Lajos és a bulgár bánság', *Századok* 34 (1900), pp. 577–615.

[–ó–o–], 'Magyar-bulgár összeköttetések', *Századok* 32 (1898), pp. 113–23.

[–ó–o–], 'Oklevelek a magyar-bulgár összeköttetések történetéhez. 1360–1369.', *Történelmi Tár* (1898), pp. 357–67.

Theiner, A., *Vetera monumenta Slavorum meridionalium historiam illustrantia*, I–II. Rome and Zagreb, 1863–75.

Theodoros Skutariotes, *Synopsis chronike*. In K. N. Sathas (ed.), *Mesaiōnikē Bibliothēkē*, VII. Venice and Paris, 1894, pp. 1–556.

Thomsen, V., *Inscriptions de l'Orkhon déchiffrées*. Helsingfors, 1896. (*Mémoires de la Société Finno-Ougrienne* v.)

Thuróczy, János, *A magyarok krónikája*. J. Horváth (trans.). Budapest, 1978. (*Bibliotheca Historica*.)

Tizengauzen, V. G., *Sbornik materialov, otnosjaščihsja k istorii Zolotoj Ordy*. I: St Petersburg, 1884; II: Moscow and Leningrad, 1941.

Todorova, E., 'Otnošenijata na Dobrotica s genuezcite', in *Srednovekovna B"lgarija i Černomorieto (sbornik dokladi ot naučnata konferencija) Varna-1980*. Varna, 1982, pp. 111–18.

Trapp, E., *Prosopographisches Lexikon der Palaiologenzeit*, I. Vienna, 1976.

Trepavlov, V. V., *Gosudarstvennyj stroj mongol'skoj imperii* XIII *v*. Moscow, 1995.

Türkiye Diyanet Vakfı İslâm Ansiklopedisi, I–XXIII. Istanbul, 1988–2003. (Series continues.)

Uspenskij, F. I., 'Bolgarskie Aseneviči na Vizantijskoj službe', *Izvestija Russkogo Arheologičeskogo Instituta v Konstantinopole* 13 (1908), pp. 1–16.

'K istorii krestjanskogo zemlevladenija', *Žurnal Ministerstva Narodnogo Prosveščenija* 225 (1883), p. 339.

Obrazovanie vtorogo bolgarskogo carstva. Odessa, 1879. (*Zapiski Imperatorskogo Novorossijskogo Universiteta* 27.)

'Značenie vizantijskoj i južnoslavjanskoj pronii', in *Sbornik statej po slavjanovedeniju, sostavlen i izdan učenikami V. L. Lamanskogo*. St Petersburg, 1883, pp. 1–32.

Valenciennes, H., *Histoire de l'empereur Henri de Constantinople*. J. Longnon (ed.). Paris, 1948.

Vásáry, István, *Az Arany Horda*. Budapest, 1986.

'History and Legend in Berke Khan's Conversion to Islam', in *Aspects of Altaic Civilization* III. Bloomington, 1990, pp. 230–52.

'Mediaeval theories concerning the primordial homeland of the Hungarians', in *Popoli delle steppe: Unni, Avari, Ungari, 23–29 aprile 1987*, I. Spoleto, 1988, pp. 213–44. (*Settimane di studio del Centro italiano di studi sull'alto medioevo* XXXV.)

Vasiliev, A. A., *History of the Byzantine Empire*, I–II. Madison, 1928–9; 2nd edition, 1952.

Veress, E., 'Originea stemelor Ţărilor Române', *Revista Istorică Română* (1931), pp. 230–1.

Vernadskij, G., 'Zolotaja Orda, Egipet i Vizantija v ih vzaimootnošenijah v carstvovanie Mihaila Paleologa', *Seminarium Kondakovianum* I (1927), pp. 73–84.

Veselovskij, N. I., 'Han iz temnikov Zolotoj Ordy: Nogaj i ego vremja', *Zapiski Rossijskoj Akademii Nauk po otdeleniju istoričeskih nauk i filologii* 13 (1922), pp. 1–58.

Vetera monumenta historica Hungariam Sacram illustrantia . . . A. Theiner (ed.). I: 1216–1352, II: 1352–1526. Rome, 1859–60.

Veterum scriptorum et monumentorum historicorum, dogmaticorum, moralium amplissima collectio, I–IX. Edmund Martene and Ursinus Durand (eds.). Paris, 1724–33.

Waddingus, Luca, *Annales Minorum seu trium ordinum a S. Francisco institutorum*, I–VIII, Rome, 1731–3 (2nd edition); I–X, 1931–2 (3rd edition).

Wendt, Heinz F., *Die türkischen Elemente im Rumänischen*. Berlin, 1960. (*Berliner Byzantinistische Arbeiten* 12.)

Wertner M., *A középkori délszláv uralkodók genealogiai története*. Temesvár, 1891.

Wittek, P., 'La descendance chrétienne de la dynastie Seldjouk en Macédoine', *Échos de l'Orient* 30 (1934), pp. 409–12.

'Les Gagaouzes = les gens de Kaykāūs', *RO* 17 (1951–3), pp. 12–29.

'Yazijioghlu Alī on the Christian Turks of the Dobruja', *BSOAS* 14 (1952), pp. 639–68.

Wolff, R. L., 'The Second Bulgarian Empire: origin and history to 1204', *Speculum* 1949, pp. 167–206.

Wyngaert, A. van den, *Sinica Franciscana* I: *Itinera et relationes fratrum minorum saeculi* XIII. *et* XIV. Quaracchi and Florence, 1929.

Yüce, Kemal, *Saltuknâme'de Tarihî, Dinî ve Efsanevî Unsurlar*. Ankara, 1987. (*Kültür ve Turizm Bakanlığı yayınları*.)

Zachariadou, Elizabeth A., 'Hoi Christianoi apogonoi tou Izzeddin Kaikaous B stē Beroia', *Makedonika* 6 (1964–5), pp. 62–74.

'Observations on some Turcica of Pachymeres', *REB* 36 (1978), pp. 261–7.

Trade and Crusade: Venetian Crete and the Emirates of Menteshe and Aydin (1300–1415). Venice, 1983. (*Library of the Hellenic Institute of Byzantine and Post-Byzantine Studies* 11.)

Zakonik Stefana Dušana cara srpskog. 1349 i 1345. Stojan Novaković (ed.). Belgrade, 1870.

Zlatarski, V. N., *Istorija na b"lgarskata d"ržava prez srednite vekove*, I–III. Sofia, 1918–40.

'Potekloto na Petra i Asenja, vodačite na v"zstanieto v 1185 god', *Spisanie na B"lgarskata Akademija na Naukite* 45 (1933), pp. 7–48.

Zimmerman, F., Werner, K., and Müller, G. (eds.), *Urkundenbuch zur Geschicte der Deutschen in Siebenbürgen*, I: 1191–1341 (nos. 1–582), II: 1342–90 (nos. 583–1259). Hermannstadt, 1892–7.

Živojinović, M., 'Žitije arhiepiskopa Danila II kao izvor za ratovanja Katalanske Kompanje', *Zbornik radova Bizantinološkog instituta* 19 (1980), pp. 251–73.

Životi kraljeva i arhiepiskopa srpskih, napisao arhiaepiskop Danilo i drugi, Č. Daničič (ed.). Zagreb, 1866.

Zsoldos A., 'Téténytől a Hód-tóig (Az 1279 és 1282 közötti évek politikatörténetének vázlata)', *Történelmi Szemle* 39 (1997), pp. 69–98.

Žuglev, K., 'Kakvo razbira Valensien pod "Blaquie" i "Blakie le Grant"', *Izvestija na B"lgarsko istoričesko družestvo* 22–4 (1948), pp. 159–67.

Index